Current Dynamics in Business and Economics: Theoretical Approaches and Empirical Discoveries

Seda Bayrakdar /
Patrycja Chodnicka-Jaworska (eds.)

Current Dynamics in Business and Economics: Theoretical Approaches and Empirical Discoveries

PETER LANG

Berlin - Bruxelles - Chennai - Lausanne - New York - Oxford

Library of Congress Cataloging-in-Publication
A CIP catalog record for this book has been applied for at the Library of Congress.

Bibliographic information published by the Deutsche Nationalbibliothek
The Deutsche Nationalbibliothek lists this publication in the Deutsche Nationalbibliografie; detailed bibliographic data is available on the Internet at http://dnb.d-nb.de.

ISBN 978-3-631-92478-5 (Print)
E-ISBN 978-3-631-92469-3 (E-PDF)
E-ISBN 978-3-631-92999-5 (E-PUB)
DOI.10.3726/b22541

Published by Peter Lang GmbH, Berlin, Germany

info@peterlang.com - www.peterlang.com

This publication has been peer-reviewed.

Seda Bayrakdar & Patrycja Chodnicka Jaworska

Foreword

Our book called "Current Issues and Contemporary Perspectives in Business & Economics, Theoretical and Empirical Studies" consists of 28 chapters. 57 authors have contributed to our book. This book contains trends and innovations in the field of economy and business. The target audience of this book is researchers, students and academics interested in business and economics. We think that it is a book in which you can find various topics and read with pleasure. We would like to express our gratitude to our publisher PETER LANG for the care they have taken in the preparation of the book.

Table of Contents

List of Contributors

Łukasz Marecki,
Warsaw School of Economics (SGH), College of Management and Finance, Warsaw, Poland

Agnieszka Wojcik-Czerniawska,
Warsaw School of Economics (SGH), College of Management and Finance, Warsaw, Poland

Andrew Enaifoghe
University of Zululand, Faculty of Commerce, Administration and Law, Empangeni, South Africa

Makhosazana Vezi-Magigaba
University of Zululand, Faculty of Commerce, Administration and Law, Empangeni, South Africa

Sipho Nkonde
University of Zululand, Faculty of Commerce, Administration and Law, Empangeni, South Africa

Constantinos Challoumis
N.K.U.A. (National and Kapodistrian University of Athens), Athens, Greece

Terezija Berlančić
Josip Juraj Strossmayer University of Osijek /Faculty of Economics in Osijek, Croatia

Ivana Fosić
Josip Juraj Strossmayer University of Osijek /Faculty of Economics in Osijek, Croatia

Ana Živković
Josip Juraj Strossmayer University of Osijek /Faculty of Economics in Osijek, Croatia

Piotr Misztal
Casimir Pulaski Radom University, Faculty of Economics and Finance, Poland

Valentina Ninova
Tsenov Academy of Economics, Bulgaria

Mesiet William Kamihanda
Euromed University of Fes, UEMF, Morocco

Hafsa El Bekri
Euromed University of Fes, UEMF, Morocco

Pedro Fernandes da Anunciação
Setúbal Polytechnic University, School of Business, Setúbal, Portugal

Cátia Susana Claro Chasqueira
INDEG-ISCTE, Executive Education, Lisboa, Portugal

Denis Ribeiro Patrocínio
Setúbal Polytechnic University, School of Business, Setúbal, Portugal

Patricia da Silva Alves Schütz
Setúbal Polytechnic University, School of Business, Setúbal, Portugal

Filipe António de Lemos
Setúbal Polytechnic University, School of Business, Setúbal, Portugal

Oriana Helena Negulescu
Transilvania University of Brasov, Romania

Raul Florentin Drenta
Technical University of Cluj-Napoca, Baia Mare, Romania

Raluca Georgiana Robu
Bucharest University of Economic Studies, Bucharest, Romania

Maria Leonor Pires
Instituto Politécnico de Setúbal, ESTSetúbal, Setúbal, Portugal

Alexandru Trifu
University "Petre Andrei" of Iasi, Romania

Aliya Akhmedieva
Tashkent State University of Economics, Uzbekistan

Abdurashid Kadirov
Research center "Scientific bases and issues of economic development of Uzbekistan" under the Tashkent State University of Economics, Uzbekistan

Bahtiyor Mamurov
Research center "Scientific bases and issues of economic development of Uzbekistan" under the Tashkent State University of Economics, Uzbekistan

Ulugbek Musabekov
Research center "Scientific bases and issues of economic development of Uzbekistan" under the Tashkent State University of Economics, Uzbekistan

Shoh-Jakhon Khamdamov
Mamun University, Khiva city, Uzbekistan

Samariddin Makhmudov
International School of Finance and Technology, Tashkent, Uzbekistan & Tashkent State University of Economics, Tashkent, Uzbekistan

Nargiza Bakhriddinovna Talapova
Tashkent State University of Economics, Tashkent, Uzbekistan

Zokir Mamadiyarov
Alfraganus University, Tashkent, Uzbekistan

Naima Berdiyerovna Rejapova
International Nordic University Department of Foreign Languages, Tashkent, Uzbekistan

Sayyora Khushbakovna Valieva
Tashkent State University of Economics, Tashkent, Uzbekistan

Tulkin Nasirovich Pardayev
Tashkent State University of Economics, Tashkent, Uzbekistan

Turayev Nurbek Muxammadovich
Tashkent State University of Economics, Tashkent, Uzbekistan

Sadokat Ilkhomjonovna Khalikchaeva
Tashkent State University of Economics, Tashkent, Uzbekistan

Azizbek Khamzaev Nematovich
Tashkent State University of Economics, Tashkent, Uzbekistan

Feruza Rajabovna Jumaniyazova
Tashkent State University of Economics, Tashkent, Uzbekistan

Sarvar Umarkhonovich Rejabbaev
Tashkent State University of Economics, Tashkent, Uzbekistan

Khayrilla Kurbonov
Tashkent State University of Economics, Tashkent, Uzbekistan

Nizomjon Shukurullaevich Khajimuratov
Tashkent State University of Economics, Tashkent, Uzbekistan

Rahimjon Makhmudov
Tashkent State University of Economics, Tashkent, Uzbekistan

Ravshanbek Sadullaevich Urunov
Tashkent State University of Economics, Tashkent, Uzbekistan

Hakimjon Hakimov
Tashkent State University of Economics, Tashkent, Uzbekistan

Dilorom Mahammadzhanovna Mutalova
Tashkent State University of Economics, Tashkent, Uzbekistan

Menglikulov Bakhtiyor Yusupovich
Tashkent State University of Economics, Tashkent, Uzbekistan

Norov Akmal Ruzimamatovich
Tashkent State University of Economics, Tashkent, Uzbekistan

Nadir Muratovich Shamsiev
Tashkent State University of Economics, Tashkent, Uzbekistan

Muyassarhon Ganievna Umarkhodjaeva
Tashkent State University of Economics, Tashkent, Uzbekistan

Makhbuba Mirkhalilovna Ismailova
Tashkent State University of Economics, Tashkent, Uzbekistan

Andrea Betti
Universidad Pontificia Comillas, Department of International Relations, Madrid, Spain

Pablo Biderbost
Universidad de Salamanca, Department of Sociology and Communication, Salamanca, Spain.

Esther Vaquero
Universidad Pontificia Comillas, Department of Financial Management, Madrid, Spain.

Trisha Ramsuraj
Department of Information and Corporate Management, Durban University of Technology, South Africa

Juliya S. Tsertseil
Plekhanov Russian University of Economics, Academic Department of Sustainable Development Finance, Moscow, Russia

Aleksei Ilyich Bolvachev
Plekhanov Russian University of Economics, Academic Department of Sustainable Development Finance, Moscow, Russia

List of Figures and Graphs

List of Tables

Łukasz Marecki & Agnieszka Wojcik-Czerniawska

The Future of Bitcoin Opportunities and Challenges

1. Introduction

Cryptocurrencies are digital financial instruments that are exchanged utilizing cryptography technologies. Sellers and buyers interact and transfer ownership via the Internet, eliminating the need for a reputable outside middleman such as a financial institution. It is an asset of value as it has inherent worth. Because cryptocurrencies aren't backed by any tangible assets like gold, they carry a huge risk for holders. A blockchain is a publicly accessible, digitally dispersed, decentralized ledger that is shared via a network of nodes. Blockchain technology is used by cryptocurrencies to generate, circulate, exchange, and archive information. In the initial article about Bitcoin (Nakamoto, 2008), the term "cryptocurrency" usually refers to a "coin" or "wallet." It also implies that the initial creators of Bitcoin tried to create a centralized digital exchange system for digital cash that would allow payments to be transferred among peers without the involvement of a banking institution. The idea essentially included the establishment of a cryptography-based electronic method of payment that operated independently of other parties. The current system for money transfers and settlement requires the full involvement of a financial organization that establishes the guidelines that must be adhered to for activities involving digital securities.

The banking institution's software determines ownership and assigns ownership, transferring the advantages to the party with contract obligations. The entire industry used paper for operations at first, but in the 1960s, mainframe computer systems were introduced, revolutionizing the field and leading to the development of modern powerful computers. The financial service provider oversees and monitors these extremely secure systems and bears responsibility for any theft, loss, or malfunction that occurs during the payment or payment process. They are legally obligated to reimburse the parties involved in the agreement for any damages. The technology behind Blockchain, which facilitates electronic transactions, is used by cryptocurrencies. Blockchain technology allows data related to transactions to be managed in a publicly accessible, decentralized database (Raymaekers, 2015).

Without the need for a middleman or other third party, such as a financial institution, bank, or regulatory authority, it enables transactions between individuals. Blockchain maintains the anonymity of user data while validating and permanently recording all transactions. With the electronic ledger, information is kept as codes. It is a decentralized, open platform that transforms the way trades are conducted globally (Radziwill, 2018). Blockchain technology may be used for a variety of purposes. Whenever an exchange involves the transfer of a financial asset, it keeps track of previous transactions, completing the transition of ownership confirmation process. Since it is incredibly difficult to change the prior entries on the blockchain, counterfeiting is almost impossible to do. The most recent cryptocurrencies to be released have innovative characteristics and apps built in to facilitate the use of financial payment.

The Ethereum cryptocurrency has grown rapidly in popularity throughout the years. Even if some of its users are inexperienced, they possess the ability to overcome the difficulties of becoming the most potent virtual currency due to its robust support system. Since its launch, the number of daily operations involving the Ethereum cryptocurrency has grown significantly. Recent cryptocurrencies have undergone multiple enhancements that have improved their total market cap and enabled the development of numerous decentralized apps on them, in contrast to previous ones. (N Reiff, 2022). The "Ethereum Virtual Machine" allows the network to facilitate several tiny transactions, such as derivatives as well as return payouts on financial instruments, besides serving as a means of exchange. It enables the settlement of work contracts for the acquisition of pricey goods.

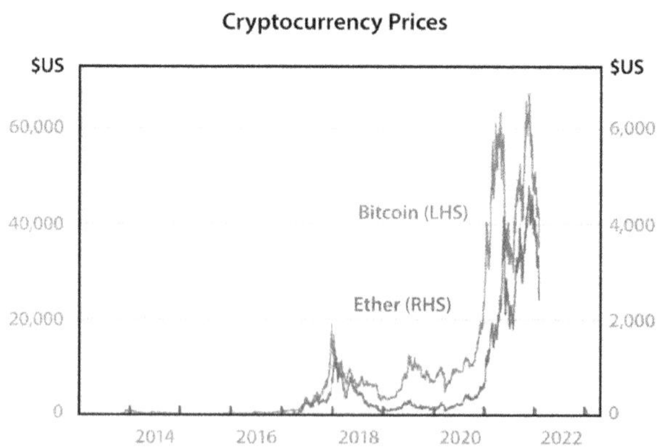

Figure 1. Cryptocurrency prices

Source: Reserve (2023)

Lacking the involvement of any centralized authority enables a fully decentralized payment process. With peer-to-peer digital transfers that don't require the involvement of a middleman to verify and validate the transaction, cryptocurrencies open up a new and creative avenue for investment exchanges. A large body of research has been written in favor of cryptocurrency technology, including methods to verify contracts on the distributed ledger throughout the network and creative tools for examining transactions on the blockchain. Initial coin products and services, or ICOs, are a significant source of funding for tech-focused businesses whose blockchain-enabled business models rely on innovation (Javed et al. , 2020). International authorities must assess it rigorously to determine whether to classify cryptocurrency assets as electronic currencies, securities, or any other type of financial transaction that creates value for the economy and safeguards shareholders (Momtaz, 2020).

2. Opportunities

With the help of cryptocurrency, it may be possible to move towards developing a secure and reliable market that would allow for faster and safer settlement and payment processes without the need for outside monetary institution interference. As a peer-to-peer system, cryptocurrency closes the gap in the present financial system and addresses issues with traditional banking. It facilitates unbanked consumers' internet transactions without the need for a middleman. Global transaction completion is possible without mysterious middleman costs.

2.1. High Return

According to Briere et al. (2015), the unique characteristics of cryptocurrencies and their capacity to fit certain economic functions make them a special asset. The past demonstrates that although Bitcoin is an extremely volatile money, investors may nevertheless expect significant returns. In addition, Bitcoin's risk is decreased because it is a part of several, different investments. Investors know that purchasing goods at lower prices and reselling them for a higher price is the greatest approach to maximise their returns on investment. Böhme et al. (2015) argue that those who purchased Bitcoin in the early going may have doubled or tripled their initial investment. Ciaran et al. (2016) researched demand and supply variables related to conventional currencies as well as digital indicators such as currency attractiveness. He also researched how the factors that determine pricing combine. The proposition suggests that demand from the market will drive up the cost of Bitcoin overall, especially when the amount of Bitcoins in existence surpasses its current level. Four times a year, the number of Bitcoins is half, a sign that there will be fewer new Bitcoins created which means more stability.

Figure 2. The price of Bitcoin
Source: Asgari and Chipolina (2024)

2.2. Fractionalization

The capacity to fractionalize any asset is one of the main benefits of the Internet. The ability to divide digital assets into more transportable and reasonably priced pieces opens up the possibility of increased liquidity and investor variety.

2.3. High Liquidity

A more standardized method of selling for presently inaccessible assets, like as corporate bonds, is made possible by partial ownership and selling of digital currencies within secondary markets, which unleash liquid in formerly illiquid marketplaces and create whole new transferable assets, like real estate cryptocurrencies. Additionally, the obstacles to issuing a security or holding an asset have been greatly reduced, providing smaller issuers with more opportunities, while larger issuers gain from the introduction of novel securities. The field of digital assets has reached a substantial level of maturity, and development in areas like post-trade, control, and settlement – all of which continue to be crucial tasks in supervised financial markets – is now driving this forward motion (Sabry et al., 2020).

2.4. Cost of Transaction

Humans have used money of some type for daily transactions throughout history. With mutual consent, individuals traded or traded their products under the concept of barter, which was the first form of trading. Fiat money was created so that people could trade easily and without needing to bring large items with them as the times changed. With the start of the twenty-first century, cryptocurrencies have swept the market. Large international corporations have been known to use Bitcoin as their medium of exchange as well as for paying their staff members' salaries every month (Angel & McCabe, 2014). Currently, cryptocurrencies and Bitcoin charges for transactions are less expensive than those of other traditional currencies. The decentralized and unregulated characteristics of cryptocurrencies are what contribute to their cheap transaction costs (Kim, 2017). There have been significant problems with the financing and payroll card payment system that is now in use. A user may end up in financial ruin due to the excessively high-interest rates applied to those who miss payments (Angel & McCabe, 2015). This hasn't been the case with cryptocurrencies, where the currency is only remitted until end-to-end users have agreed to trade.

2.5. Absence of Regulatory Burden

Adherence to regulatory mandates entails expenses. Investors do not have to pay the regulatory costs associated with cryptocurrencies.

2.6. Simple Access and Departure

Compared to other financial instruments, the entry and departure process for cryptocurrencies is significantly less difficult since they are not centralized or controlled by a central body.

3. Challenges

The need for electronic transactions and paperless currency is rising globally. Businesses, commercial concerns, and financiers are searching for a practical, secure, and risk-free method of completing transactions without the involvement of a bank or other third party. Since these transactions are untraceable and outside the jurisdiction of government agencies and law enforcement agencies, they may draw in criminal activity and other unlawful activities. The primary challenges facing the cryptocurrency sector are its total worth, unreliability, and extreme volatility. Even if it doesn't seem trustworthy right now, it doesn't indicate it will in the years to come. As a result, customers find Bitcoins to be a more alluring method of payment when buying goods or services. These businesses therefore act as Bitcoin middlemen.

This is not a securities deal; rather, it is a real-world Bitcoins trade. The distributed ledger of information on transactions does not distinguish between the two as a result. The protocol used by Bitcoin places a high premium on maintaining the most recent version of the blockchain. The idea of compensation has been developed to motivate the network's participants to work diligently and truthfully to support the network's expansion. In a way, new Bitcoins are given out as recompense. A breakthrough that the remainder of the world hasn't yet seen is Bitcoin's incentive structure. The Bitcoin protocol keeps a steady rate of keeping track of transactions since the total quantity of Bitcoins circulating is limited and measured over time. Because of the way the system is designed, there will eventually be fewer Bitcoins than there are in total – 21 million at most. The entire amount of Bitcoins is predicted to reach an important turning point in 2140 (Ghosh et al., 2020).

3.1. Price Discovery

The cost of purchasing or selling an item is its price. In an economy with free markets, demand as well as supply ultimately decide costs, and this also applies to the cost of financial assets. To a certain degree, it is simple to ascertain the possible supply and demand for existing financial assets. Even though the identical process works for cryptocurrencies, it can be challenging to determine the correct price due to increased uncertainty, an unclear market size, an absence of product knowledge, an elevated degree of investment, and the fact that cryptocurrencies are common and have no territorial limits.

3.2. Controlling Volatility

Speculation creates volatility, which eventually helps the financial markets become more liquid. No money market in the entire globe can provide traders with liquid without some degree of volatility. Unregulated fluctuation, nevertheless, is also a major danger to market security and is a major factor in trust among investors being shaken. Markets for digital currencies operate similarly, with the true risk to investors coming from unbridled volatility brought on by its decentralized structure.

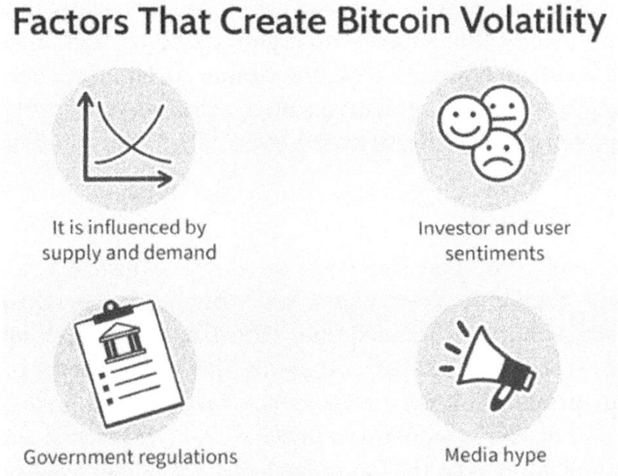

Figure 3. Factors that create bitcoin volatility
Source: Reiff (2024)

3.3. Portfolio Building

The easiest and best way to handle the risks in the financial markets is to diversify. Financial holdings that are negatively correlated are added to a portfolio to increase its diversity and allow investors to safeguard and profit from what they are investing in. Diversity is a crucial technique for handling risks since it lowers the likelihood of losses while simultaneously raising the likelihood of gains. An investor requires a range of assets to be featured in each inventory to establish one. The market breadth for cryptocurrency with negatively linked assets is either nonexistent or not easily accessible (Krichen et al., 2022). Furthermore, traders find it very challenging to evaluate the fundamentals of an individual cryptocurrency and determine how it relates to other currencies. As a result, investing in cryptocurrency asset building is challenging and somewhat of a blind bet.

3.4. Awareness

Social media is typically the greatest place to learn about cryptocurrencies. Investors use various online resources, like as social networking sites and YouTube channels, to learn about setting up accounts, transferring money, and buying and selling cryptocurrency. If you examine carefully, you will see that these outlets and social media platforms are mostly to blame for the excitement that has been generated regarding cryptocurrencies. Particularly among younger people, the use of beautiful animations, high-tech jargon, and financial suggestions draw a lot of attention. As with many other social media domains, it can be challenging to verify the veracity of the information offered by these outlet operators or influencers on the internet.

4. Future of Bitcoin

The emergence of cryptocurrencies will undoubtedly have a significant effect on the world economy. Researchers, investors, and economists all must make substantial efforts to broaden their knowledge of the technology known as blockchain (Fauzi et al., 2018a). To ensure that the possibilities for cryptocurrencies are genuine and not a coincidence, further study on their potential, technology, and danger is required as they have not yet reached a mature stage in terms of time. Moreover, the looming challenges do not absolve stakeholders of the melancholy associated with financial losses. To mitigate the 51 % attack on the blockchain mining network, further research has to be done in the future (Shi, 2016). The security protocol ought to safeguard the client's financial assets more effectively than the traditional centralized banking system, if not exactly. The groundbreaking testimonials from industry experts about the security aspect of users are warranted, as they will instill faith and trust in blockchain technology, enabling users to conduct their everyday transactions online with confidence.

A model known as the Moran process was presented by Bornholdt and Sneppen (2014) for a newly developing cryptocurrency. The market wherein currencies are bought and sold is simulated by the model. Cocco et al. (2015) state that the model can mimic the interaction between users participating in market transactions, the trading activity of the representatives, and the constant rate of freshly produced coins. Each of the currencies are transferable into other currencies with the account owner' consent. It was also found that Bitcoin may be traded for several currencies. This implies that interesting coins with potentially better attributes may eventually take the place of the highly suggested Bitcoin. Therefore, investigating these features – like security, return on investment, and low mining costs – will aid in determining which emerging digital currency will ultimately replace Bitcoin. Becker et al. have emphasised the use of work evidence in subsequent projects (2013). The reuse of the evidence of labor is one way to make the most of its byproduct. The reuse of this byproduct means that a user who has once received recognition for their efforts in solving a mathematical challenge can do so again by recognizing another user for a job well done. Utilizing the energy produced during the mining process to convert electrical energy to thermal energy is another recommendation.

This is possible in nations with cold climates, where residential buildings and other heat-intensive household tasks may be heated with the significantly excessive heat energy created during the calculation of solving the logic challenge. According to Dyhrberg's (2016) research, Bitcoin can act as an insurance policy between the US currency and the financial stock market. It was suggested that Bitcoin can reduce risk in the markets, much like gold, which is independent of any centralized authority. In the near run, Bitcoin's users' frequent and vigorous trading activity makes it possible by demonstrating its hedging qualities. This suggests that Bitcoin has minimal oversight of risks and a definite perspective in the global stock market portfolio research.

Dyhrberg (2016) asserts that bitcoin and gold are useful instruments for reducing investment risk. Although it is still too soon to compare the value of Bitcoin to that of gold, this claim shows potential and opens up a line of inquiry. It is agreed that a full grasp of the technology known as blockchain would be necessary to minimise the negative impacts of using bitcoins in day-to-day operations (Fauzi, 2018). Therefore, while specialists in this field should collaborate with lawmakers and government agencies when crafting laws and rules guiding a country's stance on cryptocurrencies. Researchers and business players need to enhance information management in order to better educate the public on the advantages and hazards of using Bitcoin. Since they have information resources that help the community learn more about certain concerns, even specialists from higher education institutions should interact with the public (Fauzi et al., 2018).

5. Conclusion

Due to their effectiveness in closing systemic gaps and the backing of the development community plus traders who view them as speculative assets, cryptocurrencies have the potential to evolve into a revolutionary technology. Robust cryptocurrency networks and apps are required to provide the peer-to-peer swapping of digital assets lawfully. Laws about cryptocurrencies provide these trades with legitimacy and significantly contribute to the creation of economic value and enhanced social welfare. Further investigation is required to assess the several elements that affect Bitcoin pricing and assist investors in managing price fluctuations (Morton, 2020). If the cryptocurrency is backed by an assortment of assets through which it may derive its worth, as opposed to the present system where its worth is derived from market request, which is the primary cause of unexplained fluctuation, then shareholders will be able to take calculated chances and it will attract greater funding. The collaboration of the contracting parties is just as important to the Bitcoin market's success as technological advancements. By establishing an auditing and grading system, ethical values might be included in an undetectable system such as cryptocurrencies. The transactions might be overseen and monitored by software.

To verify and audit if both parties to the contract are following procedures and upholding identity transparency, third parties may be engaged. Publicly sharing the audit's results might boost purchasers' trust in the legitimacy of the suppliers. Although this kind of system may be incredibly costly, it has the potential to significantly alter the cryptocurrency market, improve the condition of society, and create value for the economy. If purchasers' confidence is established through transaction transparency, cryptocurrency will undoubtedly cause a revolution in the financial system. The availability of knowledge to the public enables investors to make well-informed decisions, therefore mitigating ethical dangers. Protecting market players is becoming more and more important. Researchers in the areas of finance, economics, and other associated fields must conduct extensive study and engage in ongoing reflection. Different cryptocurrency exchanges need to be aware of how security holes might result in a hacking assault. Constant price volatility raises the risk and deters businesses and individuals from making bitcoin investments. Regulation of cryptocurrency exchanges, mitigation of hacking issues, and enforcement of identity transparency among contract parties are necessary. Parties who disregard the identity transparency policy and the grading and auditing system may be subject to regulations. To transition technology to a regulated environment, it might be highly beneficial to have an international organization oversee and monitor the transaction. Because they are unique from conventional assets and offer diversity, cryptocurrencies do not appreciate value together with other assets. Even though they might not satisfy every condition to be accepted as legitimate money for transactions, they are nonetheless very helpful to speculative investors. Cryptocurrency is a sign of a revolutionary technology that will revolutionize the established financial system.

References

Angel, J. J., & McCabe, D. M. (2014). The ethics of payments: Paper, plastic, or Bitcoin? *Social Science Research Network* [Preprint]. https://doi.org/10.2139/ssrn.2379233.

Asgari, N., & Chipolina, S. (2024). Bitcoin's Wall Street takeover frustrates crypto's true believers. *Financial Times*, 12 January. https://www.ft.com/content/f626d6f7-3210-48f2-abb1-3e9b4c3af17e.

Becker, J. et al. (2013). Can we afford integrity by Proof-of-Work? Scenarios inspired by the Bitcoin currency. in *Springer eBooks*, pp. 135–156. https://doi.org/10.1007/978-3-642-39498-0_7.

Böhme, R. et al. (2015). Bitcoin: Economics, technology, and governance. *The Journal of Economic Perspectives*, *29*(2), pp. 213–238. https://doi.org/10.1257/jep.29.2.213.

Bornholdt, S., & Sneppen, K. (2014). Do Bitcoins make the world go round? On the dynamics of competing crypto-currencies. *arXiv (Cornell University)* [Preprint]. https://arxiv.org/pdf/1403.6378.

Brière, M., Oosterlinck, K., & Szafarz, A. (2015). Virtual currency, tangible return: Portfolio diversification with bitcoin. *Journal of Asset Management*, *16*(6), pp. 365–373. https://doi.org/10.1057/jam.2015.5.

Ciaian, P., Rajčániová, M., & Kancs, D. (2015). The economics of Bitcoin price formation. *Applied Economics*, *48*(19), pp. 1799–1815. https://doi.org/10.1080/00036846.2015.1109038.

Cocco, L., Concas, G., & Marchesi, M. (2015). Using an artificial financial market for studying a cryptocurrency market. *Journal of Economic Interaction and Coordination (Print)*, *12*(2), pp. 345–365. https://doi.org/10.1007/s11403-015-0168-2.

Dyhrberg, A. H. (2016). Hedging capabilities of bitcoin. Is it the virtual gold? *Finance Research Letters*, *16*, pp. 139–144. https://doi.org/10.1016/j.frl.2015.10.025.

Fauzi, M. A. et al. (2018a). An integrative model of knowledge sharing in Malaysian Higher Learning Institute. *Kybernetes*, *47*(5), pp. 1031–1052. https://doi.org/10.1108/k-10-2017-0388.

Fauzi, M. A., Tan, C. N.-L., & Ramayah, T. (2018b). Knowledge sharing intention at Malaysian higher learning institutions: The academics' viewpoint. *Knowledge Management & E-learning: An International Journal*, pp. 163–176. https://doi.org/10.34105/j.kmel.2018.10.011.

Ghosh, A. et al. (2020). Security of Cryptocurrencies in blockchain technology: State-of-art, challenges and future prospects. *Journal of Network and Computer Applications*, *163*, p. 102635. https://doi.org/10.1016/j.jnca.2020.102635.

Javed, M., Hasan, M., & Khan, R. (2020). Future of bitcoin in India: Issues and challenges. *Journal of Statistics and Management Systems*, *23*(2), pp. 207–214. https://doi.org/10.1080/09720510.2020.1724621.

Kim, T. (2017). On the transaction cost of Bitcoin. *Finance Research Letters*, *23*, pp. 300–305. https://doi.org/10.1016/j.frl.2017.07.014.

Krichen, M. et al. (2022). Blockchain for modern applications: A survey. *Sensors*, *22*(14), p. 5274. https://doi.org/10.3390/s22145274.

Momtaz, P. P. (2020). Initial coin offerings. In *PLoS ONE*, *15*(5). https://doi.org/10.1371/journal.pone.0233018

Morton, D. T. (2020). The future of cryptocurrency: An unregulated instrument in an increasingly regulated global economy. *16*(1), p. 129. https://lawecommons.luc.edu/cgi/viewcontent.cgi?article=1219&context=lucilr.

Nakamoto, S. (2008). Bitcoin: A peer-to-peer Electronic Cash system. 2008. https://bitcoin.org/bitcoin.pdf

Radziwill, N. (2018). The Blockchain Revolution: How the technology behind bitcoin is changing money, business, and the world. *Quality Management Journal*, *25*(1), 64–65. https://doi.org/10.1080/10686967.2018.1404373

Raymaekers, W. (2015). Cryptocurrency Bitcoin: Disruption, challenges and opportunities. *Journal of Payments Strategy & Systems* [Preprint]. https://hstalks.com/article/1069/cryptocurrency-bitcoin-disruption-challenges-and-o/.

Reiff, N. (2022). Bitcoin vs. Ethereum: What's the difference? 2022. https://www.investopedia.com/articles/investing/031416/bitcoin-vs-ethereum-drivendifferent-purposes.asp

Reiff, N. (2024). Why is Bitcoin volatile? https://www.investopedia.com/articles/investing/052014/why-bitcoins-value-so-volatile.asp.

Reserve, B. O. (2023). Digital Currencies | Explainer Education. https://www.rba.gov.au/education/resources/explainers/cryptocurrencies.html.

Sabry, F. et al. (2020). Cryptocurrencies and artificial intelligence: Challenges and opportunities. *IEEE Access*, *8*, pp. 175840–175858. https://doi.org/10.1109/access.2020.3025211.

Shi, N. (2016). A new proof-of-work mechanism for bitcoin. *Financial Innovation*, *2*(1). https://doi.org/10.1186/s40854-016-0045-6.

Łukasz Marecki & Agnieszka Wojcik-Czerniawska

Impact of AI and Automation on the Job Market

1. Introduction

Four technological revolutions have swept across human civilization since the start of the twentieth century's industrial revolution, but each one may be seen as a further development of automated technology. When humans are replaced by robots, there is a perpetual conflict that must be resolved in order to balance employment and efficiency (Liu, 2018; Morgan, 2019). When people begin to grasp the current stage of mankind's social and economic development triggered by advanced technical innovation, they must embrace the "creative destruction" carried forth by the cyclical renewal of fresh technologies (Forsythe et al., 2022). The issues of where innovation will ultimately take humankind, how much artificial intelligence will alter how people interact with their jobs, and if increased productivity would result in widespread permanent unemployment have all been raised.

One of the main components of the fourth industrial revolution is artificial intelligence (AI). AI works in tandem with advances in a computer system, mechanical in nature, and electrical engineering to propel the growth and revolution of the internet-based economy. The Web-based economies have undoubtedly contributed significantly to the stability of job opportunities and financial promotion through the quick iteration and widespread adoption of overall computer technological advances; however, this is primarily due to the "employment effect" brought on by the ongoing development of creative thinking in the discipline of social manufacture and the ever-evolving times. A number of the jobs that were previously completed by human workers will unavoidably be replaced by digital technology. Owing to the country's labor market and job structure, several businesses have need assistance in hiring personnel in the past few years. Robots are doing repetitive and standardised activities because some businesses have accelerated the pace of "machine replacement," fueled by the fast development of machine learning technologies.

The digital age presents new difficulties for corporate personnel in terms of their career prospects, since deep learning and artificial intelligence allow robots to operate systems to do more complicated tasks. The World Economic Forum's

Future of Jobs 2020 report states that over the next five years, automation and the resulting division of labour between machines and humans are going to disrupt 85 million positions across 15 industries globally. The report also states that the COVID-19 pandemic-related recession and the rapid advancement of automation technology are altering the job the marketplace much more quickly than anticipated. The need for professional workers in fields like accounting, entering data, and managerial assistance has been severely impacted. On the other hand, white-collar workers' impression of an economic crisis has been made worse by this development (Duan et al., 2023). According to the research, there exists a high risk of professional replacement in the fields of agriculture, forestry, animal husbandry, fisheries, mining, production, both of and construction – all of which are expected to require a high level of intelligence. It is yet unclear if the increasing digital efficiency of AI, massive data sets, and smart manufacturing technologies will significantly alter the biological makeup of capital and hence reduce labor employment. A robot, sometimes known as the "pearl at the very top of the manufacturing crown," is a vital component of AI technology and intelligent manufacturing as it manifests in machinery and equipment. It is also a key metric for gauging a nation's high-end manufacturing sector.

Research Questions

- How may AI change the nature of work in the future?
- What kinds of occupations relating to artificial intelligence could be established in the future?

2. Methodology

This study primarily applies an explanatory model-based, inductive method based on case studies. Review of earlier research, journal articles, reports, and surveys by market research consultancies, corporations, and others is included with the compilation of case studies. To address the research questions, broad insights are shown through qualitative analysis, which aligns with the interpretative research approach. The tools that scientists employ to gather, analyze, and interpret data are referred to as research philosophies. They might have different purposes and be either quantitative or subjective. Considering the type of study being conducted, the exploratory method is still up in the air. We conduct a preliminary writing assessment utilising the following electronic informative indexes: Web of Science, PsycINFO (OVID), Scopus, and Wiley Online Library, in order to determine the extent to which attribution supposition was accepted with regard to development demonstrate. Several sources compile Google Scholar and provide a manual search of full-text scholarly publications.

3. Results and Discussion

3.1. The Direct Influence of AI on Employment

A new breed of intelligent machines that can carry out normal, monotonous, and regular manufacturing jobs requiring human decision-making, solving issues, and ability to analyse has arisen as a result of advancements in big data, machine learning, computational intelligence, and other techniques. Automating processes using robotic technology can be extremely helpful in processing large amounts of data because it can mimic and learn from workers' repetitive new tasks, such as data collection, report running, data replicating, integrity of data checks, reading, the process, and email delivering. With an economy dominated by technology and information technology, businesses are pressuring employees to take on more imaginative assignments. According to the integrative task structure hypothesis, the main advantage of productiveness gain achieved by advances in technology is the creation of new demands, or tasks. Along with updating the current tasks, these freshly created task packages also provide new work combination with more challenging technological requirements. Despite being widely employed in many areas, intelligent technology may cause people to be replaced, which might result in technical unemployment. But as a fresh wave of breakthroughs in technology and revolution emerges, high efficiency fosters the emergence of several new sectors and has a positive impact on employment creation. The result of technological advancement is the creation of new jobs.

The generation and refilling of jobs is the first effect of AI. The improved "human-machine cooperation" work style will be facilitated by the based on artificial intelligence smart manufacturing model. In a highly advanced technological civilization, the social situation of shared wealth benefits the most disadvantaged groups of people because of the enhanced productivity of labor and specialized factories caused by the division of labour. Technological innovation exerts both financial and price impacts by boosting manufacturing efficiency, lowering the sales price of the end result, and promoting social usage. These factors in turn encourage related enterprises to rise in the size of their manufacture, which raises consumer demand for work (Li et al., 2021). People often see robots as rivals to humans, yet this perspective merely reflects the materialist perception of conventional equipment. It is not an impossible task for humans and machines to cohabit. As the objective shifts from "collaboration for all" to "collaboration between man and machine," the total productivity of factors is maximised and production limitations are reduced, leading to the creation of new collaborative responsibilities and additional jobs (Balsmeier & Woerter, 2019). In addition, materialised AI technology may increase efficiency in manufacturing between both the upstream and downstream businesses in the manufacturing cycle along the value chain, as well as the overall factor product performance in ways appropriate for its component endowments structure.

The development of business production size and reproducing will be facilitated by this improvement in the efficiency of the market, and their combined impact will encourage parallel development of the labour demand for a variety of talents, which will have a creative consequence. artificial intelligence (AI), a driving factor behind the fourth industrial age, would unavoidably alter humans social standing and the composition of the work force (Chen, 2023). By automation repetitive jobs, AI and robotics raise productivity of labour while developing worker skills and elevating the value of employment. Consequently, jobs that are low-skilled will vanish in a machine-for-machine job model whereas new, as-yet-unrealized work categories arise. We may even contend that robot interactions, computational intelligence, and technological advancements are assisting in the training of highly competent robots and increasing their associated pay (Yoon, 2023).

Thus, human workers in nonprogrammed positions, like technology and knowledge, will have additional competitive advantages when intelligent company evolution replaces their initial programme responsibilities with more complicated new ones.

3.2. AI Affects Jobs and the Economy

The McKinsey Global Institute, a consultancy, estimates that AI could greatly increase global economic output by about thirteen billion dollars in the coming years and by the year 2030, or approximately 16 % more accumulative GDP when compared to today, at the median approval and consumption rate across the world and the developments in AI indicated by their modeling. This corresponds to an additional 1.2 % increase in gross domestic product every year. If this were to come to pass, the impact would be comparable to that of past advances in technology over history. This will largely come from increased innovation in goods and services as well as the replacement of humans in the workforce by technology. According to the poll, by 2030, the median model predicts that over 70 % of firms will have adopted artificial intelligence (AI) and deployed at least one type of AI technology; however, fewer than 50 % would have completely integrated every one of the five kinds. Forbes claims that one of the most significant technological advancements in history, computational intelligence (AI) has enormous potential and will impact economies all around the globe (Polák, 2021).

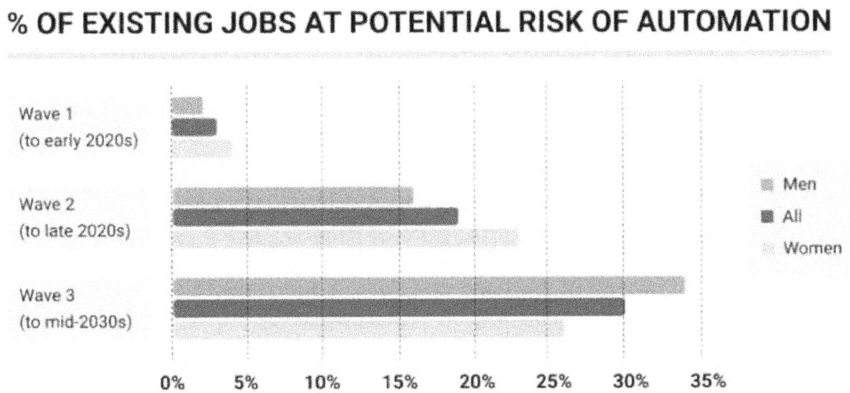

Figure 1. Percentage of existing jobs at potential risk of automation.
Source: (Pérez, 2023)

A study conducted by financial giant Goldman Sachs suggests that artificial intelligence (AI) could take over three hundred million full-time positions. Not only may technology replace 25 % of work tasks in the US and the European Union, but it may also increase production and create new jobs. It may also ultimately lead to a 7 % increase in the global yearly cost of items and services generated. Furthermore, the study predicts that approximately 25 % of jobs could potentially be performed exclusively by AI while approximately two thirds of employment opportunities in the US and Europe "are vulnerable to a particular degree of AI digitization." According to study from Open Artificial Intelligence (AI) and the University of Pennsylvania, skilled white-collar workers earning a maximum of $80,000 yearly are among the most likely categories to be affected by labour automation.

AI will cause unemployment in the future, just as other forms of technology have in the past, and dangerous societal upheaval may be sparked much more quickly. The economic disparity between the richest and poorest will widen if unemployment stays high. As AI owners of capital increase their wealth and certain employees may not gain, inequality in earnings will increase. AI may result in unemployment, but it may also lead employees to lose their dignity. It might worsen racial conflict, crime, rioting, social unrest, murder, and other kinds of contemporary society problems. However, unemployment and a lack of professional possibilities are often the primary causes of these problems (Ramos et al., 2022). Businesses have already started to develop AI technology, which will replace the antiquated method of work mechanisation. A number of nations have already replaced employment with basic automation technologies. AI will accelerate job automation and have a more widespread impact. This is because traditional automation involves particular programming, which raises manufacturing costs because it requires a lot of work from humans.

3.3. Change of Employment Structure: Substitution and Complementation of Artificial Intelligence for Employment

The system of employment has been dismantled and reorganised by the use of computational intelligence, leading to the elimination and substitution of an increasing number of positions. In particular, there is a variation in the extent to which AI replaces workers with varying degrees of education and expertise. Kong et. al., (2022) discovered that workers with lower skill levels and worse quality are more likely to be replaced, resulting in "technical unemployment". In particular, Binder, Based on the idea of a changing makeup of the labour force. Due to this issue, middle-skilled, low-educated people in administrative tasks categorised as white-col and blue-col are gradually disappearing from the workforce. The employment prospects of males with low levels of education are particularly falling. Agrawal (2019) argues that the main reason for this problem is because individuals with a lower degree of expertise and training do not possess the basic skills necessary for success in the marketplace for high-end technology. The emergence of AI has therefore put the employment status of uneducated and underqualified individuals to examination and has had a major impact on low-skill intensive industries. Simultaneously, the advancement of artificial intelligence enhances the efficiency of the industrial structure, generates fresh forms and occupations, and has a novel impact on employment, garnering significant interest from academic circles. To provide more job prospects, businesses will invest more money into AI research and development. According to Hui Wei (2020), there are two sorts of complementing effects of AI on employment: complement and recombine. This effect is larger than the replacement effect, resulting in in job augmentation.

AI's replacement impact is more pronounced in labor-intensive businesses and more pronounced in highly trained and competent industries when seen from the perspectives of different industries. The benefits that lie ahead for artificial intelligence as a universal technological advances, among them its widespread adoption, data-driven nature, and systemic intelligence, have significantly altered conventional research and development as well as manufacturing methodologies. In light of this, we should consider how AI may "substitute" and "create" jobs to prevent widespread unemployment. In particular, we can create jobs via a variety of means, encourage the modernization and change of traditional sectors, fully grow the modern service sector, actively foster new forms such as cultural tourism, healthy pensions, and cleaning services, enhance social services such as employment programs, and promptly hire "overflowing" employees in hopes of achieving balanced growth for people of different educational experiences and socioeconomic classes.

3.4. What Jobs Are Most Likely to be Automated?

- **A representative of customer service**

Nowadays, the vast majority of phone calls to assistance agents are handled online. Most of the time, customers come with repeated queries and problems. Answering these questions does not need a high level of psychological or social skills. As an outcome, artificial intelligence may be able to produce automatic responses to frequently asked questions.

- **Front desk employees**

Currently, machines staff front desks in the large majority of enterprises around the globe. AI now manages the calls as well. For example, AimeReception can see, hear, understand, and communicate with customers and visitors.

- **Bookkeepers and accountants**

Many organizations employ automation and artificial intelligence (AI) for accountancy processes. Because AI-powered bookkeeping services are provided as online services, they give flexibility, security, and an efficient accounting system. Artificial intelligence can guarantee that the procedures used to collect, store, and evaluate the data are correct. Using an AI financial solution costs considerably less than paying someone's wage to complete the same activity.

- **Retailers**

Salespeople are no longer necessary for retail and marketing goals in firms. The web and social networking sites are becoming the new focal points of marketing.

With the use of social media platforms' integrated customised advertising tools, marketers may create original content for a range of user demographics.

- **Investigation and evaluation**

In the field of evaluation and study areas, artificial intelligence is now used to locate new data with no human participation and to simplify procedures. The computing power of modern computers allows for effective data sorting, extrapolation, and analysis. With the development of computational intelligence, human participation in knowledge investigation and evaluation may become obsolete.

- **Work at a warehouse**

Increasingly automated processes and systems are required to efficiently and rapidly load goods onto delivery trucks as the online retail industry continues to grow. One area that has received attention for simplifying processes is the use of automation. Streamlined retrieval and reloading may be performed by artificial intelligence (AI) in future in order to improve shipping capacities. In the meantime, basic automated operations and manufactured distribution in the storage facility provide for easy access to automated systems that direct workers and locate shipments.

- **Writing of insurance**

While assessing the insurance applicant's viability, their most crucial task is usually to analyze the available data and incorporate it into a series of structures or formulas. Automation is capable of doing these tasks with ease and is always developing to tackle tasks that become more complicated. Consequently, a company can require fewer underwriters than initially estimated.

- **Shops**

Self-checkout machines are an example of robotics in the commerce sector; they have grown more prevalent in big-box retailers and grocery stores. Companies use self-checkout areas as a result of their cost-benefit analysis. Giving customers the ability to identify their own items might increase stealing, however the company will save more money since fewer employees would be required to run cash registers.

4. Conclusion

It is undeniable that automation and digitalization have had a significant influence on how well every social subsystem in society functions. Technology's worth (awareness) is determined only by how it is applied in the social environment in which it is developed; technological advancement on its own does not give technology meaning. With its robust word processing skills and conversation with humans, the US computer science startup OpenAI's smart Chatbot ChatGPT, which was just launched, has aroused worries about how it can affect jobs in related industries around the world.

The labour demand and supply map is greatly impacted by automation technology, which is embodied by manufacturing that is intelligent. It also has a major influence on social and economic growth. Artificial intelligence has the potential to boost job creation and economic expansion. The method of destruction is substitution; technological advances will eventually supplant outdated technology, which means that occupations involving technological advances will eventually become unemployed. Technological advancements will lower prices and improve the efficiency of resources. The breakthrough process's saving impact will lower the requirement for labor, which would raise the unemployment rate . In the labour market, new technologies produce the winners and the losers. Despite the fact that they raise living standards and production, they alter the relative responsibilities of the trades. Mechanism analysis demonstrates how AI creates jobs through mechanisms that support greater worker productivity, specialization of labour, and capital development. The geometric numerous enhance the impacts of accumulation and the amalgamation process; digital commerce, which results from technological advances and online platforms as well has supported the change of traditional commercial aggregates into the virtual collections; and the built flow of network a forum is particularly susceptible to the free transference of information, advances in technology and science, and inventiveness. Artificial Intelligence is now driving job creation through industrialised virtual agglomeration, a new mechanism and essential conduit that will increase worker autonomy, improve work fit, and encourage employers to spread worker wellbeing throughout "cultivation areas."

5. Recommendations

Technology is agnostic; how it is used is what matters. As an open-source, new general technological advances, artificial intelligence (AI) technology is a major productivity advance and a vital catalyst that has the ability to accelerate economic growth. Both the high-end manufacturing of domesticated robots and research and development expenditures in AI should be raised. The advancement of artificial intelligence (AI) has not only increased production efficiency but also caused a shift in the corporate and labour structures, creating new occupations as AI replaces human labour. Government agencies are advised to enhance the social security program and stabilise employment through a variety of means. The first channel involves assessing and keeping an eye on how AI might eliminate the lower-class labour force. This is made possible by businesses and government collaboration to create pertinent information channels, increase labour market transparency, and predictably reduce permanent joblessness. The full value of big data ought to be realised, including the establishment of a dependable platform for tracking national job statistics, actual time tracking of rapid fluctuations in work in essential groups, critical areas, and significant positions, the public release of employment status data, and the provision of early alert, projections, and forecasting services related to job creation. It is recommended that higher education departments advance a coordinated expansion of industry-university studies and support reforms to the system of higher education and training. As new digital production elements, enormous amounts of data, the World of Things, and artificial intelligence (AI) have permeated daily economic operations, causing changes in the industrial landscape as well as in the dynamics of supply and demand in the labour market.

References

Agrawal, A., Gans, J. S., & Goldfarb, A. (2019). Artificial intelligence: The ambiguous labor market impact of automating prediction. *The Journal of Economic Perspectives*, *33*(2), pp. 31–50. https://doi.org/10.1257/jep.33.2.31.

Balsmeier, B., & Woerter, M. (2019). Is this time different? How digitalization influences job creation and destruction. *Research Policy*, *48*(8), p. 103765. https://doi.org/10.1016/j.respol.2019.03.010.

Chen, Z. (2023). Ethics and discrimination in artificial intelligence-enabled recruitment practices. *Humanities & Social Sciences Communications*, *10*(1). https://doi.org/10.1057/s41599-023-02079-x.

Duan, S. X., Deng, H., & Wibowo, S. (2023). Exploring the impact of digital work on work–life balance and job performance: A technology affordance perspective. *Information Technology & People*, *36*(5), pp. 2009–2029. https://doi.org/10.1108/itp-01-2021-0013.

Forsythe, E. et al. (2022). Where have all the workers gone? Recalls, retirements, and reallocation in the COVID recovery. *Labour Economics*, *78*, p. 102251. https://doi.org/10.1016/j.labeco.2022.102251.

Hui Wei, Jiang Wei. (2020). Artificial intelligence, labor force employment and income distribution: Review and prospect[J]. *Journal of Beijing University of Technology (Social Sciences)*, *20*(05), pp. 77–86.

Kong, G., Huang, J., & Li, S. (2022). Digital transformation and within-firm pay gap: Evidence from China. *Emerging Markets Finance & Trade*, *59*(6), pp. 1748–1766. https://doi.org/10.1080/1540496x.2022.2149262.

Li, Z., Hong, Y., & Zhang, Z. (2021). The empowering and competition effects of the platform-based sharing economy on the supply and demand sides of the labor market. *Journal of Management Information Systems*, *38*(1), pp. 140–165. https://doi.org/10.1080/07421222.2021.1870387.

Liu, L. (2018). Occupational therapy in the Fourth Industrial Revolution. *Canadian Journal of Occupational Therapy*, *85*(4), pp. 272–283. https://doi.org/10.1177/0008417418815179.

Morgan, J. (2019). Will we work in twenty-first century capitalism? A critique of the fourth industrial revolution literature. *Economy and Society/Economy and Society*, *48*(3), pp. 371–398. https://doi.org/10.1080/03085147.2019.1620027.

Pérez, R. M. (2023). The Impact of Artificial Intelligence on Job Market, 14 April.

Polák, P. (2021). Welcome to the digital era – The impact of AI on business and society. *Society*, *58*(3), pp. 177–178. https://doi.org/10.1007/s12115-021-00588-6.

Ramos, M. E., Garza-Rodríguez, J., & Romero, D. E. G. (2022). Automation of employment in the presence of industry 4.0: The case of Mexico. *Technology in Society*, *68*, p. 101837. https://doi.org/10.1016/j.techsoc.2021.101837.

Yoon, C. (2023). Technology adoption and jobs: The effects of self-service kiosks in restaurants on labor outcomes. *Technology in Society*, *74*, p. 102336. https://doi.org/10.1016/j.techsoc.2023.102336.

Andrew Enaifoghe, Makhosazana Vezi-Magigaba,
& Sipho Nkonde

Challenges and Contribution of Small and Medium Enterprises (SMEs) in Enhancing Global Economic Development

1. Use This Style for Level One Headings (Introduction)

The study acknowledged the developmental role and challenges of Small and Medium Enterprises (SMEs) in enhancing global economic development in creating jobs and foster innovation. However, the globalization of the economy is seen as a chance for both developed and developing nations to increase their economic prosperity through engaging with international trade (Ahmedova, 2015). WTO (2016), states that its two main areas of focus are the globalization of production, which is concerned with sourcing goods from around the globe to benefit from social differentiation in production costs, and the globalization of markets, which lessens trade barriers across international borders (Enaifoghe, 2023a).

The focus of economic globalization is on cross-border activities that create the global business environment for all endeavors, including international trade, international investment, and strategic contracts for product development, production, sourcing, and marketing (Chew & Yeung, 2001; Sener et al., 2014). It is common to overlook the role that small and medium-sized businesses (SMEs) play in promoting constructive social, environmental, and economic change. Nonetheless, these companies have a big impact on how our local, regional, and worldwide economies develop, innovate, and endure. There is proof that SMEs add more to the prosperity of their country than they should.

According to The World Bank, SMEs account for about 90 % of all businesses, 50 % of jobs globally, and up to 40 % of GDP in developing nations (Enaifoghe, 2023a). Analyzing national data, the McKinsey research Beyond Financials (Prasanna et al., 2019), Helping SMEs thrive discovered that while midsize businesses make up 1.6 % of all businesses in Canada, they account for 12 % of the country's GDP (Chew & Yeung, 2001). Although medium businesses make just 2 % of all businesses in Malaysia, nevertheless make up around 40 % of the nation's GDP. Those smaller businesses have a disproportionate impact.

2. Research Methodology

In this study, which is qualitative, the secondary resource content data analysis method was employed. This approach enables researchers to examine and interpret textual materials that may be in the public or private domain (Kothari and Garg, 2016). This implies that the researcher evaluates the materials they review for relevance in light of their importance to the investigation (Mogalakwe, 2006). The majority of secondary sources used to gather the qualitative data were books, papers, magazines, policy briefs, journals, articles, news bulletins, and government documents on the strategies to enhance the role of Small and Medium Enterprises (SMEs) as they are vital to national economies all over the world, because they create jobs, generate value, and foster innovation.

The paper reviewed several research papers published in different databases such as Google Scholar, Scopus and other reputable publishing companies. Over 100 pieces of literature were sourced in different domains using advanced searches from Google scholars and Scorpius on the subject. The collected data were analysed based on content and relevance, but only 70 pieces of literature were used that were found relevant to inform the study.

3. The Socio-Political Economy of SMEs

Political, Economic, Social, Technological, Environmental, and Legal elements, or PESTEL for short, is a strategic planning and marketing research method that assists organizations in identifying the macroenvironmental aspects that affect their operations and in making more informed decisions. PESTEL has two main purposes, according to Yuksel (2012): first, it helps the business define the environment in which it operates; second, it gives it data and knowledge that helps it anticipate events in the future. In order to make better judgments, all businesses need to be aware of PESTEL aspects. Before drafting business plans or making choices, SMEs should do an external environment scan to look at the political, economic, social, technological, environmental, and legal influences on the company (Rakesh, 2014).

PESTEL analysis is also necessary for SMEs to be aware of their competition because these businesses have a great potential to spread industries, encourage entrepreneurship, create jobs, and bring in foreign exchange for the nation. An method to strategy formulation known as the resource-based view focuses on using the organization's resources to gain a competitive advantage (Ong et al., 2010b). A resource-based view, according to Barney (1991), enables firms to search internally rather than outside for competitive advantage.

However, a firm's resource base predicts that the firm's unique resources can produce superior performance and a competitive advantage (Ainuddin et al., 2007). SMEs have more challenges than large companies in gaining access to export resources and competencies, which makes them more difficult to penetrate international markets (Xie & Suh, 2014).

According to the resource-based view, SMEs may be able to obtain resources – tangible or intangible – through interorganizational partnerships, which will improve the performance of the business (Rice et al., 2012; Hessels & Parker, 2013). It follows that SMEs will only benefit when they build the proper network to obtain the resources required for their success (Zaheer & Zaheer, 2001).

Freeman developed the stakeholder theory, which emphasizes the significance of a company's relationships with important stakeholders. According to research, employees, customers, and partners/suppliers are all important for long-term organizational performance (Fonseca et al., 2016). In conclusion, the corporate world in a free trade environment is related to the ideologies of the theories that have been explored. Thus, theories often point to the significance of developing or strengthening firm stability circumstances via increased competitiveness.

4. The Difficulty of International Trade Competition

Currently, economic competition is observed in international arenas. It intensified following economic globalization in the 1980s and intensified further following entry into the WTO trade regime in 1995 (Gunday et al., 2011). Due to industry-specific characteristics like a low technology base, a high concentration in the labor-intensive sector, low entry barriers, relatively low fixed costs of production, and a focus on producing price-taker goods, SMEs are more vulnerable to the effects of economic competition than other industries. This is especially important as SMEs grow increasingly important to the economies of both developed and developing nations (Sener et al., 2014; Prasanna et al., 2019).

Currently, the World commerce Organization (WTO) is the principal multilateral entity that oversees international commerce and advances free trade agreements worldwide economy. Due to trade liberalization, which makes it easier for successful foreign manufacturers and retailers to enter undeveloped and remote markets, small and medium-sized enterprises (SMEs) will be more affected by the competition in the global economy if their productions are highly localized and segmented (Singh et al., 2009). According to the United Nations Economic and Social Commission for Asia and the Pacific's report (United Nations, 2009), trade liberalization, quickly advancing technology, and a constantly rising and shifting demand for unique, high-quality intermediated and final goods and services that satisfy ever-tougher international standards are the main features of the current global economy among SMEs in the Asia and Pacific region.

It is difficult for SMEs to remain competitive in such a setting, especially in their own market. The growing worldwide economic competitiveness has made product innovation a challenging process for SMEs (Gunday et al., 2011; Gherghina et al., 2019). Mustafa and Yaakub (2018) compiled a list of the main obstacles to innovation and technology adaptation based on research conducted in Malaysia. These obstacles included a lack of funding, resources, and research and development; low productivity as a result of inefficient technologies; difficulties in increasing capacity and improving product quality; and a failure to use new knowledge to develop new products. Mustafa and Yaakub (2018) stressed that SMEs should make thoughtful decisions about planning and operation because implementing innovations can be difficult.

The experts advise using this tactic to ask for help from the government. They use an example from Malaysia to accentuate this approach. According to Jinjarak and Wignaraja (2016), in order for a company to be successful on a worldwide scale, it must first overcome financial obstacles, have enough capital, manage cash flows well, and have easy access to global funding. Most small businesses struggle to get finance, particularly those in developing nations. According to Stein et al. (2013), over 17 million businesses, or 60 % of SMEs, have an excess demand for loanable capital.

Removing the financial obstacles increases the firms' competitiveness. Therefore, enterprises with less financial constraints exhibit a greater inclination towards exporting (Jinjarak & Wignaraja, 2016). Additionally, financing flexibility plays a crucial role in exporting. According to the WTO's 2016 report, Levelling the Trading Field for SMEs, prompt action is required to address the aforementioned problems to increase the SMEs' products' ability to compete in the world market. More generally, Doh and Kim (2014) state that the dynamic and positive roles played by SMEs are essential to building competitive regional economies in the global marketplaces. For instance, in South Korea, where giant conglomerates have taken over major economic markets, the performance and sustainability attained by SMEs through their proactive and dynamic conduct have demonstrated critical value.

Additionally, improving financial circumstances, investigating R&D, utilizing human capital, and collaborating with dynamic institutions – including universities at local and international levels – will increase SMEs' chances of competing globally (Sener et al., 2014). According to research by Ren et al. (2015), marketing has a key role in determining the success of SMEs in international market competition. Therefore, poor marketing is a major barrier to SMEs' ability to compete both locally and internationally (Asare et al., 2015). Businesses are influenced by economic competition to be on the lookout for innovations in their business strategies (Gunday et al., 2011). Businesses begin to understand the importance of innovation in light of the intensifying global market competitiveness when technology advances quickly and when fierce competition quickly erodes the value-added of already-produced goods and services (Garcia et al., 2020, and Kijkasiwat & Phuensane, 2020).

Sener et al. (2014) state that high value-added goods and services will increase SMEs' competitiveness in the global marketplace in relation to innovation basis. Ahmedova (2015) suggests that shifting business focus from low-value industries to specialized markets with specific competitive advantages and high-value products could equip small and medium-sized enterprises (SMEs) for success in the global marketplace. According to Singh et al. (2008), in certain cases, lifting government sanctions will increase SMEs' competitiveness on the international market. Reducing trade barriers exposes local SMEs to international competition and provides them with the international experience they need to compete in the global market (Jeppesen, 2005).

5. Discussion

5.1. Impact of the Global Challenges of SMEs

In the age of economic globalization, researchers have examined a variety of issues that SMEs in both developed and developing nations have to deal with. Andalib and Darun (2018), Qureshi et al. (2011), and Gregar et al. (2018) are a few of the topics that have been highlighted in the literature regarding these issues. According to Noe et al. (2017), from the perspective of company management, three competitive problems were identified: the global challenge, sustainability challenges, and technical challenges.

SMEs, or small and medium-sized businesses, are important players in the world economy. These organizations play a critical role in promoting innovation, employment creation, and economic expansion (Fonseca & Filipe, 2019). But if you're a small- or medium-sized business owner, you also know how difficult it can be for SMEs to grow and expand due to a variety of obstacles. This is especially true given the current state of the economy, which is marked by rising interest rates and inflation, disruptions to the supply chain, and geopolitical difficulties. Here, we examine in more detail the top ten problems that SMEs will be facing in 2023.

5.2. Availability of Funds

The largest obstacle facing SMEs is getting financing. This is especially true for smaller enterprises, as banks and other financial organizations frequently extending credit to these companies with caution, motivated by concerns about their scale and risk profile (Baker, 2014). This implies that shareholders are frequently obliged to use their own assets as security for any borrowing, which can make it difficult for small enterprises to grow, hire staff, or invest in new equipment.

5.3. Management of Cash Flow

For SMEs, cash flow management is essential. If you are a business owner, you must make sure your company has enough cash on hand to pay its bills and make expansion-related investments. Planning should be aided by creating a budget and projecting financial flows (Gamage et al., 2019). Your cash flow may be affected by client late payments, unforeseen costs, and changes in revenue. When pricing pressures and inflation have an impact, this gets worse as it affect the key inputs.

5.4. Rivalry

SMEs must contend with fierce rivalry from other companies. It might be especially difficult to compete with larger businesses because they frequently have greater resources and well-known brands. Being a manager or owner of a small to medium-sized enterprise (SME) requires you to figure out how to stand out from the competition and get market share.

5.5. Management of Talent

SMEs frequently face resource constraints and fierce rivalry from larger companies, which makes it difficult to find and keep talented workers. According to the study conducted by Enaifoghe, 2023a), Offering comparable salary and benefits in comparison to these organizations may provide a challenge for you. Rather, ascertain the advantages of your company, especially those that pertain to your staff and future hires, and center your hiring and retention tactics around these advantages (Enaifoghe & Ramsuraj, 2023). For instance, if your company has a fantastic culture, you may highlight it in your job postings and post employee endorsements on your social media pages.

5.6. Adherence to Regulations

SMEs have a lot of laws and regulations to follow and manage. Making ensuring you're complying with employment and tax laws may be costly and time-consuming (Enaifoghe, 2023b). You must also abide by any laws that are particular to your industry. It is advisable to enlist the help of a professional, such as an accountant or lawyer, to expedite the procedure and guarantee compliance.

5.7. The Shift to Digital

One of the biggest obstacles for SMEs may be the digital transformation, especially if they lack the knowledge and resources needed to keep up with the latest innovations in the market. Examining the use of cutting-edge technology such as cloud computing and e-commerce might expand your clientele and boost sales (Enaifoghe & Vezi-Magigaba, 2023). Furthermore, automation may occasionally make your activities run more quickly and effectively. Rather than viewing digital transformation as a challenge, view it as an opportunity.

5.8. Promotion and Client Outreach

To draw in new business and keep existing clients, SMEs must spend money on marketing and customer acquisition (Enaifoghe, 2023a). The secret is to concentrate on creating a powerful brand and comprehensive marketing plan. This can entail spending money on outside assistance to expand your clientele and strengthen your brand.

5.9. Controlling Expansion

For SMEs, rapid expansion can be a double-edged sword that presents both fresh chances and difficulties. Scaling businesses, adding additional staff, and managing cash flow may all be difficult, so it's critical that you prepare for development and make sure you have the tools necessary to handle it.

5.10. Security Online

SMEs are subject to cyber dangers just like any other type of organization. Many, meanwhile, lack the means and know-how necessary to put in place efficient security measures (Julita & Hasrudy, 2019) . It is imperative that you invest in cybersecurity services or, at the absolute least, install suitable security software on any internet-connected devices in order to safeguard your data and systems against viruses, hackers, and cyberattacks (Kijkasiwat & Phuensane, 2020).

5.11. Uncertainty in the Economy

SMEs have been severely damaged by the recent economic volatility and uncertainty, which makes it harder than usual to predict shifts in consumer demand

and supply chain interruptions. This emphasizes how important it is that you are ready for uncertain economic times. Having a solid backup plan can help you weather any downturns.

Numerous obstacles could obstruct the growth of your small and medium-sized company. You can improve your business's resilience and set it up for greater success by being aware of the main problems you can encounter and reducing risks through business and emergency preparedness (Garcia et al., 2020). Given that the exploring the global problem is the subject of this study, the review initially used content analysis techniques to divide the global challenges into eight thematic groups based on the chosen literature. The market competition, global capital and economic crises, information and communication technology (Enaifoghe, 2023a), multinational firms, multinational terrorism and religious conflicts, international trade war, international dumping, and MNCs are the first, second, third, and fourth.

6. Conclusion

It examined how global issues affect SMEs, what can be learned from the experiences of various businesses, and important elements that must be altered and improved. Eight global challenges – market competition, global capital and economic crisis, information and communication technology, multinational corporations, MNCs, international terrorism and religious conflicts, international trade war, and international dumping – were identified by the review as affecting SMEs in the era of economic globalization.

For SMEs, market competitiveness is an ongoing, significant obstacle. Local businesses and multinational corporations compete more as a result of globalization. Globalized marketplaces are essential to the operations of multinational corporations (MNCs) and transnational corporations (TNCs), which have the capacity to eliminate global competitive difficulties more effectively than SMEs. The pre-suggestions to face global competition are as follows: managing cash flows, having enough capital, overcoming financial barriers, and being willing to access global capital.

To meet the demands of the global competitive landscape, it is imperative to address the deficiencies in the utilization of new technologies, marketing, and management. Additionally, human resources training needs to be improved, partnerships with innovative organizations should be established, and low-value manufacturing should be shifted to niche markets that rely on high-value productions.

It is not cost-effective for MNCs to produce every facet of a particular product on their own in the current international market. In addition, SMEs face other challenges such limited markets, technology, expertise, and resources.

References

Ahmedova, Sibel. (2015). Factors for increasing the competitiveness of Small and Medium-Sizes Enterprises (SMEs) in Bulgaria. *Procedia-Social and Behavioral Sciences, 195*, 1104–1112.

Ainuddin, R. Azimah, Pawl W. Beamish, John S. Hulland, & Michael J. Rouse. (2007). Resource attributes and firm performance in international joint ventures. *Journal of World Business, 42*, 47–60.

Andalib, Tarnima Warda, & Mohd Ridzuan Darun. (2018). An HRM model for manufacturing companies of Bangladesh mapping employee rights' protocols and grievance management system. *Indian Journal of Science and Technology, 11*, 1–14.

Asare, Roland, Mavis Akuffobea, Wilhelmina Quaye, & Kwasi Atta-Antwi. (2015). Characteristics of micro, small and medium enterprises in Ghana: Gender and implications for economic growth. *African Journal of Science, Technology, Innovation and Development, 7*, 26–35.

Baker, David Mc. A. (2014). The effects of terrorism on the travel and tourism industry. *International Journal of Religious Tourism and Pilgrimage, 2*, 58–67.

Barney, Jay. (1991). Firm resources and sustained competitive advantage. *Journal of Management, 17*, 99–120.

Chew, Yoke-Tong, & Henry Wai-Chung Yeung. (2001). The SME advantage: Adding local touch to foreign transnational corporations in Singapore. *Regional Studies, 35*, 431–448.

Doh, Soogwan, & Byungkyu Kim. (2014). Government support for SME innovations in the regional industries: The case of government financial support programme in South Korea. *Research Policy, 43*, 1557–1569.

Enaifoghe, A. (2023b). The challenges hampering the South African economic growth integration process in the sub-region. *International Journal of Research in Business and Social Science* (2147–4478), *12*(7), 235–243.

Enaifoghe, A., and Ramsuraj, T. (2023). Examining the function and contribution of entrepreneurship through small and medium enterprises as drivers of local economic growth in South Africa. *African Journal of Inter/Multidisciplinary Studies, 5*(1), 1–11.

Enaifoghe, A., & Vezi-Magigaba, M. F. (2023). Conceptualizing the role of entrepreneurship and SME in fostering South Africa's local economic development. *Research in Business & Social Science.* (IJRBS), *12*(4) (2023), 96–105.

Enaifoghe, A. O. (2023a). Exploring entrepreneurship and Small and Medium Enterprises in advancing local economic development. In Hasim Özüdoğru, Muhammed Veysel Kaya and Ufuk Kaya (eds.), *Social & economic studies within the framework of emerging global developments* – Volume 4. Peter Lang Publihers, pp. 177–190. ISBN 978-3-631-90842-6.

Fonseca, Luis, Amilcar Ramos, Alvaro Rosa, Ana Cristina Braga, & Paulo Sampaio. (2016). Stakeholders satisfaction and sustainable success. *International Journal of Industrial and Systems Engineering, 24*, 144–157.

Fonseca, Luis, & Filipe Carvalho. (2019). The reporting of SDGs by quality, environmental, and occupational health and safety-certified organizations. *Sustainability, 11*, 5797.

Gamage, Sisira Kumara Naradda, E. M. S. Ekanayake, G. A. K. N. J., Abeyrathne, R. P. I. R. Prasanna, J. M. S. B. Jayasundara, & P. S. K. Rajapakshe. (2019). *Global challenges and survival strategies of the SMEs in the era of economic globalization: A systematic review.* Mihintale: Rajarata University of Sri Lanka.

Garcia, Guadalupe Manzano, Juan Carlos, & Ayala Calvo. (2020). Entrepreneurial orientation: It's relationship with the Entrepreneur's subjective success in SMEs. *Sustainability, 12*, 4547.

Gherghina, Stefan Cristian, Mihai Alexandru Botezatu, Alexandra Hosszu, & Liliana Nicoleta Simionescu. (2019). Small and Medium-Sized Enterprises (SMEs): The engine of economic growth through investment and innovation. *Sustainability, 12*, 347.

Gregar, Ales, Ladislav Kudlacek, Sisira Kumara Naradda Gamage, & Hewa Ravindra Kuruppuge. (2018). Employment choice of non-family professionals in family firms. *International Scientific Day*, 2018, 1168–1177.

Gunday, Gurhan, Gunduz Ulusoy, kemal Kilic, & Lutfihak Alpkan. (2011). Effects of innovation types on firm performance. *International Journal of Production Economics, 133*, 662–676.

Hessels, Jolanda, & Simon C. Parker. (2013). Constraints, internationalization and growth: A cross-country analysis of European SMEs. *Journal of World Business, 48*, 137–148.

Jeppesen, Soeren. (2005). Enhancing competitiveness and securing equitable development: Can Small, Micro and Medium-Sized Enterprises (SMEs) do the trick? *Development in Practice, 15*, 463–474.

Jinjarak, Yothin, & Ganeshan Wignaraja. (2016). An empirical assessment of the export-financial constraint relationship: How different are small and medium enterprises? *World Development, 79*, 152–163.

Julita, J., & Hasrudy, T. (2019). Development of porter generic strategy model for Small and Medium Enterprises (SME's) in dealing with Asean Economics Community (AEC). *International Journal of Recent Scientific Researches, 8*, 20262–20269.

Kijkasiwat, P., & Pongsutti, P. (2020). Innovations and fir performance: The moderating and mediating roles of firm size and small and medium enterprise finance. *Journal of Risk and Financial Management, 13*, 97.

Kothari, C.R. and Garg, G. (2016). Research Methodology: Methods and Techniques. 3rd Edition, New Age International Publishers, Delhi, 104–106.

Mogalakwe, M. (2009). The Documentary Research Method – Using Documentary Sources in Social Research. *Eastern Africa Social Science Research Review, 25*, 43–58.

Mustafa, H. K., & Yaakub, S. (2018). Innovation and technology adoption challenges: Impact on SMEs' company performance. *International Journal of Accounting, Finance and Business*, 3, 57–65.

Noe, Raymond A., John R. Hollenbeck, Barry Gerhart, & Patrick M. Wright. (2017). *Human resource management: Gaining a competitive advantage*, 9th ed. New York: McGraw-Hill.

Ong, Jeen Wei, Hishamuddin Bin Ismail, & Gerald Guan Gan Goh. (2010b). The competitive advantage of Small and Medium Enterprises (SMEs): The role of entrepreneurship and luck. *Journal of Small Business and Entrepreneurship, 23*, 373–391.

Prasanna, RPIR, JMSB Jayasundara, Sisira Kumara Naradda Gamage, EMS Ekanayake, PSK Rajapakshe, and GAKNJ Abeyrathne. (2019). Sustainability of SMEs in the competition: A systemic review on technological challenges and SME performance. *Journal of Open Innovation: Technology, Market and Complexity, 5*: 100.

Qureshi, Muhammad Imran, Khalid Zaman, & Mansoor Nazir Bhatti. (2011). The impact of culture and gender on leadership behavior: Higher education and management. *Management Science Letters, 1*, 531–540.

Rakesh, C. (2014). Pest analysis for micro small medium enterprises sustainability. *Journal of Management and Commerce, 1*, 18–22.

Ren, Shengce, Andreas B. Eisingerich, & Huei-Ting Isai. (2015). How do marketing research and development capabilities, and degree of internationalization synergistically affect the innovation performance of Small and Medium-Sized

Enterprises (SMEs)? A panel data study of Chinese SMEs. *International Business Review, 24*, 642–651.

Rice, John Lewis, T-Sb Liao, NC Martin, & Peter Galvin (2012). The role of strategic alliances in complementing firm capabilities. *Journal of Management and Organization, 18*, 858–869.

Sener, Sefer, Mesut Savrul, & Orhan Aydın. (2014). Structure of small and medium-sized enterprises in Turkey and global competitiveness strategies. *Procedia-Social and Behavioral Sciences, 150*, 212–221.

Singh, Rajesh K., Suresh K. Garg, & S. G. Deshmukh. (2008). Strategy development by SMEs for competitiveness: A review. *Benchmarking: An International Journal, 15*, 525–547.

Singh, Rajesh K., Suresh K. Garg, & S. G. Deshmukh. (2009). The competitiveness of SMEs in globalized economy, observations from China and India. *Management Research Review, 33*, 54–65.

Stein, Peter, Oya Pinar Ardic, & Martin Hommes. (2013). *Closing the credit gap for formal and informal micro, small, and medium enterprises.* Washington: International Finance Corporation, World Bank.

United Nations. (2009). *Globalization of production and the competitiveness of small and medium-sized enterprises in Asia and Pacific: Trends and prospects.* New York: Economic and Social Commission for Asia and the Pacific.

WTO. (2016). *World trade report – Levelling the trading field for SMEs.* Washington: World Trade Organization.

Xie, Henry, & Taewon Suh. (2014). Perceived resource deficiency and internationalization of small- and medium-sized firms. *Journal of International Entrepreneurship, 12*, 207–229.

Yüksel, I. (2012). Developing a Multi-Criteria Decision Making Model for PESTEL Analysis. *International Journal of Biometrics, 7*, 52.

Zaheer, Srilata, & Akbar Zaheer. (2001). Market micro structure in a global B2B network. *Strategic Management Journal, 22*, 859–873.

Andrew Enaifoghe

Entrepreneurship Education at the Institute of Higher Learning for Sustainable Development

1. Introduction

The study aimed to examine entrepreneurship education at the Institute of Higher Learning (IHE) for sustainable development in South Africa. South Africans have historically looked to the public and private sectors for employment. This can be demonstrated by the number of youth actively in entrepreneurship (Enaifoghe & Ramsuraj, 2023). However, South African youth must foster an atmosphere that promotes job creation and economic growth because the formal and public sectors are finding it increasingly difficult to accommodate the expanding number of job searchers (Kew, 2012). Many young people see businesses as little more than short-term sources of income until they discover a better opportunity in the official sector (Herrington et al., 2011). This is problematic, given that in economically poor times; young people are often unable to obtain better jobs in the formal sector.

Consequently, the amount of individuals who must rely on beginning a business after leaving school is probably going to rise more than the number of young graduates to survive. Students must view themselves as prospective job creators rather than job seekers after completing their undergraduate degree (Kew, 2012). The European Commission (2008) states that fostering entrepreneurial attitudes and abilities helps society even when they are not used in new company initiatives and views education as a crucial tool for encouraging young people's entrepreneurial ambitions. The effectiveness of entrepreneurship education has been questioned by a few studies (Enaifoghe & Vezi-Magigaba, 2023; Martinez et al., 2010, Pittaway & Cope, 2007).

According to studies like (Enaifoghe & Vezi-Magigaba, 2022; Martinez et al., 2010; Fiet, 2001; Pittaway & Cope, 2007), entrepreneurship education in HEIs is insufficient and does not address societal challenges like youth unemployment and graduates who are prepared for the workforce to take part in entrepreneurial endeavours. Furthermore, Verheul et al. (2001) made a distinction between general education and entrepreneurship education, asserting that "the promotion of entrepreneurship and stimulating entrepreneurial skills and knowledge of which has shown little influence in youth employment" was the special focus of university entrepreneurship education.

1.1. Research Methodology

This is a qualitative study that adopts a desktop research methodology. A thorough assessment of the literature was done to gather relevant data for the study. The body of existing literature deemed essential for the study is called the SLR (Rajasekar et al., 2006). SLR is defined as "the process of accessing published secondary data" by academics. Two distinct aspects of SLR – that it uses only secondary data that has been published – are explained by the definition (Stangor, 2011; Maxim, 1999). Publications include books, journals, articles, indexes in numerous databases, and reports from both organizations and non-organizations.

The secondary sources for the literature search on the interplay of the role of entrepreneurship education in the South African Institute of Higher Learning for sustainable development were chosen. The search engines Scopus and Google Scholar were used to find relevant literature related to the topic under study. These search engines were preferred over others because of the abundant information they provided. The authors utilized advanced keyword searches across several databases for the data collection process.

2. Exposure to Technology Innovation and University Entrepreneurship Education

According to Pittaway and Cope (2007), skill-building courses in leadership, negotiation, new product creation, creative thinking, and exposure to technology innovation must be a part of university entrepreneurship education. According to Co and Mitchell's (2006) research on entrepreneurship education in South African HEIs, although it is still in its infancy, it is thought to be crucial for raising the stature of these institutions by turning forth graduates who are prepared to start their businesses. Additionally, the survey indicates that academic, research, and outreach institutions are becoming more and more committed to entrepreneurial initiatives.

Co and Mitchell (2006) state that entrepreneurial education research on entrepreneurship in South Africa is viewed as less significant than research in other management disciplines, with universities placing more emphasis on traditional classroom delivery methods like lectures. According to Kabongo and Okpara's (2010) research, educational offerings, the provision of entrepreneurship education, and entrepreneurial universities have all aided in our understanding of the connections between the formation of new businesses and the delivery of entrepreneurship education from the standpoint of external influences or the macro view of entrepreneurship.

According to the findings of Co and Mitchell's (2006) study, higher education institutions (HEIs) can foster an entrepreneurial mindset in youth by teaching them how to identify and seize opportunities, create and destroy businesses, and clearly understand risks and rewards. According to Rae (2010), four main factors affect how entrepreneurship is evolving. The first of them is the cultural and economic background, wherein economic difficulties influence the social and economic Recognition is required for spaces for entrepreneurship as well as for initiatives toward environmental awareness, ethics, and accountability.

Secondly, things are evolving expectations from students in an era of graduate unemployment, as their connections with institutions shift. Third, the nature of the relationship between teachers and students is evolving. Examples of this include the personalization of instruction, the entrepreneurial learning that comes from schools, the use of technology, the evaluation of real-world applications through experiential and work-based learning, and the redesign of the entrepreneurial curriculum. Fourth, there is tremendous demand for universities to alter how they operate due to budgetary, human resources, and other constraints. This results in the ongoing modifications to the teaching and learning culture of entrepreneurship.

2.1. Theoretical and Conceptual Frameworks for Entrepreneurship

Providing the theoretical and conceptual frameworks that support entrepreneurship is the main goal of entrepreneurship education, yet this is not the case at the moment (Paco et al., 2010). This philosophy is presented didactically, with reading recommendations and lectures, and does not do anything to the practicality of entrepreneurship. According to a study by Hynes (1996), the teacher serves as an expert by guiding and supporting the student's learning process. This provides a comprehensive description of how formal entrepreneurship education operates. These entrepreneurship education methods are evaluated through formal exams that measure knowledge and skills.

On the other hand, the goal of the informal components of entrepreneurship education is to merge and blend the formal aspects of education. Although the effects of this are still unknown, Kim and Park (2008) claim that entrepreneurship education is becoming more and more important in emerging nations. The extremely low number of company start-ups by graduates in South Africa suggests that entrepreneurship education may not be sufficient (Tshikovhi

& Shambare, 2012). Considering the concept of entrepreneurship provided by Kim and Park (2008) Action-based entrepreneurship is then enforced by education.

The action-based entrepreneurship is defined as the process of giving people the knowledge, abilities, and attitudes to act on economic possibilities as well as the ability to recognize them (Rasmussen & Sorheim, 2006). Due to these worries, South Africa's TEA is ranked among the lowest in Sub-Saharan Africa and the entire globe (Xavier et al., 2012). From a small number in 1970 to over 400 in 1995, and nearly all institutions worldwide recently, there has been a sharp increase in the number of universities providing courses in entrepreneurship (Vesper & Gartner, 1997). According to this study, action-based entrepreneurship education in addition to academic instruction in entrepreneurship will help achieve sustainable development among the youth.

2.2. Evaluation of Entrepreneurship Education

Evaluations of courses and programs in entrepreneurship education reveal that there is a great deal of variation in the goals, pedagogy, content, goals, and outcomes (Fiet, 2001). According to Laukkanen (2000), the foundation of academic entrepreneurship education has been giving students more theory than real-world entrepreneurial training. Thus, it would seem that these people would be more inclined to launch new businesses after graduating, but this hasn't happened. The report on GEM South Africa, authored by Herrington et al. (2011), highlighted the fact that 50.9 % of South Africa's unemployed people are among youth unemployment is said to be caused by a shortage of skilled young people as well as a lack of interest in entrepreneurial activity (Herrington et al., 2011).

Few graduates pursue entrepreneurship in the face of rising unemployment, and even fewer receive practical training or internships that do not support their career route (Gregory, 2011). Klassen and Woolard (2008) claim that South Africa has been home to some of the highest unemployment rates worldwide. When comparing South Africa to the other members of the BRICS, it is evident that there is a need for efficient, action-based entrepreneurship education that will result in graduates who are prepared to pursue entrepreneurship. According to Nicolaides (2011), entrepreneurship in the context of South Africa is the process of conceptualizing, organizing, and launching a business opportunity and then, through innovations, nurturing it into a potentially high-growth venture in a complicated and uncertain environment.

2.3. Entrepreneurship Education in the South African Context

In South Africa, entrepreneurship education is still in its infancy but has neglected to foster good attitudes toward entrepreneurship and the development of young graduates' skills and competencies (Co & Mitchell, 2006). The higher education system in South Africa is insufficient to develop entrepreneurial abilities. It has a history of being overly theoretical and insensitive to the talents that employers value in the business sector. According to some, the issue arises in elementary and secondary education (Ahmed et al., 2011). Today's universities struggle to turn out graduates who are prepared to pursue entrepreneurial endeavours.

According to Fayolle et al. (2006), entrepreneurial education has been deficient, and graduates from colleges are not prepared to pursue entrepreneurial endeavours (Gregory, 2011). As a result, action-based entrepreneurship education has become a popular add-on program to curricula at most colleges (Vesper & Gartner, 1997). According to African Economic Outlook (2012), young people between the ages of 15 and 25 make up 45 % of the labour force and more than 60 % of Africa's overall population. By 2015, over 75 % of the world's population is expected to reside in sub-Saharan Africa.

Due to their lack of skills, many young people are largely shut out of a productive economic life. Because education and skill requirements are becoming more and more significant, individuals with some education frequently display skills that are irrelevant to the demands of the market. Millions of young people are unemployed or underemployed as a result of this (Xavier et al., 2012).

3. Re-thinking Entrepreneurship Education in South African Higher Education

The study argued for the necessity of theory to come before practice, not the other way around. As a result, the main task is to provide the optimal way to think about entrepreneurship education in South African higher education. Following Mwasalwiba's (2010) argument that entrepreneurship education should be supported by a robust theoretical framework. A helpful framework for creating entrepreneurial education is the 5Cs concept, which was first proposed by Morris and Kuratko (2014). Convictions, connections, competencies, conceptualization, and character are the five construct elements that make up the 5C framework.

According to the author, conceptualization is the most important component of the 5C framework since choices made regarding conceptualization will undoubtedly have a big influence on other components. One way to influence the conviction factor is to build entrepreneurship education around the 'best practice' configuration, which limits the amount of learning that can happen outside of the classroom. The facilitator is mentioned as being important under the conceptualization factor by Morris and Kuratko, but in this adaption, the author has left it out of the description because they felt the convictions element better captures the role of the facilitator. Even while entrepreneurship modules are increasingly being included in programs, at most, the share of credits from entrepreneurship modules to overall program credit hovers at 20 %.

The results support the observation made by Musetsho and Lethoko (2017) that the majority of the entrepreneurial curricula offered in various public universities in South Africa are not unique and are not structured as a stand-alone degree; rather, they are typically created as a component of another business management degree. Therefore, it would not be shocking if these students decided that they would prefer to pursue careers in their selected program specializations over careers in entrepreneurship.

4. Research Findings and Discussion

This section provides the research findings on the role of entrepreneurship education in the South African Institute of Higher Learning for sustainable development in the face of youth unemployment. Findings show that the unemployment rate in South Africa decreased from 32.6 % in the previous quarter to 31.9 % in the third quarter of 2023 – the lowest level in a year (Statistics South Africa, 2017). The labour force increased by 326 thousand to 24.6 million, the number of employed people increased by 399 thousand to 16.7 million, and the number of unemployed people declined by 72 thousand to 7.8 million (Statistics South Africa, 2017). Additionally, the number of persons who were discouraged from seeking employment decreased by 26,000 to 3.2 million, while the number of people who were not economically engaged for any other reason decreased by 160 thousand to 13.1 million.

The Q2 of 2023 saw a decrease from 42.1 % to 41.2 % in the enlarged definition of unemployment, which takes into account people who are discouraged from looking for work. The two industries with the largest job growth, according to sectors, were banking (+237 thousand) and community & social services (+119 thousand). The industries with the largest losses were manufacturing (-50 thousand), mining (-35 thousand), and transportation (-20 thousand). The percentage of young people without jobs, or those between the ages of 15 and 24, fell to 58 %, a level not seen in more than a year. (South African Statistics, 2023).

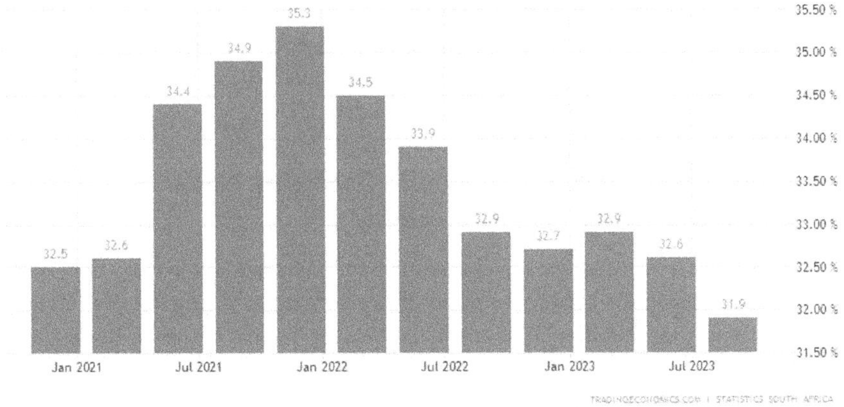

Figure 1. Statistics South Africa, 2017

According to Statistics South Africa (2023), the country's unemployment rate is 31.90 Sep 2023 far higher than the 14 % goal set in the National Development Plan for 2020 and the 6 % goal set for 2030 (National Planning Commission, 2012). Growing enrollment in postsecondary education combined with a comparatively high percentage of unemployed graduates unable to find work in the formal sector is a contributing factor (Muofhe & Du Toit, 2011; Nel & Neale-Schutte, 2013). Neither the public sector nor the private sector can absorb graduates (Fatoki, 2010) and, thus, entrepreneurial start-ups have been encouraged as the solution to the unemployment crisis in South Africa (Chimucheka, 2014; Kabonga & Okpara, 2010).

Findings show that the promotion of entrepreneurship education ought to strengthen people's intent to launch their businesses (Collet, 2013). In a similar vein, Abebe (2015) asserts that graduates of entrepreneurship programs ought to change from being job searchers to being employment producers. In contrast, 400 South African final-year undergraduate students studying business, law and management, engineering and the built environment, health sciences, and the humanities participated in a relatively recent study that revealed the students' low levels of entrepreneurial intentions and preference for employment. It is also noteworthy that, in contrast to other sub-Saharan African nations, South Africa has the lowest rate of overall entrepreneurial activity, with only around 10.6 % of higher education programs focused on entrepreneurship.

It is evident that there are not enough entrepreneurs coming out of South Africa's higher education system, and this may have something to do with the design and delivery of entrepreneurship curricula. The term "systematic innovation," coined by Drucker (1985) to refer to a planned, organized search for change combined with a methodical examination of the opportunities it presents, is used to connect innovation and change.

5. Entrepreneurship Education in Fostering National Development in the 21st Century

A call for entrepreneurship to drive growth has been issued by the World Economic Forum (2011) to solve some of the difficulties facing the 21st century. Research has long indicated that entrepreneurship fosters national development (Acs & Amington, 2004; Berkowitz & Dejong, 2005; Carree & Thurik, 2008), and more recently, studies in African nations have confirmed this relationship (Adusei, 2016). Hence, the contention that entrepreneurship is crucial to the expansion of economies (Baumol, 2014; Zhang, 2017), the promotion of innovation (Fritsch, 2008) and, in some instances, the execution of solutions for social upliftment (Littlewood & Holt, 2018).

Furthermore, since entrepreneurship is closely associated with the creation of jobs (Folster, 2000; Zhang, 2017), self-employment has been used as a stand-in for entrepreneurship in several studies (Bjuggren et al., 2012). The initial definition of entrepreneurship given by Schumpeter (1934) was the beginning of innovative activity and the introduction of new products to the market. Some people use the concept of opportunity to characterize entrepreneurship. Entrepreneurship, for instance, might be defined as the process by which people find chances to add value (Oluseye et al., 2017) or as being aware of prospects for profit (Kirzner, 1978).

6. Conclusion

The study looked at entrepreneurship education at the South African Institute of Higher Learning (IHE) for sustainable development. One argument is that strong economies are more likely to give entrepreneurs more chances to launch new goods and services into the market. Moreover, their low unemployment rate, which ranges from 3.9 % to 5.6 %, can be less a result of the structure of entrepreneurial education and more due to strong economies. Should the argument be refuted, then a nation such as South Africa that adheres to the "best practice" model – which appears to be the case – should be able to produce enough entrepreneurs to have a beneficial effect on the unemployment rate.

Furthermore, it would be understandable and far too optimistic to suggest that enhancing entrepreneurial education by adding more modules to various programs or offering a stand-alone program could be a potential answer to achieving sustainable development through entrepreneurship. The study's conclusions imply that because business management students receive their entrepreneurial training through participation in group projects, their knowledge and instruction in entrepreneurship are superior to that of the majority of regular South African students.

6.1. Implication

The provision of entrepreneurship education and entrepreneurial universities will aid in our understanding of the connections between the formation of new businesses and the delivery of entrepreneurship education from the standpoint of external influences or the macro view of entrepreneurship.

References

Abebe, A. (2015). Attitudes of undergraduate students towards self-employment in Ethiopian public universities. *International Journal of Business and Management Review*, *3*(7), 1–10.

Acs, Z. J., & Armington, C. (2004). Employment growth and entrepreneurial activity in cities. *Regional Studies*, *38*, 911–917.

Adusei, M. (2016). Does entrepreneurship promote economic growth in Africa?. *Africa Development Review*, *28*(2), 201–214.

African Economic Outlook. (2012). Youth unemployment: Five challenges for North Africa. Available: www.africaneconomicoutlook.org [Accessed 11/01/2023].

Ahmed, I., Nawaz, M. M., & Ramzan, M. (2011). Do external factors influence students' entrepreneurial inclination. *Actual Problems of Economics*, *11*, 348–355. Central Intelligence Agency 2013. The World Factbook.

Baumol, W. J. (2014). Stimulating growth amid recession: Entrepreneurship, innovation, and the Keynesian revolution. *Journal of Policy Modelling*, *36*, 629–635.

Berkowitz, D., & Dejong, D. N. (2005). Entrepreneurship and post-socialist growth. *Oxford Bulletin of Economics and Statistics*, *67*(1), 25–46.

Bjuggren, C. M., Johansson, D., & Stenkula, M. (2012). Using self-employment as proxy for entrepreneurship: Some empirical caveats. *International Journal of Entrepreneurship and Small Business*, *17*(3), 290–303.

Carree, M., & Thurik, R. (2008). The lag structure of the impact of business ownership on economic performance in OCED countries. *Small Business Economics, 30*, 101–110.

Chimucheka, T. (2014). Entrepreneurship education in South Africa. *Mediterranean Journal of Social Sciences, 52*(2), 403–416.

Co, M. J., & Mitchell, B. (2006). Entrepreneurship education in South Africa. *Education + Training, 48*, 59–348.

Collet, H. (2013). Entrepreneurship education in higher education: Are policy makers expecting too much?. *Education and Training, 55*(8), 836–848.

Drucker, P. F. (1985). *Innovation and entrepreneurship.* New York: Harper and Row.

Enaifoghe, A., & Ramsuraj, T. (2023). Examining the function and contribution of entrepreneurship through small and medium enterprises as drivers of local economic growth in South Africa. *African Journal of Inter/Multidisciplinary Studies, 5*(1), pp. 1–11.

Enaifoghe, A., & Vezi-Magigaba, M. F. (2023). Conceptualizing the role of entrepreneurship and SME in fostering South Africa's local economic development. *Research in Business & Social Science.* (IJRBS), *12*(4), (2023), 96–105.

Enaifoghe, A. O., & Vezi-Magigaba, F. N. 2022. Rethinking the sustainability of local economic development: Entrepreneurship in South Africa. *Expert Journal of Business and Management, 10*(2), 77–90.

European Commission. (2008). Progress in promoting entrepreneurial attitudes and skills through primary and secondary education. Final report of the expert group "Education and Training". Brussels, Belgium: Enterprise Directorate General of the European Commission.

Fatoki, O. O. (2010). Graduate entrepreneurial intention in South Africa: Motivations and obstacles. *International Journal of Business Management, 5*(9), 87–98.

Fayolle, A., Gailly, B., & Lassas-Clerc, N. (2006). Assessing the impact of entrepreneurship education programmes: A new methodology. *Journal of European Industrial Training, 30*, 701–720.

Fiet, J. O. (2001). The theoretical side of teaching entrepreneurship. *Journal of Business Venturing, 16*, 1–24.

Folster, S. (2000). Do entrepreneurs create jobs?. *Small Business Economics, 14*(2), 137–148.

Fritsch, M. (2008). How does new business formation affect regional development? Introduction to the special issue. *Small Business Economics, 30*(1), 1–14.

Gregory, M. (2011). *The strategic and planning value of institutional research in tracking graduate employment.* British Council and the Association of the Commonwealth Universities.

Herrington, M., Kew, J., Simrie, M., & Turton, N. (2011). *Global entrepreneurship monitor South Africa.* Cape Town: University of Cape Town.

Hynes, B. (1996). Entrepreneurship education and training – Introducing entrepreneurship into non-business disciplines. *Journal of European Industrial Training, 20,* 10–17.

Kabongo, J. D., & Okpara, J. O. (2010). Entrepreneurship education in sub-Saharan African universities. *International Journal of Entrepreneurial Behaviour & Research, 16,* 296–308.

Kew, J. (2012). A co-ordinated approach is critical to promote youth entrepreneurship. *Opinion Obstacles and Opportunities for Youth Entrepreneurship,* 33–37.

Kim, J., & Park, J. (2008). The status of entrepreneurship education in Korea. *News Letter.* Korea Federation of Small and Medium Business (KBIZ).

Kirzner, I. M. (1978). *Competition and entrepreneurship.* University of Chicago Press, Chicago, IL.

Klassen, S., & Woolard, I. (2008). Surviving unemployment without state support: Unemployment and household formation in South Africa. *Journal of African Economies, 18,* 1–51.

Laukkanen, M. (2000). Exploring alternative approaches in high-level entrepreneurship education: Creating micro-mechanisms for endogenous regional growth. *Entrepreneurship & Regional Development, 12,* 25–47.

Littlewoo, D., & Holt, D. (2018). Social entrepreneurship in South Africa: Exploring the influence of environment. *Business and Society, 57*(3), 525–561.

Martinez, A. C., Levie, J., Kelley, D. J., Saemundsson, R. J., & Schoott, T. (2010). Global entrepreneurship monitor special report: A global perspective on entrepreneurship education and training.

Maxim, P. S. (1999). *Quantitative research methods in the social sciences.* New York: Oxford University Press.

Morris, M. H., & Kuratko, D. F. (2014). Building university 21st century entrepreneurship programs that empower and transform. In S. Hoskinson & D. F. Kuratko (eds.), *Innovative pathways for university entrepreneurship in the 21st century, advances in the study of entrepreneurship, innovation and economic growth,* vol. 24, pp. 1–24, Emerald Publishing Limited, Bingley, UK.

Musetsho, T. R., & Lethoko, M. X. (2017). An evaluative study on the effect of entrepreneurial education curriculum on students at the University of Venda,

South Africa. *The Independent Journal of Teaching and Learning, 12910*, 74–89.

Muofhe, N.J., & Du Toit, W.F. (2011). Entrepreneurial education's and entrepreneurial role models' influence on career choice. SA Journal of Human Resource Management/SA Tydskrif vir Menslikehulpbronbestuur, 9(1), Art. #345, 15 pages.

Mwasalwiba, E. S. (2010). Entrepreneurship education: A review of its objectives, teaching methods, and impact indicators. *Education + Training, 52*(1), 20–47.

National Planning Commission (2012). National Development Plan 2030: Our Future—Make It Work.

Nel, H. & Neale-Shutte, M. (2013). Examining the evidence: Graduate employability at NMMU. South African Journal of Higher Education, 27(2), 437–453.

Nicolaides, A. (2011). Entrepreneurship – The role of higher education in South Africa. *Educational Research, 2*, 1043–1050.

Oluseye, A. M., Adebayo, K. F., Olulanu, O. I., Adesola, O. O., & Omonike, A. O. (2017). Effect of Entrepreneurship education on self-employment initiatives among Nigerian Science and Technology students. *Journal of Education and Practice, 8*(15), 44–51.

Paco, A. D., Ferreira, J., Rasposo, M., Rodrigues, R. G., & Dinis, A. 2010. Universities' entrepreneurship education and regional development: A stakeholders' approach. *Texto Para Discussao, 2*, 1–20.

Pittaway, L., & Cope, J. (2007). Entrepreneurship education – A systematic review of the evidence. *International Small Business Journal, 25*, 477–506.

Rae, D. (2010). Universities and enterprise education: Responding to the challenges of the new era. *Journal of Small Business and Enterprise Development, 17*, 591–606.

Rajasekar, S., Philominathan, P., & Chinnathambi, V. 2006. Research methodology. Ar XIV Physics [Online]. Available: http://arxiv.org/abs/physics/0601009v2 [Accessed 08/01/2023].

Rasmussen, E. A., & Sorheim, R. (2006). Action-based entrepreneurship education. *Technovation, 26*, 185–194.

Schumpeter, J. A. (1934). *The theory of economic development*. Harvard University Press, Cambridge, MA.

Stangor, C. (2011). *Research methods for the behavioral sciences.* USA, Wadsworth.

Statistics South Africa. (2023). Statistics South Africa on Quarterly Labour Force Survey quarter three 2023. Available: https://www.gov.za/news/media-statements/statistics-south-africa-quarterly-labour-force-survey-quarter-three-2023-14#:~:text=The%20official%20unemployment%20rate%20was,the%20second%20quarter%20of%202023 Accessed: 13/01/2024

Statistics South Africa. (2017). *Quarterly labour force survey: Quarter 4.* Government Press, Pretoria, South Africa.

Tshikovhi, N., & Shambare, R. (2012). Entrepreneurship intentions of students in free enterprise at Tshwane University of Technology. *Academy of Markets & Commerce*, 1, 1–5.

Urban, B. (2011). *The entrepreneurial mind-set* (book 2: Perspectives in entrepreneurship: A research companion), Pearson Education, Cape Town.

Verheul, I., Wennekers, S., Audretsch, D., & Thurik, R. (2001). *An eclectic theory of entrepreneurship*. Amsterdam: Tinbergen Institute.

Vesper, K. H., & Gartner, W. B. (1997). Measuring progress in entrepreneurship education. *Journal of Business Venturing, 12*, 403–421.

World Economic Forum. (2011). Unlocking entrepreneurial capabilities to meet the global challenges of the 21st century: Final report on the entrepreneurship education workstream, World Economic Forum Global Education Initiative, Geneva, Switzerland.

Xavier, S. R., Kelley, D. J., Kew, J., Herrington, M., & Vorderwulbecke, A. (2012). Global Entrepreneurship Monitor: Global report. Babson College, Universidad del Desarrollo, Universiti Turi Abdul Razak and London Business School.

Zhang, D. (2017). Investigating the perception of university entrepreneurship education. *Journal of Entrepreneurship Education, 20*(2), 1–18.

Constantinos Challoumis

Impact Factor of Liability Using the Sensitivity Method

1. Introduction

The quantification analysis of the sensitivity of the tax system to the liability is done by the application of the the Sensitivity Method (Bergh, 2009; Bourdin & Nadou, 2018; Challoumis, 2020c, 2020a, 2021c; Corti et al., 2020; Ginsburgh & Weber, 2020; Levi, 2021; Ortun et al., 2017; Paes-Sousa et al., 2019; Rumayya et al., 2020; Tvaronavičienė et al., 2018; Urwannachotima et al., 2020; Woody & Viney, 2017; Παπακωνσταντίνου et al., 2013). The background of this method stands on the behavior analysis of mathematical equations. According to bibliography (Challoumis, 2018a, 2018b, 2020b, 2020a, 2021b, 2021a, 2022b, 2022a, 2023n, 2023d, 2023l, 2023e, 2023b, 2023m, 2023i, 2023h, 2023a, 2023c, 2023g, 2023j, 2023k, 2023 f, 2024a, 2024d, 2024b). The cycle of money is the theory where the Q.E. method and also the Sensitivity Method have been applied. The Sensitivity Method is based on the concept of how sensitive is a variable. To achieve this there are two steps:

- It should be defined as the equation that is under examination, according to the applied theory.
- Following the same concept of the Q.E. method it is the case that one variable is there in the one case, and the other case is omitted. The basic difference between the Sensitivity Method to the Q.E. method is that Sensitivity does not use the generator, to produce random values, but there is each time a condition that should be satisfied.

The S.M. (Sensitivity Method) is plausible to be applied using a combination of mathematics and programming. The quantification of quality data is the concept of the S.M. (the same happens with the Q.E. method, but from a different point of view." Then, it is plausible to quantify quality data. In our analysis, this method is used for clarification of the behavior of the impact factor of the global tax revenue.

2. Literature Review

The impact factor of tax revenues of countries which are tax heaves, *s* according to the bibliography. It is determined as that:

$$s = \frac{k+l}{r+c+t+i} \tag{1}$$

"Therefore are countries that receive the products that are taxed in different countries. This allocation of profits between profits and losses permits the enterprises that participate in controlled transactions of the transfer pricing activities to maximize their utility. But, contemporaneously the tax revenue from a global view is declined (Androniceanu et al., 2019; Brakke, 2023; Challoumis, 2020a, 2021d; CYSTAT, 2018; Deng & Li, 2011; Feinschreiber, 2004; Prestianawati et al., 2020; Richard Barker et al., 2022; Soboleva I.V., 2019; Tydir N.I., 2019; Woody & Viney, 2017; Zayats O.I., 2019). Then, the loss of tax income from some countries is more than the profits that make the countries which are tax havens. Thereupon, the symbol of s the impact factor of tax revenue from a global view, and there are some coefficients which are $k, l, r, t,$ and c. Thus, the symbol of k is about the impact factor of capital, l is the impact factor about the liability of the authorities on the tax system. The interpretation of the liability is about how unbalanced it is the tax system. The parameter of r is about the ris, the t is about how much trustworthy is the tax system from the view of risk. The symbols with the "~" are accordingly the same thing but from the view of the uncontrolled transactions. Moreover, for $\tilde{s}$:

$$\tilde{s} = \frac{\tilde{k}+\tilde{l}}{\tilde{r}+\tilde{c}+\tilde{t}+\tilde{i}} \tag{2}$$

It is determined the aggregate impact factor of tax revenues, which is symbolized by $\hat{s}$, and is defined by the next equation:

$$\hat{s} = s + \tilde{s} \tag{3}$$

Based on the prior equations it is plausible to proceed to the identification of the behavior of the impact factors of tax revenues in the case of tax heavens and the case of the non-tax heavens. Then, s is a factor that allows the comparison between the controlled with the uncontrolled transactions. Thence is plausible to have a standalone behavior analysis of controlled transactions and a combined behavior analysis between the controlled transactions with the uncontrolled transactions. The next section analyzes the impact factor of tax revenues with the rest impact factors."

This methodology is illustrated below:

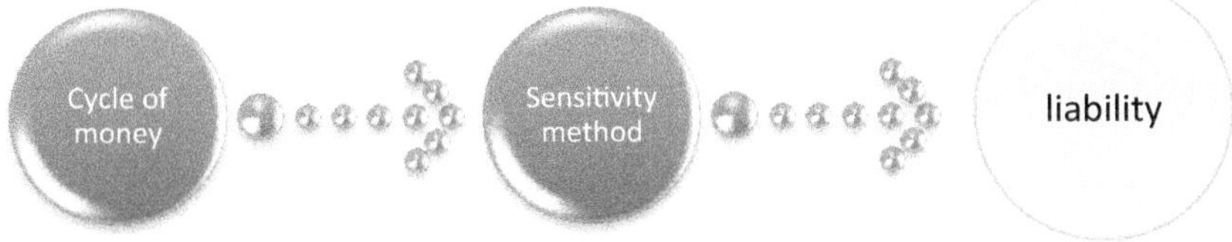

Figure 1. S.M. (Sensitivity Method)

The previous scheme followed the methodology of Sensitivity Method to determine the behavior of the global tax revenue in the case that the existence of the liability and the ideal case that this factor is avoided.

3. Results

The liability is in interaction with the impact factor of tax revenues. In this behavioral analysis is determined the model which clarifies the behavior of the impact factor of tax revenues with the existence and with the avoidance of the impact factor of tax (Challoumis, n.d.-a, n.d.-b, 2018c, 2019, 2021e, 2022a, 2023o, 2023a, 2023m, 2023j, 2023p, 2024a, 2024e, 2024 f, 2024c). Then, for the application of the Sensitivity Method:

$$t > l > i > r > k > c \tag{4}$$

Therefore, it is plausible to proceed to a quantity analysis using equations (1), (2), and (4). Therefore, applying the Sensitivity Method and choosing the appropriate magnitudes for the coefficient:

Table 1. Compiling coefficients

Factors	Values of s	Values of s'
k	0,4	0.4
i	0.6	0.6
l	0.7	-
r	0.5	0.5

(continued)

Table 1. Continued

Factors	Values of s	Values of s'
c	0.3	0.3
t	0.8	0.8
fs	<0.3	<0.3
f_i	<0.3	<0.3

The prior table presents the data that are under examination to be able to compile the model and confirm that the impact factor of liability increases the tax revenue.

Therefore, using the Sensitivity Method:

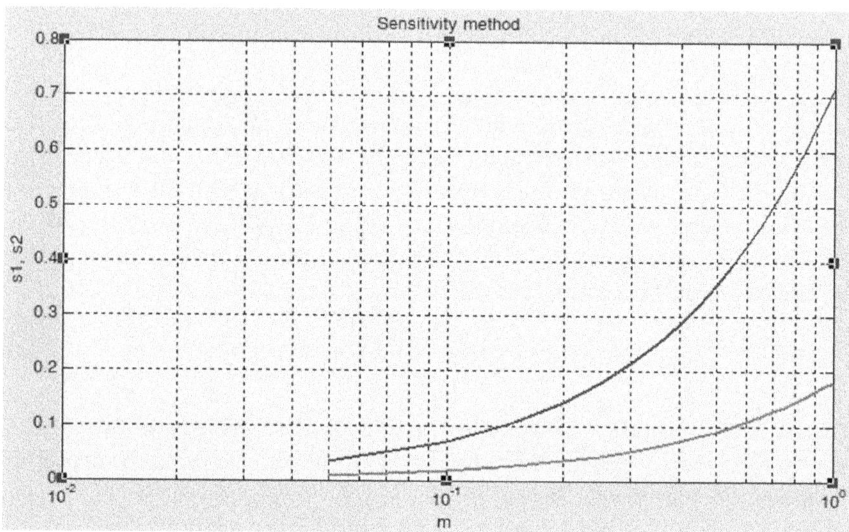

Figure 2. Application of S.M. (logarithmic form

In logarithmic forms, the green line is about the case that there doesn't exist liability, and the blue line is the case that there does exist liability. It is confirmed by the theoretical background of the theory of the money cycle (or the theory of the cycle of money) that liability increases tax revenue.

4. Conclusions

The case of liability and its relationship to worldwide tax income were investigated in this essay. It makes sense that businesses involved in controlled activities would favor tax settings with erratic legal frameworks and unpredictable economies. Because they can more effectively allocate their earnings and losses, more companies that engage in controlled transactions will be impacted by this. Then, a rise in liabilities may result in an increase in tax revenue.

Appendix

```
% Sensitivity Plot of Cycle of money (C)(R)2024 Constantinos
Challoumis
m=0:0.05:1;
k=0.4*m;
l=0.7*m;
%j=0.6*m;
%r=0.5*m;
%c=0.3*m;
%t=0.8*m;
p=0.6*m+0.5*m+0.3*m+0.8*m;
s1=k+l/p*m;
s2=k/p*m;
i=0;

plot(m,s1,m,s2)
grid on
title('Sensitivity method')
xlabel('m')
ylabel('s1, s2')

while (s1(i)>s1(i+1))
  i=i+1;
end

m(i)
s1(i)
```

References

Androniceanu, A., Gherghina, R., & Ciobănaşu, M. (2019). The interdependence between fiscal public policies and tax evasion. *Administratie Si Management Public, 2019*(32). https://doi.org/10.24818/amp/2019.32-03

Bergh, J. C. J. M. va. den. (2009). The GDP paradox. *Journal of Economic Psychology*, *30*(2). https://doi.org/10.1016/j.joep.2008.12.001

Bourdin, S., & Nadou, F. (2018). French tech: A new form of territorial mobilization to face up to global competition? *Annales de Geographie*, *2018*(723–724). https://doi.org/10.3917/ag.723.0612

Brakke, K. (2023). *Dividing a Segment into Three Equal Parts*. https://facstaff.susqu.edu/brakke/rulerandcompass/09-threeparts.html

Challoumis, C. (n.d.-a). The impact factor of Tangibles and Intangibles of controlled transactions on economic performance. *Economic Alternatives*.

Challoumis, C. (n.d.-b). The inflation according to the cycle of money (C.M.). *Economic Alternatives*.

Challoumis, C. (2018a). Analysis of the velocities of escaped savings with that of financial liquidity. *Ekonomski Signali*, *13*(2), 1–14. https://doi.org/10.5937/ekonsig1802001c

Challoumis, C. (2018b). Identification of significant economic risks to the international controlled transactions. *Economics and Applied Informatics*, *2018*(3), 149–153. https://doi.org/https://doi.org/10.26397/eai1584040927

Challoumis, C. (2018c). Methods of controlled transactions and the behavior of companies according to the public and tax policy. *Economics*, *6*(1), 33–43. https://doi.org/10.2478/eoik-2018-0003

Challoumis, C. (2019). The R.B.Q. (Rational, Behavioral and Quantified) Model. *Ekonomika*, *98*(1), 6–18. https://doi.org/10.15388/ekon.2019.1.1

Challoumis, C. (2020a). Analysis of the theory of cycle of money. *Acta Universitatis Bohemiae Meridionalis*, *23*(2), 13–29. https://doi.org/https://doi.org/10.2478/acta-2020-0004

Challoumis, C. (2020b). Impact factor of capital to the economy and tax system. *Complex System Research Centre*, *2020*, 195–200. https://www.researchgate.net/publication/350385990_Impact_Factor_of_Capital_to_the_Economy_and_Tax_System

Challoumis, C. (2020c). The impact factor of education on the public sector – The case of the U.S. *International Journal of Business and Economic Sciences Applied Research*, *13*(1), 69–78. https://doi.org/10.25103/ijbesar.131.07

Challoumis, C. (2021a). Chain of cycle of money. *Acta Universitatis Bohemiae Meridionalis*, *24*(2), 49–74.

Challoumis, C. (2021b). Index of the cycle of money – The case of Belarus. *Economy and Banks*, *2*.

Challoumis, C. (2021c). Index of the cycle of money – The case of Latvia. *Economics and Culture*, *17*(2), 5–12. https://doi.org/10.2478/jec-2020-0015

Challoumis, C. (2021d). Index of the cycle of money – The case of Ukraine. *Actual Problems of Economics, 243*(9), 102–111. doi:10.32752/1993-6788-2021-1-243-244-102-111

Challoumis, C. (2021e). Index of the cycle of money – The case of Bulgaria. *Economic Alternatives, 27*(2), 225–234. https://www.unwe.bg/doi/eajournal/2021.2/EA.2021.2.04.pdf

Challoumis, C. (2022a). Conditions of the CM (Cycle of Money). In *Social and Economic Studies within the Framework of Emerging Global Developments, Volume – 1, V. Kaya* (pp. 13–24). https://doi.org/10.3726/b19907

Challoumis, C. (2022b). Impact factor of the rest rewarding taxes. In *Complex System Research Centre*. https://doi.org/10.2139/ssrn.3154753

Challoumis, C. (2023a). A comparison of the velocities of minimum escaped savings and financial liquidity. In *Social and Economic Studies within the Framework of Emerging Global Developments, Volume – 4, V. Kaya* (pp. 41–56). https://doi.org/10.3726/b21202

Challoumis, C. (2023b). Capital and risk in the tax system. In *Complex System Research Centre* (pp. 241–244).

Challoumis, C. (2023c). Chain of the cycle of money with and without maximum and minimum mixed savings. *European Multidisciplinary Journal of Modern Science, 23*(2023), 1–16.

Challoumis, C. (2023d). Chain of the cycle of money with and without maximum mixed savings (Three-Dimensional Approach). *Academic Journal of Digital Economics and Stability, 34*(2023), 43–65.

Challoumis, C. (2023e). Chain of the cycle of money with and without minimum mixed savings (Three-Dimensional Approach). *International Journal of Culture and Modernity, 33*(2023), 22–33.

Challoumis, C. (2023f). Comparisons of the cycle of money based on enforcement and escaped savings. *Pindus Journal of Culture, Literature, and ELT*, 3(10), 19–28.

Challoumis, C. (2023g). Comparisons of the cycle of money with and without the mixed savings. *Economics & Law*. http://el.swu.bg/ikonomika/

Challoumis, C. (2023h). Currency rate of the CM (Cycle of Money). *Research Papers in Economics and Finance, 7*(1).

Challoumis, C. (2023i). Elements of the theory of cycle of money without enforcement savings. *International Journal of Finance and Business Management (IJFBM)*, Vol. 2, No. 1, 2023, *2*(1), 15–28. https://journal.multitechpublisher.com/index.php/ijfbm/article/view/1108/1202

Challoumis, C. (2023j). From savings to escape and enforcement savings. *Cogito, XV*(4), 206–216.

Challoumis, C. (2023k). G7 – Global minimum corporate tax rate of 15%. *International Journal of Multicultural and Multireligious Understanding (IJMMU), 10*(7).

Challoumis, C. (2023l). Impact factor of bureaucracy to the tax system. *Ekonomski Signali, 18*(2), 12.

Challoumis, C. (2023m). Impact factor of liability of tax system according to the theory of cycle of money. In *Social and Economic Studies within the Framework of Emerging Global Developments Volume 3, V. Kaya* (Vol. 3, pp. 31–42). https://doi.org/10.3726/b20968

Challoumis, C. (2023n). Index of the cycle of money – The case of Canada. *Journal of Entrepreneurship, Business and Economics, 11*(1), 102–133. http://scientificia.com/index.php/JEBE/article/view/203

Challoumis, C. (2023o). Risk on the tax system of the E.U. from 2016 to 2022. *Economics, 11*(2).

Challoumis, C. (2023p). Utility of cycle of money without the escaping savings (Protection of the Economy). In *Social and Economic Studies within the Framework of Emerging Global Developments Volume 2, V. Kaya* (pp. 53–64). https://doi.org/10.3726/b20509

Challoumis, C. (2024a). Approach on arm's length principle and fix length principle mathematical representations. In *Innovations and Contemporary Trends in Business & Economics.*

Challoumis, C. (2024b). Estimations of the cycle of money without escape savings. *International Journal of Multicultural and Multireligious Understanding, 11*(3).

Challoumis, C. (2024c). From economics to economic engineering (The Cycle of Money): The case of Romania. *Cogito, XVII*(2).

Challoumis, C. (2024d). Impact factors of global tax revenue – Theory of cycle of money. *International Journal of Multicultural and Multireligious Understanding, 11*(1).

Challoumis, C. (2024e). Index of the cycle of money – The case of Switzerland. *The Index of the Cycle of Money: The Case of Switzerland. Journal of Risk and Financial Management, 2024, 17, 135, 17*(4), 1–24. https://doi.org/https://doi.org/10.3390/jrfm17040135

Challoumis, C. (2024f). Rewarding taxes on the cycle of money. In *Social and Economic Studies within the Framework of Emerging Global Developments* (Vol. 5).

Corti, I. N., Roldán, C. D., & Benito, S. M. R. (2020). Fiscal pressure and fraud, predisposition to pay taxes and personal satisfaction in Spain. *Revista Espanola de Investigaciones Sociologicas, 172.* https://doi.org/10.5477/cis/reis.172.101

CYSTAT. (2018). *Η ευρωπαϊκή οικονομία από την αρχή της χιλιετίας – ΕΝΑ ΣΤΑΤΙΣΤΙΚΟ ΠΟΡΤΡΕΤΟ*. https://library.cystat.gov.cy/Documents/Publication/European_Economy_Digital-2018-EL.pdf

Deng, Y., & Li, H. (2011). Retracted Article: Measures of public economic policy under the financial crisis in China. In *2011 International Conference on E-Business and E-Government, ICEE2011 – Proceedings*. https://doi.org/10.1109/ICEBEG.2011.5877027

Feinschreiber, R. (2004). *Transfer pricing methods an application guide*. John Wiley & Sons.

Ginsburgh, V., & Weber, S. (2020). The economics of language. *Journal of Economic Literature, 58*(2). https://doi.org/10.1257/JEL.20191316

Levi, S. (2021). Why hate carbon taxes? Machine learning evidence on the roles of personal responsibility, trust, revenue recycling, and other factors across 23 European countries. *Energy Research and Social Science, 73*. https://doi.org/10.1016/j.erss.2020.101883

Ortun, V., Lopez-Valcarcel, B. G., & Pinilla, J. (2017). Tax on sugar sweetened beverages in Spain. *SSRN Electronic Journal*. https://doi.org/10.2139/ssrn.3004464

Paes-Sousa, R., De Andrade Schramm, J. M., & Pereira Mendes, L. V. (2019). Fiscal Austerity and the health sector: The cost of adjustments. *Ciencia e Saude Coletiva, 24*(12). https://doi.org/10.1590/1413-812320182412.23232019

Prestianawati, S. A., Mulyaningsih, S., Manzilati, A., & Ashar, K. (2020). *Rethinking Tax Leakage: Is It the Impact of Public Policy Failure?* https://doi.org/10.2991/aebmr.k.200606.024

Richard Barker, Lennard, A., Stephen Penman, & Alan Teixeira. (2022). Accounting for intangible assets: Suggested solutions. *Accounting and Business Research, 52*(6).

Rumayya, Rammohan, A., Purwono, R., & Harymawan, I. (2020). The local economy and Re-election of incumbent district leaders in Indonesia. *Heliyon, 6*(5). https://doi.org/10.1016/j.heliyon.2020.e04098

Soboleva, I. V. (2019). Instrumental support for the implementation of the state antimonopoly policy. *Actual Problems of Economics, 12*(222).

Tvaronavičienė, M., Tarkhanova, E., & Durglishvili, N. (2018). Sustainable economic growth and innovative development of educational systems. *Journal of International Studies, 11*(1). https://doi.org/10.14254/2071-8330.2018/11-1/19

Tydir, N. I. (2019). Conceptual issues of Ukraine's tax policy in the conditions of the forming a socially oriented market economy. *Actual Problems of Economics, 12*(222).

Urwannachotima, N., Hanvoravongchai, P., Ansah, J. P., Prasertsom, P., & Koh, V. R. Y. (2020). Impact of sugar-sweetened beverage tax on dental caries: A simulation analysis. *BMC Oral Health*, *20*(1). https://doi.org/10.1186/s12903-020-1061-5

Woody, W. D., & Viney, W. (2017). A history of psychology: The emergence of science and applications, Sixth Edition. *A History of Psychology: The Emergence of Science and Applications, Sixth Edition*, 1–599.

Zayats O. I. (2019). Category the competitive force of the country. *Actual Problems of Economics*, *12*(222).

Παπακωνσταντίνου, Α., Κανάββας, Λ., & Ντόκας, Ι. (2013). Οικονομία & μικρές επιχειρήσεις. In *Ινστιτούτο μικρών επιχειρήσεων* (pp. 1–208).

Terezija Berlančić, Ivana Fosić, & Ana Živković

Exploring Intergenerational Differences in Attitudes towards Work in the Context of Healthcare Institutions

1. Introduction

The dynamic working environment of modern organizations faces challenges arising from generational differences that shape employees' attitudes and perceptions of work. Attitudes towards work are a key factor influencing employee productivity and engagement in organizations. Understanding these cross-generational differences is essential for leading successful teams and improving the work atmosphere. The paper analyses relevant studies and research that address generational differences in attitudes towards work, with a focus on medical staff. The research methodology describes the participants, the data collection instruments and the statistical analyses used for data processing. The main research findings are presented, including the differences in attitudes to work between the different generations of medical staff. The conclusion summarises the main research findings and their significance for understanding intergenerational dynamics in the world of work. The limitations of the research are outlined and recommendations are made for future research that could deepen understanding of the topic.

2. Literature Review

Generation is conceptually defined as a group of individuals with similar birth years and shared key events in their lives, which may be philosophical, socio-political or historical in nature, that shape their culture, attitudes and perspectives (Sandeen, 2008). Many generations have been defined throughout history, but four main generations are currently observed. In today's society, increasing attention is being paid to generational theory as a framework for understanding behaviours, social behaviour and attitudes towards family, work and finance. According to Strauss and Howe (1991), the differences between generations are defined by the concept of "peer personalities"," which are a caricature of a typical member of the generation. Each generation characterises collective attitudes towards various aspects of life such as family values, sexual roles, politics and religion. These attitudes are characterised by a range of traits such as security, aggressiveness, extroversion or spirituality.

Generational theories trace how these personalities develop and influence culture and society (Strauss & Howe, 1991:63 cited in Sandeen, 2008). Most academic authors describe generation intervals as periods of 20 years. This time frame corresponds to the average period from birth to the moment when a new generation is formed or a new cycle begins. At the same time, this 20-year interval reflects the four basic phases of human life: youth, adulthood, middle age and old age (Strauss & Howe, 1991:60 cited in Sandeen, 2008).

There are obvious differences in the definition of the boundaries between the generations as well as in the names and the number of generations identified. For example, while some authors define only four main generations (Silent Generation, Baby Boomers, Generation X, Millennials), others list additional sub-generations or subdivisions within each generation. There are also differences in the years assigned to each generation, which in some cases leads to overlaps. Furthermore, some authors introduce new generations such as post-millennials or the digital generation, while others use terms such as Gen-Xers or Nexters. All this shows that the differences between generations are very heterogeneous and that there is no generally accepted or standardised understanding of the division into generations. For the definition of generations in this article, the classification according to Strauss and Howe from 1991 is used, with modifications for the transition of Generation Y (Millennials) and Generation Z according to the classification of the Pew Research Centre (Strauss & Howe, 1991:63 cited in Dimocki, 2019). As already mentioned, there are currently four active generations in the labour market. The Baby Boomer generation, which once dominated the labour market, is now in the late stages of their careers and considering options for living or retirement. Generation X is in the career stability and retention phase. Millennials are in the career progression and development phase, while Generation Z is just entering the labour market. Below will be explained detailed descriptions of the characteristics of each of the generations mentioned, including key aspects of communication, strategies for overcoming challenges, life circumstances and personality traits.

The Baby Boomers, who were born between 1946 and 1964, have dominated the labour market in recent decades. Unlike previous generations where children played a less active role in the family, they grew up in a family environment where children were the central figures (Sandeen, 2008). Long working hours often led to a neglect of family life, resulting in an increase in divorce and a decrease in the birth rate (Sandeen, 2008). As the oldest actively working generation, Baby Boomers are often recognised as experts in their field and frequently take on important management positions in companies (Potter, 2018). They favour managers who value their professional opinions and care about their needs, which leads to a stronger team spirit and more motivation. They also value loyalty to the organisation and rarely change jobs (Krasulja et al., 2015). These characteristics often lead to a longer working life, even when it is time to retire.

Generation X comprises people born between 1965 and 1980 and is often referred to as the middle child of the generation, as it lies between the Baby Boomers and the Millennials. They grew up in times of global crises such as the Chernobyl nuclear disaster and the advent of AIDS, but also experienced the advent of MTV, the first video games and the internet (Krasulja et al., 2015). They often grew up in complex family structures, with up to 40 % of them growing up in single-parent households. This generation was the first to experience divorce to such an extent, making them more independent and flexible (Sandeen, 2008; Kapoor & Solomon, 2011; Krasulja et al., 2015). Members of Generation X are often sceptical of authority and prefer a clear and sophisticated management style with constant feedback on work performance. They prefer to work independently and with flexible working hours, but tend to work in teams and are seen as creative and entrepreneurial (Weeks & Schaffert, 2019). Although their academic skills are rated lower than those of Baby Boomers, they are rated higher in the areas of negotiation skills, consumer awareness and interpersonal skills. They are financially conservative, but money is not their only motivator for work, although it can affect their motivation when their income decreases (Sandeen, 2008

Generation Y, also known as Millennials, comprises people born between 1981 and 1996. They are the children of younger members of the Baby Boom generation or older members of Generation X and are characterised by rapid technological progress and the internet (Krasulja et al., 2015). Millennials are highly educated, entrepreneurial and able to multi-task and embrace change with optimism (Fry et al., 2018). They emphasise the importance of independence and flexibility in their work and prefer functional and goal-oriented tasks that focus on achieving business objectives (Krasulja et al., 2015; Dowd-Higgins, 2013).

Generation Z comprises people born after 1997 and represents the youngest cohort in the labour market just entering the workforce. They grow up in small families, often with an older or single parent, and this shapes their attitudes and values. Generation Z favours working environments that are flexible, encourage continuous learning and personal development and allow the expression of skills, knowledge and potential. An ideal workplace for them combines creativity with complex tasks (Krasulja et al., 2015). This generation is characterised by a high willingness to change, a fast-paced lifestyle and active use of the internet and modern technologies. As they have been exposed to modern technologies from an early age, they have shaped their freedom of expression, thought and behaviour. They also tend to collaborate and enjoy fun activities (Bencsik et al., 2016). If a company does not show respect to Generation Z, they will in turn feel less respect towards the company. They particularly value managers with whom they can communicate and have an open dialogue, while they perceive those who are inaccessible or unknown as authorities (Krasulja et al., 2015; Bencsik et al., 2016).

In the healthcare sector, as in other service industries, medical staff are a key factor in the quality of services. Staff attitudes towards their work play a crucial role in shaping and maintaining the level of service quality. Attitudes are defined as evaluative statements or judgements about things, people and feelings that are complex, change over time and are influenced by various external and internal factors (Robbins & Judge, 2013:69). Most research in the field of organisational behaviour analyses three basic types of attitudes towards work: job satisfaction, job commitment and organisational commitment. In addition, there are other important types of attitudes, such as perceived organisational support and organisational commitment (Robbins & Judge, 2013:73). Job satisfaction is a central aspect of analyzing employees' attitudes and describes their positive or negative feelings towards the workplace based on an assessment of its characteristics (Robbins & Judge, 2013:74). A study by Kvist et al. (2012) shows that hospitals in which employees express a high level of job satisfaction achieve the best quality of treatment and care. In addition, job satisfaction is related to various factors such as pay, recognition, collaboration, support from superiors, working conditions and demographic characteristics (Mosadeghrad & Ferdosi, 2013). Job engagement measures the degree to which employees identify with their work and the importance they attach to their contribution (Robbins & Judge, 2013:74). Avolio et al. (2004) have shown that good nurse leaders encourage employee involvement in decision making, which leads to a greater sense of job importance among employees. Organizational commitment refers to employees' identification with the organization and its goals and their desire to remain in the organization (Robbins & Judge, 2013:75). Most research emphasizes emotional commitment to the organization as a key component of employee retention (Sanner-Stiehr, 2021; Poslovni.hr/Hina, 2022). The professional attitude of healthcare professionals is of paramount importance for their long-term commitment to healthcare organizations, especially given the high mobility between different institutions within and outside the country and the general shortage of healthcare personnel (Sanner-Stiehr, 2021 et al.; Poslovni.hr/Hina, 2022).

3. Methodology and Research Results

The survey covered healthcare facilities and the sample consisted exclusively of healthcare professionals employed in these facilities, but with different profiles, such as doctors, nurses/technicians, radiology and laboratory technicians, physiotherapists and pharmacists. The participants took part in the study voluntarily and anonymously by completing a written questionnaire consisting of a general socio-demographic section and scales on job satisfaction.

The first part of the questionnaire, the general socio-demographic questionnaire, serves as a starting point for the study and provides basic information about the participants. It consists of 18 questions, including both open and closed questions. This part of the study aims to collect basic information about the participants, including age, gender, place of residence, household, age of the participant's parents, education, employment status and characteristics of the work environment and organisation in which the participant works. This segment serves as the basis for further data analysis and interpretation and allows for the creation of a context for understanding the research findings. The Job Satisfaction Scale and the Multidimensional Generational Questionnaire for Nurses were used for the purposes of the study. The Job Satisfaction Scale is a comprehensive measure of the key dimensions of job satisfaction that was originally developed in Finland. This instrument has undergone numerous tests and translations into several languages to ensure its reliability and validity.

The KUHJSS research instrument consists of 37 items that assess various aspects of job satisfaction and are divided into seven subscales: leadership (7 items), job demands (8 items), motivational factors (6 items), work environment (4 items), well-being at work (4 items), participation in decision-making processes (4 items) and sense of belonging (4 items). Participants rate each item on a Likert scale ranging from 1 to 5, with higher scores indicating more desirable results. Previous testing and validation of the questionnaire has confirmed the reliability of the scale, expressed by Cronbach's alpha coefficients of 0.64 to 0.92, 0.65 to 0.92 and 0.661 to 0.910, indicating strong internal consistency of the research instrument (Kvist et al., 2012; Ylitörmänen et al., 2018, cited in Sanner-Stiehr, 2021). The MNGQ is a questionnaire developed in Finland to investigate generational differences among nurses (Stevanin et al., 2017). The research questionnaire consists of fifty-four items divided into eight subscales. The subscales include intergenerational conflict (10 items), perception of patient safety (11 items), intergenerational relationships (8 items), working in a multigenerational team (6 items), change orientation (7 items), working while sick and desire to work (5 items), job attractiveness, intention to leave (3 items), and flexibility and availability (4 items). Participants rated each item on a Likert scale from 1 to 5, with a higher value representing more desirable results. The range of the Cronbach's alpha coefficient is between 0.61 and 0.81.

Data processing involves the application of various statistical methods. The Kolmogorov-Smirnov test was used to check the normality of the data distribution. In addition, differences between groups were tested using the Mann-Whitney U test for the comparison of two groups and the Kruskal-Wallis test for three or more groups. The significance level was set at alpha = 0.05. The reliability of the scales was assessed using the Cronbach's alpha coefficient. The data was analysed using SPSS software (IBM SPSS Statistics for Windows, 2015).

The study included 144 participants whose demographic characteristics were analysed according to generational categories: Baby Boomers, Generation X, Millennials and Generation Z. Baby Boomers make up 12.50 % of the sample, Generation X 22.90 %, Millennials 54.90 %, making them the most represented generation among the respondents, while Generation Z accounts for 9.70 % of the total number of participants. In terms of gender, 27.10 % of participants are male, while 72.9 % are female. In terms of education level, 56.90 % of the participants have vocational training, 19.40 % have higher vocational training, 20.10 % have higher education, 2.10 % have a Master's degree and 1.40 % have a PhD. In addition, 77.80 % of the participants are nurses/technicians, 16.00 % are doctors and 6.20 % fall into other categories.

The analysis of the duration of employment shows that the majority of participants have a long professional experience, both overall (33.60 % have a duration of employment of more than 21 years) and in the current institution (31.00 % have a duration of employment of more than 21 years). Most participants work full-time (84.00 %), with the majority working 40 hours per week (82.60 %) in shifts (54.20 %). In terms of place of residence, the majority of participants live in urban areas (55.60 %).

The statistical analysis revealed significant differences between the generations in terms of demographic characteristics. The Baby Boomer generation and Generation X, for example, work longer than Generation Z and the Millennials. In addition, Generation Z is more likely to live in rural areas compared to the other generations. These findings emphasise the importance of understanding the demographic differences between generations in the context of the healthcare workforce and highlight the need to design workforce management strategies to meet the specific needs and preferences of different generations.

According to the research results, the KUHJSS scale showed high reliability (Cronbach's alpha = 0.959), confirming its validity as a tool for assessing job satisfaction among healthcare professionals. However, the "motivating workplace factors" subscale did not show satisfactory reliability (Cronbach's alpha = 0.457), suggesting that the metric items in this area of research need to be revised or replaced.

The analyses conducted did not reveal any statistically significant differences between the generations in the assessment of job satisfaction according to the KUHJSS scale and its subscales. Overall, respondents were satisfied with their jobs in the organisation where they currently work, with a median score of 141 on the KUHJSS scale (IQR 123.25–163.25). The Baby Boomer generation showed the highest satisfaction in all subscales except leadership, where members of Generation Z scored the highest, followed by Generation X. Generation X showed the lowest satisfaction in five subscales: leadership, motivating workplace factors, work environment, well-being at work and sense of unity. Millennials rated the leadership, sense of belonging and work environment subscales the lowest, although the results were comparable to those of Generation X. Generation Z rated the necessary work factors and participation in decision-making subscales the lowest.

In the study on intergenerational relationships among healthcare professionals, the Job Satisfaction Scale MNGQ was used, which consists of eight subscales (intergenerational conflict, perception of patient safety, intergenerational relationships, working in a multigenerational team, openness to change, presenteeism, intention to leave, flexibility and availability). The overall reliability coefficient of the entire MNGQ scale, expressed by Cronbach's alpha coefficient, is 0.778, which indicates a good reliability of the questionnaire in assessing job satisfaction in the selected sample. However, the "openness to change" subscale did not show satisfactory reliability (Cronbach's alpha = 0.467), suggesting limited usefulness in assessing willingness to change in relation to job satisfaction.

In contrast to the KUHJSS, the MNGQ scale, i.e. its subscales, shows statistically significant differences in the segments of job satisfaction between the different generations, as can be seen in Table 1.

Table 1. Generational differences according to the MNGQ and its subscales Median (Interquartile Range)

Baby Boom		*Generation X*	*Millennials*	*Generation Z*	*Total*	*P*.*
Total MNGQ	189 (165,75–209,25)	185 (176,50–194)	190 (176–201)	191,50 (185,75–201,75)	189 (176,25–201)	0,610
Conflicts between the generations	32,5 (19,50–37,25)	30 (22–33,50)	30 (27–34)	30,50 (27,75–36,50)	30 (27–34)	0,641
Opinion on patient safety	42 (38,25–46)	43 (37,50–49)	40 (34–44)	40 (36–44,50)	41 (36–45,75)	**0,031**
Relationships between the generations	21 (9,75–28,25)	20 (13–25)	22 (18–25)	24 (17–27)	21 (17–25)	0,260
Working in a multi-generational team	27,50	26	26	28	27	0,287
	(25–29,25)	(23,50–28,50)	(23–29)	(24,50–29)	(23–29)	
Orientation towards change	27,50	28	31	31,50	29,50	**0,029**
	(21,50–30,25)	(25–33)	(27–33)	(27–33,25)	(26–33)	
Presenteeism	22,50 (21–25)	21 (19–23)	20 (17–21)	19 (16–21)	20 (18–22)	**0,001**
Intention to leave	3	6	7	5,50	6	**0,046**
	(3–7)	(3–9)	(4–9)	(3–11,25)	(3,25–9)	
Flexibility and availability	16	16	16	15,50	16	0,548
	(12,75–19)	(14–18)	(14–18)	(13,75–16)	(14–18)	

Source: Author's own work

According to the research results, statistical differences were found between the generations in several subscales. Generation X has a stronger focus on patient safety compared to millennials ($p = 0.031$), while Baby Boomers and millennials are more willing to change in the "orientation towards change" subscale compared to Generation X ($p = 0.031$)". Baby Boomers show a greater willingness to work when ill and a tendency to work despite illness than Generation Z and Millennials "($p = 0.001$) in the "presenteeism" subscale", and they are more inclined to leave their current job than Millennials in the "intention to leave" subscale ($p = 0.046$)".

Millennials are characterised by high scores in the subscales intention to quit and flexibility and availability, while their lowest scores are in working in a multigenerational team, perception of patient safety and intergenerational conflict. On the other hand, Generation Z scores highest in the subscales intergenerational relationships, working in a multigenerational team and orientation to change, while their lowest scores are in perception of patient safety, where they are on par with Millennials, presenteeism and flexibility and availability. Baby Boomers also achieve high scores, particularly in the subscales intergenerational conflict, presenteeism and flexibility and availability, while their lowest scores come from the subscales orientation to change and intention to leave. Finally, Generation X scores the lowest on the MNGQ scale, particularly in the intergenerational conflict, intergenerational relationships and working in a multigenerational team subscales, while their highest scores are recorded in the patient safety perception and flexibility and availability subscales.

Comparing the research conducted with previous studies points to similarities and differences between the groups studied and provides valuable insights into the dynamics between generations in the work environment. Understanding these differences is important for developing strategies to successfully manage diverse teams and increase employee satisfaction. (Sanner-Stiehr et al., 2021). In analysing the impact of intergenerational differences on attitudes towards work, researchers have highlighted key factors that influence employee satisfaction and organisational commitment. Interpersonal relationships in organisations that are complex and evolving reflect the different perspectives of generations on work. Significant differences between generations were found in perceptions of the work environment and motivational factors. The study by Sanner-Stiehr et al. (2021), conducted in the US, Finland and Italy among healthcare professionals, including Generation Z and physicians, provided insights into the differences between generations. Millennials frequently expressed the highest levels of job satisfaction, while Generation X frequently reported lower levels of satisfaction. Differences were also found between countries, with Italian Baby Boomers being the most satisfied and Millennials the least. The results of the study suggest that different generations place different value on aspects of the working environment and motivation. While Baby Boomers often emphasised the importance of patient safety, Millennials showed an inclination towards change and opportunities for advancement. Generation X was often characterised by their emphasis on change and working in intergenerational teams.

4. Conclusion

The paper highlights the importance of understanding the differences between generations in healthcare organisations to facilitate communication and collaboration between staff. Different generations, such as Baby Boomers, Generation X, Millennials and Generation Z, have different priorities and expectations of their workplace, which necessitates an adaptation of leadership approaches. Baby Boomers, who prioritise work and loyalty to the company, differ from Millennials, who seek a work-life balance and are more open about their dissatisfaction. A transformational leadership style offers an adaptable approach that promotes individuality and encourages active employee engagement. Considering the different needs and preferences of the generations, it is crucial to create communication that is acceptable and understandable for all employees. This not only improves the organisation of work and the delivery of healthcare services, but also promotes the personal and professional development of each team member. In today's organisations, including healthcare facilities, the diversity of the workforce with its different experiences requires management structures to adapt to new ways of working and communicating. Employee loyalty is no longer just linked to the start of a career, but also to ongoing communication, team relationships and work-life balance. Limitations of the research conducted include a random sample with a small number of respondents who are predominantly female and an uneven distribution of healthcare workers. In addition, the majority of respondents belonged to the Millennial generation, which limits the generalisability of the results. For further research, it is recommended to use a larger and more diverse sample from different healthcare settings, including clinics, ambulance services and clinical hospitals and centres.

References

Avolio, B. J., Zhu, W., Koh, W., & Bhatia, P. (2004). Transformational leadership and organizational commitment: Mediating role of psychological empowerment and moderating role of structural distance. *Journal of Organizational Behavior, 25*(8), pp. 951–968.

Bencsik, A., Horváth-Csikós, G., & Juhász, T. (2016). Y and Z generations at workplaces. *Journal of Competitiveness*, *6*(3), pp. 90–106.

Dimocki, M. (2019). Defining generations: Where Millennials end and Generation Z begins. *Pew Research Center*. [Online]. Available at: https://www.pewresearch.org/fact-tank/2019/01/17/where-millennials-end-and-generation-z-begins/ [Accessed on December 2023].

Dowd-Higgins, C. (2013). How to play together in the multi-generational sandbox at work. *Huffington Post*. [Online]. Available at https://www.huffpost.com/entry/how-to-play-together-in-t_b_2989568. [Accessed on March 2024].

Fry, R., Igielnik, R., & Patten, E. (2018). How Millennials today compare with their grandparents 50 years ago. *Pew Research Center*. [Online]. Available at: https://www.pewresearch.org/fact-tank/2018/03/16/how-millennials-compare-with-their-grandparents/ [Accessed on January 2024].

IBM Corp. Released 2015. IBM SPSS Statistics for Windows (no date). Armonk, NY: IBM Corp.

Kapoor, C., & Solomon, N. (2011). Understanding and managing generational differences in the workplace. *Worldwide Hospitality and Tourism Themes*. Madera, J.M. (ur.) 3(4), pp. 308–318.

Krasulja, N., Radojević, I., Janjušić, D., & Vujić, N. (2015). Multigeneracijska radna snaga- prednost ili nedostatak za suvremene organizacije. *Praktični menadžment: stručni časopis za teoriju i praksu menadžmenta*, *6*(1), 59–68.

Kvist, T., Mäntynen, R., Partanen, P., Turunen, H., Miettinen, M., & Vehviläinen-Julkunen, K. (2012). The job satisfaction of Finnish Nursing Staff: The development of a job satisfaction scale and survey results. *Nursing Research and Practice*, 2012, pp. 1–11.

Mosadeghrad, A., & Ferdosi, M. (2013). Leadership, job satisfaction and organizational commitment in healthcare sector: Proposing and testing a model. *Materia Socio Medica*, *25*(2), p. 121.

Poslovni.hr/Hina. (2022). Koliko nam zapravo manjka zdravstvenog kadra?. [Online]. Available at: https://www.poslovni.hr/hrvatska/koliko-nam-zapravo-manjka-zdravstvenog-kadra-4330782 [Accessed on March 2024].

Potter, S. B. (2018). What would a transfer of power from Baby Boomers to Generation X look like?. Available at: https://insight.factset.com/what-would-a-transfer-of-power-from-baby-boomers-to-generation-x-look-like [Accessed on March 2024].

Robbins, S. P., & Judge, T. (2013). *Organizational behavior*. 15th ed. Boston: Pearson.

Sandeen, C. (2008). Boomers, Xers, and Millennials: Who are they and what do they really want from continuing higher education?. *Continuing Higher Education Review*, *72*, pp. 11–31.

Sanner-Stiehr, E. Stevanin, S., Mikkonen, S., & Kvist, T. (2021). Job satisfaction and generational nursing characteristics among registered nurses in the United States, Italy and Finland: Results of a survey study. *Journal of Nursing Management*, *29*(8), pp. 2364–2373.

Stevanin, S., Bressan, V., Vehviläinen-Julkunen, K., Pagani, L., Poletti, P., & Kvist, T. (2017). The multidimensional nursing generations questionnaire: Development, reliability, and validity assessments. *Journal of Nursing Management*, *25*(4), pp. 287–296.

Strauss, W., & Howe, N. G. (1991). *Generations: The history of America's future, 1584 to 2069*. 1 ed. New York, NY: Morrow.

Weeks, K. P., & Schaffert, C. (2019). Generational differences in definitions of meaningful work: A mixed methods study. *Journal of Business Ethics*, *156*(4), pp. 1045–1061.

Ylitörmänen, T., Turunen, H., & Kvist, T. (2018). Job satisfaction among registered nurses in two Scandinavian acute care hospitals. *Journal of Nursing Management*, *26*(7), pp. 888–897.

Table 1. Continued

Institution	definition
World Bank	A CBDC is a central bank liability that is digitally created and recorded on centralized or decentralized ledgers, denominated in an existing unit of account, and convertible in physical cash, commercial bank money and other forms of money on demand by the holder at authorized entities.

Source: Own preparation.

A retail CBDC is one that is designed to be used for everyday transactions by individuals and businesses. A retail CBDC differs from other types of cashless payment instruments (such as credit transfers, direct debits, card payments, and e-money) in that it is a direct claim on a central bank rather than a liability of a private financial institution. In contrast to a retail CBDC, a wholesale CBDC caters to a distinct set of end consumers. Wholesale CBDCs are designed for transactions involving banks, central banks, and other financial organizations. As a result, wholesale CBDCs would function similarly to today's central bank reserves or settlement balances. Wholesale CBDCs, on the other hand, may provide financial institutions with access to new tokenisation-enabled functions such as composability and programmability.

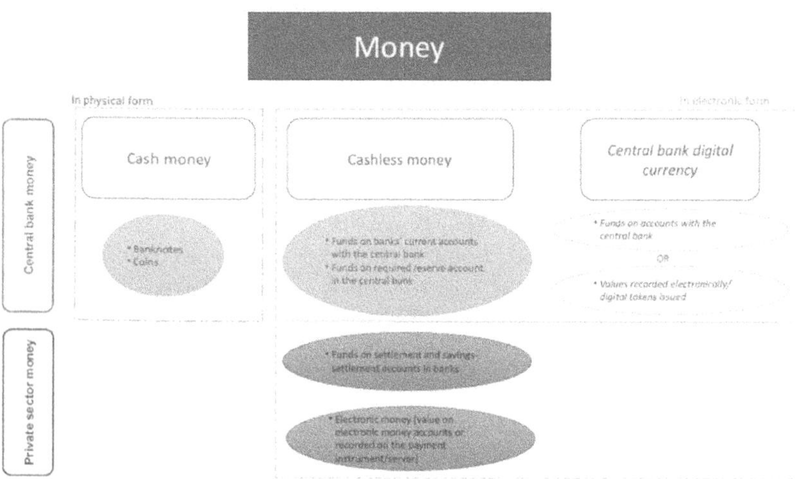

Figure 1. Physical and electronic form of money

Source: NBP (2021).

Piotr Misztal

Current Status and Prospects of Central Bank Digital Currency in the World Economy

1. The Essence of Central Bank Digital Currency

Central Bank Digital Currency (CBDC) is a digital representation of a country' fiat currency produced and regulated by the central bank. In general, CBDC are a type of digital money denominated in the national unit of account that i a direct obligation of the central bank (Ricci et al., 2024). CBDCs are central ized and issued by a country's monetary authority, such as the central bank, a opposed to decentralized cryptocurrencies like Bitcoin or Ethereum, which us blockchain technology to operate (Agur et al.,2022).

Table 1. Central Bank Digital Currency definitions by international institutions

Institution	definition
Federal Reserve Bank	A CBDC is defined as a digital liability of a central bank that is widely available to the general public
BIS	A CBDC would be a digital banknote. It could be used by individuals to pay businesses, shops, or each other (a "retail CBDC"), or between financial institutions to settle trades in financial markets (a "wholesale CBDC")
IMF	IMF staff defined CBDC as "a new form of money, issued digital by the central bank and intended to serve as legal tender."
CPMI	A new form of central bank money. That is, a central bank liability, denominated in an existing unit of account, which serves both as a medium of exchange and a store of value
G20	CBDC has been defined as central bank money in a digital format, denominated in the national unit of account, that is a direct liability of the central bank and can be used for retail payments and/or wholesale settlement. (Notice that copies the CPMI verbatim.)
G7	A retail CBDC would be a digital form of central bank money, denominated in the national unit of account, distinct from electronic reserves (which cannot currently be accessed by individuals) and physical cash. As a direct liability of the central bank, CBDCs would also be distinct from commercial bank money. If issued, CBDCs, as a form of central bank money, could act as both a liquid, safe settlement asset and as an anchor for the payments system

(*continued*

CBDC can be issued in two ways, depending on the location and type of electronic recording:

(a) Account-based – the CBDC concept is based on accounts held with the central bank.
(b) Token-based are digital representations of value that can be held on a central bank issued electronic device, such as a prepaid card, SIM card, or phone application, or in a distributed ledger.

Table 2. Account-based approach vs Token-based approach

Feature	Account-based	Token-based
Access	KYC/AML practices	Universal
Anonymity	Not anonymous	Different levels of anonymity can be established
Transfer	Centralised	Decentralised
Cash-like	Not	Yes
Custody	Custodian approach	Non-custodian approach

Source: NBP (2021).

There are significant discrepancies between the aforementioned CBDC models. The CBDC model, which is based on a system of accounts kept with a central bank, involves direct adjustments to the account balances of the transaction parties. In the second situation, when a payment is executed using CBDC stored in the distributed ledger or locally on a payment instrument or device, the digital representation of the transaction value must be transferred between the payer and the payee.

2. Central Bank Digital Currency Pros and Cons

Central Bank Digital Currency has various possible advantages and downsides, which might differ based on the design, execution, and environment. This is an overview:

(a) Financial Inclusion

CBDCs can give access to financial services for the unbanked or underbanked because they can be accessed and transacted on digital devices such as smartphones. This can help to close the gap between people who have access to traditional financial services and those who don't.

Financial inclusion is frequently a top policy priority for a retail CBDC, particularly in emerging and low-income nations. CBDCs, if appropriately structured to address financial inclusion barriers, have the potential to achieve adoption as a payment channel for financially excluded people. CBDCs can be designed to replicate some of the desirable properties of cash, such as the ability to make payments without a bank account, the trust associated with central bank money, low or no fees, and less stringent identity requirements for low-risk populations who struggle to obtain formal identification. However, complete compliance with financial integrity rules is important. A CBDC could also provide benefits other than income, such as the building of a financial history to assist broaden access to credit. A CBDC can thus serve as an important entry point into the official financial system. CBDCs, as a public-sector venture with no profit incentive, have the potential to foster competition by lowering payment and financial service prices. Furthermore, CBDCs can meet the needs of rural and low-income communities who are underserved by the private sector by making resources available on a range of hardware devices and in offline contexts. However, a CBDC alone is not a silver bullet to financial inclusion, as it can face challenges common for digital products, such as gaps in digital and financial knowledge, and access to electricity and digital networks. A CBDC may not be the optimal financial inclusion solution for every country, thus policymakers should consider a variety of policies and initiatives, including but not limited to CBDCs, to promote financial inclusion.

(b) Efficiency

Digital currencies have the potential to improve payment systems by reducing transaction time and costs, particularly for cross-border payments. This efficiency can benefit both individuals and corporations, resulting in higher production and economic growth.

In some nations, payments systems are dominated by a few large corporations that charge high rents and do not necessarily provide compatible services. In some circumstances, CBDC could discipline the market to provide better and cheaper services while also increasing innovation. It might also function as a backbone to promote interoperability, since payment service providers (PSPs) could settle claims against each other in CBDC.

(c) Reduced Counterfeit Risk

CBDCs can assist combat counterfeiting because they are issued by the central bank and can be electronically validated. This lowers the possibility of counterfeit currency flowing in the economy, increasing general trust in the monetary system.

Cyberattacks, power failures, and other types of malfunctions may cause disruptions to digital payments. Cash is a valuable option when payment methods are temporarily unavailable; nonetheless, it is inconvenient and unsuitable for e-commerce and other digital settings. Furthermore, in other areas, cash use is fast declining. CBDC could be built as an alternative payment system that functions independently of other payment systems. As such, it has a good possibility of being operational as a "back up" in the event of a major outage. Furthermore, CBDC might be designed from the beginning to be more resilient than conventional payment systems, for example by adding innovative offline technologies and assuring high cybersecurity readiness.

(d) Monetary Policy Control

CBDCs allow central banks to exercise more direct influence over monetary policy. Central banks can execute more effective economic stabilization programs such as interest rate adjustments or quantitative easing by better monitoring the movement of money.

(e) Monetary Sovereignty

CBDCs have the ability to mitigate the risk of non-fiat e-money replacing fiat money, preventing the loss of monetary policy sovereignty. There is a risk that a more liquid or handy form of international CBDC will impact the velocity of local currency and consequently monetary policy.

CBDCs have the potential to influence the macroeconomic environment that supports monetary policy transmission. A CBDC provides a secure store of value and an efficient means of payment, which can boost competition for deposit funding, increase banks' share of wholesale funding, and reduce bank profits. A CBDC might potentially improve financial inclusion and prevent dollarization or cryptoization. These changes in the macroeconomic environment have the potential to strengthen the channels of monetary policy transmission if CBDC is properly structured. In normal circumstances, the effects on monetary policy transmission are predicted to be minimal for CBDC holdings of moderate magnitude. However, these consequences may be more pronounced in a context of low interest rates or financial market stress, when the relative value of a CBDC rises. A non-remunerated CBDC may harden the zero lower bound on interest rates. Finally, during market stress, a CBDC may enhance the danger of flight to safety from retail bank savings.

CBDC benefits cannot be fully realized unless there is greater and higher quality connectivity between economies through distributed computing and public digital infrastructure; expanded global and regional trade and investment opportunities via digital access to capital and free trade; and increased and diversified regional public goods such as distributed ledger and blockchain for trade traceability, identity, supply chain financing, and product tokenization.

Central bank digital currencies are also associated with certain risks:

(a) Privacy Concerns

CBDCs raise privacy issues because central banks will have access to precise transaction data. This raises concerns about individuals' privacy rights and the possibilities for government surveillance. Protecting user privacy while adhering to anti-money laundering (AML) and know-your-customer (KYC) rules is a major concern.

(b) Cybersecurity Risks

CBDCs would be vulnerable to cyberattacks, necessitating strong security measures to prevent theft and fraud. The digital nature of CBDCs makes them appealing targets for hackers, and any breach could have serious ramifications for financial stability and customer trust.

(c) Impact on Commercial Banks

If households and companies may open accounts directly with the central bank, the traditional banking model may be disrupted and commercial banks' position in the financial system reduced. This might disrupt the banking sector, resulting in employment losses.

(d) Operational Challenges

Implementing and managing a CBDC infrastructure will necessitate substantial investment in technology and expertise. Central banks would need to provide secure and user-friendly digital platforms, educate the public on how to use CBDCs responsibly, and assure interoperability with existing financial systems.

(e) Legal and Supervision Risk

Many countries' central banks have legal loopholes in digital currency issuance, use, circulation, and supervision, such as how CBDCs are treated in deposit insurance. There are issues in monitoring and supervising CBDCs. For example, with traditional money supervision, banks may detect and remove physical counterfeits from the system. However, digital cash does not exist in physical form but can be accessed using software and hardware e-wallets. Its counterfeiting and supervision methods differ. If a software bug exists, the loss can be significant and broad. When hackers steal or a system fails, the security issue may be more serious than it is with traditional currency.

(f) Financial Exclusion

With a lack of digital literacy, a basic comprehension of financial concepts, and an inability to trust technology, parts of the population, such as the poor and elderly, may be excluded or alienated from digital infrastructure. It is important to develop open public digital financial infrastructure, as without it, more individuals will be excluded than included. Another concern emerges in terms of digital and financial literacy. Digital and financial, or simply fintech, illiteracy can lead to exclusion. In this sense, a CBDC might have a negative influence on the economy and society. These exclusion concerns can be mitigated by developing digital infrastructure, increasing digital literacy among the vulnerable population, and empowering small companies through CBDC education programs.

Balancing the benefits of financial inclusion and efficiency against concerns about privacy, cybersecurity, and the impact on current financial institutions will be critical in the creation and implementation of CBDCs. Despite these issues, several central banks are actively investigating and experimenting with CBDCs, and some countries have already piloted, planned, or launched their own digital currencies.

3. Literature Review

Meaning et al. (2021) claim that CBDCs make negative nominal interest rates and helicopter money more effective, but they believe that central banks can still use such policy tools without them. The paper's principal findings indicate that, assuming a universally available, freely convertible, and interest-bearing CBDC design choice, central banks can continue to use present monetary policy techniques with no practical modification. The report also claims that CBDC policy rate transmission to the secondary lending market and the actual economy would be stronger.

Agur et al. emphasize that a CBDC can be built to have characteristics comparable to cash or deposits, as well as to be interest bearing: a CBDC that competes closely with deposits reduces bank credit and output, but a cash-like CBDC may cause currency to evaporate. The best CBDC design thereby balances bank intermediation with the social utility of retaining a varied range of payment mechanisms. When network effects are important, an interest-bearing CBDC mitigates the central bank's trade-off.

According to Arauz (2021), governments may find direct payments to households appealing, especially in light of declining demand, rising youth unemployment, and global wealth inequities.Some governments may hope to engineer effective demand in order to impose demand-side policies by incorporating programmability into digital money vouchers.However, such an ambition would spark another debate over the roles of governments and central banks, potentially leading to excessive economic involvement.

Hermawan et al. (2023) use a structural New Keynesian Phillips curve framework with an explicit velocity term to investigate the possible effects of CBDC issuance on aggregate fluctuations in the Indonesian economy. According to the study, a 10 % fall in money velocity, assisted by a CBDC issue, would cut inflation by 0.6–1.7 %. The authors emphasize the necessity of incorporating money velocity in policy decisions. The study also concludes that a larger-scale model is required to provide more precise estimates about the possible influence of CBDC issuance on aggregate volatility and monetary policy.

According to Edwards (2021), CBDC could completely drown out bank deposits in weaker economies, emphasizing the risk of currency substitution. Inadequate countries with weak monetary and fiscal institutions in the global hierarchy may see increased currency substitution unless CBDC policies are properly implemented to defend local currencies. Current cryptocurrency ownership data may support this idea.

According to Armelius et al. (2018), an interest-bearing digital euro might make monetary policy more effective by improving the pass-through of policy rate adjustments, so changing the conditions under which liquidity exists.If the central bank boosts both its policy rate and interest rates on digital euros, banks may need to raise their own interest rates to dissuade clients from converting deposits into digital euros.

Bolt et al. (2022) propose the digitalization of public money through the use of CBDCs to defend the interests of state instruments, as private digital currencies grow rapidly. The article proposes that authorities should create a balance between private stable coins and public CBDCs in order to avoid impeding creative financial sector activities. The proposed high-level system foresee tighter controls in response to rising private money acceptance, while also calling for convertibility between the two kinds of money.

4. Empirical Data

CBDCs are being considered by 134 nations and monetary unions, accounting for 98 % of world GDP.In May 2020, the number was only 35. Currently, 68 countries are in advanced stages of exploration (development, piloting, or launch). The development phase includes the technical build and early testing of a CBDC in a controlled environment. The pilot phase involved small-scale testing of a CBDC in the real world with a limited number of individuals. However, the launch phase indicates that a CBDC has been issued for extensive retail and/or wholesale use.

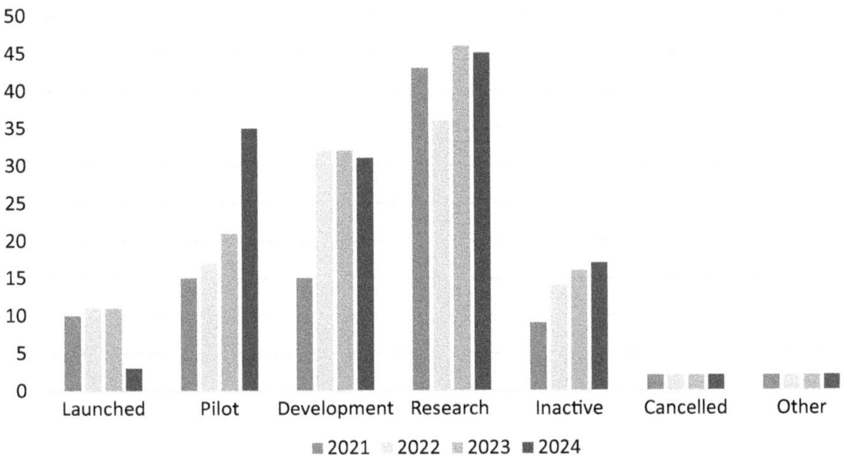

Figure 2. Number of countries and currency unions exploring CBDC in the period 2021–2024

Source: cbdctracker.org (2024).

As many as 19 of the G20 countries are currently in the advanced stages of CBDC development.Eleven of those countries are already in the pilot stage. This covers Brazil, Japan, India, Australia, South Korea, South Africa, Russia, and Turkey. So date, only three countries – the Bahamas, Jamaica, and Nigeria – have fully implemented a CBDC.The Eastern Caribbean Currency Union, which consists of eight countries, has paused the availability of DCash owing to technical concerns and is creating a new pilot. The number of current CBDC pilots has reached a new high of 36, including the digital euro.CBDCs in advanced retail projects are dispersed through intermediaries such as banks, financial institutions, and payment service providers. In China, a direct CBDC is available through a central bank application.

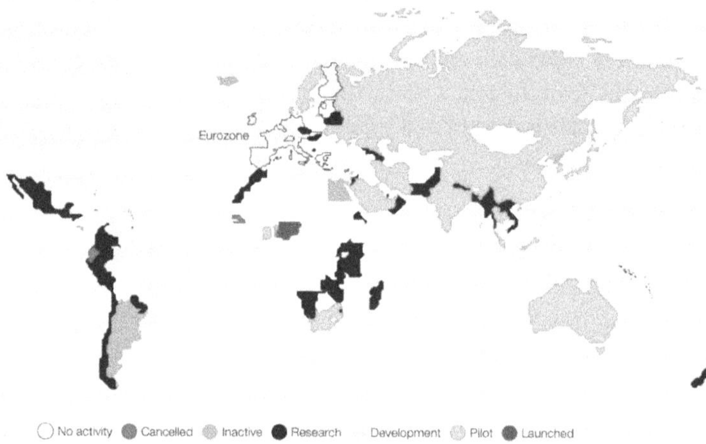

Figure 3. The map of CBDC phase of exploration
Source: cbdctracker.org (2024).

Since Russia's invasion of Ukraine and the subsequent G7 sanctions response, wholesale CBDC development has increased.There are presently 13 cross-border wholesale CBDC projects, including mBridge, which connects China, Thailand, the UAE, and Hong Kong, and will expand to 11 additional countries this year. China's digital yuan (e-CNY) is the world's largest CBDC trial, reaching 260 million wallets across 25 cities.Since 2022, it has been employed in a variety of scenarios, including transportation, healthcare, and crude oil purchases. In 2024, the pilot will focus on maximizing foreign tourist use and expanding cross-border e-CNY applications. In Asia-Pacific countries, the most popular reason for implementing digital money was to broaden the scope of digital payments for retail recipients. In the case of wholesale payments, the primary reason for implementing the central bank's digital money was to improve payment efficiency, stability, and safety.

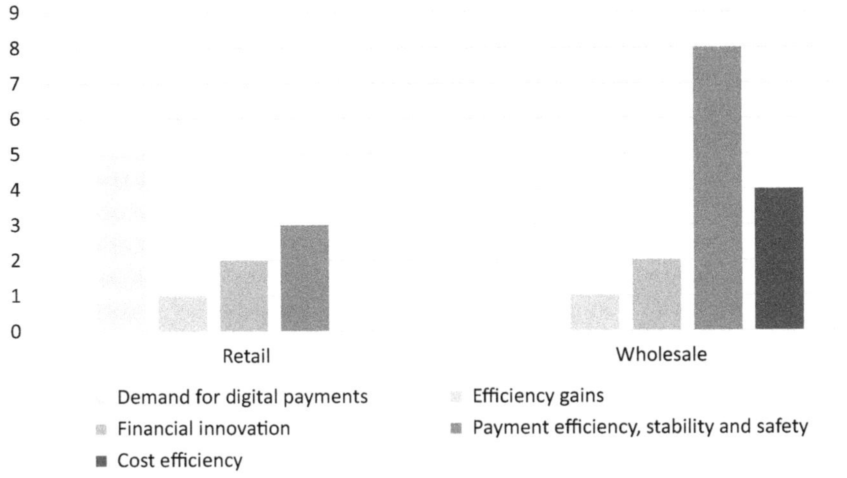

Figure 4. Motivations for issuing a CBDC in Asia-Pacific countries (APAC)
Source: IMF survey (2024).

5. Perspectives of Central Bank Digital Currency in Euro Area

People in the Eurozone benefit from a widely accepted form of payment – euro cash – that they may easily use throughout our monetary union. Cash has distinct properties: it is widely available and free to use throughout the Eurozone; it ensures the highest level of privacy protection; it is inclusive and does not require an online connection; it is secure and risk-free; it allows for instant payment settlement and can be used for both person-to-person and point-of-sale transactions. No digital payment method currently provides all of these benefits. A digital euro would bridge this gap. It would be a digital form of payment that provides the same advantages as cash. While the Eurosystem would continue to keep euro cash available, in response to Europeans' growing preference for digital payments, the digital euro would serve as an alternative.

A digital euro would be available to everyone and could be used to make all digital payments, both online and offline, throughout the Eurozone for free.A digital euro would be designed to provide a higher level of anonymity than other digital payment systems. Central banks have little interest in people's payment patterns or commercial goals. By legal and technical design, the ECB would be unable to identify the identity or payment patterns of those who use digital euros. A digital euro would leave no one behind; it would be inclusive and simple to use, ensuring that all of us had access to digital payments, including those without an internet connection, bank account, or credit card.

Payments are a crucial aspect of our daily lives, and a digital euro would ensure that our payment system continues to run smoothly. Unlike existing digital payment methods, it would strengthen our resistance to catastrophes such as cyberattacks and power outages. Similarly, it would decrease our reliance on non-European payment suppliers. A digital euro would be intended for usage in retail, online, and in-person transactions. It also provides some extra advantages over cash: it encourages more innovation in the private sector by boosting market competitiveness. Taking European integration a step further, a digital euro would provide a standardized means of payment for all payment needs across the Eurozone. It would offer an unprecedented European platform for innovative payments.

The essential legal framework will be provided by laws adopted by co-legislators in the European Union (EU). In an increasingly digital world, introducing a digital euro would be a natural next step in the evolution of our currency. It would ensure that we can preserve the same levels of trust and stability that money and payments have today, while simultaneously providing a new, digital option that overcomes the constraints of present payment methods.

According to the results of the Bundesbank's April 2021 poll of German householders, the prospective features of a digital euro include some of the user needs for currency and preexisting cashless payment devices. The most crucial aspects of a digital euro are ease of usage, privacy, data security, and global usability. A digital euro is acknowledged as having significant promise, particularly in terms of data protection. Individuals have a high level of faith in the central bank to manage their data honestly and safely. The possibility to eliminate private payment service providers, particularly in e-commerce, is viewed as a key element of the digital euro.

In contrast, the notion (Deutsche Bundesbank Monthly Report, 2021) that a digital euro is central bank money, and hence a fail-safe mode of payment, has minimal impact in many people's daily lives. Furthermore, people's present payment behaviour, routines, and general attitude towards digitization have a significant impact on their preferences for a digital euro. In particular, dedicated cash users are more skeptical about the digital euro. A digital euro is unlikely to provide the same amount of privacy as cash, which is why fears of surveillance, excessive data transparency, and, more broadly, data misuse are important sources of pessimism among this group.

The interviewees saw a digital euro as a complementary currency rather than a replacement for cash. This reinforces the Eurosystem's plan to offer the digital euro in addition to, rather than instead of, currency, if it is decided to deploy it. A digital euro would be a new auxiliary payment instrument with unique capabilities, available alongside cash and standard cashless payment methods. Its usage would be more general than physical cash, allowing users to pay with central bank-issued money in a digital setting, offsetting an increasing reliance on private payment systems. A digital euro could serve as a helpful complement to currency, but it cannot replace it.

Implementing a new payment mechanism is not an easy undertaking. It necessitates the involvement of numerous stakeholders in implementing their respective components of the solution. It entails stakeholder involvement, technology development, and testing across different systems. A roll-out plan is consequently required. If and when the decision is made to issue a digital euro, the Eurosystem will roll it out in two stages for priority use cases. This gradual approach is usual with complicated payment instruments such as the digital euro. It would reduce risks, facilitate issue resolution, and allow people to progressively become acquainted with the digital euro.

Following a two-year study phase, the ECB's Governing Council has decided to proceed to the next phase, digital euro preparation. During this preparation phase, the Eurosystem will concentrate on more testing of the design, user experience, privacy, financial inclusion, and environmental footprint of a digital euro. This will entail more work on the digital euro scheme rule book and the development of a selection process for potential service providers. The planning phase will run concurrently with the legislative deliberations.

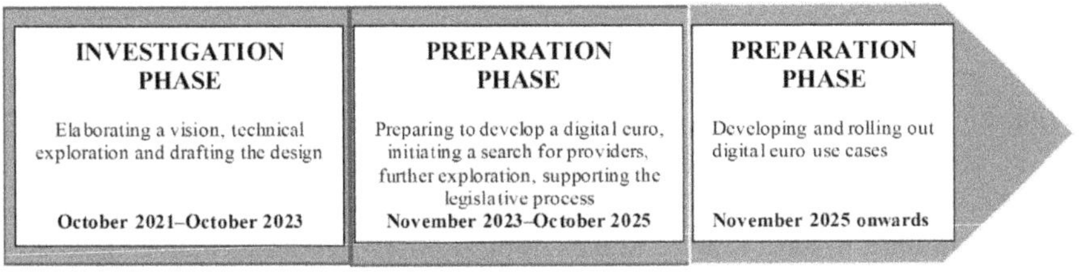

Figure 5. Phases of the introduction of the digital euro
Source: ECB (2023).

The ECB is prepared to maintain its regular communication with EU legislators on this issue and will examine any changes to the digital euro architecture that may result from legislative deliberations. The preparation phase began on November 1, 2023 and will last for two years. Based on the results of the first step of the preparation phase and legislative developments, the Governing Council will decide whether to proceed to the next step, which will work toward operational preparedness for the possible future issue and roll-out of the digital euro.

6. Conclusion

Digital currency, in whatever shape it takes, has the potential to be the fundamental tool for the digital economy's transformation. Asian governments are investing in digital infrastructure, currency and asset market monitoring, CBDC issuance, and financial architecture to combat the threat of stable coins like Diem. Cambodia, the PRC, Singapore, and Thailand have taken the lead. Issues such as needs, goals, digital financial infrastructure, and others should be recognized and debated before authorities contemplate implementing a CBDC. While many factors will influence how, when, and what is implemented, effective public-private sector partnership may be critical to its success. Before adoption, it is critical to assess interoperability. Strong national policies in the three nations studied closely in this research have already resulted in CBDC tests and implementation.

However, in order for these emerging technologies to gain widespread adoption, they may need to interact via intermediaries and across boundaries. These programs and initiatives are analogous to bilateral or multilateral trade agreements in terms of phase and program alignment. Interoperability is critical in economies with cross-border trade. Future focus areas may include exploring new multilateral platforms, global stable coin arrangements, and CBDCs to address cross-border payment challenges while maintaining minimum supervisory and regulatory standards to prevent monetary and financial instability. These projects may promote global financial inclusion and sustainability by bridging the gap between diverse CBDC initiatives and existing payment networks and digital currencies, ensuring global success. Analysts believe that borderless, worldwide trade will be enabled via an interoperable protocol, as our global economic system is too complex to be replaced by a single currency. Some may have an impact on different locations or utilities, and ongoing study is critical in improving any CBDC and digital infrastructure design to capitalize on new technological breakthroughs.Continuously upgrading CBDCs, researching future paths, and modifying implementation plans are increasingly critical central bank responsibilities. Finally, digital money will be the future, with a large "impact surface".

Countries are now ready to take part in international regulatory coordination, promote regulatory consensus, and create unified regulatory standards.

Unavoidably, the only and best way to accomplish this is to be familiar with the technology, learn from implementation, constantly analyze existing regulations, and improve anytime international dynamics alter the landscape.

Practical evidence from existent use cases is currently limited. The most common application for retail CBDCs is in Nigeria, where adoption remains low despite being mandated in society. This enforcement has put social stability at jeopardy. Meanwhile, useful empirical data from such a large-scale real-world experiment remain to be acquired. Several other central banks are ready to bring their CBDC networks online. Overall, as the primary purpose of R&D operations shifts from design to implementation, use cases fail to provide the essential feedback loops to determine the reality of potential benefits and risks associated with specific design qualities.

Literature

Agur, I., Ari, A., & Dell'Ariccia, G. (2022). Designing central bank digital currencies. *Journal of Monetary Economics, 125*, 62–79, https://doi.org/10.1016/j.jmoneco.2021.05.002.

Arauz, A. (2021). The international hierarchy of money in cross-border payment systems: Developing countries' regulation for central bank digital currencies and Facebook's Stablecoin. I*nternational Journal of Political Economy*, *50*(3), 226–243.

Armelius, H., Boel, P., Claussen, C. A., & Nessén, M. (2018). The e-krona and the macroeconomy. *Sveriges Riksbank Economic Review, 4*, 52.

Bolt, W., Lubbersen, V., & Wierts, P. (2022). Getting the balance right: Crypto, stablecoin and central bank digital currency. *Journal of Payments Strategy & Systems*, *16*(1), 39–50.

Deutsche Bundesbank Monthly Report. (2021). What do households in Germany think about the digital euro? First results from surveys and interviews, October.

ECB. (2023). Digital Euro The next step in the advancement of our currency, October, 18.

Edwards, S. (2021). Central bank digital currencies and the emerging markets: The currency substitution challenge. *Challenge*, *64*(5–6), 413–424. https://doi.org/10.1080/05775132.2021.2004738.

Hermawan, D., Lie, D., Sasongko, A., & Yusan, R. (2023). Money velocity, digital currency, and inflation dynamics. *MPRA Paper*, 116906. https://mpra.ub.uni-muenchen.de/116906/.

Meaning, J., Dyson, B., Barker, J., & Clayton, E. (2021). Broadening narrow money: Monetary policy with a central bank digital currency. *International Journal of Central Banking*, *17*(2), 1–42.

NBP. (2021).Central Bank Digital Currency, Payment Systems Department, May.

Ricci, L. A, Ahokpossi C,. Belianska, A., Khandelwal, K., Lee, S., Li, G., Mu, Y., Quayyum, S. N., Nunez, S., Ree, J., Souto, M. R., & Simione F. (2024). Central Bank Digital Currency and Other Digital Payments in Sub-Saharan Africa: A Regional Survey 001.

Valentina Ninova

Artificial Intelligence and Insurance: A Bibliometric Analysis

1. Introduction

The application of AI is being initiated and enforced across all industries, predicated in large part by the increased volume of available data, advanced computing capabilities, and the ever-changing expectations and attitudes of consumers. AI holds colossal transformative potential for industries in particular and society as a whole, the large-scale deployment of which could revolutionize any industry that relies heavily on data. The evolution of AI is affecting several sectors, including insurance, „pushing it" towards accelerated development (Aleksandrova et al., 2023). In this evolution, insurance is making a kind of „leap" from its current state of „detect and fix" to "predict and prevent," transforming every aspect of the industry in the process (Balasubramanian et al., 2021).

In practice, AI has spawned a new stage of innovation and efficiency in insurance, the result of a rapidly evolving risk landscape, unprecedented technological advances, and growing demand from potential insureds for more personalized services (Snowflake Inc., 2023). Possessing the ability to analyze massive amounts of data in a short amount of time, AI is emerging as a kind of insights backbone for the insurance business (Ladva & Grasso, 2023).

A study conducted by Conning highlights a surge in AI adoption by the insurance industry (R&I Editorial Team, 2024), and its application in this specific economic activity is along the following lines: (i) risk modelling; (ii) data forecasting; (iii) claims processing; (iv) and contact centre operations, with plenty of potential opportunities in the pipeline (Scattaglia et al., 2023). Projections for future developments are that the pace of change will also accelerate as brokers, consumers, financial intermediaries, insurers and providers become more adept at using advanced technology to improve decision-making and productivity, lower costs and optimise the customer experience (Balasubramanian et al., 2021).

The capabilities it holds in terms of decision-making can be a titanic step for business efficiency and new solutions. Wider adoption of AI applications is transforming insurance and society, bringing benefits that include: (i) increased efficiency; (ii) new products; (iii) and fewer repetitive tasks (About Allianz Global Corporate & Specialty, 2018). AI models have the potential to enable future scenarios, improve the accuracy of risk assessment and drive better pricing (Scattaglia et al., 2023). The insurance industry is on the verge of a kind of seismic, technology-driven shift, with four AI-related trends shaping insurance: (i) the explosion of data from connected devices; (ii) increased prevalence of physical robotics; (iii) open-source and data ecosystems; (iv) advances in cognitive technologies (Balasubramanian et al., 2021).

The introduction of technological innovations at any stage of the industrial revolution, including the current large-scale application of AI, is inevitably accompanied by challenges and risks that definitively need to be assessed. AI-based applications increase the vulnerability of businesses to cyber-attacks and technical failures, resulting in wider business disruption and the realisation of scenarios of severe financial loss or, at best, lost profits. The potential results of the increasingly widespread application of AI in the insurance industry, and the resulting challenges it faces, are provoking research interest, becoming a catalyst for generating research in this area. This is the real reason that gave rise to the idea of tracking current trends in the specialized literature on AI and insurance.

Through this work, an in-depth and detailed review of the publication activity of existing research in the field of AI and insurance available in the bibliographic arrays of Scopus is presented. The research objective is to trace the evolutionary development of publications on the presented topic by conducting a bibliometric analysis including: extracting trends in terms of the number of papers on the topic by year; highlighting co-authorships as well as leading researchers/authors about the number of papers and citations; the most widely used keywords and their co-occurrence, emblematic papers and leading countries. The presented study is aimed at scientific researchers whose goal is related to familiarization with the directions, development and trends of scientific publications dedicated to AI and insurance.

The results of the bibliometric analysis are directed to all scientific researchers whose scientific interests and searches coincide or are indirectly related to the studied topic, allowing them to get acquainted with current trends and directions of development, thus orienting them in a great variety and quantity of scientific publications dedicated to the topic of "AI and insurance".

The presented document is structured in five sections. The introduction focuses on the topicality of the subject matter and presents an overview of the research. Section 2 includes a brief overview of publications on the topic of "AI and insurance", describing its various subtopics in the context of the diversity of publications/ papers. Section 3 details the research algorithm and methodology, and describes how the data required to conduct the research was collected. Section 4 presents and discusses the results obtained as a consequence of the analyses of (i) scientific publications by year; (ii) co-authorship, most active and most cited authors; (iii) co-occurrences analysis of keywords and top ten most frequent keywords; (iv) document analysis; and (v) analysis by countries. The last section, Section 5 of the study, summarizes the results and conclusions drawn, outlines the limitations of the study and traces the directions for future research on the topic.

2. Literature Review

A more detailed review of the scientific publications indexed in Scopus on the topic of "AI and insurance" allows us to define the main sub-thematic directions, representing in practice the diversity of focuses and perspectives of their authors. They are extremely diverse, and their tracking successfully illustrates the evolution in theory and practice, the broad aspect of the subject of research and the increasingly narrow profile of the titles. In the context of the general finding just made, within the framework of the present literature review, the emphasis is placed on publications that we consider significant and whose added value on the subject of "AI and insurance" we subjectively assess as indisputable.

The insurance sector has undergone significant development over the past few decades due to changes in technology, including the use of AI, regulation and consumer needs (Sundari et al., 2024, Chen, 2023, Harvey & Gowda, 2021). The role of AI in insurance is aimed at helping the insurance industry improve customer service and understand their behaviour (Sharma & Sood, 2022). AI can help in several ways to address fundamentally different challenges facing the insurance industry, as well as to improve customer satisfaction (Ayaz et al., 2023), and also to create value in insurance (Riikkinen et al., 2018). AI technologies have the potential to mediate the process of conducting effective communication with customers, reducing costs, developing new products and services, and improving the competitive environment (Ceylan, 2022). The role of AI is also key in terms of accelerating societal resilience to climate disasters through effective risk management (Sheehan et al., 2023).

In their study, a group of authors (Khan & Khan, Maier et al., 2023) argue that AI-powered technologies are resulting in significant changes in life insurance companies, improving efficiency, decision-making processes and the overall employee experience, contributing significantly to the overall success of these types of organisations. The use of AI in property and casualty insurance has a wide range of applications, such as combating fraudulent claims, making rapid business decisions, predictive analytics, and improving customer experience (Rajagopal, 2020). AI can serve to reduce customer retention management costs

(Thawakar & Srivastava, 2021). In the specialized scientific literature, there is also research that has a result – a presentation of the idea of how the life result serves as the main engine for risk management of implemented algorithmic insurance systems (Maier et al., 2020).

Some researchers believe that the application of AI in insurance is still in its infancy, but they also note that innovation in the insurance industry and emerging technologies will create additional challenges for AI professionals (Singh & Chivukula, 2020, Moyo et al., 2022). On the other side are those scientists who promote the adoption of artificial intelligence with change management (Heijari, 2020). The application of AI is about more accurately predicting the probabilities of loss and transforming some risks, and this in turn is forcing insurance companies to rethink traditional insurance coverage (Eling et al., 2022). The adoption of AI in insurance is also influenced by the challenge faced by humanity, namely the COVID-19 pandemic (Agarwal et al., 2022, Ninova & Ninov, 2023).

Conducted research focuses on the technology-organization-environment framework, examining the factors influencing the behavioural intention of employees in the insurance industry to adopt AI-enabled applications (Gupta et al., 2022). A survey of AI adoption attitudes in insurance in India in 2023 identified the role of artificial intelligence in the Indian insurance industry, and the results demonstrate the extent of active use of the technology by specific organizations, and the intentions of others who do plans for its future integration in your business (Srinivas & Gandra, 2023).

Empirical findings made in 2023 in Vietnamese non-life insurance companies concluded that the most important determinant influencing the adoption of AI technology is the attitude towards the adoption of new technological solutions (Nguyen et al., 2024).

The scientific publication also deserves attention (Lamberton et al., 2017) which discusses the implications that AI and robots may have on human society and employment (particularly in the insurance industry).

3. Materials and Methods

3.1. Bibliometric Analysis

Bibliometric analysis is a reliable and strictly specific method for conducting scientific research and analysis, while working with large volumes of scientific data, allowing the discovery of evolutionary nuances in a specific scientific field (Donthu et al., 2021). Bibliometric methods or "analysis" have become an integral part of research evaluation methodology, primarily in the scientific and applied fields (Ellegaard & Wallin, 2015). The application of bibliometric analysis is aimed at revealing emerging trends in the presentation of articles and journals, fixing patterns of collaboration and research components, as well as exploring the intellectual structure of a specific field in the existing literature (Donthu et al., 2021, Vermaa & Gustafsson, 2020, Redzwan & Ramli, 2022).

When conducting scientific research, different software and software tools can be used individually or complexly (within one study) to carry out bibliometric analysis (Long Island University, 2024): (i) BibExcel; (ii) CiteSpace; (iii) Netdraw; (iv) Pajek; (v) Sci2; (vi) PoP (Publish or Perish); (vii) RStudio; (vii) SITKIS; (ix) UCInet; (x) VOSviewer. The present study was carried out by applying a specialized software tool for creating maps based on network data and for visualizing and exploring these maps – VOSviewer (Nees Jan van Eck and Ludo Waltman; Version 1.6.20). In the research process, the instructions for using the specific version of the software tool compiled by Nees Jan van Eck and Ludo Waltman were followed (Jan van Eck & Waltman, 2023). VOSviewer has superb visualization and allows loading and exporting information from many sources (Moral-Muñoz et al., 2020). In this line of thought, VOSviewer is a software tool that is used to construct and visualize bibliometric networks. It also offers text-mining functionality to construct and visualize co-occurrence networks of important terms extracted from scientific literature (Long Island University, 2024). In the grid view, items are represented by their label and by default also a circle, with the size of the item's label and circle determined by the item's weight (Jan van Eck & Waltman, 2023).

3.2. Data Collection

The data collection method followed an algorithm containing four main steps applied to the Scopus database to identify only publications on the topic of „AI and insurance". A string of keywords is the result of a search in the specified database, where search within is carried out as follows: (TITLE-ABS-KEY (artificial AND intelligence) AND TITLE-ABS-KEY (insurance)). The search result as of April 2, 2024, found a total of 1695 documents according to the set criteria.

An additional limitation was imposed on the next phase of data collection for conducting the study (TITLE-ABS-KEY (artificial AND intelligence) AND TITLE-ABS-KEY (insurance)) AND (LIMIT-TO (LANGUAGE, „English")) as a result, 1633 documents were selected. It is important to note that in the process of data collection, no additional restrictions regarding document type (Article, Conference paper, Review, Book chapter, Editorial, etc.) were applied. Another no less essential „technical detail" of the analysis is that the task is to analyze the documents indexed in Scopus for the period 1985–2024. The choice of the starting year of the research period – in this case – 1985, is not random but is based on the identification of an indexed publication on the subject under consideration. Here is the place to make another important clarification related to the fact that the first dating of publicly disclosed information on the subject of "intelligence exhibited by machines, in which machines imitate the cognitive functions associated with the human mind; cognitive functions include all aspects of learning, perception, problem-solving and reasoning" dates back to the early 1950s (Anyoha, 2017).

Ultimately, as a result of applying the selected search criteria for scientific publications on the subject in Scopus, the bibliometric analysis was officially performed on 1633 documents. The search criteria for scientific publications and their sequence of application are presented in Figure 1.

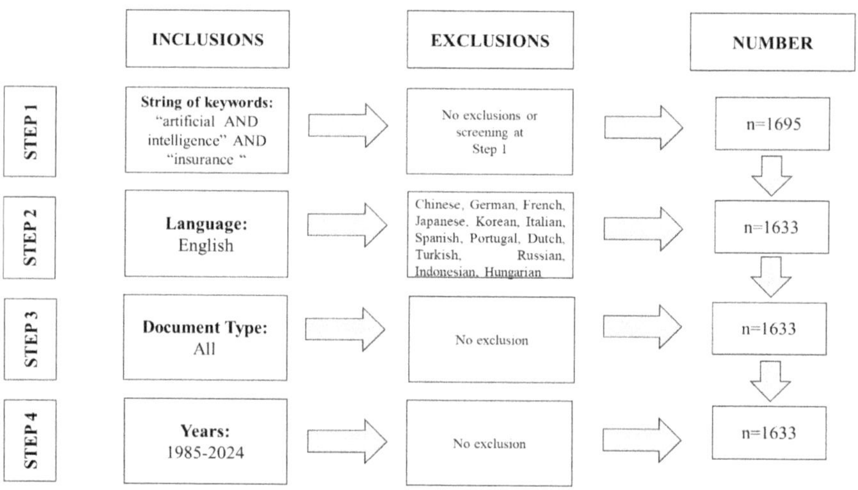

Figure 1. Search Criteria For Scientific Publications
Source: Author's data based (Chandrarathne et al., 2023)

4. Results and Discussion

4.1. Scientific Publications by Year

Figure 2 presents the documents that are relevant according to the criterion – the year of publication. The results generated for the selected period 1985–2024 are characterized by a dynamic that, especially after 2014, has a clear trend towards an increase in the number of documents indexed in Scopus. A peculiar peak of published papers on the subject under consideration is marked in 2023, the explanation for which could be sought in the increasing application of AI in several industries, including insurance, for which we consider the catalyst to be the COVID-19 pandemic. The causal link between the global pandemic and the boom in terms of the discussion and practical application of AI in insurance is axiomatic and beyond doubt, and the result is tangible, which explains the "proliferation" of publications on this undoubtedly topical subject for science, business and consumers. It is necessary to mention the fact that the extraction of information from the Scopus database was carried out by April 2, 2024, which is logically reflected in the results, evident from the direction of the trend for this year within Figure 2.

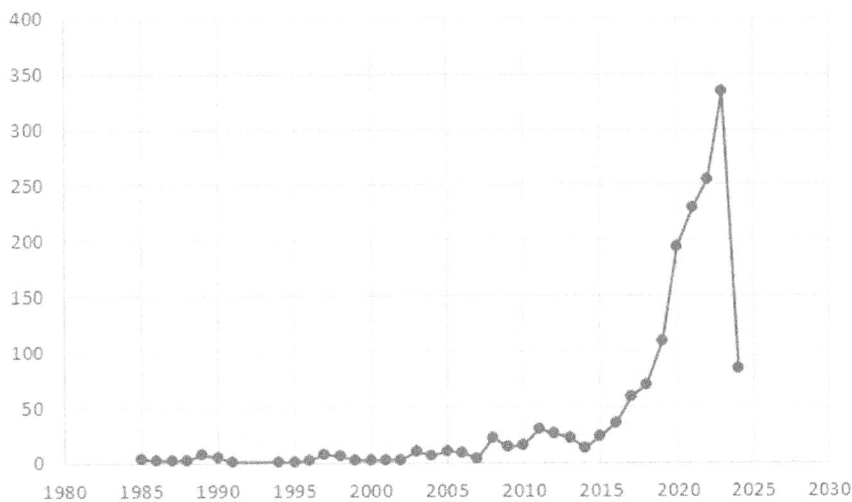

Figure 2. Documents Trends By Year
Source: (Elsevier, 2024)

Table 1 presents the five years within which the most papers on the subject have been published, and this not coincidentally covers the years 2019 to 2023, the genesis of which trend we have already clarified above in the text. Of the 1633 scientific publications identified in Scopus, 1122 are the documents published in the 5 years mentioned or approximately 68.71 % of the total of all the documents covered by this bibliometric analysis.

Table 1. Top Five Years With The Most Documents

No.	Year	Number of documents
1	2023	334
2	2022	255
3	2021	229
4	2020	194
5	2019	110

Source: Authors based on (Elsevier, 2024)

4.2. Co-authorship Analysis, the Most Active and Most Cited Author

The co-authorship analysis is performed using VOSviewer. Authors are represented by their label and by a circle, the size of the label and the circle of the item being determined by the weight is relative to the occurrences (Jan van Eck &Waltman, 2023). Figure 3 shows the largest set, consisting of 40 items grouped into 3 clusters, with 385 links (weights – document).

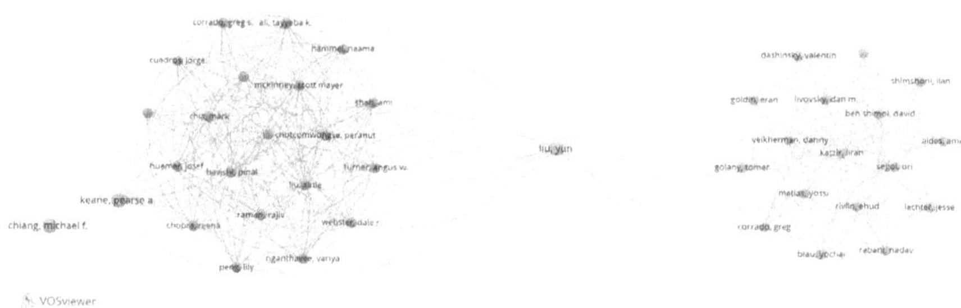

Figure 3. Co-Authorship Network Visualisation: Author: Largest Set

The largest of the resulting clusters is Cluster 1 (red, $n = 20$) and includes the authors Pinal Bavishi (1 document, 21 citations, and 21 TLS), Mark Chia (1 document, 21 citations, and 21 TLS), Reena Chopra (1 document, 21 citations, and 21 TLS), Peranut Chotcomwongse (1 document, 21 citations, and 21 TLS), and Naama Hammel (1 document, 21 citations, and 21 TLS). In the framework of Cluster 2 (green, $n = 18$) authors present Yun Liu (2 documents, 39 citations, and 38 TLS), Valentin Dashinsky (1 document, 18 citations, and 17 TLS), Yochai Blau (1 document, 18 citations, and 17 TLS), Ori Segol (1 document, 18 citations, and

17 TLS), and Tomer Golany (1 document, 18 citations, and 17 TLS). Cluster 3 (blue, $n = 2$) consists of Michael F. Chiang (2 documents, 91 citations, and 1 TLS) and Pearse A. Keane (2 documents, 49 citations, and 22 TLS).

The largest of the resulting clusters is Cluster 1 (red, $n = 20$) and includes authors Pinal Bavishi (1 paper, 21 citations and 21 TLS), Mark Chia (1 paper, 21 citations and 21 TLS), Reena Chopra (1 paper, 21 citations and 21 TLS), Peranut Chotcomwongse (1 paper, 21 citations and 21 TLS) and Naama Hammel (1 paper, 21 citations and 21 TLS). Within Cluster 2 (green, $n = 18$), the authors present Yun Liu (2 papers, 39 citations and 38 TLS), Valentin Dashinski (1 paper, 18 citations and 17 TLS), Yohai Blau (1 paper, 18 citations and 17 TLS), Ori Segol (1 paper, 18 citations and 17 TLS) and Tomer Golani (1 paper, 18 citations and 17 TLS). Cluster 3 (blue, $n = 2$) consists of Michael F. Chang (2 papers, 91 citations, and 1 TLS) and Pierce A. Keene (2 papers, 49 citations and 22 TLS).

Table 2 shows the top ten most active authors on the topic "AI and insurance". The criterion set to determine the ranking is the number of indexed documents.

Table 2. The Top Ten Most Active Authors

No.	Author	Documents
1	Simon Grima	6
2	Priti Ranjan Sahoo	5
3	Martin Mullins	5
4	Lizhen Cui	4
5	Chunyan Miao	4
6	Han Yu	4
7	Ravi Shankar Jha	4
8	Richard A. Bauder	4
9	Taghi M. Khoshgoftaar	4
10	Kiran Sood	4

Within Table 3, the top 10 authors according to the "citations" criterion are presented. The authors are required to have a minimum number of documents of an author in the Scopus database – 2. As a result of the set control, the representative sample of the number of authors was defined to be 5475, with only 286 of them meeting the specified requirement.

Table 3. The Ten Most Cited Authors With At Minimum 2 Documents

No.	Author	Documents	Citations	TLS
1	I. Glenn Cohen	3	863	3
2	W. Nicholson Price	3	548	3
3	Peter Szolovits	2	448	1
4	Rifat Atun	3	416	1
5	Effy Vayena	2	305	1
6	Santosh Kumar	2	258	2
7	Holger Fröhlich	2	244	1
8	Dino Pedreschi	3	180	4
9	Taghi M. Khoshgoftaar	4	148	3
10	Salvatore Ruggieri	2	144	4

* TLS= Total link strength

4.3. Co-occurrence Analysis of Keywords and Top Ten Most Frequent Keywords

Figure 4 shows the keyword co-occurrence network. The minimum number of occurrences per keyword is set to six occurrences. This requirement is tailored to the version of the software application and more specifically to the specifics of – by default, a maximum of 1000 rows representing the 1000 strongest relationships between elements are displayed. In the network visualisation, keywords are represented by their label and by default also by a circle (Jan van Eck & Waltman, 2023). The label's size and the keywords' circle are determined by the weight of the occurrences and in general, the more similar the two keywords are, the stronger their relatedness (Jan van Eck & Waltman, 2023). The study identified 11670 keywords. When a minimum threshold of six occurrences was introduced, their number was reduced to 878.

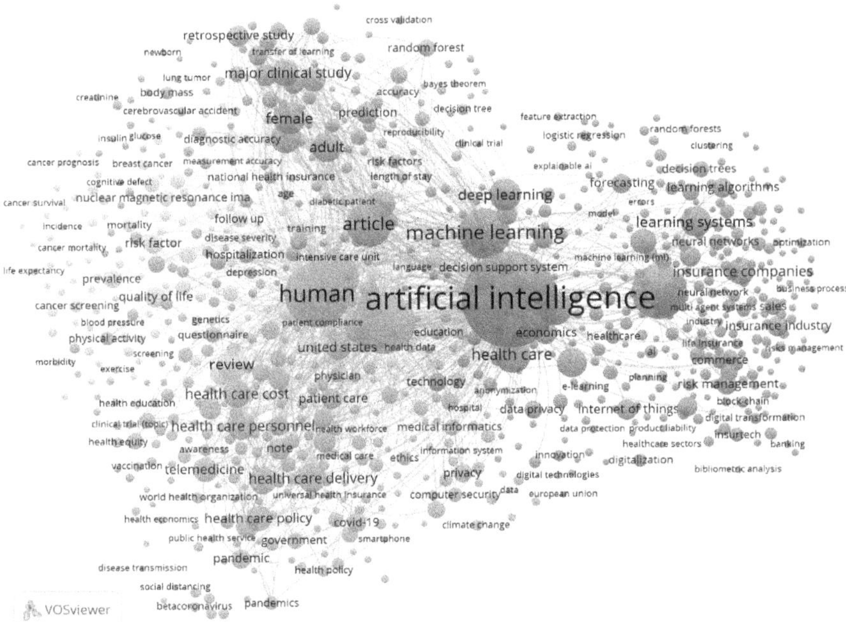

Figure 4. Co-Occurrences Of Keywords Network Visualisation

The results obtained from co-occurrences analysis of keywords, automatically grouped within six clusters, which we will present in operational order:

i. Cluster 1 (red, n = 343) is the largest and includes the keyword "artificial intelligence", which is part of the scientific works of various authors (Shneiderman, 2020; Alami et al., 2020; Singh et al., 2020). In addition, Cluster 1 also contains other terms, the use of which is closely related to the topic of AI, such as: "machine learning" (Finlayson et al., 2019; Vayena et al., 2018, Nemesure et al., 2021), "deep learning" (Xu et al., 2021), "learning system" (Datta et al., 2016), "health care" (Chen et al., 2019; Forcier et al., 2019; Silverman et al., 2015), "insurance companies" (Eckert & Osterrieder, 2020) and other keywords also fall into this cluster.
ii. Cluster 2 (green, n = 219) is the second largest and combines the keywords "human" (Schuetz & Venkatesh, 2020, Aizenberg & Hoven, 2020), "health insurance" (Kim et al., 2021; Zarifis et al., 2020), "climate change" (Sacchelli et al., 2017) etc.
iii. Cluster 3 (blue, n = 139) is third in the order and includes the keywords "article" (Denecke et al., 2024; Monlezun, 2023), "adult" (Imam et al., 2023), "random forest" (Katiyar et al., 2023; Seyedtabib & Kamyari, 2023) etc.

iv. Cluster 4 (yellow, $n = 132$) includes the keywords „Alzheimer disease“ (Abdulazeem et al., 2023; Kim et al., 2023), „atrial fibrillation“ (Krittanawong & Scheuring, 2023), „bioinformatics“ (Arivazhagan &Van Vleck, 2023) etc.
v. Cluster 5 (purple, $n = 44$) includes the keywords „anxiety“ (Hughes et al., 2023), „behaviour change“ (Kario, 2023), „blood glucose monitoring“ (Maahs et al., 2022) etc.
vi. Cluster 6 (light blue, $n = 1$), includes a single word „electronic health records“ (Marks et al., 2023).

Table 4 contains occurrences of the keywords, their Total link strength, and cluster. The data from the results highlights how strong the importance/influence of AI on health insurance and health care is, which „traces“ and thickly highlights the close relationship that exists between them. On the other hand, the human element is also significant and integral when researching AI and insurance.

Table 4. The Top Ten Most Frequent Keywords In Artificial Intelligence And Insurance And Occurrences In Scopus

No.	Keyword	Occurrences	TLS	Cluster
1	Artificial intelligence	1232	16244	1
2	Human	557	12447	2
3	Health insurance	516	10170	2
4	Humans	349	8204	2
5	Machine learning	334	5400	1
6	Article	265	6232	3
7	Health care	159	2540	1
8	Decision making	147	2105	1
9	Female	134	3394	3
10	Deep learning	130	1870	1

* TLS= Total link strength

4.4. Document Analysis

The following analysis is intended to present the most cited documents on the subject (AI and insurance). This analysis was performed by extracting information from the Scopus database. A total of 1633 documents were identified in the bibliographic array at the date of the study. In the network visualization, documents are represented by their label through a circle (Jan van Eck & Waltman, 2023). The weight of the citations determines the size of the label and the circle of documents. Thus, the more similar the two documents are, the stronger their connectivity (Jan van Eck & Waltman, 2023). A minimum requirement of at least 2 citations per document was previously set, resulting in 867 documents out of 1633 being detected by the control. The following figure visualizes the final result, presenting the largest set consisting of 37 documents categorised into the following 10 clusters: Cluster 1 (red, $n = 5$), Cluster 2 (green, $n = 5$), Cluster 3 (blue, $n = 4$), Cluster 4 (yellow, $n = 4$), Cluster 5 (purple, $n = 4$), Cluster 6 (light blue, $n = 4$), Cluster 7 (orange, $n = 3$), Cluster 8 (brawn, $n = 3$), Cluster 9 (violet, $n = 3$), and Cluster 10 (pink, $n = 2$).

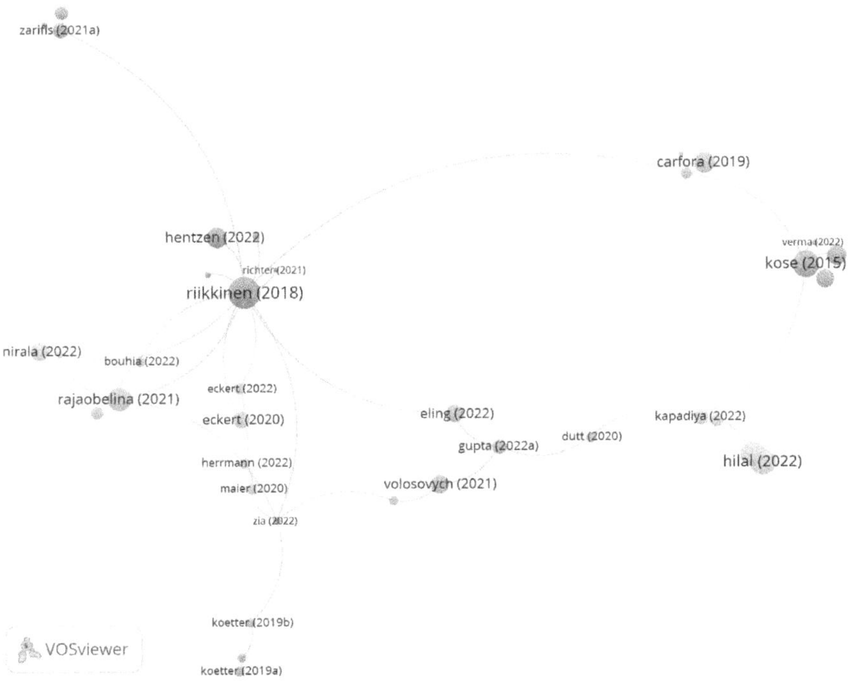

Figure 5. Network Visualisation Of Citation Analysis Of Documents

In the following lines, we will present part of the subject matter, respectively the thematic focus of the scientific publications falling within the list of documents selected according to the "citation" criterion, covered within the above 10 clusters. The diversity of scientific issues related to the use of "AI and insurance" is found in publications related to (i) presenting a literature review in the field of AI in financial services, applying a combined use of different scientific databases (Hentzen et al., 2022); (ii) research of chatbot software application from a theoretical and technological point of view (Rajaobelina et al., 2021; Nirala et al., 2022); (iii) analysis of the impact of AI on the insurance sector (Eling et al., 2022); (iv) structural equation modelling to test which variables significantly influence employees' behavioural intentions to adopt AI in the insurance industry (Gupta et al., 2020); (v) exploring the impact of the COVID-19 pandemic leading to a major transformation in the insurance industry through the progressive use of innovative AI-based insurance technologies (Volosovych et al., 2021); (vi) approving an approach aimed at identifying driver behaviour, exploring the use of unsupervised machine learning techniques, for car insurance purposes (Carfora et al., 2019); (vii) demonstrating the feasibility of applying AI for healthcare insurance purposes and the potential of their collaboration (Kose et al., 2015; Dutt, 2020).

Within the following table are the ten most cited documents by number of citations.

Table 5. The Ten Most Cited Documents By Number Of Citations From Scopus

No.	Author(s)	Document Title	Source	Citations
1	(Kusner et al., 2017)	Counterfactual fairness	Advances in neural information processing systems	703
2	(Hsieh et al., 2019)	Taiwan's National Health Insurance Research Database: past and future	Clin Epidemiol	692
3	(Price & Cohen, 2019)	Privacy in the age of medical big data	Nature Medicine	540
4	(Burton et al., 2021)	The Lancet Global Health Commission on Global Eye Health: vision beyond 2020	The Lancet Global Health	529
5	(Ling & Li, 1998)	Data Mining for Direct Marketing: Problems and Solutions	KDD-98	528
6	(Finlayson et al., 2019)	Adversarial attacks on medical machine learning	SCIENCE	495
7	(Datta et al., 2016)	Algorithmic Transparency via Quantitative Input Influence: Theory and Experiments with Learning Systems	2016 IEEE Symposium on Security and Privacy (SP)	433

Table 5. Continued

No.	Author(s)	Document Title	Source	Citations
8	(Cai et al., 2018)	A high-performance and in-season classification system of field-level crop types using time-series Landsat data and a machine learning approach	Remote Sensing of Environment	341
9	(Feng et al., 2015)	Applying deep learning to answer selection: A study and an open task	2015 IEEE Workshop on Automatic Speech Recognition and Understanding (ASRU)	287
10	(Vayena et al., 2018)	Machine learning in medicine: Addressing ethical challenges	PLoS Med	285

Source: (Kusner et al., 2017; Hsieh et al., 2019; Price & Cohen, 2019; Burton et al., 2021; Ling & Li, 1998; Finlayson et al., 2019; Datta et al., 2016; Cai et al., 2018; Feng et al., 2015; Vayena et al., 2018)

4.5. Analysis by Countries

As a next step in the present study, an analysis of the bibliographic coupling of countries was performed based on information extracted from the Scopus database. After setting the minimum requirements in terms of (i) a minimum number of documents of a country – 1; and (ii) a minimum number of citations of a country – 1, the final result was reduced to 121 countries, out of the 136 countries identified. The visualisation of the result obtained is presented in the following figure, within which the largest set consisting of 107 items (countries) is present. In the network visualisation: (i) countries are represented by their label through a circle (Jan van Eck & Waltman, 2023); (ii) the weight of the document determines the size of the label and the circle of countries (Jan van Eck &Waltman, 2023). For each of the 121 countries, the total strength of bibliographic links to other countries is calculated.

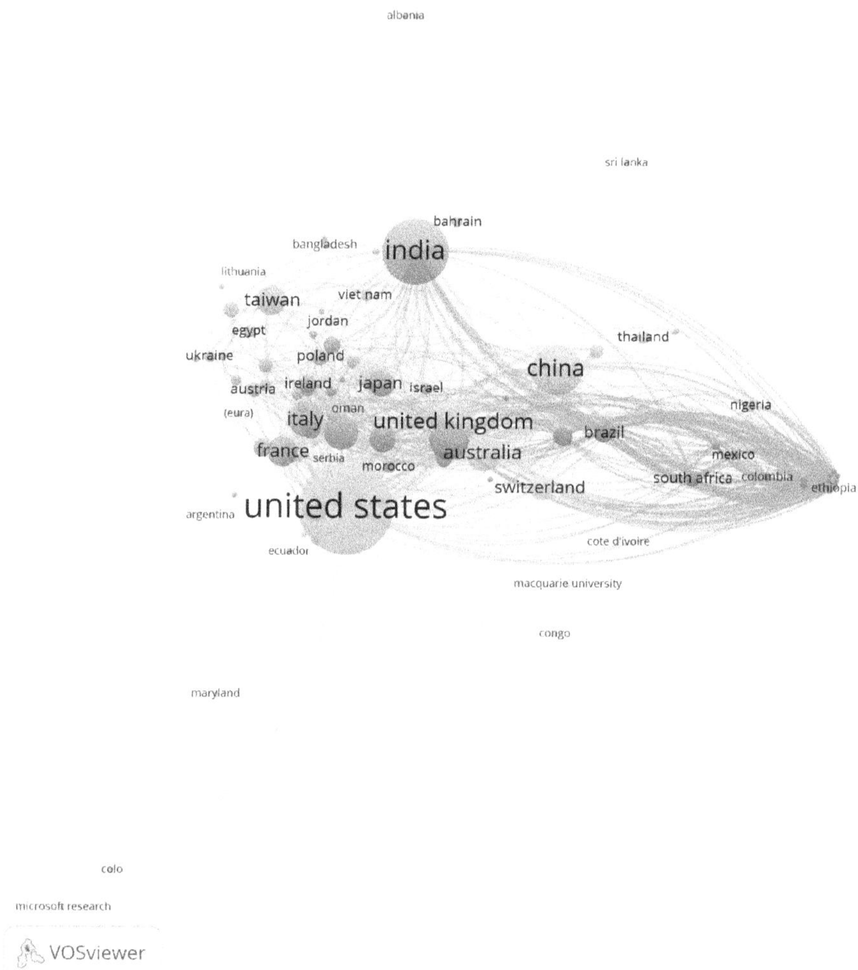

Figure 6. Network Visualisation Of Bibliographic Coupling Of Countries

The United States had the highest total link strength (25635), the highest number of documents (n = 483), and the citations (n = 10917) regarding bibliographical links with other countries. Therefore, it can be concluded that the United States is considered a leading country regarding the number and citations of scientific publications.

To illustrate the research results, a tabular ranking is presented (Table 6), including the ten countries with the highest number of scientific publications on the topic of "AI and insurance", the total number of citations of each country, and the Total link strength.

Table 6. The top ten countries by the number of documents

No.	Country	Documents	Citations	TLS
1	United States	483	10917	25635
2	India	247	2012	13205
3	China	141	1926	12431
4	United Kingdom	110	2825	16339
5	Germany	85	1471	11010
6	Australia	74	1495	11279
7	Italy	69	760	6671
8	Canada	64	1744	5719
9	Taiwan	50	1346	2432
10	France	50	551	2943

* TLS= Total link strength

The interpretation of the results in the table is unambiguous and eloquently reports the leadership of the United States in this ranking – with exactly 29.58 % of the total share of documents retrieved from the Scopus database on the topic (Sheth et al., 2024; Mathauera & Oranje, 2024; Biju et al., 2024; Mello et al., 2024). The second position is given to India with a share of 15.13 % of thematic studies conducted (Tomar & Sharma, 2023; Hemachandran & Rodriguez 2023; Kewal & Saxena, 2023; Pathak & Bansal, 2023). In the top 10, third place goes to China, which is also cementing itself as a driving force in terms of published research on "AI and insurance" (Guo et al., 2024; Deng et al., 2024; Sai et al., 2023; Lin et al., 2023), with a share of 8.63 %. United Kingdom, Germany, Australia, Italy, Canada, Taiwan and France round out the top ten.

5. Conclusion

Following the stated algorithm and adhering to the adopted methodology, it can be concluded that the outcome of this research work is the fulfilment of the stated main research objective. The latter consists in performing a thorough bibliometric analysis of the document flow on the topic "AI and insurance" for the period 1985–2024, based on extracted publications from the bibliographic arrays appearing in the abstract and indexing full-text database Scopus, using the software tool VOSviewer (as of April 2, 2024). In the course of the analysis, the following scientific generalizations were made:

i. regarding the topic of "AI and insurance", there is an unconditional and definite evolution – evidenced on the one hand by the 1,633 papers identified in Scopus (according to predefined criteria), on the other hand by the diversity of publications on the topic with a narrow focus presented in the literature review, and on the third hand by the visualized trend of "increasing productivity" on the topic;
ii. as for the most prolific period for authors of publications on the topic of "AI and insurance", it is undoubtedly the five consecutive years from 2019 to 2023, with a score of 68.71% of the universe of all papers covered by this bibliometric analysis. The five-year period coincides with the pandemic of COVID-19, which logically became a catalyst for revolutions in many sectors of the economy and social life, a key feature of which was namely the forced application of AI-based technological innovation, including in Insurance;
iii. it was found that the leading author according to the criterion for the number of published papers on the topic "AI and insurance", according to the analysis is Simon Grima with 6 publications on the topic, and according to the citation criterion, with at least 2 documents, the author generating the largest number of citations is I. Glenn Cohen with 863 citations. In this line of thought, the top three most cited documents are also identified: (Kusner et al., 2017) – 703 citations, (Hsieh et al., 2019) – 692 citations, and (Price & Cohen, 2019) – 540 citations;
iv. also identified the countries that generated the largest number of documents for the period under review on the topic of "AI and insurance", the leader among which is the United States (holding 29.58% of the total share of documents on the topic), followed by India and China, with 483, 247 and 141 documents respectively. The remaining countries in the top 10 for this criterion are the United Kingdom, Germany, Australia, Italy, Canada, Taiwan and France, respectively;
v. in terms of cooccurrence analysis of keywords, the results demonstrate a combination of keywords such as "artificial intelligence", "machine learning", "deep learning", "learning systems", and "insurance companies", among others. The analysis also shows that there is an increased interest, mostly focused on "artificial intelligence" (1232 occurrences), "human" (557 occurrences), "health insurance" (516 occurrences), "humans" (349 occurrences), and "machine learning" (334 occurrences).

The findings based on this comprehensive bibliometric analysis of publications on the topic of "AI and insurance" carry new semantic information needed to optimize and streamline insurance business and science.

5.1. Limitations

For networking, only files from the Scopus bibliographic database were used. The choice of the mentioned database was driven by the fact that Scopus has a rigorous selection process and is one of the largest citation databases (Baas et al., 2020). Outside the scope of the study, documents from the following databases Web of Science and Dimensions remain. Lens and PubMed files and reference manager files (i.e., RIS, EndNote, and RefWorks files) were also not included.

No restrictions were placed on scientific publications in terms of document type, source title, subject area, affiliation, funding sponsor, country/territory, and open access when conducting Scopus data collection.

5.2. Guidelines for Future Research

The focus of future research, based on bibliometric analysis, could be directed, for example, towards the implementation of AI in specific forms of insurance – life insurance or non-life insurance.

FUNDING: This research was funded by The Bulgarian National Science Fund at the Bulgarian Ministry of Education and Science, Funding Competition for financial support for projects of junior researchers and postdocs – 2022, Funding number: KII-06-M65/2 from 12 December 2022, Project title: "Artificial intelligence in the economic perspective", Project coordinator: Aleksandrina Aleksandrova, PhD.

References

Abdulazeem, H., Whitelaw, S., Schauberger, G., & Klug, S. J. (2023). A systematic review of clinical health conditions predicted by machine learning diagnostic and prognostic models trained or validated using real-world primary health care data. *PLoS ONE, 18*(9), e0274276.

About Allianz Global Corporate & Specialty. Allianz. [Online].; 2018. Available from: https://commercial.allianz.com/content/dam/onemarketing/commercial/commercial/reports/AGCS-Artificial-Intelligence-Outlook-and-Risks.pdf.

Agarwal, P., Swami, S., & Malhotra, S. K. (2022). Artificial Intelligence adoption in the post COVID-19 new-normal and role of smart technologies in transforming business: A review. *Journal of Science and Technology Policy Management, 15*(3), 506–529.

Aizenberg, E., & Hoven, Jvd. (2020). Designing for human rights in AI. *Big Data & Society, 7*(2).

Alami, H., Rivard, L., Lehoux, P., Hoffman, S. J., Cadeddu, S. B. M, Savoldelli, M., et al. (2020). Artificial intelligence in health care: Laying the Foundation for Responsible, sustainable, and inclusive innovation in low- and middle-income countries. *Global Health, 16*(52).

Aleksandrova, A., Ninova, V., & Zhelev Z. (2023). A Survey on AI implementation in finance, (Cyber) insurance and financial controlling. *Risks, 11*(5), 91.

Anyoha, R. SITN: Science in the News. [Online].; 2017. Available from: https://sitn.hms.harvard.edu/flash/2017/history-artificial-intelligence/.

Arivazhagan, N., & Van Vleck, T. T. (2023). Natural language processing basics. *Clinical Journal of the American Society of Nephrology, 18*(3), 400–401.

Ayaz, M., Sharma, T., & Rao, S. H. (2023). Disruptive artificial intelligence (AI) use-cases in insurance. *AIP Conference Proceedings, 2782*(1).

Baas, J., Schotten, M., Plume, A., Côté, G., & Karimi, R. (2020). Scopus as a curated, high-quality bibliometric data source for academic research in quantitative science studies. *Quantitative Science Studies, 1*, 377–386.

Balasubramanian, R., Libarikian, A., & McElhaney D. McKinsey & Company. [Online].; 2021. Available from: https://www.mckinsey.com/industries/financial-services/our-insights/insurance-2030-the-impact-of-ai-on-the-future-of-insurance.

Biju, A. K. V. N., Thomas, A. S., & Thasneem, J. (2024). Examining the research taxonomy of artificial intelligence, deep learning & machine learning in the financial sphere – A bibliometric analysis. *Quality and Quantity, 58*(1), 849–878.

Burton, M. J., Ramke, J., Marques, A. P., Bourne, R. R. A., Congdon, N., Jones, I., et al. (2021). The Lancet Global Health Commission on global eye health: Vision beyond 2020. *The Lancet Global Health, 9*(4), e489–e551.

Cai, Y., Guan, K., Peng, J., Wang, S., Seifert, C., Wardlow, B., et al. (2018). A high-performance and in-season classification system of field-level crop types using time-series Landsat data and a machine learning approach. *Remote Sensing of Environment, 210*, 35–47.

Carfora, M. F., Martinelli, F., Mercaldo, F., Nardone, V., Orlando, A., Santone, A., et al. (2019). A "pay-how-you-drive" car insurance approach through cluster analysis. *Soft Computing, 23*, 2863–2875.

Ceylan, I. E. (2022). The effects of artificial intelligence on the insurance sector: Emergence, applications, challenges, and opportunities. In Bozkuş Kahyaoğlu, S. *The impact of artificial intelligence on governance, economics and finance*. Springer;.

Chandrarathne, W., Gamage, S., & Perera, D. (2023). Research in microinsurance: A bibliometric analysis and review. *Journal of Management, Social Sciences and Humanities. 4*(2), 25–57.

Chen, CCh. Regulation of the use of artificial intelligence for investment in the insurance industry. In Remolina, N., & Gurrea-Martinez, A. *Artificial Intelligence in finance*: Edward Elgar Publishing. 2023; 271–292.

Chen, I. Y., Szolovits, P., & Ghassemi, M. (2019). Can AI help reduce disparities in general medical and mental health care? *AMA Journal of Ethics, 21*(2), E167–E179.

Datta, A., Sen, S., & Zick, Y. (2016). Algorithmic transparency via quantitative input influence: Theory and experiments with learning systems. 2016 IEEE Symposium on Security and Privacy (SP), 598–617.

Denecke, K., May, R., & Rivera-Romero, O. (2024). Transformer models in healthcare: A survey and thematic analysis of potentials, shortcomings and risks. *Journal of Medical Systems, 48*(23).

Deng, S., Zhang, J., Lin, Z., & Li, X. (2024). Service staff makes me nervous: Exploring the impact of insecure attachment on AI service preference. *Technological Forecasting and Social Change, 19*, 122946.

Donthu, N., Kumar, S., Mukherjee, D., Pandey, N., & Lim, W. M. (2021). How to conduct a bibliometric analysis: An overview and guidelines. *Journal of Business Research, 133*, 285–296.

Dutt, R. (2020). Chapter 11 – The impact of artificial intelligence on healthcare insurances. *Artificial Intelligence in Healthcare*, 271–293.

Eckert, C., & Osterrieder, K. (2020). How digitalization affects insurance companies: overview and use cases of digital technologies. *ZVersWiss, 109*, 333–360.

Eling, M., Nuessle, D., & Staubli, J. (2022). The impact of artificial intelligence along the insurance value chain and on the insurability of risks. *The Geneva Papers on Risk and Insurance – Issues and Practice, 47*, 205–241.

Ellegaard, O., & Wallin, J. A. (2015). The bibliometric analysis of scholarly production: How great is the impact? *Scientometrics, 105*, 1809–1831.

Elsevier BV. Scopus. [Online].; 2024. Available from: https://www.scopus.com/term/analyzer.uri?sort=cp-f&src=s&sid=700ef17495b878783dc6f6e938f81d79&sot=a&sdt=a&sl=69&s=%28TITLE-ABS-KEY%28Artificial+intelligence%29+AND+TITLE-ABS-KEY%28insurance%29%29&origin=resultslist&count=10&analyzeResults=Analyze+results.

Feng, M., Xiang, B., Glass, M. R., Wang, L., & Zhou, B. (2015). Applying deep learning to answer selection: A study and an open task. In 2015 IEEE Workshop on Automatic Speech Recognition and Understanding (ASRU). Scottsdale, AZ, USA: IEEE. pp. 813–820.

Finlayson, S. G., Bowers, J. D., Ito, J., Zittrain, J. L., Beam, A. L., & Kohane, I. S. (2019). Adversarial attacks on medical machine learning. *Science, 363*, 1287–1289.

Forcier, M. B., Gallois, H., Mullan, S., & Joly, Y. (2019). Integrating artificial intelligence into health care through data access: Can the GDPR act as a beacon for policymakers. *Journal of Law and the Biosciences, 6*(1), 317–335.

Guo, Y., Li, Y., Liu, D., & Xu, S. X. (2024). Measuring service quality based on customer emotion: An explainable AI approach. *Decision Support Systems, 17*, 114051.

Gupta, S., Ghardallou, W., Pandey, D. K., & Sahu, G. P. (2022). Artificial intelligence adoption in the insurance industry: Evidence using the technology–organization–environment framework. *Research in International Business and Finance, 63*, 101757.

Harvey, H. B., & Gowda, V. (2021). Regulatory issues and challenges to artificial intelligence adoption. *Radiologic Clinics, 59*(6), 1075–1083.

Heijari, N. Driving the Adoption of Artificial Intelligence with Change Management – Case Study from Insurance Industry. 2020.

Hemachandran, K., & Rodriguez, R. V. *Artificial intelligence for business: An implementation guide containing practical and industry-specific case studies.* Taylor and Francis; 2023.

Hentzen, J. K., Hoffmann, A., Dolan, R., & Pala, E. (2022). Artificial intelligence in customer-facing financial services: A systematic literature review and agenda for future research. *International Journal of Bank Marketing, 40*(6), 1299–1336.

Hsieh, C. Y., Su, C. C., Shao, S. C., Sung, S. F., Lin, S. J., Kao Yang, Y. H., et al. (2019). Taiwan's National Health Insurance research database: Past and future. *Clinical Epidemiology, 11*, 349–358.

Hughes, M. S., Addala, A., & Buckingham, B. (2023). Digital technology for diabetes. *New England Journal of Medicine, 389*(22), 2076–2086.

Imam, M., Soliman, H. Y., & Abdel-Atty, H. M. (2023). Future applications of artificial intelligence for the Egyptian universal health insurance system. *Journal of Health Management, 25*(4), 709–714.

Jan van Eck, N., & Waltman, L. (2023). VOSviewer. [Online]. Available from: https://www.vosviewer.com/documentation/Manual_VOSviewer_1.6.20.pdf.

Kario, K. (2023). Digital hypertension towards to the anticipation medicine. *Hypertension Research, 46*, 2503–2512.

Katiyar, P. B, Chase, H. M. M, Lenke, L. G. M., Weidenbaum, M. M., Sardar, Z. M. M. M. (2023). Using Machine Learning (ML) models to predict risk of venous thromboembolism (VTE) following spine surgery. *Clinical Spine Surgery, 36*(10): E453–E456.

Kewal, T., & Saxena, C. (2023). Transition from traditional insurance sector to InsurTech: Systematic analysis and future research directions. In Swaroop, A., Polkowski, Z., Correia, S. D., & Virdee, B. (eds.), International Conference on Data Analytics and Management, ICDAM 2023: Springer Science and Business Media Deutschland GmbH. pp. 473–487.

Khan, A. A, & Khan, N. A. (2023). Role of artificial intelligence in life insurance organization: In respect of human resource functions. *Journal of Management and Entrepreneurship.*

Kim, B. J. (2023). The intersection of technology and humanity: Exploring the ethics and potential of artificial intelligence in medicine. *Journal of Clinical Neurology, 19*(3), 215–216.

Kim, J. O., Jeong, Y. S., Kim, J. H., Lee, J. W., Park, D., & Kim, H. S. (2021). Machine learning-based cardiovascular disease prediction model: A cohort study on the Korean National Health Insurance Service Health Screening Database. *Diagnostics, 11*(6), 943.

Kose, I., Gokturk, M., & Kilic, K. (2015). An interactive machine-learning-based electronic fraud and abuse detection system in healthcare insurance. *Applied Soft Computing, 36*, 283–299.

Krittanawong, C., & Scheuring, R. A. (2023). Space and precision cardiovascular health: future perspectives of space travel. *European Heart Journal, 44*(37), 3498–3500.

Kusner, M. J., Loftus, J., Russell, C., & Silva, R. (2017). Counterfactual fairness. *Advances in Neural Information Processing Systems,* 30.

Ladva, P., & Grasso, A. (2023). Swiss Re. [Online]. Available from: https://www.swissre.com/risk-knowledge/advancing-societal-benefits-digitalisation/how-to-ensure-ai-helps-business.html.

Lamberton, C., Brigo, D., & Hoy, D. (2017). Impact of Robotics, RPA and AI on the Insurance Industry: Challenges and opportunities. *Journal of Financial Perspectives, 4*(1).

Lin, W., Yu, S., & Huang, L. (2023). Application of artificial intelligence technology based on deep learning in identification of lung cancer properties. *Revista de Psiquiatria Clinica, 50*(6), 71–77.

Ling, C. X., & Li, C. (1998). Data mining for direct marketing: Problems and solutions. *Kdd, 98*, 73–79.

Long Island University. (2024). LIU Post. [Online]. Available from: https://liu.cwp.libguides.com/c.php?g=225325&p=4966525.

Maahs, D. M., Addala, A., & Shalitin, S. (2022). Diabetes technology and therapy in the pediatric age group. *Diabetes Technology & Therapeutics, 24*(S1).

Maier, M., Carlotto, H., Sanchez, F., Balogun, S., & Merritt, S. (2019). Transforming underwriting in the Life Insurance Industry. *Proceedings of the AAAI Conference on Artificial Intelligence, 33*(01), 9373–9380.

Maier, M., Carlotto, H., Saperstein, S., Sanchez, F., Balogun, S., & Merritt, S. (2020). Improving the accuracy and transparency of underwriting with AI to transform the Life Insurance Industry. *AI Magazine, 41*(3), 78–93.

Marks, M., & Haupt, C. E. (2023). AI Chatbots, health privacy, and challenges to HIPAA compliance. *JAMA, 330*(4), 309–310.

Mathauera, I., & Oranje, M. (2024). Machine learning in health financing: Benefits, risks and regulatory needs. *Bulletin of the World Health Organization, 102*(3), 216–224.

Mello, M. M., & Rose, S. (2024). Denial – Artificial Intelligence tools and health insurance coverage decisions. *JAMA Health Forum, 5*(3), e240622.

Monlezun, D. J. (2023). Percutaneous coronary intervention mortality, cost, complications, and disparities after radiation therapy: Artificial intelligence-augmented, cost effectiveness, and computational ethical analysis. *Journal of Cardiovascular Development and Disease, 10*(11), 445.

Moral-Muñoz, J. A., Herrera-Viedma, E., Santisteban-Espejo, A., Cobo, M. J. Moral-Muñoz, J. A., & Herrera-Viedma. (2020). Software tools for conducting bibliometric analysis in science: An up-to-date review. *Profesional De La información Information Professional, 29*(1).

Moyo, J., Watyoka, N., & Chari, F. (2022). Challenges in the adoption of artificial intelligence and machine learning in Zimbabwe's Insurance industry. In 1st Zimbabwe Conference of Information and Communication Technologies (ZCICT). Harare, Zimbabwe: IEEE. pp. 1–6.

Nemesure, M. D., Heinz, M. V., Huang, R., & Jacobson, N. C. (2021). Predictive modeling of depression and anxiety using electronic health records and a novel machine learning approach with artificial intelligence. *Scientific Reports, 11*(1980).

Nguyen, T. H. D., Nguyen, X. T., & Le, T. H. T, & Bui, Q. A. (2024). Determinants influencing the adoption of artificial intelligence technology in non-life insurers. *Corporate Governance and Organizational Behavior Review, 8*(1), 205–212.

Ninova, V., & Ninov, N. (2023). The effect of the COVID-19 pandemic on the health insurance market in Bulgaria: Empirical analysis of market concentration. *Optimizing Energy Efficiency During a Global Energy Crisis*, 165–177.

Nirala, K. K., Singh, N. K., & Purani, V. S. (2022). A survey on providing customer and public administration based services using AI: chatbot. *Multimedia Tools and Applications, 81*, 22215–22246.

Pathak, A., & Bansal, V. Factors influencing the readiness for artificial intelligence adoption in Indian Insurance Organizations. In International Working Conference on Transfer and Diffusion of IT, TDIT 2023; 2023: Springer Science and Business Media Deutschland GmbH.

Price, W. N., & Cohen, I. G. (2019). Privacy in the age of medical big data. *Nature Medicine, 25*, 37–43.

R&I Editorial Team. (2024). Risk & Insurance. [Online]. Available from: https://riskandinsurance.com/insurance-industry-increasingly-adopting-ai-technologies-study-shows/.

Rajagopal, S. K. P. (2020). A review on artificial intelligence in property and casualty insurance. *International Journal of Innovative Research in Science, Engineering and Technology (IJIRSET), 9*(7), 5251–5254.

Rajaobelina, L., Prom Tep, S., Arcand, M., & Ricard, L. (2021). Creepiness: Its antecedents and impact on loyalty when interacting with a chatbot. *Psychology & Marketing, 28*(12), 2339–2356.

Redzwan, N., & Ramli, R. (2022). A bibliometric analysis of research on stochastic mortality modelling and forecasting. *Risks, 10*(10), 191.

Riikkinen, M., Saarijärvi, H., Sarlin, P., & Lähteenmäki, I. (2018). Using artificial intelligence to create value in insurance. *International Journal of Bank Marketing, 36*(6), 1145–1168.

Sacchelli, S., Fabbrizzi, S., Bertocci, M., Marone, E., Menghini, S., & Bernetti, I. (2017). A mix-method model for adaptation to climate change in the agricultural sector: A case study for Italian wine farms. *Journal of Cleaner Production, 166*(10), 891–900.

Sai, S., Chamola, V., Choo, K. K. R., Sikdar, B., & Rodrigues, J. J. P. C. (2023). Confluence of blockchain and artificial intelligence technologies for secure and scalable healthcare solutions: A review. *IEEE Internet of Things Journal, 10*(7), 5873–58971.

Scattaglia, S., Adesman-Navon, I., & Henderson, J. (2023). KPMG International. [Online]. Available from: https://kpmg.com/xx/en/home/insights/2024/03/ai-in-insurance-a-catalyst-for-change.html.

Schuetz, S., & Venkatesh, V. (2020). Research perspectives: The rise of human machines: How cognitive computing systems challenge assumptions of user-system interaction. *Journal of the Association for Information Systems, 2*, 21.

Seyedtabib, M., & Kamyari, N. (2023). Predicting polypharmacy in half a million adults in the Iranian population: comparison of machine learning algorithms. *BMC Medical Informatics and Decision Making, 23*, 84.

Sharma, V., & Sood, D. (2022). The role of Artificial Intelligence in the insurance industry of India. Big Data analytics in the insurance market. *Emerald Studies in Finance, Insurance, and Risk Management*, 287–297.

Sheehan, B., Mullins, M., Shannon, D., & McCullagh, O. (2023). On the benefits of insurance and disaster risk management integration for improved climate-related natural catastrophe resilience. *Environment Systems and Decisions, 43*, 639–648.

Sheth, S., Baker, H. P., Prescher, H., & Strelzow, J. A. (2024). Ethical considerations of artificial intelligence in health care: Examining the role of generative pretrained transformer-4. *Journal of the American Academy of Orthopaedic Surgeons, 32*(5), 205–210.

Shneiderman, B. (2020). Bridging the gap between ethics and practice: Guidelines for reliable, safe, and trustworthy human-centered AI systems. *ACM Transactions on Interactive Intelligent Systems, 10*(4), 26.

Silverman, B. G., Hanrahan, N., Bharathy, G., Gordon, K., & Johnson, D. (2015). A systems approach to healthcare: Agent-based modeling, community mental health, and population well-being. *Artificial Intelligence in Medicine, 63*(2), 61–71.

Singh, R. P., Hom, G. L., Abramoff, M. D., Campbell, J. P., & Chiang, M. F. (2020). Current Challenges and Barriers to Real-World Artificial Intelligence Adoption for the Healthcare System, Provider, and the Patient. *Translational Vision Science & Technology* , *9*(45).

Singh, S. K., & Chivukula, M. (2020). A Commentary on the application of artificial intelligence in the Insurance Industry. *Trends in Artificial Intelligence, 4*(1), 75–79.

Snowflake Inc. (2023). Snowflake Inc.. [Online]. Available from: https://www.snowflake.com/trending/role-ai-insurance/.

Srinivas, B., & Gandra, P. K. (2023). Role of artificial intelligence in Indian Insurance Industry: Challenges and opportunities from sustainability perspectives. *Journal of Informatics Education and Research, 3*(2).

Sundari, D., Melinasari, S., Suryani, E., & Fadilah, H. F. (2024). Implementation of artificial intelligence at The Insurance Company. Proceeding of the International Conference on Multidisciplinary Research for Sustainable Innovation, *1*(1), 249–255.

Thawakar, S., & Srivastava, V. (2021). Artificial intelligence-based cost reduction for customer retention management in the Indian Life Insurance Industry. In

Applied Advanced Analytics. Springer Proceedings in Business and Economics. Springer.

Tomar, K., & Sharma, S. (2023). A proposed artificial intelligence and blockchain technique for solving health insurance challenges. In Chand, M., Jain, V., & Ajmera, P. *Data-driven technologies and artificial intelligence in supply chain: Tools and techniques.* CRC Press, pp. 31–57.

Vayena, E., Blasimme, A., & Cohen, I. G. (2018). Machine learning in medicine: Addressing ethical challenges. *PLoS Medicine, 15*(11), e1002689.

Vermaa, S., & Gustafsson, A. (2020). Investigating the emerging COVID-19 research trends in the field of business and management: A bibliometric analysis approach. *Journal of Business Research, 118*, 253–261.

Volosovych, S., Zelenitsa, I., Kondratenko, D., Szymla, W., & Mamchur, R. (2021). Transformation of insurance technologies in the context of a pandemic. *Insurance Markets and Companies, 12*(1), 1–13.

Xu, B., Wang, W., Guo, L., Chen, G., Wang, Y., & Zhang, W., et al. (2021). Evaluation of deep learning for automatic multi-view face detection in cattle. *Agriculture, 11*(11), 1062.

Zarifis, A., Kawalek, P., & Azadegan, A. (2020). Evaluating If trust and personal information privacy concerns are barriers to using health insurance that explicitly utilizes AI. *Journal of Internet Commerce,* 20(1), 66–83.

Mesiet William Kamihanda & Hafsa El Bekri

Do International Business Legitimate through SDGs? A Case of African Multinational Banks

1. Introduction

Legitimacy is a perception of approval of an organization's actions (Schmidtke et al., 2023). Multinational Enterprises (MNEs) are seen as having legitimacy after complying with the minimum standards of a specific social identity prototype. Some research holds that legitimacy is a requirement of all corporations (Dingwerth et al., 2020)

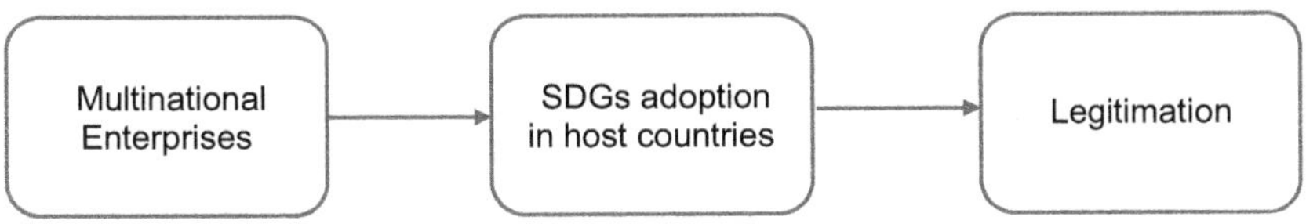

Figure 1. Legitimacy of MNEs
Source: Authors

According to Schiopoiu-Burlea and Popa (2013), legitimacy theory explains organizations' behavior in implementing and developing voluntary social and environmental disclosure of information to fulfill their social contract, (Claro & Esteves 2021) which enables the recognition of their objectives and survival in a jumpy and turbulent environment. Schmidtke and Lenz (2023) demonstrated that MNEs scale up self-legitimation to defend their organizations' legitimacy in light of public criticism and strengthen self-legitimation to mobilize additional support from relevant audiences when their authority increases. (Vaara & Tienari, 2008, 2011) examined legitimation in multinational corporations by focusing on critical discourse analysis (CDA) in which they interpreted the central role of texts in legitimation and institutionalization processes in MNC. Specifically, CDA clarifies the linkages between microlevel textual processes and functions and macrolevel social phenomena. The MNEs use CDA in a conscious attempt to employ discourse analytical tools for controversial societal or social issues (Phillips et al., 2004). The scholars suggested that legitimation creates a sense of positive, beneficial, ethical, understandable, necessary, or otherwise acceptable action in a specific setting.

(Vaara & Tienari, 2004, 2008) Highlighted that legitimacy are created with specific discourses which provide the frame in which people make sense of particular issues and give sense to them (Fairclough & Thomas, 2004). Vaara & Tienari (2011) highlighted that MNEs often face different kinds of struggles that are controversial actions particularly connected with global capitalist or neo-liberal (Fairclough, 2009) ideologies. Hence, discursive frameworks by MNEs are often legitimated as "necessary" in global framework (Fairclough & Thomas, 2004). According to (Dingwerth et al., 2020), MNEs have long relied on a functional narrative, although they differ in the extent and manner of narratives.

MNEs constantly seek to strengthen their identity (Whetten, 2006) and gain legitimacy in the host countries by creating confidence and trust among stakeholders (de Perea et al., 2019) due to the liability of newness and foreignness faced by Emerging Markets MNEs.(Marano et al., 2017). In this manner, Corporate Social Responsibilities (CSR) are also used by MNEs that wish to establish legitimacy (Arvidsson, 2010; Khan et al., 2012), gain a public perception of being a good corporate citizen (Băleanu et al., 2011), improve competitiveness and boost brand awareness (Scharf & Fernandes, 2013) balance corporate profits with society's prosperity (Tjia & Setiawati, 2012), and build a good corporate image in the host countries (Ebo-Hinson, 2011).

This is not a surprise since maintaining legitimacy is critical for the survival and success of organizations (Ozdora-Aksak & Atakan-Duman, 2015). Firms still need to gain legitimacy to get accepted (Biloslavo et al., 2020) not only social, but also political legitimacy. MNEs are in constant moves to gain legitimacy (Méndez-Suárez et al., 2020).

(Vaara & Tienari, 2008, 2011) spotlighted the role of texts in legitimation and institutionalization processes in MNEs but confessed that, "we have not focused here on intertextuality, that is, the linkages between specific texts in discussions around particular phenomena, which is a central issue in terms of being able to map out the impact of specific texts on others in legitimation processes." Therefore, considering the increasing interest in adoption and implementation of SDGs by MNEs in host countries, especially developing ones, this chapter accesses the use of SDGs to gain legitimacy (phenomenon) by using discursive typology from texts of the 4 Moroccan MNBs' CEOs' letters for the years 2012 to 2023 and how SDGs adoption as narrated through CDA impact or relate to their legitimation in host African countries. Moreover, according to (Sarfraz et al., 2018) foreign MNBs are more motivated to undertake CSR initiatives than domestic banks. Whether it is out of symbolic legitimacy seeking or substantive motive, the adoption and disclosure of SDGs remain a question that has not yet been answered (Lodhia, 2022). Companies' commitment to SDGs, was a mixture of symbolic and substantive legitimation strategies (Eng, 2023). Companies that frequently adopt sustainability practices to gain legitimacy and a positive reputation (Fiaschi et al., 2017). This indicates a void to be filled in the SDGs adoption and legitimation nexus.

1.1. Moroccan MNBs Cross-border Expansion

Banks from emerging economies are becoming more prominent investors, especially in small developing countries and countries where income levels are low (low and lower-middle-income), where they portray the significance of the markets which they do business in (Claessens et al., 2011). The three largest Moroccan banks (Attijariwafa Bank (AWB), Banque Centrale Populaire (BCP) and Bank of Africa (BOA)/MCE Group) built their presence in Africa largely through acquiring existing banks. For instance, BCP acquired Banque Atlantique in 2012, while BMCE group became the main shareholder of BOA in 2010. In 2008, AWB bought a French-based bank, "Credit Agricole's African operations (CBWAS, 2020). Furthermore, AWB acquired 100 % of the Barclays Bank Egypt's company, currently among the bank's big branches (IMF,2016; Banks' Annual reports, 2020). Moroccan banks have diversified their operations in highly emerging countries such as China, Mexico, and South Korea and in developed countries including Europe, America, Japan, and Canada (Aarhus, 2021).

Interestingly, different from the decade of 2005 to 2015, when their main concern was expansion and internationalization along with growth, from late 2015 onwards, Moroccan Banks are observed to redirect their efforts more into inclusive growth and sustainability (Gondwe,2001). The adoption of Sustainable Development Goals in late 2015 significantly impacted this move (UN, 2016). The banks' efforts were more channeled on green project financing, responsible employment, gender economic inclusion, and the creation of opportunities such as education and employment for the marginalized groups in the countries' societies in which they are present, which can be defined as increasing the adoption of SDGs.

1.2. Legitimation Theory

Legitimacy can be defined as "a generalized perception or assumption that the actions of a firm/corporation or entity are proper, desirable, and appropriate within a certain socially context and system of beliefs, norms and definitions (Schiopoiu Burlea & Popa, 2013; Schmidtke & Lenz, 2023)

Legitimacy theory has been used for a decade to underline why firms report environmental and social (Deegan, 2019). According to (Fiaschi et al., 2017), speech and press freedom in the host countries have a significant influence on emerging markets MNEs' corporate social irresponsibility in a sense that firms are less likely to do-harm when investing in countries with strong speech and press freedoms. Therefore, due to the sensitive nature of the activity, MNBs are subject to a high level of scrutiny from host counties' local sociopolitical actors, especially the regulator and the media (Fiaschi et al., 2017). The pressure for companies to contribute to the SDGs has been built up by persistent stakeholders, for instance, media, governments, and shareholders and the pressure to comply host countries' regulations (Deegan, 2019) and such pressure and expectations are likely to threaten the firms' legitimacy if they are not addressed (Ivanaj et al., 2021; van Zanten & van Tulder, 2018). (Duque-Grisales et al., 2020), the authors found that adopting sustainability initiatives is conditioned by institutional pressures to meet stakeholder expectations.

2. Literature Review

2.1. Legitimation through Communication and Discursive Typology in MNBs

A study by (Simcic-Brønn & Vidaver-Cohen, 2008), underlined that MNEs use sustainability as a legitimacy factor and with the motive to Remain Competitive (other than the Profitability factor). Similarly, (Chiu & Sharfman, 2011) found that its firms' visibility to stakeholders had a larger impact on managers' decisions regarding how much corporate social performance their firms exhibit than

Forcadell et al. (2020) extended the theory of the firm by including Corporate Sustainability and the findings revealed that MNBs find the complementarity between digitalization and Corporate Sustainability to be an efficient way to confront the threat of new entrants (reputation and competitiveness). On the other hand, (Wu et al., 2017) identified that banks engaged in more CSR exhibited better Financial Performance (financial motives).

Caussat et al. (2019) showed that legitimation strategies aim to diffuse a positive image of the organization and give a prominent role to communication with and public relations with important legitimacy providers. (Deegan, 2019) identified that reporting offers a one-way communication channel from a corporation to its stakeholders to manage their legitimacy. Research has found that legitimacy concerns drive sustainability and embed companies in social and environmental reporting.

MNEs from emerging are more likely to face the liabilities of origin, that is, the negative perceptions in host countries about these firms' willingness and ability to build legitimate businesses (Marano et al., 2017); hence, from a legitimacy perspective, companies can overcome the liability of foreignness by improving their legitimacy among stakeholders in host countries (Luo et al., 2002) This legitimacy can be improved by being responsive and giving back to society (Wood, 1991). By implementing CSR and sustainability initiatives, companies can enhance their acceptance among stakeholders in host countries and overcome the liability of foreignness (Caussat et al., 2019).

(Maruyama & Wu, 2015) indicated that firms try to gain reputation and overcome the liability of foreignness by improving moral legitimacy attained by conducting CSR activities. (Silva, 2021)'s findings indicated that two-thirds of companies tend to address the SDGs by mapping them to existing activities to legitimize their contributions. On the other hand, MNEs are keener in considering their negative externalities in host countries and tend to actively address SDGs in their business strategies contrary to addressing SDGs following stakeholders' pressure and liability of foreignness (Claro, 2021)

According to Mijatovic et al. (2019), the firms that observed regulations, which have a higher employee relations level and are more social and community-involved, were more likely to have higher levels of environmental practice, including observing environmental SDGs.

(Lopez, 2020) identified that the CSR strategy can be linked with the SDGs when stakeholder theory and creating a shared value are two observed goals. Sustainability appears to be an antecedent of corporate reputation and a tool to enhance stakeholders' acceptance and perceptions on companies' activities (Gomez-Trujillo et al., 2020)

Numerous studies have indicated that SDG involvement by multinationals is inspired by a mixture of legitimacy and institutional motives (van der-Waal & Thijssens, 2020).

Calabrese et al. (2022) highlighted that the adoption and general contribution to the SDGs by multinational firms is still symbolic and mostly a matter of legitimacy-seeking. Calabrese et al. (2022) further indicated that firms are more likely to contribute to the SDGs that are related to environmental and economic targets. Therefore, MNEs with different business strategies implemented different SDGs, with more focus on SDGs 13,5,8,9,12 (Lodhia, 2022)

Moreover, MNEs are more engage with SDGs targets that are actionable and relevant with their business model (value chain) and more engaged on SDGs targets that within "avoid harm" rather than those that "do good" (Hult et al., 2018; van Zanten & van Tulder, 2018) the MNEs' international legitimacy is at risk if they do harm in the conduct of their business (Fiaschi et al., 2017). Therefore, it is important to assess whether SDGs adaptation narrated through CDAs are driven by legitimation motives of MNEs, specifically MNBs from emerging market economies (Gomez-Trujillo, 2024)

H1: Legitimation in discourse and communication has a positive effect on the adoption and implementation of SGDs by MNBs from Africa

3. Methodology

3.1. Variables Computation

As specified by (Vaara et al., 2006), CDA helps us understand the inherently political nature of such discursive legitimation. This chapter uses content analysis of the Critical Discursive Approach (CDA) following (Vaara & Tienari, 2008, 2011). Non-financial statements and consolidated non-financial statements analysis have been used in studies like (Avrampou et al.,2019). Two researchers employed manual/hand content analysis to reduce the risk of inter-coder reliability. The official definitions of the 17 SDGs on the United Nations website were used for SDGs.

3.1.1. Legitimation

We used the Banks' communication and discourse from the CEOs' or presidents' annual letters and annual sustainability reports from 2012 to 2023. We first identified different types of accreditations/recognitions the banks publish on sustainability annual reports and communicate in CEOs' annual letters, which act as a sign of gaining legitimacy/image. These included industry awards, certifications, rankings, or partnerships with high-level/renewed or influential organizations. Then, scores were assigned on each accreditation/recognition based on the perceived significance. The scores ranged from 5 (highest) to 1 (lowest). The third stage involved applying the weightings (2 being the highest weight and 1.5 the lowest) to the scores depending on the endorsing organization or entity's importance and calculating the weighted total score.

3.1.2. SDGs Adoption

It was identified by thoroughly reading the sustainability reports and CEOs or presidents' letters; we grouped the respective SDGs communicated directly (by stating the goal such as SDG 5) or indirectly (by stating the undertaken activity related to the certain SDG). For each year, the frequencies of each SDG were specified from SDG1–17 with the frequency of zero (0) if a certain SDG was not communicated at all, followed by the calculation of SDG adaptation by each bank. An equal weight for all SDGs was assumed (1/17). Lastly, the SDGs adoption index was calculated by summating all the weighted frequencies for each bank in a year to get each years' index. The same was done for all years and all banks.

3.2. Data Analysis

The coded data were analysed using STATA17 and a Structural Equation Model (SEM).

Table 1. Model Operationalization

Variable	Description	Acronym	Hypothesis
Legitimation (exogeneous)	Sustainability's Discursive and communication	Legitimation	H1
SDGs adoption (endogenous)	SDGs adoption index on SDGs 1–17	SDGs-adoption	NA

Source: Authors

4. Results and Discussion of the Findings

4.1. Results

Since the announcement of SDGs by the United Nations, sustainability and MNEs have caught great attention in International Business Research (IBR) (Sachs & Sachs, 2021; Van Tulder et al., 2021). This chapter proposes the explanatory model that examines the nexus of African Multinational Banks' (AMNBs), legitimation through discourse typology and SDGs adoption. Our findings highlight a positive and statistically significant relationship between legitimation and SDGs adoption.

Our results suggest that Legitimation has a positive and significant impact on the SDGs adoption (significant are 1 % (0.010)). Specifically, the results suggest that other factors, being constant, for each percent increase in legitimation through CDA, tend to increase SDGs adoption by AMNBs by 29.7 %, hence supporting Hypothesis 1.

The observed structural relationship ($\beta = 0.297$; ρ-value < 0.010) adoption by AMNBs confirms the impactful role of legitimation in the adoption and implementation of Sustainable Development Goals (SDGs) by AMNBs. The results concur with the previous studies, which stressed that MNEs seek to gain legitimacy and hence tend to engage more in sustainability practices; specifically, SDGs adoption and implementation are mainly due to legitimation. That is gaining trust, acceptance and confidence among the stakeholders as well as overcoming liabilities of newness/foreignness in the host countries (Gomez-Trujillo & Gonzalez-Perez, 2022; Maruyama & Wu, 2015; Claro, 2021; Calabrese et al., 2022; van der-Waal & Thijssens, 2020; Marano et al., 2017; Gomez-Trujillo & Gonzalez-Perez, 2020)

The legitimation having a positive impact on SDGs adoption shows that the more African MNBs seek to increase their legitimation in African host countries, the more are likely to adopt more SDGs in those host countries. Our findings contribute to the consensus that legitimation is critical in adopting SDGs by MNEs, specifically African MNBs. Furthermore, the results imply that the more MNBs from emerging markets seek legitimacy in host countries mainly African countries, the more they will likely adopt and implement more SDGs in those countries. Therefore, the overall findings of this study underscore the significance of legitimation on SDGs adoption by MNBs in host countries.

Table 2. Assessment of the Path Model

Structural relationships	**Coefficients**	**Standard error**	**Probability: p>IzI**
Legitim -> SDGsadopt	0.297	0.116	0.010
LR test of the model vs. saturated	χ^2=(3)=7.345		Prob.χ = *0.000*
R-squared	.592731		

Lastly, in assessing model calibration, the chi-square test (χ^2), it plays a critical role, where the lower test statistic (t-statistic) implies a better model fit. While the conventional probability threshold is set at 5 % (0.05), the sensitivity of chi-square test to sample size is a crucial consideration. In our results, the chi-square statistic, together with probability value (prob>chi2 = 0.000) validates the robust fit of this study's model to the data, indicating its significance. Additionally, the R-squared (goodness of fit) value of 59 % implies that variations in SDGs adoptions are explained by the model predictors (internalization performance, strategy, and legitimation). Both chi-square statistic and the R-squared results validate that the model is not Suspicious. Our results highlight that legitimation is highly significant for African MNBs' adoption of the SDGs. By bolding the legitimation role of SDG adoption, the results offer important insights to both MNBs and host countries' stakeholders.

4.2. Conclusion, Theory and Practice Implications

The results of this chapter offer valuable insights mainly since it is based on African Multinational Banks, contrary to other studies that observed MNEs from different industries such as manufacturing, retailing, and other service industries (Gomez-Trujillo et al., 2024; Nguyen et al., 2021; Nishitani & Kokubu, 2020; Van Zanten et al., 2018; Maruyama & Wu, 2015; Caussat et al., 2019). Moreover, its contribution is based on the context. Our study is based on MNBs from the global south, specifically African emerging market economies, different from other studies whose context were from the developed economies (Bose & Khan, 2022; Nishitani & Kokubu, 2020) or Latin America, Asian and Eastern Europe emerging markets economies and Eastern Europe (Duque-Grisales et al., 2020; Kiliç, 2016; Gomez-Trujillo & Gonzalez-Perez, 2020; Wei & Nguyen, 2020).

Our findings concur and extend the applicability legitimacy theory and the resource dependence theory by indicating how the process of seeking legitimacy through communication and discursive typology may be influential toward adoption of SDGs in African countries whose region, like other regions is stated to have a huge (unclosed) SDGs gap (Liou et al., 2021), and how SDGs adoption may act as a guiding framework for MNEs' access to valuable resources along with legitimating their present in the African) host countries within the global sustainability landscape (Kourula et al., 2017). This implies that initiatives to seek legitimacy can be a strategic move for MNEs, specifically MNBs, to adopt and implement SDGs, which can turn out to be an advantage to the host countries. However, this underlines a further research need to examine the connection between SDGs attainment (measured by counties' SDGs index) and the MNBs legitimation to measure the extent (magnitude) to which legitimation by MNBs impacts SDGs implementation in African countries in the 7 years before the elapse of the UN SDGs.

Moreover, the results give important implications to sustainability managers looking to grow and establish their firms in foreign countries, on sustainability issues precisely SDGs adoption. Understanding the link between legitimation has been stated as crucial to MNEs from emerging markets, which are likely to face liabilities of foreignness. (Maruyama & Wu, 2015; Caussat et al., 2019; Gomez-Trujillo, 2024). SGDs adoption may be a great plus for them to make informed decisions on approaching legitimacy and adopting SDGs in their countries of presence, specifically Africa, to the host countries. On the other hand, the result of this study may imply a caution on the probability of SDGs greenwashing (Heras-Saizarbitoria et al., 2022). Therefore, the stakeholder such as government to know how to well related with MNEs, in this case, MNBs.

References

Aarhus, P.(2021). Morocco's Bankig sector holds steady. *The BANKER*. Retrieved from https://www.thebanker.com/World/Africa/Morocco/Morocco-s-banking-sector-holds-steady

Arvidsson, S. (2010). Communication of Corporate Social Responsibility: A study of the views of management teams in large companies. *Journal of Business Ethics*, *96*(3), 339–354.

Băleanu, T. E., Chelcea, L., & Stancu, A. (2011). *Corporate Social Responsibility the social responsibility of the top 100 Romanian Companies. An Analysis of Corporate Websites.*

Biloslavo, R., Bagnoli, C., Massaro, M., & Cosentino, A. (2020). Business model transformation toward sustainability: The impact of legitimation. *Management Decision*, *58*(8),1643–1662.

Bose, S., & Khan, H. Z. (2022). Sustainable development goals (SDGs) reporting and the role of country-level institutional factors: An international-evidence. *Journal of Cleaner Production*, *335*.

Calabrese, A., Costa, R., Levialdi-Ghiron, N., Tiburzi, L., & Villazon Montalvan, R. A. (2022). Is the private sector becoming cleaner? Assessing the firms' contribution to the 2030 Agenda. *Journal of Cleaner Production*, *363*.

Caussat, P., Prime, N., & Wilken, R. (2019). How multinational banks in India gain legitimacy: Organizational practices and resources required for implementation. *Management International Review*, *59*(4), 561–591.

CBWAS. (2020). Central Bank of West-African States Annual-reports.

Chiu, S. C., & Sharfman, M. (2011). Legitimacy, visibility, and the antecedents of corporate social performance: An investigation of the instrumental perspective. *Journal of Management*, *37*(6), 558–1585.

Claro, P. B. O., & Esteves, N. R. (2021). Sustainability-oriented strategy and Sustainable Development Goals. *Marketing Intelligence & Planning*, *39*(4),613–630.

Claessens, S., van Horen, N., Gurcanlar, T., & Mercado Sapiain, J. (2011). Foreign Bank presence in developing countries 1995–2006: Data and trends. *Electronic Journal.*

de Perea, J. G. Á., Ramírez-García, C., & Del Cubo-Molina, A. (2019). Internationalization business models and patterns of SMEs and MNEs: A qualitative multi-case study in the agrifood sector. *Sustainability*, *11*(10).

Deegan, C. M. (2019). Legitimacy theory: Despite its enduring popularity and contribution, time is right for a necessary makeover. *Accounting, Auditing and Accountability Journal*, *32*(8), 2307–2329.

Dingwerth, K., Schmidtke, H., & Weise, T. (2020). The rise of democratic legitimation: Why international organizations speak the language of democracy. *European Journal of International Relations*, *26*(3),714–741.

Duque-Grisales, E., Aguilera-Caracuel, J., Guerrero-Villegas, J., & García-Sánchez, E. (2020). Can proactive environmental strategy improve Multilatinas' level of internationalization? The moderating role of board independence. *Business Strategy and the Environment*, *29*(1), 291–305.

Ebo-Hinson, R. (2011). Online CSR reportage of award-winning versus non-award-winning banks in Ghana. *Journal of Information, Communication and Ethics in Society*, *9*(2), 102–115.

Fairclough, N., & Thomas, D. (2004). Peripheral Vision: Discourse Analysis in Organization Studies: The Case for Critical Realism. *Organizational Studies*, *26*(6), 915–939. doi:https://doi.org/10.1177/01708406050546

Fairclough, N. (2009). A dialectical-relational approach to critical discourse analysis in social research. *Methods in Critical Discourse Analysis, 2_{nd} Edition.*

Fiaschi, D., Giuliani, E., & Nieri, F. (2017). Overcoming the liability of origin by doing no-harm: Emerging country firms' social irresponsibility as they go global. *Journal of World Business*, *52*(4), 546–563.

Forcadell, F. J., Aracil, E., & Ubeda, F. (2020). Using reputation for corporate sustainability to tackle banks digitalization challenges. *Business Strategy and the Environment*, *29*(6), 2181–2193.

Gomez-Trujillo, A. M., Gonzalez-Perez, M. A., & Baena-Rojas, J. J. (2024). Sustainable strategy as a lever for corporate legitimacy and long-term competitive advantage: An Examination of an Emerging Market Multinational. *European Business Review*, *36*(1),112–139.

Gomez-Trujillo, A. M., & Gonzalez-Perez, M. A. (2020). What do we know about organizational sustainability and international business? In *Management of Environmental Quality: An International Journal*, 31(2), 292–305.

Heras-Saizarbitoria, I., Urbieta, L., & Boiral, O. (2022). Organizations' engagement with sustainable development goals: From cherry-picking to SDG-washing? *Corporate Social Responsibility and Environmental Management*, *29*(2), 316–328.

Hult, G. T. M., Mena, J. A., Gonzalez-Perez, M. A., Lagerström, K., & Hult, D. T. (2018). A ten country-company study of sustainability and product-market performance: Influences of doing good, warm glow, and price fairness. *Journal of Macromarketing*, *38*(3),242–261.

Ivanaj, S., Ivanaj, V., McIntyre, J., & Guimaraes da Costa, N. (2021). What can multinational enterprises do to implement sustainable development goals? *Journal of Cleaner Production*, *296*, 126586.

Khan, A., Muttakin, M. B., & Siddiqui, J. (2012). Corporate governance and Corporate Social Responsibility disclosures: Evidence from an emerging economy. *SSRN Electronic Journal.*

Kiliç, M. (2016). Online Corporate Social Responsibility (CSR) disclosure in the banking industry: Evidence from Turkey. *International Journal of Bank Marketing, 34*(4), 550–569.

Kourula, A., Pisani, N., & Kolk, A. (2017). Corporate sustainability and inclusive development: Highlights from international business and management research. *Current Opinion in Environmental Sustainability, 24,* 14–18.

Liou, R. S., & Rao-Nicholson, R. (2021). Multinational enterprises and Sustainable Development Goals: A foreign subsidiary perspective on tackling wicked problems. *Journal of International Business Policy, 4*(1), 136–151.

Lodhia, S., Kaur, A. & Kuruppu, S. C. (2022). The disclosure of sustainable development goals (SDGs) by the top 50 Australian companies: Substantive or symbolic legitimation? *Meditari Accountancy Research.*

Lopez, B. (2020). Connecting business and sustainable development goals in Spain. *Marketing Intelligence and Planning, 38*(5), 573–585.

Luo, Y., Shenkar, O., & Nyaw, M. K. (2002). Mitigating liabilities of foreignness: Defensive versus offensive approaches. In *Journal of International Management* (Vol. 8).

Marano, V., Tashman, P., & Kostova, T. (2017). Escaping the iron cage: Liabilities of origin and CSR reporting of emerging market multinational enterprises. *Journal of International Business Studies, 48*(3), 386–408.

Maruyama, M., & Wu, L. (2015). Overcoming the liability of Foreignness in international retailing: A consumer perspective. *Journal of International Management, 21*(3), 200–210.

Méndez-Suárez, M., Monfort, A., & Gallardo, F. (2020). Sustainable banking: New forms of investing under the umbrella of the 2030 agenda. *Sustainability, 12*(5), 1–13.

Mijatovic, I., Maricic, M., & Horvat, A. (2019). The factors affecting the environmental practices of companies: The case of Serbia. *Sustainability, 11*(21).

Nguyen, D. K., Huynh, T. L. D., & Nasir, M. A. (2021). Carbon emissions determinants and forecasting: Evidence from G6 countries. *Journal of Environmental Management, 285.*

Nishitani, K., & Kokubu, K. (2020). Can firms enhance economic performance by contributing to sustainable consumption and production? Analyzing the patterns of influence of environmental performance in Japanese manufacturing firms. *Sustainable Production and Consumption, 21,* 156–169.

Ozdora-Aksak, E., & Atakan-Duman, S. (2015). The one presence of Turkish banks: Communicating the softer side of corporate identity. *Public Relations Review*, *41*(1), 119–128.

Phillips, N., Lawrence, T.B. & Hardy, C. (2004). DISCOURSE AND INSTITUTIONS. *Academy of Management Review, 29*(4), 635–652.

Sachs, J. D., & Sachs, L. E. (2021). Business alignment for the "Decade of Action." In *Journal of International Business Policy*, 4(1), 22–27.

Sarfraz, M., Qun, W., Hui, L., & Abdullah, M. I. (2018). Environmental risk management strategies and the moderating role of corporate social responsibility in project financing decisions. *Sustainability, 10*(8).

Scharf, E. R., & Fernandes, J. (2013). The advertising of corporate social responsibility in a Brazilian bank. *International Journal of Bank Marketing, 31*(1), 24–37.

Schiopoiu Burlea, A., & Popa, I. (2013). Legitimacy Theory. *Encyclopedia of Corporate Social Responsibility*, 1579–1584.

Schmidtke, H., & Lenz, T. (2023). Expanding or defending legitimacy? Why international organizations intensify self-legitimation. *Review of International Organizations.*

Simcic Brønn, P., & Vidaver-Cohen, D. (2008). Corporate motives for social initiative: Legitimacy, sustainability or the bottom line? In *Journal of Business Ethics*.

Silva, S. (2021). Corporate contributions to the Sustainable Development Goals: An empirical analysis informed by legitimacy theory. *Journal of Cleaner Production, 292.*

Vaara, E., & Tienari, J. (2004). Critical Discourse Analysis as a Methodology for International Business Studies. *Handbook of Qualitative Research Methods for International Business, Edward Elgar*., 342–359.

Vaara, E., Tienari, J., & Laurila, J. (2006). Pulp and paper fiction: On the discursive legitimation of global industrial restructuring, *27*(6), 789–813.

Vaara, E., & Tienari, J. (2008). A discursive perspective on legitimation strategies in multinational corporations. *Academy of Management Review*, *33*(4), 985–993.

Vaara, E., & Tienari, J. (2011). On the narrative construction of multinational corporations: An ante-narrative analysis of legitimation and resistance in a cross-border merger. *Organization Science*, *22*(2), 370–390.

van der-Waal, J. W. H., & Thijssens, T. (2020). Corporate involvement in Sustainable Development Goals: Exploring the territory. *Journal of Cleaner Production*, *252*.

Van Tulder, R., Rodrigues, S. B., Mirza, H., & Sexsmith, K. (2021). The UN's Sustainable Development Goals: Can multinational enterprises lead the decade of action? *Journal of International Business Policy*, *4*(1).

van Zanten, J. A., & van Tulder, R. (2018). Multinational enterprises and the Sustainable Development Goals: An institutional approach to corporate engagement. *Journal of International Business Policy*, *1*(3–4), 208–233.

van Zanten, J. A., & van Tulder, R. (2021). Improving companies' impacts on sustainable development: A nexus approach to the SDGs. *Business Strategy and the Environment*, *30*(8), 3703–3720.

Wei, Z., & Nguyen, Q.TK. (2020). Chinese service multinationals: The degree of internationalization and performance. *Management International Review*, *60*(6), 869–908.

Whetten, D. A. (2006). Albert and Whetten revisited: Strengthening the concept of organizational identity. *Journal of Management Inquiry*, *15*(3), 219–234.

Wood, D. J. (1991). Corporate social performance revisited. *Source: The Academy of Management Review*, *16*(4).

Pedro Fernandes da Anunciação &
Cátia Susana Claro Chasqueira

Audit of Information Systems in the Bakery Industry in Portugal

1. Introduction

Information systems audit (IS) emerges as an essential field in the contemporary business context, facing challenges and requirements with the same degree of complexity as the criticality of IS. Since the dawn of the digital age, information security has been a constant concern for organizations, especially as the integration and interoperability of information systems and technologies (ITS) grow (Laudon, et al. 2021). Derived from the relational context in which economic organizations position themselves, IS plays a central role in business operations, from data management to strategic decision-making. In the conceptual field, SI auditing emerges as a vital tool to ensure the value of information, the anatomy and metabolism of decision-making and management, and competitiveness, as it should ensure the security of systems, their effectiveness, and their compliance with relevant standards and regulations (Oliveira, 2022). The audit corresponds to a systematic process of obtaining and evaluating evidence of activities, events, or transactions and, in the field of information systems, focuses on the evaluation of the implementation, operation, and control of IS resources in the context of economic organizations (Rahman et al., 2014). In it, professional auditing assumes a central role, since, by the nature of its intervention, its analysis is reflected in the scope of the business and the ITS. In this sense, these are two areas for which it must have consolidated knowledge (Axelsen et al., 2017).

Although the IS audit should integrate higher education in the field of IS (Oliveira & Anunciação, 2022), it is not always considered with the same relevance by managers and entrepreneurs in the field of their organizations. This is a more evident fact when it comes to small and medium-sized enterprises. In a survey conducted by the Information Systems Governance European Club (ISGec, 2019), the large companies and public administration in Portugal in 2013 and 2014, referring to the practices adopted in 2011 and 2012, respectively, on the frequency of audits at the IS level, it was evidenced that, in 2011, 82.6 % reported performing audits on IS and 17.4 % did not perform them. However, taking 2012 as a reference, these values were described, showing that

75.3 % performed audits on IS and 22.2 % indicated that they did not perform them. Given these values and deepening the analysis to better understand the frequencies of these practices, it was evident that, in terms of the practice of the annual audit, in 2011, only 31.6 % performed, while in 2012 this value increased to 55.7 %. When questioned about the practice of auditing without a defined period, compared to 2011, 47.4 % assumed this realization and, in 2012, only 31.1 % did so. When the need to carry out audits when inconsistencies or incidents are detected at the IS level, in 2011 only 7.8 % did so, and in 2012 only 3.3 % of the surveyed companies. This reality, found at the level of large companies that usually have organizational areas (e.g., departments) dedicated to IS, makes us consider what will be the reality at the level of small and medium enterprises. Economic reality stresses the importance of adequate internal control systems, consistent with the nature, complexity, and risk profile of operations (Dimitrova et al., 2016), which we know is difficult in small and medium-sized enterprises.

Audit standards play a crucial role in guiding audit practices and the importance of following internationally recognized standards such as ISO/IEC 27001 and COBIT, to ensure the effectiveness and credibility of audit processes occupies a prominent place (Gelinas, et al. 2018). International audit standards focus particular attention on the importance of corporate controls in general and information systems in particular (Bedard et al., 2005). It is important to follow frameworks, standards, and models that provide clear guidelines on the security controls that must be implemented, helping organizations to continually assess and improve their posture of information security and IS (Akoka & Wattiau, 2010). In addition, risk management emerges as a key pillar. Risk identification and assessment are essential to guide audit activities and prioritize information security resources effectively. The risk management approach allows organizations to understand the potential threats they face, assess the likelihood of occurrence and the associated impact, and implement appropriate preventive and corrective measures.

However, the implementation of an IS audit process is not without challenges. One of the main challenges is the lack of awareness and understanding of its importance. Many organizations underestimate the risks associated with information security and do not dedicate the necessary resources to properly protect their IS. This can result in gaps that are exploited by hackers, resulting in data breaches and damage *to* the company's reputation. Another significant challenge concerns the complexity of modern IT environments. With the proliferation of connected devices and the adoption of emerging technologies such as cloud computing, the Internet of Things (IoT), blockchain, and artificial intelligence, among others, enterprise networks have become more difficult to secure and audit. The diversity of systems, platforms, and applications increases the attack surface and makes it more difficult for auditors to track and assess the security of all information activities (Whitman & Mattord, 2018). Organizations operate in increasingly interconnected environments, with global networks, business partners, and third-party service providers. This broadens the scope and scale of information security challenges, requiring comprehensive and coordinated audit approaches to ensure the effective protection of information systems (Pfleeger et al., 2015).

In addition to the technical challenges, the successful implementation of the IS audit also faces organizational and cultural obstacles. Resistance to change, lack of management support and lack of collaboration between different stakeholders can make it difficult to effectively implement audit processes. Organizational culture also plays a crucial role in this context, influencing how teams perceive and prioritize information security. However, the lack of specialized resources in information security is identified as one of the main barriers to effective audits (Whitman & Mattord, 2018). The shortage of qualified IS audit professionals can make it difficult to identify and mitigate cyber threats, leaving organizations vulnerable to attacks and security breaches.

In short, IS auditing plays a key role in protecting information assets and ensuring the integrity, confidentiality, and availability of business systems. However, it faces several challenges, from the complexity of information technology environments to organizational and cultural barriers. By recognizing and addressing these challenges, organizations can strengthen their information security posture and minimize the risks associated with the digital age.

2. Information Systems Auditing

The current trend of transformation of an industrial society into an Information Society continues to occur at an accelerated pace. Recent developments in industry 4.0. technological advances have produced a real technological revolution of great density and intense impact on industries. The incorporation of innovative technologies and interconnectivity between systems is increasing (Rodríguez, 2005). The dependence of businesses and organizations on IS is significant. Periods of unavailability or difficulty of interconnection can lead to significant real and opportunity costs. For these reasons, it is important to consider, at the management level, some reasons that justify the need to audit the IS, namely, the change in organizational surroundings, the trends of technological evolution, and the optimization of the performance of the IS (Carneiro, 2009).

The audit is not limited to the search for inconsistencies or deficiencies at the IS level. The audit should involve processes of planning, development, testing, and application of systems, whether examining the logical, physical, environmental, organizational structure of control, security, and data protection (Carneiro, 2009). The audit is responsible for the analysis and evaluation of controls in the processing of information, from design to installation of systems; assess all information flows, examine the efficiency of the use of IT resources, the effectiveness of pre-determined controls, and the validity of findings; verify in detail the processing of the data and the computer resources involved in it; collect and evaluate evidence to examine whether an IS guarantees data integrity, prevents its destruction and efficiently uses computer resources.

The audit aims to increase user satisfaction levels; safeguard the security of data, hardware, and software components; minimize the existence of risks in the use of information technology; and ensure greater integrity, confidentiality, and reliability of the information. However, one does not change organizations without changing responsibilities. There must be careful reflection on the controls that must be audited, on risk management, and a firm commitment to change the organization (Peret, 2023).

The curious situation experienced in the industrial and economic sector under analysis, refers to the mandatory audit, under the law, on food security. In this context, we could compare the IS audits with those concerning food safety:

1. **Objectives:**
   - o The IS audit focuses on assessing the security, integrity, and efficiency of an organization's IS, including networks, databases, applications, and cybersecurity controls.
   - o The food safety audit focuses on ensuring that food products meet established safety and quality standards, from production to distribution, including good manufacturing practices, quality control, and compliance with sanitary regulations.

2. **Scope of application:**
   - o The IS audit applies to all organizations that use IS in their operations, regardless of the sector, covering financial companies, healthcare, retailers, and manufacturing industries, among others.
   - o The food safety audit is specific to companies involved in the production, processing, storage, and distribution of food, including farms, food factories, restaurants, and supermarkets.

3. **Risks and Challenges:**
   - o In IS auditing, key risks include data breaches, cyber-attacks, service interruptions, and inadequate compliance with information security regulations.

   - In the food safety audit, the main risks involve microbiological contamination, chemical contamination, food adulteration, inadequate labeling, and non-compliance with food safety standards.

4. **Standards and Regulations:**
   - In IS auditing, widely recognized international standards include ISO/IEC 27001 for information security and COBIT for IT governance, along with industry-specific regulations such as the General Data Protection Regulation (GDPR) for data protection in the European Union.
   - In the food safety audit, standards include ISO 22000 for food safety management systems, HACCP (Hazard Analysis and Critical Control Points) for food risk control, and government regulations, such as the FDA in the United States and FSSC 22000 in the European Union.

5. **Results and Impacts:**
   - In IS auditing, audit results may include recommendations to improve security controls, identify vulnerabilities in information technology, and ensure regulatory compliance to protect information assets and mitigate cyber risks.
   - In the food safety audit, the results may include the identification of areas of non-compliance with food safety standards, suggestions for improving quality control procedures, and ensuring the production of safe and high-quality food.

In the specific information systems supported by information technologies (computer systems), as mentioned by Oliveira (2023), the Audit should translate into an intervention of analysis and diagnosis of the organization and computer management (computer system) covering all aspects, and particularly those relating to users. It should aim to analyze the importance and organization of the means (hardware, software, and personnel) and whether they are proportionate and adapted to the needs of the organization; and the verification that the achievements and results obtained attest to a rational and efficient management of the available means. In this sense, audits shall consider organizational, functional, human, management, technical and economic aspects, in particular:

- organizational aspects – the structure of the IT service and degree of centralization; organization of studies; organization of the holding; systems analysis and design methodologies; etc.
- functional aspects – adaptation of information systems to management needs; viability and response time; degree of information hierarchy; coordination aspects; system integration; etc.
- human aspects – inclusion of informatics in the organization and its brand image; levels of satisfaction of managers and users; degree of motivation of computer staff; etc.
- management aspects – functions of IT staff; management methods and techniques used; Administration's relative position vis-à-vis IT; IT policies and plans; etc.

- technical aspects – computer and configuration; operating system; informatic system; data collection; codification; controls; specific techniques (multiprogramming, real-time, virtual memory); etc.
- economic aspects – burden and allocation structure; methods of imputation; budgets and deviations; accounting (operating account, profit, and loss account, balance sheet); investments linked to the IT plan; etc.

Although IS audit and food safety audit have different approaches and objectives, both play a key role in ensuring safety, integrity, and compliance in their respective domains, contributing to consumer confidence and brand protection of organizations, highlighting the relevant role of auditing in the specific security in each of the domains.

3. Objectives and Methodology

This work was intended to assess, in an exploratory way, the maturity and valuation of IS Audit practices and skills in the context of the Bakery Industry. For this, we used a sample of 15 companies and conducted semi-structured interviews with those responsible for these companies and their IT systems, when they exist. For the proposed study, the self-assessment model proposed by Gerardus Blokdyk (2020) was adopted. In this model, seven criteria are defined to assess the level of maturity for IS audit practices:

- Criterion 1 – Recognize – This criterion allows to realize the need for change of the organization and to recognize that there are processes, controls or other variables that represent problems or opportunities for improvement.
- Criterion 2 – Define – This criterion contributes to a clear definition of the organization's problems, needs, and objectives.
- Criterion 3 – Measure – This criterion aims to help collect the necessary information to measure the current situation of the organization (As-Is).
- Analyze – Contributes to the analysis of the causes that led the organization to the current situation.
- Criterion 5 – Improve – This criterion helps to develop a practical solution to respond to the problems identified and understand how the organization can innovate, test new solutions and measure the results.
- Criterion 6 – Control – Implement the practical solution and correct any undesirable implications.
- Criterion 7 – Sustain – Recognize the positive impacts of the audit and continue in the process of continuous improvement.

Answers to a wide range of questions (between 99 and 139 questions, in the various criteria) were requested, on a Likert scale of 1 to 5 points (1 – Strongly Disagree; 2 – Disagree; 3 – Neutral; 4 – Agree; 5 – Strongly Agree).

This self-assessment was developed to understand the requirements and elements related to IS audit, based on best practices and standards in business process architecture, design, and quality management. The objective was to perceive the current practices and management procedures of the self-assessment elements clearly and quickly. With this questionnaire format any manager, even with a limited knowledge about the auditing practices of information systems, can understand the As-Is in which your organization is, the respective result can serve as a starting point for the implementation of an information system audit in the organization. This questionnaire can also serve as a basis for gathering evidence that can help support the first phase of the lifecycle of an information systems audit, known as the planning phase.

4. Analysis of the Results

In the universe of the 15 companies, all of them of an industrial nature, that is, with daily manufacture of products, the process proposed by Gerardus Blokdyk (2020) was adopted, and companies were asked to answer the questions that allowed, for each criterion, define the current state of the company in terms of auditing information systems.

Regarding criterion 1 (Recognize), 28 % of companies obtained a rating of 4 or higher, which demonstrates that there is a global recognition of the importance of IS audit for the organization. These companies are mostly certified or in the process of food certification, which, in a way, ends up influencing their closer proximity to other types of audits, specifically IS. The result shows a recognition by companies of an urgent need for better knowledge of the organization and the need to improve processes and controls. However, 72 % of companies showed little interest in IS auditing.

Regarding criterion 2, a relatively satisfactory result was found, as 28 % of companies assigned a maximum rating, and only 21 % agreed. This means that almost most companies that have recognized the need for change in their organizations have moved towards a clear definition of what or what the problems of the organization are, and what their needs and objectives are. However, we can also conclude that a significant part has not considered a specific organizational approach relevant in this field.

Regarding criterion 3 (measure), the result of companies with classification higher than 4 was 21 %, aligning with criterion 1. From the analysis of the answers to this criterion, it is clear that there is an almost perfect alignment between the first three criteria, that is, practically all organizations that recognized the need to implement changes in the organization have already implemented initiatives of clear definition about what or what are the problems, needs, and objectives of the organization and characterization of the As-Is and, in this sense, will be better prepared to support change projects to be implemented at a later stage.

From analysis to criterion 4 (Analyze), it appears that there is a lower number of companies concerned with the analysis of the causes that led the organization to the current situation (only 7 % of the companies). Most associate this type of issue with the growth of the company and the use of IS in their processes and, therefore, consider that it is only now natural to have a more active concern with the IS audit. They also consider that the investment, in this specific case, both financial and technological resources should be focused on the future and improvements, and not on identifying what went less well in the past.

In criterion 5, 36 % were companies with classification 4 or higher. It is noticed that there is a growing number of companies concerned with the improvements of IS and that they realize the importance of developing practical solutions to respond to the problems identified and realize how the organization can innovate, test new solutions, and measure results. Here, too, there is an informal relationship between the result of the evaluation on this criterion and the level of innovation the company implemented in its products, services, and processes. It is observed that there is a greater concern with the search for solutions in companies that have higher levels of maturity in terms of innovation.

In terms of criterion 6 (Control), the percentage of companies with a rating higher than 4 returns to be lower, reaching only 14 %. In the observation of the answers within this criterion, it is verified that the limitation of human resources and internal technical training in the procedures related to the audit are the main factors for a low level of implementation.

Criterion 7 (Sustain) back is aligned with criterion 6 (Control) since in organizations where the IS audit process was implemented there is a global recognition of the positive impacts of the audit and the need to continue in the process of continuous improvement.

5. Conclusions

The relevance of the IS audit in the current context of economic organizations and, above all, with strong dependence on IS and ICT. Information systems currently support a large part of organizational processes, whether financial, operational, commercial, among others, and end up having a key role also in supporting other audit processes, in this case, with a more evident focus on food security. This relevance can be easily understood when comparing the legal requirement in this sector of conducting a food safety audit with IS audits. There is an undeniable proximity and it is also emphasized in this study. However, it should also be noted that many small and medium-sized enterprises adopt these practices when required by law. This means that audits at the ISD level are usually for a secondary plan.

It was evident that factors such as the low rate of training that characterizes the sector, the high turnover of resources, and the existing weaknesses at the IS level condition the efficiency of operations and the quality of products and services delivered to customers. These weaknesses also influence the low need in the implementation of audit processes. However, there is sensitivity to this issue and the assumption of its relevance in the context of organizational development. The need to implement processes that support the continuous improvement of the company is still something required by external stakeholders, such as customers, regulatory entities or even by company partners. It was also apparent that the IS auditing is often confused with the food safety audit. the fact that these companies are not the target of major media exposure, do not have confidential information from their customers, and even are often at the beginning or middle of a value chain, makes them feel unappealing to cyber-attacks or information theft by third parties. However, when talking about the theft of product revenues or documents related to production processes, the alertness of those responsible increases considerably.

References

Akoka, Jacky & Wattiau, Isabelle. (2010). A framework for auditing web-based information systems. *ECIS 2010 Proceedings*. 58.

Axelsen, M., Green, P., & Ridley, G. (2017). Explaining the information systems auditor role in the public sector financial audit. *International Journal of Accounting Information Systems*, 24, pp. 15–31.

Bedard, J. C., Graham, L., & Jackson, C. (2005). Information systems risk and audit planning. *International Journal of Auditing*, *9*(2), 147–163.

Blokdyk, G. (2020). Information Systems Audit A Complete Guide - 2020 Edition – Paperback – March 9, 2021, 5STARCooks Publishing.

Carneiro, A. (2009). *Audit and Control of Information Systems*, FCA Publishing *(In Portuguese)*.

ISGec. (2019). Information Systems Governance. Results of surveys to Large Companies and Public Administration in Portugal, Information Systems Governance – Concepts, good practices and case studies, Information Systems Governance–Portugal, Chiado Publishing, pp. 203–239 *(In Portuguese)*

Dimitrova, J., Andonovski, M., Temjanovski, R., & Dimitrova, E. (2016). Information systems auditing–legislation and standards. In *International Balkan and near eastern social sciences conference series (IBANESS)*. Faculty of Economics. Prilep.

Gelinas, U. J., Dull, R. B., & Wheeler, P. (2018). Accounting information systems. Cengage AU.

Laudon, K. C., Laudon, J. P., & Traver, C. G. (2021). Essentials of Management Information Systems Fouteenth Edition Global Edition.

Oliveira, A., & Anunciação, P. F. (2022). Teaching of information systems in Portugal – Teaching of informatics and information systems, in the last 50 years in Portugal. Some contributions to its history. In Ramos, I., Sousa, R. D., & Quaresma, R. (eds.), (2022). *Information systems – Diagnostics and prospective*. Sílabo Publishing, pp. 57–92 *(In Portuguese)*.

Oliveira, A. (2023). Journey through the Brave World of Business Sciences – From Fernando Pessoa to the Digital Revolution, Sílabo Publishing *(In Portuguese)*

Peret, P. (2023). *Information system audit – How to control the digital disruption.*

Pfleeger et al. (2015). *Security in computing*. 5th Edition.

Rahman, A. A. B. L., Al-Nemrat, A., & Preston, D. S. (2014). Sustainability in Information Systems Auditing. *European Scientific Journal*. September 2014 / SPECIAL/ edition Vol. 3 ISSN: 1857 – 7881 (Print) e – ISSN 1857 – 7431, pp. 458–472.

Rodríguez, R. (2005). Basic concepts of information systems auditing. In *Auditing Information Systems* (pp. 1–24). IGI Global.

Whitman, M. E. & Mattord, H. (2018). *Management of Information Security*, 4th Edition.

Pedro Fernandes da Anunciação, Denis Ribeiro Patrocínio, &
Cátia Susana Claro Chasqueira

Industry 4.0 Digital Evolution Maturity Index

1. Introduction

The term Industry 4.0 (I4.0), introduced as a strategy by the German government to enhance Germany's leadership in industry, particularly in production (Yin et al., 2018), initiated a fresh industrial landscape and a new industrial revolution (Kagermann et al., 2013), the fourth one, characterized by technological advancements, like the shift from analog to digital, which had a notable influence, particularly in the electronics sector (Yin et al., 2018).

Digitalization, facilitated by electronics and Information Technologies (IT), has advanced to the creation and integration of Cyber-Physical Systems (CPS), Internet-of-things (IoT), and the Internet of Services (Jazdi, 2014). CPS, IoT, and smart factories are the three primary components of I4.0 (Kagermann et al., 2013). The electronics, software, and sensors integration, ensures network connectivity for data collection and exchange over the Internet. The incorporation of intelligent systems (CPS) into production networks has enabled the creation and operation of a virtual environment that complements the physical. This allows interaction from the virtual with physical devices and the detection and action in the real world (Negri et al., 2017). There are two key components in this Industry 4.0 environment. IoT facilitates communication between assets (Atzori et al., 2010), and CPS integrates the physical and virtual realms (Lee, 2008). These two key components, crucial for the advancement of smart factories, drive the evolution of organizational dynamics by implementing advanced automation in emerging collaborative supply chains (Radziwon et al., 2014). In the industrial setting, particularly in production, the goals of I4.0 include the advancement of the production system through smart manufacturing, involving the integration of humans, technology, and information (Kang et al., 2016), and the enhancement of products through Smart Product, enabling a product to control its production process and incorporate service concepts based on its features (Porter & Heppelmann, 2015).

This disruptive scenario highlights the need arising from the integration of technology with the economy and society. Companies must have the capability to acknowledge this evolution and incorporate these disruptive technologies into their processes, organizational dynamics, and change management. Often, many organizations fail to comprehend their implications (Porter & Heppelmann, 2015), lack the necessary technologies (Moeuf et al., 2017), or are apprehensive about the significant investments involved (Theorin et al., 2016). To address these issues and develop suitable plans, it is crucial for companies to comprehend their current maturity level concerning I4.0 (As-Is) and use this as a basis to establish a transformation roadmap (Becker et al., 2009). Only companies that grasp their current situation (As-Is) and have a clear direction will be able to progress (To-Be). Only then will they be ready to grasp and meet the innovations and demands of I4.0 (Schwab, 2017).

This is a path with no return (Anunciação, 2014). Digital transformation in the industrial context will inevitably involve the implementation of cyber-physical systems connecting processes, people, machines, and products. Companies must evolve towards critical factors of the digital economy, such as the necessity of connectivity, real-time access to information, systems with performance and outputs suitable for economic requirements, ubiquity in accessing information systems (IS), and information processing, among other examples. From an economic standpoint, Industry 4.0 is anticipated to facilitate the development of more comprehensive and interconnected ecosystems, enabling novel operational methods and the emergence of fresh business models through a more efficient and integrated link to consumers. This connection introduces another concept and associated reality concerning services. It brings forth the concept of Service 4.0, which illustrates the organization's interaction with its customers and how it adjusts its operations and offerings based on customer proximity. All these perspectives will challenge the architecture of IS, as they will necessitate responses to this new holistic, relational, and connectivity context, arising from a collaborative environment and flexible means of production. This gives rise to the concept of organizational urbanism (Anunciação, 2016) (Anunciação & Zorrinho, 2006) as a strategy to address the demands of the various contexts arising in integrated logistics chains and the array of digital distribution and customer service channels.

To this end, it is crucial in the management field for companies to evaluate their I4.0 development level. Using Maturity Models (MM) to assess the level of industrial companies is significant (Schumacher et al., 2014). Although some existing models may suggest that classification depends on evaluators' subjective opinions, implying that they may not yield accurate results and are prone to uncertainty and imprecision in real-world applications (Tan et al., 2017), and despite some confusion in the literature regarding maturity (Kohlegger et al., 2009), it is believed that adopting an objective maturity model can be a crucial tool for identifying the current state of any company and supporting the development of the most suitable strategies.

2. Understanding the Industry 4.0

Despite the high level of interest in Industry 4.0 by academics and professionals (Hermann et al., 2016), there is still a lot of confusion about vocabulary and themes. For instance, Industry 4.0 and Industrial Revolution 4.0 are frequently used interchangeably. However, the first refers to the initiative of the German government under a national program that was followed by other themes worldwide, such as the Factories of the Future in the European Commission's Horizon 2020 program. The term Industry 4.0 was introduced in research and gained popularity in society because, while individual changes in the production sector can be seen as an evolution of the current third industrial revolution, there is a consensus that the speed and impact of these advancements have led to the fourth industrial revolution (Schwab, 2017). The terms Industry 4.0 and Industrial Internet are still confusing, as it's not clear which provides a more holistic view, and they can sometimes be used interchangeably (Wang et al., 2016).

An interesting contribution comes from Thoben et al. (2014), highlighting the amount of technology required by the innovative system designed to respond to the revolution of Industry 4.0, extending the concept of Industrial Internet to the whole industry, even using the term Industrial Internet of Things (IIoT), which focuses especially on the interconnectivity of industrial assets. Its main objective is to strengthen modern industries with three pillars: process optimization, resource consumption optimization, and the creation of complex autonomous systems (Mourtzis et al., 2016). Industry 4.0 is the popular name given to a set of innovations brought about by the extensive use of intelligent industrial devices with built-in sensing and communication capabilities that can be easily interconnected (Philbeck & Davis, 2018).

3. Context of the Maturity Model for I4.0

Maturity is a theory of evolution based on stages, whose main objective is to describe the stages and trajectories of maturation through a maturity scale (Finnerty et al., 2017). In this context, MM establishes a basis for evaluating and measuring the performance of an organization and, in addition, provides a framework for the strategic planning of investments, thus ensuring continuous improvement and progression toward the company's objectives (Hackos, 1997). Since MM guides how to move forward along the maturity plan (Antunes et al., 2014), they differ considerably from techniques such as gap analysis and benchmarking. The latter are, however, very reliable methods for comparing and assessing maturity, but cannot be used as stand-alone solutions. Instead, they are complementary techniques in measuring maturity that can be used, for example, to understand the goal of an organization that intends to achieve once defined the level of maturity (Tonelli et al., 2016).

Despite the vast amount of literature, MM cannot be defined without ambiguity. The root of this problem lies in the design of MM, whose tables are often too specific in the application and object to be measured (Wendler, 2012). In recent years, useful attempts have been made to organize the design of MM, to provide the main phases of the development of generic models (De Bruin et al., 2005) and to define a structured method to develop a specific MM (Becker et al., 2009). Since the design method proposed by Becker et al. (2009) emerged in the literature, it has been widely used. The authors propose a general model of procedure in eight phases with seven requirements. Each phase meets one or more requirements, and all phases need scientific documentation. On the other hand, De Bruin et al. (2005), who can be considered pioneers in defining the design of the MM, propose a six-stage framework, the first and second stages of which determine the scope and design or architecture of the model. The first allows the establishment of external limits for the application and use of the model, by requiring the definition of the objective of the model and the actors involved in the development. The second is the basis for further development and implementation, requiring the definition of five criteria, namely the public; the method and engine of application; respondents; and finally, the final application. The other fundamental stage is the population of the model, that is, the way to gather the content. Lastly, the model is evaluated, deployed, and constantly updated (i.e., the maintenance phase).

Considerable efforts have been made to assess the level of deployment of Industry 4.0. This assessment is relevant as it allows companies to understand any delays and where more resources need to be committed to speed up the transition. A large part of the maturity evaluation models starts with a self-assessment approach, in which each company can verify the level of implementation by compiling a questionnaire, which is designed to evaluate its own maturity model. The importance of evaluating companies' readiness to adopt Industry 4.0 is due to the need for companies to introduce information and communication technologies in manufacturing processes and comprehend what is still required to accomplish this task.

4. Objectives and Methodology

The objectives of this research were to assess the degree of maturity of Industry 4.0 in the economic sector of the bakery industry. The choice of this sector derives from the cultural relevance that bread has in Portuguese food, the criticality of bread and derivatives as food products associated with primary and daily needs, the high production rates, as well as the need to show those responsible for some companies the state of maturity in which they are. The study was created in collaboration with the representative association of this economic sector, referencing companies located in the Lisbon area. A sample of companies with different market shares and turnover volumes was identified.

Although in the field of academic research, there are several understandings about the MM, it was decided to adopt the pragmatic model, adopted by a suitable entity related to the business and industrial companies in Portugal. The choice fell on the evaluation model of COTEC-Portugal (THEIA – Technological and Holistic Engagement for Industry 4.0 Assessment). COTEC-Portugal is the main Portuguese business association for the promotion of innovation and business technological cooperation with the mission of supporting the development of the industry. The THEIA is a tool that aims to improve the business of small and medium-sized enterprises, making it easier to switch to digital in close collaboration with their business. By using this model, one can assess digital maturity and transition to the new paradigm of Industry 4.0, while also identifying areas for growth in digital maturity (COTEC, w.d.).

This instrument (THEIA) allows organizations to reflect on and evaluate their digital capabilities and define their positioning strategies in the future, regarding Industry 4.0. From the identification of the As-Is, it is intended that this evaluation constitutes a starting point for the definition of a roadmap that allows to start of a path for the desired digital transformation (To-Be).

The analysis dimensions adopted in the study, according to the model, were: «Innovation and change management», «Management of intangible assets», «Operations and processes», and «Customer orientation». In each dimension, we analyzed the following subdimensions (COTEC, w.d.):

- Innovation and change management:
  - Vision and objectives are the desired direction and way the organization intends to be perceived in the market, according to ambitions, positioning in the industry, identification, and forecasting of trends, and its ability to integrate opportunities.
  - Talent requires timely identification of employee requirements and needs for new digital and technological skills, as well as appropriate acquisition strategies, such as recruitment, training actions, and partnerships.

- o Culture and leadership foster an inclusive organizational culture that provides new opportunities to employees, listens to them, and values them as key parts of the transformation.
- o Innovation eco-system establishing relationships with stakeholders to allow the organization to leverage synergies within and outside the activity sector and benefit from related value chains or joint developments of new products or solutions.
- o Innovation eco-system established relationships with stakeholders to allow the organization to leverage synergies within and outside the activity sector and benefit from related value chains or joint developments of new products or solutions.

- Management of intangible assets:
  - o Knowledge management is the ability to enjoy information that facilitates the development of necessary knowledge levels to generate competitive advantages, stimulate innovation, and promote organizational sustainability.
  - o Risk management and cybersecurity ensure the existence of a prevention policy and culture, with the implementation of a set of practices for the identification, analysis, evaluation, treatment, and reporting of major risks, as well as mitigation plans, to manage risk and safeguard the confidentiality of information.
  - o Technological integration defines an application architecture that allows the integration of platforms between the various links in the value chain, making it a connected and transparent ecosystem.

- Operations and processes:
  - o Horizontal and vertical integration in the value chain ensures information sharing and system integration between stakeholders, providing a complete view of the value chain. By creating an ecosystem that is connected, transparent, and more efficient, we can respond to changes in demand with greater agility, whether from an internal (internal) or external (external) integration perspective.
  - o Flexibility of operations creates conditions to ensure greater flexibility in operations, ensuring greater efficiency and responsiveness in time required by changes in the market and provision of personalized products/services in small quantities, with minimal impact on replenishment operations.
  - o Proactive decision-making about the adoption of technologies, such as Artificial Intelligence, which enables the ability to analyze and forecast/ identify equipment failures, changes in demand patterns or production conditions, and facilitate decision-making autonomously and immediately, acquiring knowledge through experience, changing the paradigm of response to external and internal change needs. Consequently, enhancing the efficiency and profitability of operations.
  - o Financing is the ability to define, in advance, the financing needs associated with the implementation of the technological innovation strategy, ensuring the adequacy of the budget to the defined objectives, and balancing overall budget planning and project financing.

- Customer focus:
  - o New products and services through the adoption of new processes of creation of products/ services through the use, for example, of data collected regarding the

consumption of existing products/ services, and co-creation of offers with customers or other partner entities.

- o New sources of revenue through the possibility of offering their products/services based on alternative business models, typically associated with the digital economy, such as subscription models, payment models per use or platform models (where revenue is generated through the aggregation and facilitation of interactions between two or more stakeholder groups).
- o Customer knowledge is the ability to collect and monitor data regarding the purchase and use of the products and services offered, by incorporating technologies in them (e.g. sensors, RFID, geolocation systems) and their connectivity, allowing to identify trends and customer needs.
- o Channels and connectivity as a presence in digital channels, namely on own websites, online commerce platforms, and social networks, enhancing access and acquisition of new customer segments, the collection of opinions, and the creation of communities.
- o Customer experience includes the collection and analysis of information throughout the customer experience allowing the creation and customization of experiences, and customizing the offer according to their needs, behaviors, and preferences.

The scale of evaluation and classification of the maturity of the companies was based on a scale of Likert, in which the following levels were considered: Level 1 – Non-existent maturity; Level 2 – Low maturity; Level 3 – Some digital transformation initiatives, but without strategy; Level 4 – Adoption of non-integrated strategies; Level 5 – Existence of a defined and integrated strategy.

5. Results Analysis

The analysis of the four dimensions indicated above was carried out from a sample of 15 small and medium enterprises in the bakery industry located in the region of Lisbon, Portugal. To understand their digital maturity assessment in detail, each company was asked to answer a 30-question questionnaire proposed by the THEIA model.

Regarding the first dimension, «innovation and change management», when asked about the existence of a technological innovation strategy in line with the market context and the company's overall vision, 71 % of companies consider incorporating technological innovations in their strategy. However, in only 29 % of cases, it was possible to identify a detailed action plan for achieving objectives aligned with innovation. The distance between thinking about innovation and setting clear objectives for its implementation derives, to a certain extent, from the feeling that technological innovation materializes only in the acquisition of technological equipment that allows the automating of production lines, leaving out the remaining dimensions of the manufacturing process. Other dimensions should also be considered, such as the appropriate planning of production needs and resources strictly necessary to avoid waste, the creation and maintenance of audit and quality plans that contribute to the standardization of the product, or the implementation of digital systems for traceability records and HACCP (Hazard Analysis and Critical Control Point) that allow to respond unequivocally to legal and consumer requirements. Regarding the active and regular demand for information on technological innovation trends in the sector, the entire sample answered affirmatively, invoking mainly the presence in fairs and congresses specific to the sector. Despite this, no company has stated that they will devote full-time resources to monitoring technological innovation trends.

The monitoring of the technological evolution plan was not accompanied by specific KPIs (Key Performance Indicators) by any of the companies. Regarding talent management, there is a growing concern about the technical training of human resources in technological areas, with 50 % of companies saying that they consider, in their annual training plan, actions aimed at valuing their employees in this type of skill. The low training that characterizes the human resources of the sector has been, to some extent, one of the biggest obstacles to the adoption, for example, of IS that allows for efficient management of all the operational activity of the company, creating barriers to the implementation of these systems. Regarding training focused on themes such as information security and risk management, the percentage of companies investing directly in this type of training falls to 14 %. It has been observed that risk management is only carried out in most companies through the quality management systems mandated by law within the minimum requirements stipulated by law.

From the analysis of the subdimension Culture and leadership, most innovation processes are defined in a top-down model, with little or no involvement of employees in defining the strategy.

When addressing the organizational dimension and processes, there were some encouraging results, as 57 % of managers expressed concern with horizontal and vertical integration in the value chain. In reality, significant distances are still observed, with only 21 % of companies successfully investing in integrated and future-ready IS. The managers of these companies are actively concerned about the flexibility of operations, with 71 % declaring it as a priority for their business. Here too, the execution rates are considerably low. Modernization investment is mainly aimed at purchasing more modern manufacturing equipment, leaving out the digitalization and automation of processes that enable greater global operational efficiency.

The customer orientation dimension had a more positive contribution to the level of digital maturity of the business. A continuous strategy of creating new products to respond to market needs was identified by 43 % of the companies. The growth of new digital channels has been constant and has resulted in greater proximity to the customer. There is, however, a long way to go towards the customer, towards transparency in product information, on the techniques and safety standards adopted by the company and to efficiently systematize and integrate the relevant information about the customer, what they are looking for, the level of experience perceived and what their preferences and requirements.

6. Conclusions

The digital transformation of the economy and companies is not a management option. This is a disruptive challenge that is reflected in production, information systems, and communication technologies, as well as in the relationship with partners and, above all, in the economic relationship with customers. Any of the innovations referenced, Internet-of-Things, Cloud Computing, or Artificial Intelligence will open new, competitive, and sustainable opportunities for industrial units, so their management should be attentive to this organization and economic revolution.

From the analysis of the four dimensions and subdimensions made to a sample of 15 industrial units in the bakery industry, we can conclude that the digital maturity level of the sample is low and that, although it has been evident that a positive path has been made in recent years, to some extent enhanced by the Covid-19 pandemic and the strong change in consumption patterns since then, there is still a long way to go to integrate digital transformation in the company's strategy, as a way to achieve the desired operational excellence.

It would be interesting to carry out a study broader to the sector and, above all, to be able to reflect with the generality of the respective entrepreneurs the results now obtained.

References

Antunes, P., Carreira, P., & Mira da Silva, M. (2014). Towards an energy management maturity model. *Energy Policy*, vol. 73, pp. 803–814.

Anunciação, P. F. (2016). Organizational urbanism: A value proposal for the generation of organizational intelligence to healthcare institutions – The case of a Portuguese Hospital Center. Handbook of Research on Information Architecture and Management in Modern Organizations, Chapter 21, 458–486.

Anunciação, P. F., & Zorrinho, C. (2006). *Organizational urbanism – How managing technological shock in companies*. Lisbon: Sílabo Publishing (*In Portuguese)*.

Atzori, L., Iera, A., & Morabito, G. (2010). The Internet of Things: A survey. *Computer Networks*, vol. 54, no. 15, pp. 2787–2805.

Becker, J., Knackstedt, R., & Pöppelbuß, J. (2009). Developing maturity models for IT Management, Bus. *Information Systems Engineering*, vol. 1, no. 3, pp. 213–222, 2009.

De Bruin, T., Freeze, R., Kaulkarni, U., & Rosemann, M. (2005). Understanding the main phases of developing a maturity assessment model, Australas. *Chapter of the Association for Information System*, pp. 8–19.

Finnerty, N., Sterling, R., Coakley, D., & Keane, M. M. (2017). An energy management maturity model for multi-site industrial organizations with a global presence. *Journal of Cleaner Production*, vol. 167, pp. 1232–1250.

Hackos, J. T. (1997). From theory to practice: Using the information process-maturity model as a tool for strategic planning. *Technical Communication*, vol. 44, no. 4, pp. 369–380.

Hermann, M., Pentek, T., & Otto, B. (2016, January). Design principles for industrie 4.0 scenarios. In 2016 49th Hawaii international conference on system sciences (HICSS) (pp. 3928–3937). IEEE.

Jazdi, N. (2014). Cyber physical systems in the context of Industry 4.0, 2014 IEEE Autom. Qual. Testing, Robot., pp. 2–4, 2014.

Kagermann, H., Helbig, J. Hellinger, A., & Wahlster, W. (2013). Recommendations for implementing the strategic initiative INDUSTRIE 4.0: Securing the future of German manufacturing industry; final report of the Industrie 4.0 Working Group. Forschungsunion.

Kang, H. S., Lee, J. Y., Choi, S., Kim, H., Park, J. H., Son, Y. S., Kim, B. H., & Noh, S. D. (2016). Smart manufacturing: Past research, present findings, and future directions. vol. 3, no. 1, pp. 111–128.

Kohlegger, M., Maier, R., & Thalmann, S. (2009). Understanding maturity models. Results of a structured content analysis.

Lee, E. A. (2008). "Cyber Physical Systems: Design Challenges," 2008 11th IEEE International Symposium on Object and Component-Oriented Real-Time Distributed Computing (ISORC), Orlando, FL, USA, 2008, pp. 363–369, doi: 10.1109/ISORC.2008.25.

Moeuf, A., Pellerin, R., Lamouri, S., Tamayo-Giraldo, S., & Barbaray, R. (2018). The industrial management of SMEs in the era of Industry 4.0. International journal of production research, 56(3), 1118–1136.

Moeuf, A., Pellerin, R., Lamouri, S., Tamayo-Giraldo, S., & Barbaray, R. (2018). The industrial management of SMEs in the era of Industry 4.0. International journal of production research, 56(3), 1118–1136.

Mourtzis, D., Papathanasiou, P., & Fotia, S. (2016). Lean rules identification and classification for manufacturing industry. Procedia CIRP, 50, 198–203.

Negri, E., Fumagalli, L., & Macchi, M. (2017). A review of the roles of digital twin in CPS-based production systems. *Procedia Manufacturing*, vol. 11, no. June, pp. 939–948.

Philbeck, T., & Davis, N. (2018). A quarta revolução industrial. *Journal of International Affairs*, 72, 17–22.

Porter. M. E., & Heppelmann, J. E. (2015). How smart, connected products are transforming companies. *Harvard Business Review*, vol. 2015, October, 2015.

Radziwon, A., Bilberg, A., Bogers, M., & Madsen, E. S. (2014). The smart factory: Exploring adaptive and flexible manufacturing solutions. Procedia Engineering, vol. 69, pp. 1184–1190.

Schwab, K. (2017). The fourth industrial revolution. Currency, World Economic Forum - Committed To Improving the State of the World, Edipro.

Schumacher, A., Erol, S., & Sihn, W. (2014). A maturity model for assessing Industry 4.0 readiness and maturity of manufacturing enterprises. *Procedia CIRP*, vol. 52, pp. 161–166.

Tan, Q., Tong, Y., Wu, S., & Li, D. (2017). Evaluating the maturity of CPS in discrete manufacturing shop-floor: A group AHP method with fuzzy grade approach, Mechanika, vol. 24, no. 1, pp. 100–107.

Theorin, A., Bengtsson, K., Provost, J., & Lieder, M. (2016). An event-driven manufacturing information system architecture, vol. 0, pp. 1–17, 2016.

Thoben, K. D., Busse, M., Denkena, B., & Gausemeier, J. (2014). System-integrated Intelligence–new challenges for product and production engineering in the context of Industry 4.0. Procedia Technology, 15, 1–4.

Tonelli, F., Demartini, M., Loleo, A., & Testa, C. (2016). A novel methodology for manufacturing firms value modeling and mapping to improve operational performance in the industry 4.0 era. *Procedia CIRP*, vol. 57, pp. 122–127.

Wang, S., Wan, J., Zhang, D., Li, D., & Zhang, C. (2016). Towards smart factory for industry 4.0: a self-organized multi-agent system with big data based feedback and coordination. Computer networks, 101, 158–168.

Wendler, R. (2012). The maturity of maturity model research: A systematic mapping study. *Information and Software Technology*, vol. 54, no. 12, pp. 1317–1339.

Yin, Y., Stecke, K. E., & Li, D. (2018). The evolution of production systems from Industry 2.0 through Industry 4.0. *International Journal of Production Research*, vol. 56, no. 1–2, pp. 848–861, Jan 2018.

Patricia da Silva Alves Schütz & Pedro Fernandes da Anunciação

Data Science and Unintentional Unethical Behavior

1. Introduction

The convergence of the physical and digital worlds presents several opportunities and challenges. Opportunities include increased connectivity, more personalized experiences, new business models, easier and improved decision-making, innovation and economic growth, social development, among other aspects. However, technological innovation, and particularly its usage, does not always protect, respect, or value the human person. Society's attraction to new technologies is normal, as is the desire to assimilate innovation, either as a competitive advantage for companies or as a form of social identity for most people, particularly younger generations.

These factors cause the most innovative technologies to become integral parts of people's lives and economic and social activities, especially in urban centers and developed countries. Information technologies underpin a new, more active, faster, and innovative lifestyle where data and information are accessed in real time and communication is carried out continuously online. We are permanently connected and accessible. However, technological innovation is not always accompanied by ethical and legal frameworks that protect most of people's rights and freedoms. The ability to define, develop, and adopt ethical and legal standards to protect people regarding ancestral aspects like freedom, responsibility, justice, independence, respect, safety, or morality is often developed reactively and slowly. The lack of proactivity in this area means that even when some aspects of an ethical or legal framework emerge in response to new technological contexts, they are often surpassed by the latest disruptive innovations.

The importance of the human dimension associated with technological developments, especially regarding the relationship between technological innovation and respect for human dignity in matters like privacy or data security, is a current reality widely discussed in scientific and technical forums. Industry 5.0, for example, clearly focuses on the human aspect through the development of human-centered technologies, aiming to create a super-intelligent society, known as Society 5.0, which combines the physical and digital worlds to provide a high quality of life (Mourtzis et al., 2022). The technological dynamic is an irreversible movement. Society is increasingly marked by this dimension, and technologies like 5G, virtualization, cloud computing, the Internet of Things, and artificial intelligence (AI) will continue to influence human development and challenge society to navigate a technological framework (Tyagi et al., 2023)

However, as mentioned earlier, progress is not always supported by new values, principles, and norms that enable the adoption of new technologies based on justice and human respect. In data science specifically, the field has been driven by technological innovations advancing faster than laws and compliance regulations can keep up.

It is encouraging to see the growing need to reflect on and discuss ethics in the current development framework. However, many debates lack clarity and certainty regarding the impacts of technological change. They often do not conclude whether a new ethical dimension is needed in data processing by algorithms over which there is little or no control. In many situations, it is challenging to define what should or should not be considered ethical or correct. Society's attraction to innovation often prevents it from addressing or delimiting the ethical dilemmas posed by these innovations. The rapid adoption of new technologies by individuals or companies can lead to distortions and unforeseen consequences. Furthermore, the associated dilemmas highlight the lack of training and preparation among technology professionals concerning human behavior and the social context in which their solutions will be applied.

In data science, professional competence is based on STEM areas (Science, Technology, Engineering, and Mathematics). This sector is predominantly male (STEM Women, n.d.), and the lack of diversity in teams can lead to unconscious biases that negatively influence behavior, driving decisions and actions that contradict ethical values, often without the individuals involved realizing it (Sezer et al., 2015). These biases are particularly prominent in homogeneous teams, especially in terms of gender, creating "blind spots" that foster unethical behavior, with adverse impacts on specific groups and society in general. Therefore, it is essential to go beyond usual models and tools and integrate ethical and responsible principles from conception through development and implementation, seeking economic and social benefits (Júnior & Júnior, 2023).

The objective of this article is to identify and analyze the sensitivity of future data science professionals to ethics based on the guide developed by the Royal Statistical Society (RSS) and the Institute and Faculty of Actuaries (IFoA) in the UK (RSS&IFoA, 2019). This study aims to mitigate the impact of gender biases in algorithms. One example of gender bias can be found in machine learning methods, such as "word embeddings," with a specific task suggested on a checklist to mitigate these biases (Gendered Innovations, w.d.). In summary, data science professionals should consider ethical aspects in their work to positively contribute to society while maintaining high professional standards.

2. The Importance of Ethics and a Guide for Ethical Data Science

Economic, political, and social events often highlight the importance of ethics. As a universal concept spanning all professions, ethics should be an inalienable value, respected, promoted, and encouraged by everyone. Its relevance within the Information Society context arises from the potential for asymmetrical and dichotomous societal development, specifically (Anunciação, 2014):

- A universalist dimension versus a culture of individualism, as technologies open the door to global knowledge and action but simultaneously promote widespread individualism, focused on the user's interests and aspirations;
- A confidentiality dimension versus a culture of exposure, as technologies enable personalized treatment through individualized channels, but also facilitate high exposure by allowing access to individual information; and,
- A development dimension versus a culture of exclusion, as the Information Society has a collective, social, and global dimension of development that grows with technology adoption, while creating exclusion movements for those who cannot follow it.

Ethics highlights the set of conduct norms considered more or less absolute and universally valid, which allow for the analysis and evaluation of individuals' conduct and behavior, with the aim of distinguishing between good and evil, right and wrong. (Anunciação, 2014). Ethics should establish ideal laws for human activities, against which people can and should assess their actions. In data science, according to Floridi & Taddeo (2016), data ethics is a branch of ethics that studies and evaluates moral issues related to data (generation, recording, curation, processing, dissemination, sharing, and use), algorithms (artificial intelligence, machine learning, artificial agents, and robots), and corresponding practices (responsible innovation, programming, hacking, and professional codes) in order to formulate and support morally good solutions (for example, correct conduct or values).

Analysis tools and the abundance of data sources available to organizations and individuals create a potentially rich environment, allowing for detailed insights at low costs, providing new opportunities through economic knowledge. Due to the challenges posed by data access and processing, initiatives have been developed to regulate and document a set of guidelines for data scientists. One of these initiatives is associated with the Royal Statistical Society (RSS) and the Institute and Faculty of Actuaries (IFoA) in the UK, which developed a guide for Ethical Data Science. The guide aims to promote ethical data science practices and encourage professionals to consider the potential societal implications of their work. By following the guide's principles, data scientists can contribute positively to society while minimizing harm and maintaining expected professional standards. The five domains outlined in the guide are:

- Value of data science for society: Data scientists should use their expertise to benefit society, sharing the advantages and considering the potential societal implications;
- Avoid and prevent harm: Professionals are advised to respect individual and group privacy, equality, and autonomy, denounce potential ethical violations, and fulfill legal and regulatory obligations;
- Professional competence: Professionals should adhere to best practices, use robust statistical methods, assess benefits versus risks, and regularly review models;
- Maintaining reliability: Work should be based on transparency, honesty, and stakeholder engagement to increase the reliability of work and results;
- Accountability and oversight: Ensure human oversight, understand when to delegate decisions to systems, and establish essential governance mechanisms, especially considering when delegating decision-making to systems.

Data science practices are influenced by factors such as sector, organizational structure, or previous analytical processes, as well as team diversity and skill sets. Regarding the latter, STEM Women (n.d.) reports that women represented only 26 % of the workforce in these fields in 2022. In Information Technologies, this percentage is even lower 19 % in 2022. These figures reveal a gender imbalance that, if race is also considered, could reveal other biases. Behavioral sciences have been studying unethical and dishonest behavior over the last decade. An interesting finding is that many "inappropriate" behaviors are classified as unintentional. According to Sezer et al. (2015), unintentional unethical behaviors can be promoted by three main "ethical blind spots": implicit biases, temporal distance from ethical dilemmas, and decision-making biases, which cause individuals to misjudge others' unethical behavior.

In the case of implicit biases, these can directly impact data science. Because the sector is predominantly male, the algorithms developed can contain "ethical blind spots" due to the homogeneity of professionals. The guide addresses the "Application and Maintenance of Professional Competence," highlighting the importance of following best practices and legal and regulatory requirements to demonstrate professional competence. This involves understanding data errors and distortions, using clean data, and employing robust statistical and algorithmic methods.

Professionals are encouraged to assess the benefits of their respective work against the associated risks, ensuring regular review of models to maintain their relevance and accuracy. By advocating for professional competence, data scientists can enhance the quality and integrity of their work, mitigate potential risks, and contribute to the ethical practice of data science. The guide also provides an implementation checklist for the recommendations. This dimension of competencies further references "Analysis and Development in Data Science."

To incorporate ethics into data analysis, model building, and system design, professionals should:

- Apply permitted uses and consent, professional and regulatory requirements;
- Monitor risks identified during planning and assess additional risks (harm, bias, error, privacy);
- Apply best practices, develop analytical rigor, ensure methodological quality, and foresee peer reviews;
- Minimize model and algorithm complexity and conduct thorough validation;
- Clearly communicate results and uncertainty when making recommendations.

The guide does not specifically address implicit race or gender biases in developed models. For instance, gender bias is found in machine learning methods like "word embeddings," which map words to geometric vectors. While these can capture analogies such as "man is to king as woman is to queen," they also reflect stereotypes, linking "man" to "doctor" and "computer programmer" while "woman" is linked to "nurse" and "homemaker" (Bolukbasi et al., 2016). To mitigate implicit algorithmic biases, the checklist should include an item explicitly addressing this issue.

3. Objectives and Methodology

The objective of this study was to explore the sensitivity of future data scientists to the main ethical dimensions as a framework for their future professional roles. To achieve this, we referenced the guide developed by the Royal Statistical Society (RSS) and the Institute and Faculty of Actuaries (IFoA) in the UK for Ethical Data Science. We asked a sample of postgraduate students in data science to rate the relevance of each indicated dimension on a Likert scale, considering its importance in professional practice.

The selection of RSS and IFoA was based on their mission to promote good ethical practices in data science and encourage professionals to adopt these practices. The dimensions considered were "Project Planning," "Data Management," "Analysis and Development of Models and Systems," "Implementation and Result Delivery," and "Communication and Supervision." Each dimension included:

- o **Project Planning** – Integrating ethics into Data Science projects, specifically:
  - Public interest and fairness in value distribution.
  - Ethics at the data origin.
  - Risks (privacy, harm, justice).
  - Evaluation of stakeholder perceptions.
  - Early feedback from experts.
  - Project governance (security, data handling, etc.).
- o **Data Management** – Integrating ethics in data management (acquisition, storage, and preparation):
  - Consents for legal data use.
  - Security measures and proper team training in data handling.
  - Awareness of the impacts of data processing on privacy, bias, and errors.
- o **Analysis and Development of Models and Systems** –Incorporating ethics into the models and system design:
  - Consents, professional and regulatory requirements.
  - Risk monitoring (planning, etc.) and assessment of additional risks (harm, bias, errors, privacy).
- o **Implementation and Result Delivery** – Integrating ethics in the operationalization and implementation of models and systems:
  - Transparency in decision delegation.
  - Sharing methods, results/limitations, and code with relevant parties; inviting feedback.
- o **Communication and Supervision** – Incorporating ethics in communications:
  - Communicate with stakeholders throughout the projects and assist any non-technical individuals in understanding technical and ethical issues.
  - Be honest and objective in communicating about the work.

For this purpose, 11 students with different academic backgrounds were selected, some at the beginning and others finalists in postgraduate studies in data science for enterprise, forming a focus group to share opinions on the topic under study.

4. Analysis of Results

The study sample comprised 11 postgraduate Data Science for Business students. Of these, 46 % have been studying for more than two years, 27 % started less than a year ago, and 27 % are in their final year. Professionally, 60 % of respondents currently work in data science, while 40 % expect to start soon. Of those already working, 50 % are in private institutions, 33 % in public, and 17 % in both. The remaining 40 % have not yet started working in data science. These contextual details help clarify the formation of opinions on ethics in data science and can shape how participants perceive the ethical issues explored.

- **Project Planning Dimension**

There's a strong consensus on the importance of various ethical aspects. Most respondents significantly value public interest and justice, with 60 % agreeing fully and 40 % agreeing. Data origin ethics is also highly valued, with 82 % fully agreeing and 18 % agreeing. This sentiment is reflected in the importance of risks related to privacy, harm, and justice, with a high sensitivity to potential negative impacts. Stakeholder perception assessment and early expert feedback underscore the need for diverse perspectives, though 36 % were neutral about the latter. Project governance, including security and ethical data handling, is considered crucial by 82 % of respondents. However, 40 % do not fully agree on the necessity of planning, which might affect subsequent sub-dimensions.

- **Data Management Dimension**

Respondents exhibit a strong commitment to ethical practices in data management and handling. Most acknowledge the importance of obtaining proper consents for legal data use, with 82 % fully agreeing. Similar percentages are observed for robust security measures. The need to train teams for responsible data handling is strongly emphasized, with 70 % fully agreeing. Furthermore, there's a strong awareness of the privacy impact, bias, and errors in data processing, as 64 % fully agree and 36 % agree. Regarding data quality and rigorous cleaning practices, 45 % fully agree, 45 % agree, and 10 % are neutral. For bias detection and mitigation, 73 % fully agree, and 27 % agree. This dimension shows increased percentages of neutral or agreeing responses, revealing room for stronger assertions.

- **Analysis and Development of Models and Systems**

There is a clear commitment to ethics, quality, and transparency in analytical practices. The majority of respondents (64 %) fully agree, while 36 % agree. Professional and regulatory compliance, as well as continuous risk monitoring, were less emphasized, with 45 % fully agreeing and 55 % agreeing. Compliance with legal and ethical standards is recognized, as is the potential impact of data models. Regarding best practices and analytical rigor, 55 % fully agree, and 45 % agree. While most value methodological integrity and high standards, the responses reflect challenges. For model complexity minimization, 45 % fully agree, 37 % agree, and 18 % are neutral. Despite recognizing the need for clarity and transparency, implementation challenges remain evident.

- **Implementation and Result Delivery**

Respondents adhere strongly to principles of transparency, sharing, anonymization, and quality assurance, demonstrating their commitment to responsible practices. There's robust agreement, with 73 % fully agreeing and 18 % agreeing. On transparent decision delegation and sharing methods, 55 % fully agree, 36 % agree, and 9 % are neutral. Data anonymization before publishing results is crucial, with 82 % fully agreeing and 18 % agreeing. For adequate system quality assurance, 45 % fully agree, and 55 % agree, highlighting the importance of independent validation and scientific transparency.

- **Communication and Supervision Dimension**

Respondents show a strong commitment to clear and honest communication, emphasizing ethical and community involvement in projects. Most (64 % fully agree, 36 % agree) value effective communication with stakeholders, making technical and ethical issues accessible. Honest and objective communication is widely recognized, reflecting a commitment to integrity and transparency. Most respondents (73 % fully agree, 18 % agree, and 9 % are neutral) emphasize professionals' responsibility to ensure that organizations understand and implement appropriate ethical principles. Active engagement with ethical bodies, privacy groups, and the public is valued by 55 % who fully agree, while 36 % agree and 9 % remain neutral. This highlights a dedication to transparency, responsibility, and inclusiveness in data science projects.

5. Conclusion

The analysis of survey responses on ethics in data science demonstrates a robust awareness and commitment among respondents to integrating ethical practices throughout various project phases. From data management to communication and supervision, there is a notable concern for adhering to ethical principles that ensure not only data and system integrity and quality but also transparency and social responsibility.

The issue of bias in algorithms, which often goes unnoticed by professionals due to a predominant focus on technical skills over ethical, social, and philosophical considerations, remains a challenge in the field. The topics presented in the Data Science Ethics Guide provide a framework for data scientists to address ethical considerations in their work, enabling them to contribute positively to society while mitigating potential harm and upholding high professional standards. To prevent biases, such as gender bias, the guide should explicitly include a task to "debias" potential distortions in models and systems developed in data science.

However, the results of this study, in some dimensions, fall short of strongly and significantly expressing the relevance of ethics in data science. In the future, we hope that the study will be expanded to a larger population to obtain more significant results among students and professionals associated with data science.

References

Anunciação, P. A. (2014). Ethics, sustainability and the information and knowledge society. Chiado Publishing. *(In Portuguese)*

Bolukbasi, T., Chang, K. W., Zou, J. Y., Saligrama, V., & Kalai, A. T. (2016). Man is to computer programmer as woman is to homemaker? Debiasing word embeddings. *Advances in Neural Information Processing Systems*, 4349–4357.

Floridi, L., & Taddeo, M. (2016). What is data ethics? *Philosophical Transactions of the Royal Society A*, 374 (20160360), 20160360. http://dx.doi.org/10.1098/rsta.2016.0360.

Gendered Innovations. (w.d.). Machine learning. Stanford University. Retrieved from https://genderedinnovations.stanford.edu/case-studies/machinelearning.html#tabs-2, on 25/03/2024.

Júnior, F. D. M., & Júnior, P. D. M. (2023). Opportunities and challenges of integrating the physical and digital worlds. *Computing – Brazilian Computer Society Journal*, 51, 8–12. *(In Portuguese)*

Mourtzis, D., Angelopoulos, J., & Panopoulos, N. A. (2022). Literature review of the challenges and opportunities of the transition from Industry 4.0 to Society 5.0. Energies, *15* (6276), 6276. https://doi.org/10.3390/en15176276

Royal Statistical Society (RSS) & Institute and Faculty of Actuaries (IFoA). (2019). A guide for ethical data science. Retrieved from https://rss.org.uk/RSS/media/News-andpublications/Publications/Reports%20and%20guides/A-Guide-for-Ethical-Data-Science-Final-Oct-2019.pdf, on 28/04/2024.

Sezer, O., Gino, F., & Bazerman, M. H. (2015). Ethical blind spots. *Current Opinion in Psychology*, 6, 77–81. https://doi.org/10.1016/j.copsyc.2015.03.030

STEM Women. (s.d.). Women in STEM: Statistics, progress, and challenges. Retrieved from https://www.stemwomen.com/women-in-stem-statistics-progress-and-challenges, on 26/04/2024.

Tyagi, A. K., Dananjayan, S., Agarwal, D., & Ahmed, T. H. F. (2023). Blockchain – Internet of Things applications: Opportunities and challenges for Industry 4.0 and Society 5.0. *Sensors*, 23 (947), 947. https://doi.org/10.3390/s23020947

Pedro Fernandes da Anunciação & Filipe António de Lemos

Information Systems Project Management in Multinational Companies

1. Introduction

Many companies, especially the most mature and focused on the provision and services associated with information systems and technologies (IST), often adopt a project-based approach in the development and execution of their economic activities (Kock et al., 2020). This is a relevant approach in the development of IST as a project that is conditioned to the needs and specificities of the respective clients (Durmic, 2020). The conditioning of project success to the various factors associated with it requires, in principle, a rigorous performance of those who provide this type of service. Success in Information Systems (IS) projects is a challenge (Takagi and Varajão (2020).

And, in this context of IST companies, it is important to highlight two dimensions. The first refers to nature. Any intervention at this level, whether in software development, architecture, change management, or audits, among other examples, usually presupposes interventions of functional and technical teams in a well-defined period and with well-defined resources. The temporal dimension and resources, including financial resources, are conditioned by the contractual value associated with the provision of services, previously agreed between the service provider and the customer (Zalozhnev & Peremezhko, 2022). Any deviations from deadlines and resources presuppose new negotiations between the stakeholders involved and possible budgetary corrections if agreed with the client, or the assumption of losses if the deviations are assumed by the service provider. These situations show the relevance of knowledge and experience required in project management.

The second refers to technological innovation, which, being often recent, does not allow the existence of a degree of maturity of the technical teams sufficient to explain, with a low level of risk, the allocation of resources, including temporal, inherent to the development of technological solutions to support organizational information systems. This reality often increases the complexity of the projects creating greater difficulties for the teams in justifying the viability of the projects. On the other hand, it is emphasized that there is a natural tendency of customers to adopt the latest technological innovations even if it is not clear the full exploitation of existing technological potentialities. Considering that technological innovation and economic and organizational change go "hand in hand" it is considered that a demanding project management can help in the introduction of technological innovation and help in obtaining associated economic advantages, as there is no "magic steps" for the development of IS. The development of IS corresponds to a difficult, complex, and abstract process, which must be carried out in close harmony with organizational objectives and strategies so that the associated project management is assumed as a critical success factor.

Project management thus proposes a coherent and rigorous conceptual and management approach. But sometimes is not the most appropriate approach to complex construction projects subject to successive changes (Lalmi et al., 2021). This does not mean that it can be deduced that management, in general, should not be consistent and rigorous but objectives and organization of the various resources to achieve the defined objectives dictate the need for particular attention to identification, planning, management, and control of the project to ensure an adequate level of execution, on the one hand, to what was previously planned, and strict compliance, on the other hand, with the set of commitments made between the client and the service provider.

It should also be noted that, in addition to the success of the project being directly associated with the fulfillment of the objectives and the satisfaction of the client's needs, there are still results that, although they may seem secondary, may often condition the performance of the established contract. It is normal that investments in information technologies (hardware or software), for example, are associated with expectations of efficiency, effectiveness, or productivity gains. Similarly, it may also be expected that projects of technological innovation and reorganization can expect competitive benefits (Barbiero et al., 2022). In the same line of thought, it is important to bear in mind that many of the IST projects depend on the change management associated with the introduction of new technologies, and the change may be, in some cases disruptive.

As an IS perspective, it is essential to adopt a holistic and systemic perspective for IST projects. The development of IS, the rearchitected resulting from technological innovation, the introduction of new application solutions, the realization of investment in hardware, the management of IS, and the audit of ITS, among other examples, require a systemic view at the conceptual level of the interventions to be carried out in the field of IS. Projects are conceptually unique and generate unique products or services (Varajão, 2022). This conceptual particularity forces managers to avoid standardization in their approach and management.

2. Software Houses and Project Management

A software house corresponds to a company whose economic activity focuses on IST. In this sense, it covers a set of specificities specific to the respective activity. The first aspect that should be highlighted is the proximity and dependence that has with the customer. The respective activity is directed to each client, individually and according to the specificities found, which are usually reflected in constraints in the projects developed. This dimension supports the conceptual aspect of the unique specificity of each project developed. A second dimension refers to the normal involvement and participation of those who provide the service in a value chain, which usually begins in design and ends in construction. For example, if we consider software development we will be talking about the phases of analysis, design, construction, implementation, maintenance, and training. A third dimension refers to the ICT expertise that is required in some projects. It is normal for a project to bring together a team of qualified professionals, such as software engineers, programmers, interface designers, systems analysts, project managers, among other professionals. These diverse teams must be prepared to respond to the diverse demands associated with design, design, planning, architecture, implementation, testing, and training. Outputs can match applications, web platforms, enterprise management systems (ERPs), mobile software, and more, tailored to each customer's unique needs. In addition, it is still expected that through this customization, customers will achieve higher levels of efficiency, automation, and innovation, which is a challenge to the integration of ICT in the modus operandi of customers.

Project management requires maturity and at this level, it is expected that, among other things, these companies, due to their experience, have, as a critical success factor, the ability to develop and implement management systems and control the cost and time of projects; adopt permanent practices to improve project management skills; develop integrated cost and time control practices, among other things.

To ensure the success of a project, the team must select the appropriate processes within the project management process groups that are necessary to meet the project objectives; use a precise approach to adapt the product specifications and plans, to meet the requirements of the project and the product; comply with the requirements to meet the needs, wishes and expectations of the stakeholders; and, balance the competitive requirements of scope, time, cost, quality, resources and risk, to produce a quality product (Miguel, 2009). It is certain that the success of a project beyond the fulfillment of the elements mentioned above, also depends on the project manager. It is expected a good leadership capacity includes strong interpersonal and communication skills, business and technology knowledge, competence in risk management, and a good integrator.

All these traditionally relevant elements in project management are currently exponentially valued in a new context of the software development industry resulting from the globalization of economic activities. It becomes difficult, especially after the pandemic period that has recently conditioned most companies and the economy, to justify the realization of software development projects or in the broader field of IS. Within the organizations themselves, whether suppliers or customers, for reasons of efficiency or effectiveness, most IS service providers have adopted the development of virtual projects (Miguel, 2006). It becomes less and less economical or competitive, develop software solutions within the same company or even within the same country. In this new reality, we can have members of a single team who can work from home or offices in different locations, different teams that can develop different parts of a product in different locations, or have a development team in one location and a maintenance team in another location (Hennel & Rosenkranz, 2021).

In this sense, it is important to know the challenges of international companies that develop products and services in IS as well as to understand the practices they develop to adapt to market challenges.

3. Objectives and Methodology

This paper aims to analyze the project management practices in international companies that provide services in the field of IS and adopt these practices in the development of their economic activities. To this end, through the adoption of the case study methodology (Yin, 2018), the analysis will focus on identifying the specificities of project management in a multinational company with representation in Portugal. The conceptual principles associated with project management will be taken into account in the analysis.

The methodology adopted was the establishment of a Focus group (Bloor et al., 2001), at various levels, which involved five project blinds and one country manager, aiming to identify the practices adopted in daily life and assess, according to the principles, models and conceptual tools usually identified, the benefits achieved.

The focus of analysis in the various meetings focused on the management of the scope (how the scope of the company is managed before the start of the project, after starting, during the project, reflections of the change of scope in the budget, team, etc.); Project management (how project management is prepared, team definition, planning, change management, monitoring and control, etc.); Economic and financial management (how the economic and financial management of projects is carried out, feasibility analysis, budget management, customer value identification, risk management, etc.); Evaluation and control (instruments adopted for the evaluation and control of projects, performance indicators, performance indicators, deviation, etc.); e, Team management (how project teams are managed, concerning selection, participation management, risk management, culture, leadership, etc.).

4. Case Analysis

Regarding the first point addressed, scope management, it was evident that this relationship differs from project to project. The company reveals some differentiating practices of the conceptual scope that traditionally support project management. In the Focus group it was stressed the importance of bearing in mind the specificity of the economic nature of the activities developed, which can condition the traditional phases of project development and management. The provision of services in the field of IS is often faced with some difficulties that begin as soon as the definition of the scope. It is not always easy for customers to understand or explain their IS needs. They know what they need but have difficulty in relating what is intended with the ITS and, above all, projecting the impacts of the new desired reality.

This is a difficulty that may be related to a weak domain and knowledge of the various ICTs that allow a clear perspective on the benefits and potential they can bring to the economic activity of their organizations and, even a more concrete and precise dialogue with the project manager or the technical team. If we consider the variety of interventions that can be developed, such as software maintenance and technology solutions, the identification and implementation of innovative technological solutions; development of customized solutions; maintenance and support; digital transformation; architecture; mobile application development; web development; Implementation of integrated Business Management Systems (ERPs); E-commerce solutions; Consulting; Cybersecurity, among others, it becomes difficult to often specify the needs, frame the scope of the project and, consequently, plan the project.

Thus, it was mentioned, as current practice, that the company develops before defining the scope of the project with the client, a process of approximation and eventual negotiation with the objective of "proposing/ selling" certain portfolios or projects that can meet the needs of the client. These proposals, even if more comprehensive than the needs, have the merit of alerting the customer to the systemic effects of many interventions at the IST level. This approach can be initiated by the company or by the client himself, who contacts the company explaining his needs. In this specific case, an analysis of the opportunity is carried out, being designed, and an architecture is associated with the technological solution that will respond to the specificity of the customer's needs. This proposal is prepared by the pre-sale team. Then, the same team begins the preparation of a commercial proposal, with the breakdown of unit values of equipment, and resources involved, including humans, which will serve as a basis for identifying the respective profile. The services to be provided to the client after completion of the project are also identified and detailed, resulting in a budget proposal that is sent to the client. Based on this proposal and only for management guidance is defined the expected return on investment (ROI), as well as calculated the desired financial profitability.

Another interesting aspect refers to the constitution of the project team. After the award by the client is appointed a project manager who assumes the authority and responsibility for the management of the same. After this appointment is presented the project team, which is not defined by him, but by the Manager of the corresponding Business Unit, based on the technical profile necessary to perform, with quality, the tasks to be performed. This practice results from the fact that the organization is organized by business units, and the respective "borders" are defined according to the associated technological area. Whenever there is a need for a multidisciplinary team, elements belonging to several business units are affected. From this moment, the project manager initiates the project with an internal meeting, to know the details of the project, and meetings are initiated with the technical team, in order to prepare a schedule, and consequently the project plan and the kickoff meeting. The project manager has the responsibility to consolidate the charter project producing a document, which will be sent to the client, with a set of more consolidated information and which is subject to the client's approval, in particular, presentation of the technology and its competitive advantages (technical approach), presentation of the assumptions and scope of the project, presentation of the schedule and implementation plan, presentation of the project team, presentation of the communication plan; identification of risks (documenting the risk description, category, responsible team (client or provider), impact and strategy to adopt, as foreseen in ISO 31000).

Regarding project management, it is emphasized that, during the project and respecting the defined communication plan, control points are made to monitor the development of activities. If it is necessary to assess any changes to the plan initially planned, a systemic perspective and collective responsibility is adopted, involving internally the commercial area, pre-sales and responsible for the business unit, so that there is a strategic alignment with a given change to the scope of the ongoing project. During the course of the activities, between internal control meetings and with the client, informal or formal, a financial monitoring and control is carried out, accompanying all existing costs and revenues for the project. For this purpose, we use a financial platform that is integrated in the SAP software, with several pillars of financial and accounting control, the main ones are: time value consumed by project participants, subcontracting (if necessary), travel expenses (meals or trips), value of equipment (purchases), miscellaneous expenses, billing/receipt by the customer, grants/financial provisions associated with the project, interest payable/receivable from the group to which the organization belongs. In this specific point, it is important to highlight an innovative way of managing financial resources. The company, in the field of financial control, assumes the need to manage globally the costs associated with the various projects under development, whether these current or future costs. In this sense, it is worth noting the particularity of, in this process, the business group (holding), to which the Portuguese organization belongs, being able to charge or remunerate (interest) associated with the project whenever the execution of the planned work does not follow the stipulated billing. Taking as a reference the proposed planning, if it is delayed and if at the date of control, it was expected to be invoiced a value corresponding to 75 % of the project value to the client, start to be charged late interest to the project team that will affect them to the budget initially planned and agreed with the client. However, in reverse logic, if the performance of the work is in advance of the planning and billing is in accordance with the planning of the tranches of payments to be made, the project team can credit interest in its budget associated with the project. Thus, this is a policy of internal accountability of project managers/ teams knowing that throughout the involvement in the various projects will have to manage surplus or deficits and account to top management regarding the performances achieved. On the other hand, they have the responsibility to proactively manage the payments associated with the project minimizing any risks related to possible cash difficulties of the client. Thus, although there is a financial culture of invoicing to the customer from the initial stages, this is a practice that cannot be applied inflexibly to all customers, since, in the case of public organizations, there are stricter rules that only allow invoicing to these bodies to be carried out after the completion of all activities. In this case, the risk is lower in that it is the Government that assumes the role of customer. Interestingly, still in the field of project control, some traditional indicators are not adopted in the evaluation of performance, such as the time-consuming index or the cost performance index. The assessment of compliance with planning is carried out with the support of the Gant chart associated with the project, which can lead to analysis biases that can compromise the success of the same.

Throughout the project, although the Project Manager has authority, should always alert the head of the business unit, namely, whenever the scope changes, it is necessary to allocate new resources, the project is delayed or advanced, etc. Every month the project management "reorganizes" the projects, with a view to controlling costs and income, namely, regarding the hours/ effort of the project, various expenses (equipment, transport, etc.) as well as the control of interest that must be paid or received from the holding company.

5. Conclusions

It is evident the relevance and requirement of project management. In companies where there is a close relationship with the customer, such as those that carry out their activities within the ITS, and where the products or services developed have unique characteristics related to the needs and objectives of customers, project management is a critical success factor. In the case analyzed are evident some characteristics that are usually not included in the associated literature.

The first is explained in the intervention of the commercial team, for a first negotiation of a portfolio of products or services, even if this presentation seeks to meet their needs. It can be understood that there may be a broader commercial focus than the analysis of the customer's need. On the other hand, although it was not possible to ascertain, it is the commercial team that prepares the proposal and architecture associated with the technological solution that will respond to the specificity of the customer's needs. This means that, subsequently, the project team will be conditioned to the solution presented by the commercial team. It was also not possible to ascertain whether alternatives of solutions equally suited to their needs were presented to the customer.

Another interesting aspect refers to the presentation of the project team to the project manager. This means that the project manager has no responsibility for choosing the members of the team he will lead. Among the documentation that you must present to the client, (technical approach, project team, communication plan, risk plan), it is not evident the presentation of a detailed budget that allows the client to understand the resources associated with the project and its cost.

A final aspect that should be highlighted is the adoption of an integrated perspective of project financial management and not a singular focus on each project. Through a debit or credit accounting of the benefits or losses that may occur, the financial rigor is cultivated, and the expected revenues are ensured. Still in this context, it was found that they have not adopted performance evaluation, such as the index of time spent or the index of cost performance.

5.1. Limitations and Future Work

The main limitation was the adoption of a case study. Although it is a multinational company, with significant wealth and experience in the field of project management, given the theme and relevance of the subject in companies providing services in the field of information systems and technologies, it would be interesting to develop a broader study to other companies to eventually compare the practices adopted in project management and even identify best practices. On the other hand, it would be relevant to analyze the opinion of professionals participating in projects to identify the practices adopted and the degree of success associated with them.

References

Barbiero, G., de Almeida Junior, N. S., de Araújo, C., & Sato, A. F. (2022). Good practices ITIL adoption in PMBOK based information systems projects. *Brazilian Journal of Development*, *8*(2), 10670–10691. *(In Portuguese)*

Bloor, M., Frankland, J., Thomas, M., & Robson, K. (2001). Focus groups in social research. London: Sage Publications.

Durmic, N. (2020). Information systems project success factors: Literature review. *Journal of Natural Sciences and Engineering, 2*

Hennel, P., & Rosenkranz, C. (2021). Investigating the "socio" in socio-technical development: The case for psychological safety in agile information systems development. *Project Management Journal*, *52*(1), 11–30.

Kock, A., Schulz, B., Kopmann, J., & Gemünden, H. G. (2020). Project portfolio management information systems' positive influence on performance–the importance of process maturity. *International Journal of Project Management*, *38*(4), 229–241.

Lalmi, A., Fernandes, G., & Souad, S. B. (2021). A conceptual hybrid project management model for construction projects. *Procedia Computer Science*, *181*, 921–930.

Miguel, A. (2006). *Management of software project management*. FCA Publishing

Miguel, A. (2009). *Modern Project Management – Best techniques and practices*, 4th Edition. FCA Publishing.

Takagi, N., & Varajão, J. (2020). Success management in information systems projects – Work-in-progress (2020). CAPSI 2020 Proceedings. 32.

Varajão, J., Lourenço, J. C., & Gomes, J. (2022). Models and methods for information systems project success evaluation–A review and directions for research. *Heliyon*, *8*(12).

Yin, R. (2018). *Case study research, design & methods* (5ª ed). Thousand Oaks: Sage.

Zalozhnev, A. Y., & Peremezhko, D. V. (2022). IT project management: Supply chain optimization for service operations. *IFAC-PapersOnLine*, *55*(10), 2505–2508.

Oriana Helena Negulescu

Impact of Artificial Intelligence on Companies' Strategy and Business Management for Performance

1. Introduction

Business strategy is a company's initiative to create value for the organization and its stakeholders and gain a competitive advantage in the market. It is crucial to a company's success and is needed before any goods or services are produced or delivered (Boyles, 2022).

It is known that a strategy includes a company's vision, mission, values, strategic objectives, systems, and structures that are translated into activities. In order to create and improve its strategy, a company needs relations with all its stakeholders: suppliers for materials and equipment, which requires spending money; employees to make the product or services at a margin cost; customers to sell value at a price; and shareholders to approve the statement.

The company must create and continuously update its strategic resources and competencies to implement the strategy.

On the other hand, artificial intelligence (AI) creates new opportunities for innovation and enables businesses to reinvent their operations. AI impacts nearly every industry, from manufacturing to hospitality, healthcare, and academia, by giving machines the growing capacity to learn, reason, and make decisions. Without an AI strategy, organizations risk missing out on AI's benefits (Finio, 2023).

The world of business today is experiencing continuous and rapid change. Globalization, technological advancement, climate change, and social pressure are the four most essential forces inducing change.

If globalization and the advance of technology are predominantly positive forces that lead to the creation of business development conditions, climate change, and social pressure are predominantly negative forces that are difficult to manage and inhibit company performance.

Under these conditions, the balance can be established by changing the strategy based on considering the maximum interest in AI – a product of the advance of technology.

AI is in full swing and is, for the future, the solution for the balance of forces and performance (Fig. 1)

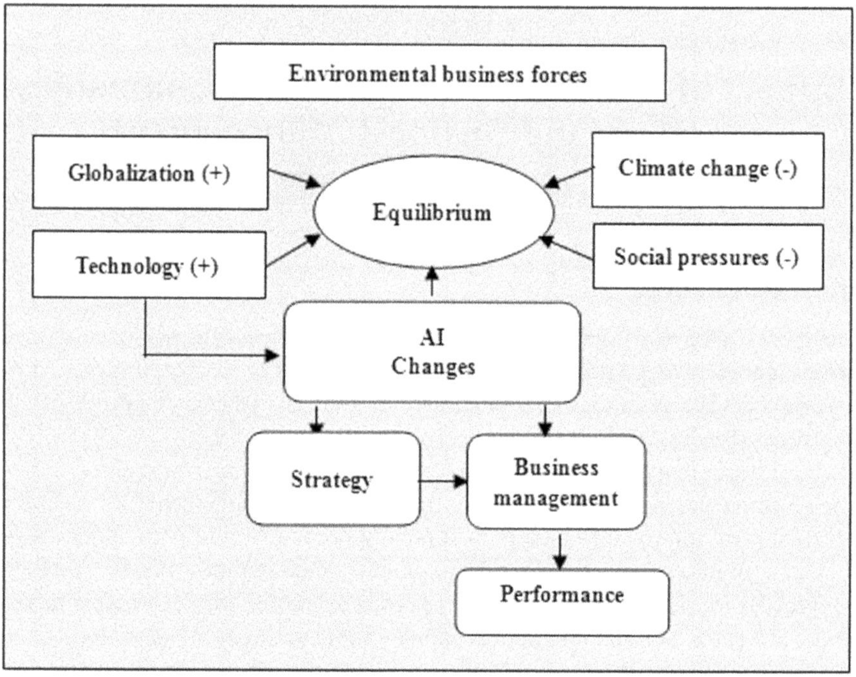

Fig. 1. AI – source for the balance of forces in business
(Source: own concept)

In the context briefly presented in Fig. 1, AI becomes the engine of changing the company's strategy and, of course, the entire management process. Therefore, the question arises: How does artificial intelligence change a company's strategy? The answer to this question is the purpose of this chapter.

The research methodology is based on grounded theory (Glaser & Strauss, 1967). This is supported by secondary data collection, structured observation, analysis, synthesis, and conceptualization.

2. General Context of AI in the Strategy and Business Management

In the context of strategy, Marvin Minsky, the pioneer of artificial intelligence research in the 1960s, spoke of artificial intelligence as a "suitcase word" – a term you can put anything you want into. Regarding this term, Atsmon (2023) stated that this is still the case, as companies should use more traditional analytics capabilities while increasing strategy automation. The author emphasizes that AI cannot replace managerial thinking with a machine. However, it could help it perform various tasks: descriptive analysis (dashboard), diagnostic intelligence, predictive intelligence, and others. Also, implementing AI for predictions better identifies what can or cannot be controlled in volatility and vulnerability to external events.

In the age of digital transformation, big data, and the need for speed to run organizations, AI advances can build on better decisions than humans in certain unique situations, and humans can make better choices when critical thinking is needed (Xing et al., 2016; Tabesh et al., 2019).

A successful AI strategy is indispensable. It supports business objectives, facilitates prioritization, optimizes talent and technology options, and ensures an orchestrated integration of AI that will support organizational success (Finio, 2023). The author proposes 9 steps for developing a practical artificial intelligence strategy, including clearly defining the objectives and building a roadmap. Instead, Montgomery (2021) considers that an enterprise that uses AI must comply with 15 principles to maintain its competitive advantage, including having governance, ethics, and security built in from the beginning.

In short, traditional businesses in almost every sector are under attack by digital disruptors that effectively harness the power of communities (Reillier, 2017).

3. The Process of Strategy and Business Management Changes Due to AI

In the current global conditions, shown in Fig. 1, AI becomes the main driver for change. In Fig. 2, the entire process of change is conceptualized. Change targets are strategy and business management; barriers and risks intervene in this process. However, positive effects are obtained at the end of the steps, beginning to be reported in the EU.

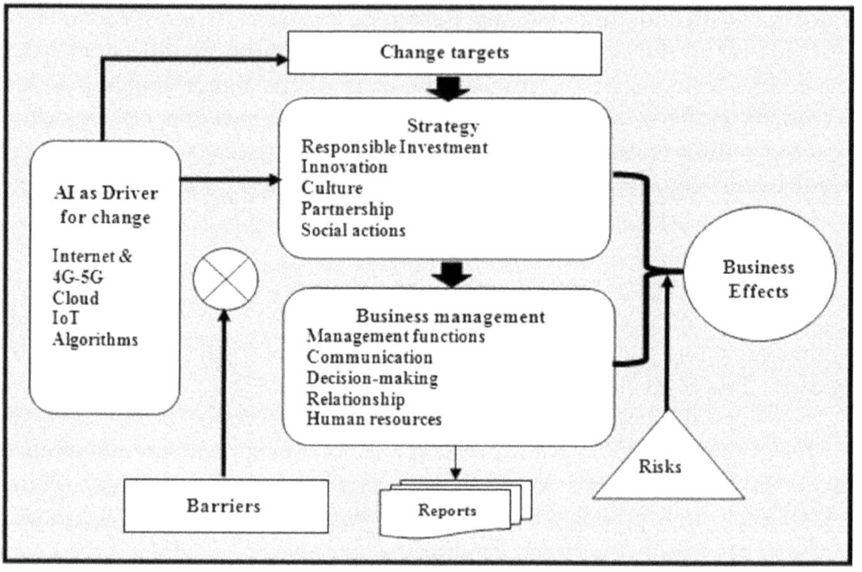

Fig. 2. Process of strategy and business management change due to AI (conceptualization)

(Source: own concept)

3.1. AI as a Driver for Change

It has been almost 30 years since the Internet was part of the lives of companies and us personally. During this time, the technology has been perfected so that the coverage area and the speed of transmission of messages and data have continuously increased through better connections, reaching 4 G and 5 G. Research is already being done for the transition to 6 G. Satellite connections they allowed the creation of the cloud, in which massive databases can be stored and found with various search engines.

At the same time, the electronics industry developed. Computers have increased capacity; smartphones have various functions, as well as TV sets. The connections between equipment and devices that work in networks, the so-called Internet of Things (IoT) based on. They allow command and control or detect environmental changes from a distance through sophisticated software.

Artificial intelligence, through increasingly technologically advanced algorithms, makes possible applications that were unimaginable not long ago. Thus, many production companies use automation, digital twins, and/or mixed teams of workers and cobots throughout the value chain.

Augmented reality allows the virtual world to be superimposed on the real world, and virtual reality is introduced through the computer and a headset into an imaginary or virtual world.

On the other hand, artificial intelligence teaches computers to process data, almost like the human brain. Based on historical data, generative technology allows the production and simulation of images, text, voice, or content used in marketing, sales, and other activities.

In this sense, artificial Intelligence platforms are used: chatbots, deep learning software, and machine learning software, each having different functions (Rajkumar, 2024).

All these advances, briefly presented, have led to profound changes in the company's strategy and business management.

3.2. Change Targets

3.2.1. Strategy Change

The stakeholders' main strategic objectives now and in the future are responsible investments- including AI, supporting innovation, organizational culture, partnerships, and social actions.

(1) Responsible Investment

Responsible investments are the key to business development. Responsible investment is an investment approach that explicitly acknowledges the relevance to the investor of environmental, social, and governance (Tabur, 2023) factors and the long-term health and stability of the market. (CISL) Investments in AI and cyber security meet these goals.

Investors are increasingly looking for ways to align their investments with their values and support companies prioritizing social and environmental responsibility, such as optimizing energy consumption with AI. In financial investments, AI offers automated investment advice and portfolio management services. Algorithms in the platforms analyze market trends and individual investor preferences to provide customized investment strategies for profitable solutions (Leadershiptribe, 2024).

Technology has evolved from capturing the imagination of customers to capturing billions of dollars in collective revenue. However, disparities remain stark within the industry. Companies on this year's AI 50 have raised $34.7 billion in funding. Almost a third of that total comes from OpenAI, thanks to about $10 billion from Microsoft (Cai, 2024).

Investments in cyber security are essential for protecting digital assets because these systems, even if they are robust, are also vulnerable to cyber threats. Cybersecurity is not a separate IT issue but a critical business function that impacts every aspect of the organization (Leadershiptribe, 2024).

Staff training, capacity management, and an in-depth understanding of the organization's specific risk landscape are as vital as technology investments (Mitchellson, 2024).

(2) Creativity and Innovation

Until recently, human creativity was the only source of artistic and intellectual production, but the capacity of AI brings it to its limits. AI developers are researching how the creativity of machines is used within ethical limits while preserving human value. Thus, creative platforms will promote an inclusive digital future and pave the way for emerging talent from every corner of the world, supporting the emergence of talent regardless of geographic and socio-economic barriers (Kazim, 2024). But, A platform business requires learning a whole new set of management rules, such as Uber, Airbnb, Amazon, and eBay (Reillier & Reillier, 2017).

(3) Culture Change

AI is changing organizational culture by encouraging people to learn algorithms and how to use them, create and innovate, respect ethical principles, and adopt and adapt to change because "AI marks a new interaction model between humans and computers" (Spataro, 2023).

Artificial intelligence enables senior management to maintain a proactive and compliant organizational culture, fostering stakeholder trust and confidence (Takyar, 2021) and identifying employee behaviors and attitudes toward change through predictive analytics and machine learning.

Resistance to change builds a proactive, resilient, change-ready culture and encourages adaptation and innovation. The automation capabilities of AI simplify administrative tasks, and managers can focus on the strategic aspects and human elements of change management (Moulton, 2014).

As organizations embrace AI, the impact on organizational culture will only grow, propelling them toward a future of endless possibilities and constant evolution (Bath, 2024).

(4) Partnership and Cooperation

Since costs are high, partnerships and cooperation are necessary to reduce costs and provide free access to AI's benefits. Partnerships are established between companies specializing in AI and user companies, including their suppliers.

Advanced AI technologies, research, and product creation may necessitate vast computer resources available only in substantial computing centers. According to some estimates, the total electricity demand for information and communications technologies (ICTs) might account for up to 20 % of the worldwide electricity demand by 2030, up from approximately 1 % (Jeevanandam, 2023).

These partnerships ensure "integrated cloud strategies, new possibilities for data-driven insights and transforming industries through intelligent automation, and developing edge solutions that move processing capabilities closer to data sources." (Tullur, 2024)

(5) Social Actions

In the new strategies involving the development of ESG, AI is present to help in social actions like social care, digital companionship with chatbots, social media communication, and digital information in the real world by using chatbots, social media tools, virtual reality (VR), and augmented reality (AR) (Rizbi, 2024; Ox, 2024; Castelfranchi, 1998).

Generative AI, such as AI chatbots, can help with various tasks in social care. However, many social activities directly affect people's human rights and well-being (Ox, 2024).

Harnessing AI responsibly and ethically encourages social interactions and a more connected and inclusive digital society instead of isolation (Rizbi, 2024).

3.2.2 Business Management Change

Changes in business management due to the use of AI affect the essential functions of management, decision-making, communication methods, and relationships with suppliers and customers, as well as human resources

(1) Basic Management Functions

The principles on which the traditional management functions are based – Planning, Organizing, Commanding/Staffing, Coordinating/Leading, and Controlling (Fayol, 1916; Koontz & O'Donnell, 2005) are changing due to the use of AI algorithms. Thus, the main implications of AI in management functions, according to Takyar (2021), are:

Planning. Predictive Analytics, forecasting models, scenario analyses, digital twins, and marketing research make planning much easier and more anchored in environmental changes. This allows companies to know customers' preferences and plan activities along the entire value chain based on them.
Organizing. The organization is made more efficient by automating processes, replacing routine work with AI tools, allocating resources and distributing tasks,
Staffing. Staffing is helped by AI tools for recruiting, training, and performance evaluation by "making data-driven decisions regarding staffing levels, skill gaps, and organizational structure" (Takyar, 2021)
Leading. Leading is helped by using AI tools to optimize time management, analyze employee skills, prioritize tasks, and customize employee training needs. Leading also assists in detecting potential conflicts and finding ways to stop or diminish their escalation.
Controlling. Using key performance indicators, controlling uses AI to monitor the results, quality control, cost control, risk control, and real-time performance. "These dashboards empower leaders to quickly identify deviations from expected targets or benchmarks, allowing for timely interventions and strategic adjustments." (Takyar, 2021)

(2) Decision-making

Using AI, managers can make decisions faster. Incorporating AI into organizations' overall plans and actions impacts business strategy. AI can assist in strategic decision-making by facilitating innovation, identifying market trends, optimizing resource allocation, and providing valuable insights. It enables businesses to optimize their competitive position, identify new growth opportunities, and adapt to shifting market conditions (Saha et al., 2023, p. 927).

With the ability to analyze vast amounts of data, AI algorithms can empower managers to make more informed decisions and pinpoint areas for improvement within their operations, such as customer preferences and personalized product recommendations.

(3) Communication

AI tools can enhance communication and collaboration within the management team by providing data analytics, scheduling assistance, and facilitating virtual meetings (Takyar, 2021).

AI technologies like natural language processing (NLP) and machine learning can refine internal and external communication. For instance, businesses use chatbots powered by NLP to ensure continual communication by providing intelligent coaching. Since AI can identify questions, you can create prompts in chatbots that answer with tutorials, answers created by humans, and more. This allows them to address issues immediately, mitigate concerns, and keep everybody in the loop about the change process (Moulton, 2014).

(4) Relationship

AI optimizes the entire process, from demand forecasting to inventory management. Companies like Walmart and Amazon use AI algorithms to analyze historical sales data and external factors to predict future demand accurately. This allows them to optimize inventory levels, reduce waste, and improve customer satisfaction (Leadershiptribe, 2024).

Supply chain planners can use AI embedded in demand planning software to estimate not only demand but also the potential impact of scenarios such as economic downturns or severe weather events on demand, as well as on their costs, production capabilities, and ability to make deliveries (Tsidulko, 2024).

With AI, the relationship with customers integrates intelligence capabilities for storing, analyzing, predicting, and automating real-time interactions. Also, an AI-powered Customer Relationship Management system integrates artificial intelligence capabilities with traditional functionalities. It is not just about storing customer data anymore; it is about analyzing, predicting, and automating real-time interactions (Vaugham, 2024).

(5) Human Resources

AI supports employees in performing tasks more efficiently, in a shorter time, with reduced physical effort, increasing productivity and satisfaction.

In addition, promoting an inclusive digital future paves the way for managers to hire talent from every corner of the world (Kazim, 2024).

3.3. Barriers

Although research in the field of AI leads to innovations almost daily, the access of many companies, exceptionally tiny and medium-sized companies, to these discoveries is restricted by a series of barriers, among which are outdated hardware and software, a shortage of financing for investment in algorithms and cyber security, a lack of AI knowledge among employees, and a lack of AI experts.

Even if some algorithms are free of charge, especially for the general public, implementing integrated systems with AI requires specialized consulting and experts in companies, which, depending on the complexity, sometimes costs a lot.

On the other hand, employee training programs are expensive because people are not yet prepared to change roles and acquire the necessary skills.

3.4. Risks

Using AI in strategy involves a series of risks, especially in company management. The most critical risks are cyber-attacks, primarily exposed in Negulescu et al. (2022) and the data. If cyber attacks can be countered by purchasing powerful and up-to-date software, the data problem is the responsibility of the companies.

The quality and quantity of the data entered into the system, with which the AI algorithms are modeled, either ensure high accuracy or do not. However, getting such information in real-life scenarios might not always be easy (Zuccarelli, 2024). Other risks relate to the ethics of data use and the departure of the best employees to companies that can afford more significant personal benefits.

Since AI systems are only as good as the data they use, we must ensure that the data used to train such models is of the highest quality. This means using high-quality data sources that can provide accurate and factual information. However, getting such information in real-life scenarios might not always be easy (Zuccarelli, 2024).

3.5. Outcomes

In any case, changes have been produced by AI. They will produce positive effects on the performance of companies in the future, thus ensuring an undeniable competitive advantage. The main positive effects can be found in a series of outputs (Fig. 3).

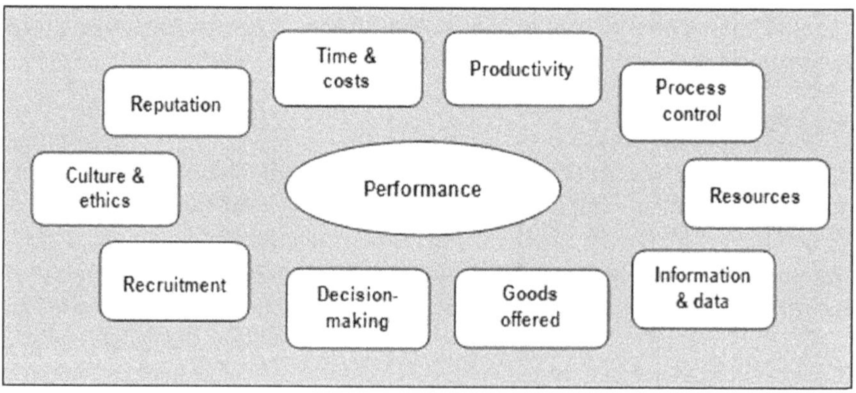

Fig. 3. Outcomes from AI utilization for performance
(Source: own concept)

Therefore, the effects of using AI can be, but are not limited to, the following:

- Reduced time and operational costs;
- Increased productivity;
- Better control of processes (suppliers' materials quality, production, standards accuracy);
- Optimizes the consumption of resources;
- Access to information and quick management of data and information;
- Personalized goods for customers and more information about consumers' needs;
- Assisted decision-making by real-time and predictive analytics;
- Automatic recruitment and employee evaluation and training;
- Strong culture for AI ethics and trust;
- Reputation.

All these benefits increase company performance. However, for these benefits to be real, it is necessary to ensure the ethical use of artificial intelligence and a just transition to an economy with zero carbon emissions (IFAC, 2023).

Before concluding, the mention related to governance reporting recently discussed within EFRAG (2023) at the European Union level regarding sustainable reporting is relevant. The document mentioned aims to guide the reporting of corporates and other companies about sustainable policies, targets, and actions on their entire value chain, including responsible investments, cooperation, and other aspects.

4. Conclusion

AI is the current and future force pushing companies to redefine strategies and business management, although it faces some barriers and risks.

The changes at the strategic level, including responsible investments in AI, sustainability, and social actions, lead to a change in organizational culture through new values, attitudes, and behaviors toward ethical principles specific to digitization. These can be found in changes in managerial functions, communication, and relationships along the value chain adapted to AI.

Therefore, AI is a determining factor in creativity, innovation, optimizing resource use, and managing a large volume of data. It also makes global connections and facilitates partnerships and alliances in proactive strategies and cyber security.

AI offers unexplored opportunities in the ever-evolving business landscape and contributes to increasing business agility.

References

Atsmon, Y. (2023). Artificial intelligence in strategy, Podcast, https://www.mckinsey.com/capabilities/strategy-and-corporate-finance/our-insights/artificial-intelligence-in-strategy.

Bath, V. (2024). Understanding the Impact of AI on Organizational Culture, Available at: https://www.globalcoachcenter.com/understanding-the-impact-of-ai-on-organizational-culture/.

Boyles, M. (2022). What is a business strategy, and why is it important? Harvard Business Scholl online, https://online.hbs.edu/blog/post/what-is-business-strategy.

Cai, K. 2024, AI 50, https://www.forbes.com/lists/ai50/?cdlcid=5d851547195063fa4f8e9bf3&sh=3d5104ae290f.

Castelfranchi, C. (1998). Modelling social action for AI agents, *Artificial Intelligence*, Volume 103, Issues 1–2, August 1998, Pages 157–182, Elsevier, https://doi.org/10.1016/S0004-3702(98)00056-3.

EFRAG. (2023). Implementation guidance for value chain (VCIG), EFRAG SRB Meeting 23 August 2023 Agenda paper 05-02, the European Union, Brussels.

Fayol, H. (1916). *Administration Industrielle et Générale*. Paris: Institute of Electrical and Electronics Engineering.

Finio, M. (2023). How to build a successful AI strategy, IBM, https://www.ibm.com/blog/artificial-intelligence-strategy.

Glaser, B., & Strauss, A. (1967). *The discovery of Grounded Theory: Strategies for qualitative research*. Mill Valley, CA: Sociology Press.

IFAC. (2023). Integrity in a changing world, Proceedings of the 22nd IFAC World Congress, Yokohama, Japan, July 9–14, 2023, Volume 56, Issue 2, Pages 1–11942, Elsevier.

Jeevanandam, N. (2023). AI Insights – How can AI help achieve sustainable development goals? Available at: https://indiaai.gov.in/article/how-can-ai-help-achieve-sustainable-development-goals.

Kazim, F. (2024). Can there be creative equity in the age of AI? World Economic Forum, https://www.weforum.org/agenda/2024/04/can-there-be-creative-equity-in-the-age-of-ai/.

Koontz, H., & O'Donnell, C. (2005). *Management: A system and contingency analysis of managerial functions*. McGraw-Hill Book Company, New York.

Leadershiptribe. (2024). Artificial Intelligence in business management: A revolution in the making, Available at: https://leadershiptribe.com/blog/artificial-intelligence-in-business-management-a-revolution-in-the-making

Mitchelson, D. (2024). Key strategies for building cyber resilience in 2024, https://www.weforum.org/agenda/2024/04/cybersecurity-key-strategies-cyber-resilience-2024/

Montgomery, M. (2021). Enterprise AI Management Principles, https://www.linkedin.com/pulse/enterprise-ai-management-principles-mark-mon tgomery/.

Moulton, T. (2014). How Artificial Intelligence (AI) Drives Change Management, *Change Management Review*, podcast, https://changemanagementrev iew.com/how-artificial-intelligence-ai-drives-change-management/.

Negulescu, O. H., Doval, E., & Stefanescu, A. S. (2022). Actual and future digital threats and their impact on civil and military cybersecurity management. *Defence Science Review*, Editorial system, Poland, PNO-00056-2022-01.

Ox. (2024). Experts call for responsible use of generative AI in adult social care, Available at: https://www.ox.ac.uk/news/2024-02-22-experts-call-responsi ble-use-generative-ai-adult-social-care.

Rajkumar. (2024). The 10 Best Artificial Intelligence Software in 2024 (AI Tool Reviews), https://www.softwaretestingmaterial.com/artificial-intelligence-software/?utm_content=cmp-true.

Reillier, L. C., & Reillier, B. (2017). *Platform strategy*. Routledge.

Rizbi, J. (2024). How AI Is Redefining Social Interactions in The Digital Age, https://www.forbes.com/sites/jiawertz/2024/03/25/how-ai-is-redefining-soc ial-interactions-in-the-digital-age/.

Saha, G. C., Menon, R., Paulin, M. S., Yerasuri, S., Saha, H., & Dongol, P. (2023). The impact of Artificial Intelligence on business strategy and decision-making processes. *European Economic Letters*, *13*(3) (2023), https://doi.org/10.52783/eel.v13i3.386.

Spataro, J. (2023). 3 Steps to Prepare Your Culture for AI. *Harvard Business Review*, https://hbr.org/2023/06/3-steps-to-prepare-your-culture-for-ai.

Tabesh, P., Mousavidin, E., & Hasani, S. (2019). Implementing big data strategies: A managerial perspective. *Business Horizon*, *62*(3), Elsevier, 347–358.

Tabur, M. (2023). ESG ratings and the investor decision-making process: A comparative analysis of rating agencies' data and its effect on financial performance, PressAcademia, pp. 167–172, DOI: 10.17261/Pressacademia.2023.1772 PAP-V.17-2023(27).

Takyar, A. (2021). AI in business management: Unveiling the next wave of operational excellence, https://www.leewayhertz.com/ai-in-business-man agement/.

Tsidulko, J. (2024). Benefits of AI in the Supply Chain. Available at: https://www.oracle.com/scm/ai-supply-chain/.

Tulluri, T. K. (2024). Accelerating Digital Evolution: The AI-driven partnership between HCLTech and Intel, Available at: https://www.hcltech.com/blogs/accelerating-digital-evolution-the-ai-driven-partnership-between-hcltech-and-intel.

Vaugham, A. (2024). The Best AI CRM for 2024, Available at: https://technologyadvice.com/blog/information-technology/ai-crm/.

Xing, E.P., Ho, Q., Xie, P., & Wei, D. (2016). Strategies and principles of distributed machine learning on big data. *Engineering*, *2*(2), Elsevier, 179–195, https://doi.org/10.1016/J.ENG.2016.02.008.

Zuccarelli, E. (2024). Building trust in AI means moving beyond black-box algorithms. Here's why. Available at: https://www.ainave.com/tech-bytes/building-trust-in-ai-means-moving-beyond-black-box-algorithms-here-s-why.

Raul Florentin Drenta & Raluca Georgiana Robu

Digitalization as a Catalyst for the Global Expansion of SMEs: Opportunities, Challenges, and Strategic Implications

1. Introduction

The world has witnessed a significant shift toward digitalization in recent years, which has profoundly impacted how businesses operate globally. This shift has been witnessed all over the world. Small and medium-sized businesses (SMEs) are not an exception to this trend; rather, they are actively working to expand their operations in international markets by utilizing digital technologies. In this context, the purpose of this article is to investigate the intricate relationship between digitalization and the global expansion of small and medium-sized enterprises, focusing on the difficulties and opportunities brought about by this process. This study sheds light on the multifaceted impact of digitalization on SMEs by conducting a comprehensive review of the existing literature. The findings of this study can provide insights that can inform policymakers, practitioners, and scholars alike.

Small and medium-sized enterprises have consistently been recognized as crucial contributors to the economy and significant employers, spanning various industries and countries. Despite receiving relatively less attention than their larger counterparts, smaller businesses' attributes, roles, and strategies have consistently fascinated business scholars. In this context, the ability of SMEs to internationalise through digitalization and their place in the global economy become attractive research subjects.

During the past two decades, the information technology revolution has significantly altered the identity and position of SMEs in relation to large companies and customers. The current era has diminished the strength of small companies in the face of global competition while equipping them with skills and possibilities to accomplish tasks and connect with previously inconceivable customers. This paper thoroughly examines existing scientific literature to determine the various opportunities and challenges that small and medium-sized enterprises (SMEs) encounter in today's business landscape, specifically in relation to digitalization and advancements in information and communication technology.

Over the past thirty years, small and medium enterprises (SMEs) have significantly contributed to global economies (Gherghina et al., 2020). SMEs are widely recognized as the primary catalysts for economic growth in all nations (Aris, 2007). Several scholars have observed that small and medium-sized enterprises (SMEs) play a substantial role in the advancement of the economy (Gherghina et al., 2020; Susman, 2007) and serve as an engine for the expansion of emerging industries while also supporting established ones (Hossain, 2015). Despite being relatively small in size and market share, SMEs represent the majority of all enterprises and play a crucial role in driving economic entrepreneurship innovation (Gherghina et al., 2020), competitiveness, and future growth (Gaweł et al., 2023), despite their limited resources and access to information (Cassetta et al., 2020). Most economies in developed and developing countries have acknowledged the significance and function of small and medium-sized enterprises in fostering social unity, generating employment, and promoting economic growth. The future progress of nations is heavily reliant on the growth of SMEs (Susman, 2007).

Due to the globalization of the world, with national borders becoming more accessible to everyone, SMEs are now facing intense competition within their own country and on a global scale. Given the challenging nature of the business landscape, with multinational corporations operating worldwide (Denicolai et al., 2021), SMEs are compelled to enhance their competitiveness and identify the key factors that contribute to the effectiveness of their operations that enable them to pursue their expansion strategies on foreign markets.

Encouraging innovation and adjusting strategies to different international markets is a effective approach to international expansion using digital technologies (Bhuiyan et al., 2021). Digitalization enables the swift and streamlined internationalization of SMEs by broadening their reach to global markets and cutting costs associated with international transactions.

This article will examine the challenges and advantages associated with the digital transformation of SMEs, which have the potential to expand their position in the global economy.

2. Problem Statement

Digitalization has changed the global business scene, creating new possibilities and difficulties for SMEs looking to develop internationally. As digital technologies progress, SMEs are under pressure to use them to compete globally. However, SMEs generally struggle with digitalization due to limited resources, digital skills, and complicated regulatory regimes.

Digitalization has several effects on SMEs across industries, regions, and nations. Some SMEs have used digital technology to grow and become more competitive, but others have failed to adapt and fallen behind in the global economy. Thus, the complicated link between digitization and SMEs' worldwide development, including its obstacles and potential, must be examined.

Digitalization presents obstacles and possibilities for SMEs pursuing worldwide expansion, according to this report. This study will examine the complex effects of digitalization on SMEs through a comprehensive literature review, serving policymakers, practitioners, and scholars. The research will also identify best practices and methods for SMEs to overcome digitalization problems and use digital technology to expand internationally.

3. Research Questions/Aims of the Research

This study aims to investigate the impact of digitalization on the internationalization capacity of small and medium-sized enterprises (SMEs) in different industries and regions.

Research Questions:

1. How has digitalization influenced the internationalization capacity of SMEs?

This research question explores the impact of digitalization on the ability of SMEs' in different industries to internationalize and expand their operations in different regions. The study will examine how digitalization has affected SMEs' competitiveness in various global markets and how it has enabled or hindered their internationalization efforts.

2. What are the main barriers and facilitators that digitalization introduces in the internationalization process of SMEs?

This research question identifies and analyses the main barriers and facilitators SMEs face when adopting digital technologies to expand their operations in international markets. The study will examine the challenges and opportunities associated with digitalization, such as limited resources, lack of digital skills, and complex regulatory environments.

3. What role do business environment and technological factors play in the success of SME internationalization through digitalization?

This research question examines how business environment and technology affect SMEs' digitalization-based internationalisation. The paper will evaluate how digital infrastructure, government regulations, market circumstances, and cultural differences effect SMEs' worldwide expansion with digital technology. It will also identify best practices and methods for SMEs to overcome digitalization difficulties and capitalise on possibilities.

4. Research Methods

The research methodology used in this study involves a thorough review of the existing literature. This systematic literature review method involves identifying, selecting, and critically analysing relevant studies to answer research questions. The review process involves searching for relevant articles in academic databases, screening them and extracting the main ideas from selected articles.

The studies included in the review are analysed using a qualitative approach. This method involves interpreting and synthesizing data from multiple sources to develop a comprehensive understanding of the research questions. Moreover, it allows a deeper exploration of the complex relationships between digitalization and SME internationalization.

The selected studies include case studies, empirical studies, and theoretical papers that provide insights into the impact of digitalization on SMEs acting in different industries and expanding internationally. The research methodology also critically appraises the selected studies to assess their quality and validity. This ensures that the review's findings are based on reliable and trustworthy evidence.

Overall, the systematic review methodology used in this study is a rigorous and systematic approach to synthesizing and analysing the existing literature on the impact of digitalization on SMEs' internationalization capacity.

5. Findings

5.1 The Impact of Digitalization on SMEs's Capacity for Global Expansion

The progress of digitalization has greatly transformed the capacity of small and medium-sized firms (SMEs) to enter and grow in global marketplaces, expediting procedures and altering conventional approaches to expansion.

Generally, digitalization has a positive role in facilitating faster SMEs' entry into foreign markets (Lee et al., 2019; Vadana et al., 2019; Cassetta et al., 2020) and benefits born-global firms in particular (Shneor, 2012).

Many studies reveal that internationalization strategies need to be adapted to opportunities and challenges brought by digitalisation and that digitalization strategies have different effects on the internationalization capacity. While born-digital firms internationalise fast (Vadana et al., 2021), many SMEs are unable to internationalise digitally (Westerlund, 2020) because they were not intended to expand in this manner from the beginning, owing to budgetary constraints or limited adaptability. Digitalization enables SMEs to tap into new markets without investing heavily upfront (Bargoni et al., 2024). It also helps them streamline their operations and become more efficient.

The benefits of digitalization on the global expansion capacity cover a wide range: it improves operational efficiency by implementing automation and leveraging data analytics technology to discern untapped markets and customer groups (Gaweł et al., 2023), enhances connectivity and access to reliable assistance, even amid global deglobalization trends (Fan, et al., 2022), strengthens business process management over the supply chain (Westerlund, 2020). But most importantly, digitalization radically alters the methods that SMEs use to enter foreign markets. Digital platforms enable SMEs to internationalize with few resources, offering them the chance to overcome limitations and get access to networks (Huijun Jin, 2018). Integrating omnichannel strategies using digital technology facilitates improved coordination between distribution channels and the market, hence promoting the generation of digitalized value in global marketplaces (Montera, 2022).

With the advent of digitalization, SMEs can now enhance their international business skills and broaden their operations on a global scale, free from the limitations of traditional methods (Cassetta et al., 2020). Through digital platforms, SMEs now can tap into international markets like never before. This newfound access allows them to connect with global consumers quickly and efficiently, all without the hefty expenses typically associated with physical expansion (Denicolai et al., 2021). Digitalization can enhance SMEs' internal skills (Dethine et al., 2020) by enabling them to better manage customer relationships and supply chains, leading to increased efficiency.

Digital orientation and strategy is a key aspect necessary to adapt to emerging technology, improving proficiency in utilizing digital platforms for marketing and sales, and expertise in managing data (Bil Kai Sia's, 2022). But digital technologies expand possibilities as geographic barriers are overcome and global markets can be accessed without the constraints of a physical presence (Joensuu-Salo et al., 2018).

Research shows that SMEs with strong entrepreneurial mindsets and effective digital strategies perform better in foreign markets. These firms innovate and adapt quickly to market changes using technology. Djou (2020) found that in the metallurgical and equipment industries, entrepreneurial orientation and digitalization affected SMEs' international performance and that digitalization required innovation capacity, proactivity, and risk-taking.

To sum up, under diverse circumstances digitalisation can have either a positive impact on SMEs expansion capacity on foreign markets, or limited benefits, mainly depending on the firms' capacity to adapt to new trends.

5.2. SME Internationalisation through Digitalization: Barriers and Enablers

According to research, several factors can hinder or facilitate SMEs' internationalization through digitalization. One key opportunity is the development of a strong digital strategy and ecosystem network. This can provide SMEs with the necessary tools and resources to expand their international presence. On the other hand, a major barrier is the lack of adequate human capacity to utilize digital technologies effectively.

Additionally, underdeveloped ecosystem networks can pose challenges for SMEs looking to go global through digitalization (Le-Dain et al., 2023). Some studies highlight the significance of social networking and entrepreneurial digital marketing in boosting the global expansion of SMEs (Yang et al., 2023). As digitalization continues to advance, it has the potential to reshape internationalization patterns by introducing new factors that hold more weight than traditional determinants like company size and age (Tippmann et al. (2023)).

Identified barriers encompass resistance to change, insufficient digital skills, and the initial costs of digitalization, which can pose significant challenges for SMEs (Gaweł et al., 2023). In certain markets, the effectiveness of digitalization and internationalization strategies can be limited by underdeveloped digital infrastructure (Thrassou et al., 2020). One of the main challenges SMEs face is the absence of a culture of innovation and limited financial resources, which hinder their ability to effectively embrace digitalization (Hervé et al., 2022). Furthermore, digitalization necessitates organizational adjustments, posing challenges for small and medium-sized enterprises that face constraints in terms of resources (Reim et al., 2022) and management capabilities (Galdino et al., 2019). Understanding the intricacies of incorporating digital technologies into current business models and cultivating specialized digital skills are crucial for successfully harnessing the potential of these technologies. In addition, the expenses related to digitalization and cyber security pose considerable challenges for SMEs (Westerlund, 2020; Anwar et al., 2022).

5.3. The Role of Business Environment and Technological Factors in SMEs' Digitalization

The success of the internationalization of SMEs through digitalization is influenced by various business environment and technological factors, making it a complex and multifaceted process. To successfully expand their operations in international markets, SMEs must access advanced digital technologies and a strong telecommunications infrastructure (Uvarova & Pobol, 2021). Technological factors, such as innovation capacity, are important in determining the international performance of SMEs (Anwar et al., 2022). Research indicates that the integration of digital technology positively impacts the performance of businesses (Hervé et al., 2021). It enables product innovations and enhances overall productivity (Wen et al., 2021). Technologies enable seamless communication and trading across distances and time zones. Today's business need strong IT infrastructure and digital technologies. These resources enable digital technology adoption, which opens up worldwide markets and boosts competitiveness. Nessrine Omrani (2022) highlights that this emphasis on technology is key for businesses to thrive in the global marketplace.

Additionally, business considerations like sustainability policy and government backing can affect results. Different criteria determine how SMEs can adopt new technology into their business plans. This highlights the significance of creating a conducive environment that fosters innovation and facilitates growth (Ta et al., 2023).

Factors like the political and economic stability of the host country (Jekanyika Matanda, 2012), legal regulations on e-commerce and data protection (Savrul et al., 2014), and business culture (Dimitratos et al., 2016; Reim et al., 2022) all determine how effectively SMEs can operate in foreign markets. Furthermore, the export intention of SMEs is also influenced by their perceptions of sustainability policies in foreign markets. Discussing environmental sustainability and embracing digital systems can significantly increase a company's intention to expand internationally (Szabó et al., 2023). On the other hand, although digitalization and sustainability are linked, when a company internationalises, they compete one having priority over the other (Denicolai et al., 2021).

To sum up, digitalization has the power to expand market opportunities and enhance the operational efficiency of SMEs. The digitalization process has had a favourable impact on the speed at which manufacturing businesses expand internationally despite global pressures causing a decrease in globalization (Fan et al., 2022). By streamlining processes and cutting costs, digitalization becomes crucial in the face of fierce global competition. Therefore, SMEs can effectively by incorporating digital technologies if they adjust to business environment factors.

6. Conclusions

Digitalization may help or hinder internationalisation for small and medium-sized firms (SMEs), as shown in this study. We found that digitalization's effects vary according to company strategy and characteristics by reviewing case studies and secondary data in the empirical literature. This emphasises the need for a complete plan that incorporates technology and context.

Digitalization has helped SMEs enter global markets and overcome offline market restrictions. However, firm characteristics and the business climate greatly affect performance. Establishing partnership networks and executing a sound digital strategy facilitate internationalisation via digitalization, but limited human resources and digital competences are the biggest hurdles.

This study closes with a thorough literature evaluation to strengthen the research. However, different sources and research methods limit the applicability of the findings to all SMEs. The study depends on pre-existing literature and case studies, which may bias data interpretation. Sectorial and regional variance need more research to understand context-specific dynamics.

By contrasting how digitization affects small and medium-sized firms' world-wide expansion, this study advances understanding. This gives policymakers, practitioners, and researchers interested in technology and international entrepreneurship new insights.

Further research is warranted to investigate the distinct ramifications of digitalization across various sectors and regions, scrutinize the influence of cultural variables, and construct prognostic models that assist small and medium-sized enterprises in optimizing the advantages of digitalization.

In the context of globalization, digitalization represents a force of transformation that presents substantial opportunities and challenges for SMEs. A comprehensive comprehension of these dynamics will enable SMEs to manoeuvre through the intricate terrain of global markets.

References

Anwar, M., Scheffler, M. A., & Clauss, T. (2022). Digital capabilities, their role in business model innovativeness, and the internationalization of SMEs. *IEEE Transactions on Engineering Management.*

Aris, N. M. (2007). SMEs: Building blocks for economic growth. *Department of National Statistics, Malaysia.*

Bargoni, A., Ferraris, A., Vilamová, Š., & Wan Hussain, W. M. H. (2024). Digitalisation and internationalisation in SMEs: A systematic review and research agenda. *Journal of Enterprise Information Management.*

Bhuiyan, M. R., & Yusuph, R. G. (2021). Influence of digitalization on business model innovation in the internationalization process of SMEs. Master Degree Project, University of Gothenburg.

Bil, Kai, Sia, Yan-Yin, Lee., M, Falahat. (2022). Digitalisation and internationalisation of SMEs in emerging markets. *International Journal of Entrepreneurship and Small Business*, *45*(3), 334–334.

Cassetta, E., Monarca, U., Dileo, I., Di Berardino, C., & Pini, M. (2020). The relationship between digital technologies and internationalisation. Evidence from Italian SMEs. *Industry and Innovation*, *27*(4), 311–339.

Ciasullo, M. V., Montera, R., Mercuri, F., & Mugova, S. (2022). When digitalization meets omnichannel in international markets: A case study from the agri-food industry. *Administrative Sciences*, *12*(2), 68.

Denicolai, S., Zucchella, A., & Magnani, G. (2021). Internationalization, digitalization, and sustainability: Are SMEs ready? A survey on synergies and substituting effects among growth paths. *Technological Forecasting and Social Change*, *166*, 120650.

Dethine, B., Enjolras, M., & Monticolo, D. (2020). Digitalization and SMEs' export management: Impacts on resources and capabilities. *Technology Innovation Management Review*, *10*(4).

Dimitratos, P., Johnson, J. E., Plakoyiannaki, E., & Young, S. (2016). SME internationalization: How does the opportunity-based international entrepreneurial culture matter?. *International Business Review*, *25*(6), 1211–1222.

Djou, L. G., Udin, U., Lukiastuti, F., & Filatrovi, E. W. (2020). The contingency approach of digitalization and entrepreneurial orientation on SMEs performance in metal and machinery industry. *International Journal of Criminology and Sociology*, *9*(1), 2235–2249.

Fan, Y., Cui, V., Feng, S., & Wu, J. (2022). Digital technologies and firm internationalization: The role of regional digitalization. In *Academy of Management Proceedings* (Vol. 2022, No. 1, p. 16656). Briarcliff Manor, NY 10510: Academy of Management.

Galdino, K. M., Rezende, S. F. L., & Lamont, B. T. (2019). Market and internationalization knowledge in entrepreneurial internationalization processes. *International Journal of Entrepreneurial Behavior & Research*, *25*(7), 1580–1600.

Gaweł, A., Mroczek-Dąbrowska, K., & Pietrzykowski, M. (2023). Digitalization and its impact on the internationalization models of SMEs. *Artificiality and Sustainability in Entrepreneurship*, *19*.

Gherghina, Ş. C., Botezatu, M. A., Hosszu, A., & Simionescu, L. N. (2020). Small and Medium-sized Enterprises (SMEs): The engine of economic growth through investments and innovation. *Sustainability*, *12*(1), 347.

Hervé, A., Schmitt, C., & Baldegger, R. (2021). Internationalization and Digitalization: Applying digital technologies to the internationalization process of small and medium-sized enterprises. *Technology Innovation Management Review*.

Hervé, A., Schmitt, C., & Baldegger, R. (2022). Digitalization and internationalization of micro-, small, and medium-sized enterprises: An overall conceptual process. *Journal of the International Council for Small Business*, *3*(4), 329–336.

Hossain, M. (2015). A review of literature on open innovation in Small and Medium-sized enterprises. *Journal of Global Entrepreneurship Research*, *5*, 1–12.

Jin, H., & Hurd, F. (2018). Exploring the impact of digital platforms on SME internationalization: New Zealand SMEs use of the Alibaba platform for Chinese market entry. *Journal of Asia-Pacific Business*, *19*(2), 72–95.

Jekanyika Matanda, M. (2012). Internationalization of established small manufacturers in a developing economy: A case study of Kenyan SMEs. *Thunderbird International Business Review*, *54*(4), 509–519.

Joensuu-Salo, S., Sorama, K., Viljamaa, A., & Varamäki, E. (2018). Firm performance among internationalized SMEs: The interplay of market orientation, marketing capability and digitalization. *Administrative sciences*, *8*(3), 31.

Le-Dain, M. A., Benhayoun, L., Matthews, J., & Liard, M. (2023). Barriers and opportunities of digital servitization for SMEs: the effect of smart Product-Service System business models. *Service Business*, *17*(1), 359–393.

Lee, Y. Y., Falahat, M., & Sia, B. K. (2019). Impact of digitalization on the speed of internationalization. *International Business Research*, *12*(4), 1–11.

Omrani, N., Rejeb, N., Maalaoui, A., Dabić, M., & Kraus, S. (2022). Drivers of digital transformation in SMEs. *IEEE Transactions on Engineering Management*.

Reim, W., Yli-Viitala, P., Arrasvuori, J., & Parida, V. (2022). Tackling business model challenges in SME internationalization through digitalization. *Journal of Innovation & Knowledge*, *7*(3), 100199.

Savrul, M., Incekara, A., & Sener, S. (2014). The potential of e-commerce for SMEs in a globalizing business environment. *Procedia-Social and Behavioral Sciences*, *150*, 35–45.

Shneor, R. (2012). *10 Born global firms, internet, and new forms of internationalization* (p. 161). Cheltenham: Edward Elgar Publishing.

Susman, G. I. (Ed.). (2007). *Small and Medium-sized Enterprises and the global economy*. Edward Elgar Publishing.

Szabó, R. Z., Szedmák, B., Tajti, A., & Bera, P. (2023). Environmental sustainability, digitalisation, and the entrepreneurial perception of distances as drivers of SMEs' internationalisation. *Sustainability*, *15*(3), 2487.

Ta, V. A., & Lin, C. Y. (2023). Exploring the Determinants of digital transformation adoption for SMEs in an emerging economy. *Sustainability*, *15*(9), 7093.

Tippmann, E., Monaghan, S., & Reuber, R. A. (2023). Navigating the paradox of global scaling. *Global Strategy Journal, 13*(4), 735–773.

Thrassou, A., Uzunboylu, N., Vrontis, D., Christofi, M. (2020). Digitalization of SMEs: A review of opportunities and challenges. In: Thrassou, A., Vrontis, D., Weber, Y., Shams, S. M. R., & Tsoukatos, E. (eds.), *The changing role of SMEs in global business. Palgrave studies in cross-disciplinary business research*, In Association with EuroMed Academy of Business. Palgrave Macmillan, Cham.

Uvarova, O., & Pobol, A. (2021). SMEs digital transformation in the EaP countries in COVID-19 time: Challenges and digital solutions. In Eastern Partnership Civil Society Forum. Obtenido de https://eap-csf. eu/wp-content/uploads/SMEs-digital-transformation-in-the-EaP-countries-during-COVID-19. pdf.

Vadana, I. I., Torkkeli, L., Kuivalainen, O., & Saarenketo, S. (2019). Digitalization of companies in international entrepreneurship and marketing. *International Marketing Review*, *37*(3), 471–492.

Vadana, I. I., Kuivalainen, O., Torkkeli, L., & Saarenketo, S. (2021). The role of digitalization on the internationalization strategy of born-digital companies. *Sustainability*, *13*(24), 14002.

Wen, H., Lee, C., & Song, Z. (2021). Digitalization and environment: How does ICT affect enterprise environmental performance?. *Environmental Science and Pollution Research*, *28*, 54826–54841.

Westerlund, M. (2020). Digitalization, internationalization and scaling of online SMEs. *Technology Innovation Management Review*, *10*(4).

Yang, M., Gabrielsson, P., & Andersson, S. (2023). Entrepreneurs' social ties and international digital entrepreneurial marketing in Small and Medium-sized Enterprise internationalization. *Journal of International Marketing*, *31*(4), 1–22.

Maria Leonor Pires

The Challenges of e-HRM – A Literature Review

1. Introduction

Fast-paced changes driven by technology were bound to affect Human Resource Management (HRM). From the last decades of the 20th century to the first quarter of the 21st century, we passed from paper to computer use, mostly as a simple recording on Word or Excel of what was prior in paper, to the first databases, and later to web-based technology and, more recently, Artificial Intelligence (AI), leading to e-HRM, which stands for electronic human resource management.

Among the multiple definitions of e-HRM, we can find a generalist approach in Berber et al. (2018), identifying the basic elements involved: web-based technologies, HRM services, management, and employees. A wider approach was proposed by Bondarouk and Ruël (2009), who introduced a reference to value creation, and the efficiency and quality of HRM enhanced by IT. They first conceptualize e-HRM as "an umbrella term covering all possible integration mechanisms and contents between HRM and Information Technologies aiming at creating value within and across organizations for targeted employees and management" (Bondarouk & Ruël, 2009. p. 507). This concept was extended to include creating long-term opportunities for the organization's stakeholders (Bondarouk & Brewster, 2016).

Lengnick-Hall and Moritz (2003) characterized the evolution of e-HRM in three stages. The first corresponds to one-way communication using the company's intranets, centered on rules and procedures. This is followed by the mechanization of transactions, replacing paper with electronic data, and providing staff and line managers with access to databases to input and update data. The third stage is centered on knowledge and managing intellectual capital, developing social capital, and operationalizing the HRM function, which is believed to result in better customer service, new goods and services, and thus value creation.

The pursuit of efficiency and value creation is not new to HRM. It is one of the pillars of strategic HRM, which considers the HRM function as a strategic partner of the organization through the management of people, with specific policies and practices aligned with a wider strategic orientation.

Indeed, Lepak and Snell's (1998) view on e-HRM was closely linked to strategic HRM. What they call "virtual HRM", was viewed as an instrument to "help the organization to acquire, develop, and deploy intellectual capital" (Lepak & Snell, 1998, p. 216). The main argument is that the competitive advantage of organizations can be attained through people, making HR a strategic partner. This means centering the management of people on employee development, hiring the best, training, career, and performance management instead of administrative and routine tasks while being more flexible and contributing to cost reduction.

Being released from these routine tasks would leave room for HR professionals to take the advocated strategic role of contributing to companies' performance and success. This is also preconized by Bondarouk et al. (2017), which envisages the adoption of e-HRM as a way of reaching administrative and strategic benefits through cost savings, and improved service delivery.

Our research questions have as their starting point the much sought-after efficiency: is it being achieved? Can we consider HRM's role as becoming more strategic? To what extent do the roles of HRM professionals change? What ethical and legal issues can be identified with IT usage over the personal data of employees and applicants?

In this study, we conducted a comprehensive literature review to address and discuss the answers to these questions or ongoing challenges in the field of e-HRM.

2. Efficiency Pursuit and the Strategic Role of HRM

One of the main questions for both practitioners and researchers is the efficiency of e-HRM systems and their association with the strategic role of HRM departments. Starting with efficiency, the potential benefits offered by e-HRM can come in several ways, such as cost reduction and better service delivery in operational areas.

All HRM functions seem to benefit from the use of technology (Fındıklı & Bayarçelik, 2015). The recruitment and selection of employees can be more effective; these systems allow access to a greater number of candidates, increase the efficiency of recruitment, shorten the process, and reduce costs. Regarding employee training and development, the use of online training systems and e-learning is a more flexible way for employees to acquire and develop skills. Performance evaluation, from the perspective of employee development, would also be facilitated through the provision of information and support systems. Compensation systems can also benefit from the automation of bureaucratic processes, reducing the time spent on these tasks.

Besides reducing the administrative load and enhancing efficiency (Stone & Deadrick, 2015), these systems would also be a means to attract and retain valuable employees by identifying their needs, allowing better HR decisions and better and faster access to information and databases for staff and line managers (Lepak & Snell, 1998). Thus, e-HRM allows for better decision-making, knowledge management, and the development of intellectual capital (Lengnick-Hall & Moritz, 2003).

However, all the anticipated benefits are far from assured. The work of Ruël et al. (2004) found support for cost reduction and administrative burden reduction with middle management and employees being involved in HR tasks, but not in upgrading employees' competencies.

Data collected by Fındıklı and Bayarçelik (2015) from an HR manager sample showed a reduction in organizational costs and better communication between managers and employees; however, respondents also considered e-learning ineffective. Other researchers claim that even though technology offers increased efficiency and cost savings, it may not help attract, motivate, and retain talent since all technologies have limitations and in the specific case of training, the opportunities for feedback and practice may not be adequate for the needs of trainees (Stone & Deadrick, 2015).

Stone and Dulebohn (2013) pointed out several benefits, such as increased efficiency, reduced costs, and administrative burden, but also drew attention to unwanted results, namely not achieving the expected degree of efficiency in the processes, not meeting the expectations of some stakeholders, and the danger of invasion of privacy.

The study of Parry and Tyson (2011) provided mixed evidence because they found that although the aims of efficiency, service delivery, and standardization were achieved, and despite the HR department having the time and information to support business strategy, their involvement in decision-making remained unaltered.

Another important question here is that the implementation and use of e-HRM are not only context-dependent, but HR managers also play an essential role in the adoption process and its success. Bondarouk et al. (2017) also emphasize that human involvement is vital in the adoption and impact of e-HRM. Factors such as organizational culture, acceptance of new technology, belief in its importance and value, and efficient training are crucial.

A study conducted by Yusliza and Ramayah (2012) on the adoption and utilization of e-HRM by HR professionals found that goal clarity, satisfaction, perceived value, support, social influence, and ease of use all contributed to a favorable attitude toward its implementation, as well as adequate technical support (Ma &Ye, 2015).

With the mechanization of more routine tasks, in addition to the desired efficiency gains, two additional things are expected to occur: the cut down on HRM staff previously engaged with less strategic functions (Lengnick-Hall & Moritz, 2003; Ulrich & Dulebohn, 2015) and to allow HR professionals to focus on organizational change activities, direct their competencies toward business issues, and thus supporting HRM as a strategic partner (Bondarouk et al., 2017).

Concerning the expected transformation of HRM, progressing from an administrative to a strategic role, Bondarouk and Ruël (2013) research offers interesting insights. Despite personnel reduction in the HR department, e-HRM failed to achieve the expected strategic role or enable operational efficiency benefits. Nevertheless, HR professionals felt more confident in using e-HRM, perceiving a shift in their roles in people management and business partnership. Additionally, both line managers and non-managers were involved in more HR activities, but line managers reacted negatively to their increased involvement.

We can add another dimension to this discussion, that is where the strategic value of e-HRM lies. For Stone et al. (2015), the question is whether e-HRM should focus on efficiency or attract, motivate, and retain employees. In terms of effectiveness, if that is the goal to reach, they point out the danger of creating distance between employees and, given its tendency toward passiveness and impersonality, transforming HR into a management tool, risking its true strategic value. On the employees' side, the author's research also concluded that interaction and interpersonal relations were still preferred over the use of technology.

Another important question is that, while implementing e-HRM to increase efficiency, we might neglect the human element of HRM. This takes us back to the debate on "hard" versus "soft" HRM models. The "hard" model, with its roots in strategic management theories, emphasizes "resources" and efficiency, views labor as a commodity, and tries to reduce its costs. While the "soft" model stresses the importance of motivation, commitment, and satisfaction for higher performance. Here, HR plays a pivotal role in managing labor and promoting organizational engagement. Some key features of the soft model include advanced recruitment, job security, extensive training, employee involvement, competitive compensation, performance management, work-life balance, and inclusivity (Marchington, 2015).

Although e-HRM can be used in both models, companies must decide what will be the focus of technology, an efficiency-centered model, or a human-centered model. A strong argument favoring the latter can be found in the work of Cleveland et al. (2015). These authors present an understanding of HRM function as not only being influenced by internal contexts, such as structure, culture, leadership, and social responsibility but also recognizing that HRM can also directly affect the external context, for instance, with its employment policies and recruitment practices. Organizations and HRM, as a whole, are inserted into an always-changing dynamic environment; to be successful, they must adapt, but they can also be an instrument of change in the direction of human development.

3. The Role of HRM Professionals

HRM professionals play a crucial role in the success or failure of e-HRM implementation and achieving its goals. An important question is what this implies for them since their tasks and roles are changing.

As we've seen previously one of the answers comes from the efficiency perspective. With the efficiency gains, HR would have the time and the tools to make strategic decisions, act like internal consultants, and be able to provide value for the organization (Bondarouk & Ruël, 2009).

We believe that Snell and Lepak (1998) were among the first to identify the adjustments that HR managers must make, such as having a stronger grasp of connections and information and seeing their work in terms of value added. They also recognized that HR professionals needed a different skill set.

This subject has been addressed by Ceric and Parton (2024) who refer to the need for e-HRM knowledge and skills to conduct or enable its implementation, which goes by understanding the technical aspects and being able to communicate efficiently with the IT technicians providing a better understanding of this tools. Another important skill, to be able to contribute strategically to the company, would be data analytic skills, which should be added to their training. Their research also shows the importance of HR professionals as enablers of e-HRM, providing training, support, and advocacy to leadership about its benefits and usage.

In addition to the more technical skills and the role of strategic partner, Ulrich and Dulebohn (2015) propose new skills, like advocates of change in the organization, helping align culture with strategy, being innovators in their field, and technology defenders, to help the company position itself regarding stakeholders. For Cohen (2015) beyond the specific knowledge of HR functions, there would be also a place for other skills such as ethics, communication, consultation, critical evaluation, and relationship management. We believe that while these competencies are not exactly new they are now as needed, or even more than ever.

Another question arising is the shift in the perception of the HRM department, by line managers and also employees. With e-HRM both these groups can access information, analyze data, and make decisions; employees have greater input and control over their personal information and updating records, therefore the HR professional's role will be of consultant, to help when necessary (Lengnick-Hall & Moritz, 2003).

Nevertheless, the results of the work of Al-Harazneh and Sila (2021) show the existence of an unexpected perceived negative effect of the HR professionals on e-HRM system usage, which brings the authors to wonder about an eventual negative perception of the monitoring role of HR professionals, being suggested that an improvement in the image and nature of their services is needed.

HR professionals can be called to new tasks where their intervention seems fundamental, and that are consequence of the growing use of data science and AI in HR.

Among the major challenges in the area, as identified in the work of Tambe et al. (2019) there is the complexity of HR, the responsibility regarding fairness and ethical and legal restraints, and the possible negative reactions of employees to management choices based on algorithms. The way to overcome these challenges would be to rely on HR professionals to deal with complexity, understand the problems, and contribute to decisions with their specific knowledge, which would be crucial regarding legal and ethical problems.

A qualitative study by Radonjić et al. (2022), exploring the pros and cons of the use of AI, concluded that despite the high quality of the information generated, it has to be subjected to human evaluation to judge its validity and appropriateness in account of legal or internal restraints. Also, it is acknowledged that an impartial human intervention in algorithms must be ensured so that unbiased data can be generated. It is also noteworthy that emotionless decision-making is considered a limitation regarding employee involvement. The need for new skills, albeit not identified, and close cooperation with data specialists are also acknowledged as the way to overcome operational problems.

4. Ethical and Legal Challenges

When going over the main ethical and legal issues arising from e-HMR and the recent use of AI we find data security, invasion of privacy, discrimination, the possibility of data errors that lead to poor decisions, fairness, and legal compliance (Lukaszewski & Stone, 2024; Tambe et al., 2019).

Data security is a major issue for any organization and the use of IT on employee data only increases the problems and its scope. Security breaches can now affect employees' private data, and misuse of security credentials or access errors can expose private information. In addition, we can also question the access to employee mail communications by organizations, even if legitimate it might not be accepted as ethical. Part of these questions also apply to applicants in recruitment processes, with the data collected, and also when extending data collection and analyses not only to applications and interview content but also to social media. Regarding this specific subject, Tambe et al. (2019) add what they call the "adaptative response" of applicants and employees, when feeling scrutinized they will opt to behave according to social desirability in those means, leading to results that machines cannot interpret thus requiring specific human knowledge.

This is also true in the decision-making stage, especially when algorithms are involved. First, they can introduce or replicate undesirable bias. Second, when it comes to explaining the "algorithm choices" there is not only the problem of formal complexity of how it works but we would say of the potential perceived lack of legitimacy and responsibility, which can affect perceptions of procedural and informational justice, again human action, knowledge, and reasoning is necessary.

In fact, organizational justice is one of the two main ethical problems identified by Wasserman and Fisher (2020), the other relates to outsourcing. Regarding justice, the authors underline the importance of informational justice and procedural justice. Both applicants and employees should perceive the use of information and its sharing as fair. On the side of procedural justice, it is important to guarantee due process to those affected by decision-making based on algorithms. We believe that distributional justice should also be considered. Distributional justice refers to the fairness of outcomes received (like payment) with job contributions (Greenberg, 2009). When line managers are called upon to carry out HR administrative management tasks, now redistributed thanks to technology, shouldn't these new tasks and responsibilities also be translated into material rewards and compensation increases, in the name of fairness? If not, we risk that it will just be seen as an unnecessary burden, and this could also be an obstacle to line managers accepting this new role.

The other important issue is the ethical accountability of organizations regarding outsourcing, and the treatment of contract workers, specifically in their working conditions, wages and benefits, and development opportunities, and all of this is particularly true in the case of freelancers and gig workers (Wasserman & Fisher, 2020). Although they can be out of reach in legal terms, we can see them as new stakeholders to which companies must also be socially responsible.

5. Conclusion

In this paper, we have tried to find answers to some of the new challenges in the field of HRM that arise from the use of e-HRM. The first question is that of efficiency, and although this is not a guarantee, the answer is that there are gains to be made in the use of IT, by reducing operating costs and even the size of the HR department.

As for the desired strategic role for HRM, the answer is not simple, although in some cases professionals feel they have more time to devote to more global or strategic issues, this does not always seem to be the case, which leads us to consider that perhaps it is the companies themselves that are neglecting the strategic role of HRM.

Or perhaps the answer is partly related to the need for new competencies on the part of HR professionals. The answer is not straightforward. Though there is a call for the ability to understand more of the technical aspects of e-HRM systems to better communicate with the technical staff and of data analytic skills it becomes clear that communication, analysis and evaluation, ethics, and relations management, which aren't new, are also needed and maybe of greater importance in this new context surrounded by technology.

The darker side of e-HRM, the ethical and legal problems that surfaced, regarding privacy, the use of algorithms, and problems with fairness have been recognized and must be dealt with. In our view, this is a domain where HRM professionals can and should have an important role, guaranteeing compliance and ethics on the various processes involving people and on the proactive development of policies and procedures for stakeholders and organizations (Lukaszewski & Stone, 2024) as a part of their strategic role that we believe can be aligned with a developmental understanding of the HR function.

References

Al-Harazneh, Y. M., & Sila, I. (2021). The impact of E-HRM usage on HRM effectiveness: highlighting the roles of top management support, HR professionals, and line managers. *Journal of Global Information Management* (JGIM), *29*(2), 118–147.

Berber, N., Đorđević, B., & Milanović, S. (2018). Electronic human resource management (e-HRM): A new concept for digital age. *Strategic Management-International Journal of Strategic Management and Decision Support Systems in Strategic Management*, *23*(2).

Bondarouk, T. V., & Ruël, H. J. M. (2009). Electronic human resource management: Challenges in the digital era. *The International Journal of Human Resource Management*, *20*, 505–514

Bondarouk, T., & Ruël, H. (2013). The strategic value of e-HRM: results from an exploratory study in a governmental organization. *The International Journal of Human Resource Management*, *24*(2), 391–414.

Bondarouk, T., & Brewster, C. (2016). Conceptualising the future of HRM and technology research. *The International Journal of Human Resource Management*, *27*(21), 2652–2671.

Bondarouk, Parry, & Furtmueller (2017) Electronic HRM: four decades of research on adoption and consequences, *The International Journal of Human Resource Management*, *28*(1), 98–131, DOI: 10.1080/09585192.2016.1245672

Ceric, A., & Parton, K. (2024). What prevents organisations from achieving e-HRM potential?. *Australasian Journal of Information Systems*, *28*.

Cleveland, J. N., Byrne, Z. S., & Cavanagh, T. M. (2015). The future of HR is RH: Respect for humanity at work. *Human Resource Management Review*, *25*(2), 146–161.

Cohen, D. J. (2015). HR past, present and future: A call for consistent practices and a focus on competencies. *Human Resource Management Review*, *25*(2), 205–215.

Fındıklı, M. A., & beyza Bayarçelik, E. (2015). Exploring the outcomes of electronic human resource management (E-HRM)?. *Procedia-Social and Behavioral Sciences*, *207*, 424–431.

Greenberg, J. (2009). Everybody talks about organizational justice, but nobody does anything about it. *Industrial and Organizational Psychology*, *2*(2), 181–195.

Lengnick-Hall, M. L., & Moritz, S. (2003). The impact of e-HR on the human resource management function. *Journal of Labor Research*, *24*(3), 365.

Lepak, D. P., & Snell, S. A. (1998). Virtual HR: Strategic human resource management in the 21st century. *Human Resource Management Review*, *8*(3), 215–234.

Lukaszewski, K. M., & Stone, D. L. (2024). Will the use of AI in human resources create a digital Frankenstein?. *Organizational Dynamics*, 101033.

Ma, L., & Ye, M. (2015). The Role of Electronic Human Resource Management in Contemporary Human Resource Management. *Open Journal of Social Sciences*, *3*(4), 71–78.

Marchington, M. (2015). Human resource management (HRM): Too busy looking up to see where it is going longer term?. *Human Resource Management Review*, *25*(2), 176–187.

Parry, E., & Tyson, S. (2011). Desired goals and actual outcomes of e-HRM. *Human resource management journal*, *21*(3), 335–354.

Radonjić, A., Duarte, H., & Pereira, N. (2022). Artificial intelligence and HRM: HR managers' perspective on decisiveness and challenges. *European Management Journal*.

Ruël, H., Bondarouk, T., & Looise, J. K. (2004). E-HRM: Innovation or irritation. An explorative empirical study in five large companies on web-based HRM. *Management Revue*, 364–380.

Stone, D. L., & Deadrick, D. L. (2015). Challenges and opportunities affecting the future of human resource management. *Human Resource Management Review*, *25*(2), 139–145.

Stone, D. L., & Dulebohn, J. H. (2013). Emerging issues in theory and research on electronic human resource management (eHRM). *Human Resource Management Review, 23*(1), 1–5.

Stone, D. L., Deadrick, D. L., Lukaszewski, K. M., & Johnson, R. (2015). The influence of technology on the future of human resource management. *Human Resource Management Review*, *25*(2), 216–231.

Tambe, P., Cappelli, P., & Yakubovich, V. (2019). Artificial intelligence in human resources management: Challenges and a path forward. *California Management Review*, *61*(4), 15–42.

Ulrich, D., & Dulebohn, J. H. (2015). Are we there yet? What's next for HR?. *Human Resource Management Review*, *25*(2), 188–204.

Wasserman, M., & Fisher, S. (2020). Sailing in Stormy Weather: Digitalization, Ethics and e-HRM. In T. Bondarouk & S. Fisher (Ed.), *Encyclopedia of Electronic HRM* (pp. 156–162). Berlin, Boston: De Gruyter Oldenbourg.

Yusliza, M. Y., & Ramayah, T. (2012). Determinants of attitude towards E-HRM: An empirical study among HR professionals. *Procedia-Social and Behavioral Sciences*, *57*, 312–319.

Alexandru Trifu

Is the Happiness Decisive in Providing Prosperity and Competitiveness?

1. Introduction: The Focus on Economic and Productive Entities

As the source of the human actions aimed at reaching the desired goals, *the happiness, the state of happiness is the main ingredient.* Why? Because, the happiness is considered a permanent state, synonymous with contentment and prosperity (author's note).

Happiness is a feeling that depends on the attitude you take in life towards each person's actions and behavior (www.totcum.com 2020). We are not dealing with a universally accepted definition of happiness; it can vary from person to person.

Moreover, the neuropsychological research has shown that the happiness is the best food for the brain. To achieve the desired state of happiness, each in his own way and having very different goals and motivations, we need personal experiences, as well as mental associations – shortcuts in thinking called *heuristics* (Tversky & Kahneman, 2019). The article published in Science in 1974, vol. 185 *relates to the decisions that people make* ***under conditions of uncertainty*** (author's note), as the vast majority of situations existing in the external or internal environment of businesses are.

The material highlights that people can rely on a small number of heuristics (the shortcuts in thinking, a rule of thumb, a quick practical way of solving a problem):

a. Representativeness;
b. Availability;
c. Adjustment and anchoring.

In the first case, people make estimates and judgments about things and other people based on the similarity thereof to existing stereotypes and representative types.

In the second case of heuristics, there is the availability; people go for the first thing that comes to their minds. This is fast and useful, but it can lead to erroneous decisions, given the complexity of today's activities and also the complexity of challenges that strike in structural economic-social systems.

In the third case, people tend to start from whatever initial value they were given. Too often this value is not only wrong, but people are reluctant to stray too far from it. This is *the anchoring effect*.

Certainly, this approach also supports the modern decision theory and it shows us the somewhat simplistic method of judgment that must take into account many more objective and subjective variables, especially since we are discussing happiness as an enhancer of performance and competitiveness.

But we are interested in what the targets of happiness would be. One would be the achievement of *prosperity* that is the state of being *successful and prosperous*[1].

The performance is the other target in the present situation and which in the present case relates to *the efficiency* of the proposed and performed actions[2]. *The competitiveness* is also inextricably linked to this target, i.e. the ability to face the competition, through the strong desire to be more successful than others[3].

Is *the money a goal of happiness* and *can money buy happiness*? Answers have been given, some taking into account the current generational structure (see Morgan, 2023).

For the first question some figures were advanced related to incomes of £50,000, for example, or $70–80,000, according to calculations made by two renowned Nobel Prize winning economists, Daniel Kahneman and Angus Deaton, in a 2010 study (Rampono, 2023). Having money, being prosperous, having everything you want and even more, is a goal that brings less happiness than the satisfaction of having everything that can be bought and owned.

To the second question, both our personal opinion and the answers received and analyzed indicate a categorical answer: No, it cannot.

Let us specify, however, that money/welfare can buy access to public utility services, to the areas of the materialization of the Human Capital, but desired and obtained jobs truly increase the happiness and they have beneficial effects on entities and households (Nortje, 2023).

We are also interested in *the competitiveness of the economic regions of the European Union*, because we are talking about economic and social units related to the regional economy, i.e. the European Union.

---

1 *** (2024) Merriam-Webster Dictionary, *Prosperity*, www.merriam-webster.com/dictionary/prosperity/ retrieved on April 2, 2024.

2 *** (2024) Merriam-Webster Dictionary, *Performance,* www.merriam-webster.com/dictionary/performance/ retrieved on March 30, 2024.

3 *** (2024) Merriam-Webster Diuctionary, *Competitiveness,* www.merriam-webster.com/dictionary/competitiveness/ retrieved on April 2, 2024.

The territorial competitiveness is the ability of a region to offer an attractive and sustainable environment where businesses and residents can live and carry out their activities (Luca, 2023). So, the central idea of the present work is the attractiveness of economic entities, both from the financial and utility viewpoint.

The more developed regions, including capital regions, are more competitive and attractive for young graduates, for the skilled workforce, and the gaps between them tend to decrease and the score compared to the European average (100 %) must decrease.

According to a map of the Price of Happiness on the Globe (Rampono, 2023), the developed countries, the developed regions have a much higher cost of happiness compared to the rest of the areas and regions. The causal relationship of imposition goes from the appropriate state of mind to the activity in a business environment and region with potential, the achievement of the proposed goals and a welcome feedback for the continuation of the activity with the help of timely corrections.

But, to complete the picture with the positioning of the various territorial units in the European Union, we present the following situation from December 2023, regarding the GDP per inhabitant (Pălăngean, 2023):

1.	**Bruxelles**	**66.200 euros**
2.	**Praha**	**65.800 euros**
3.	**Hamburg**	**61.900 euros**
4.	**Copenhagen (Hovedstaden)**	**57.700 euros**
5.	**Paris (Ile-de-France)**	**56.900 euros**
6.	**München (Oberbayern)**	**56.600 euros**
7.	**Stockholm**	**55.300 euros**
8.	**Amsterdam (Noord-Holland)**	**54.400 euros**
9.	***Bucharest (București-Ilfov)***	***53.900 euros***
10.	**Warsaw (Warszawski Stoleczny)**	**53.700 euros**

As noted, this is a ranking for *capital regions and adjacent areas only*. Therefore, the analysis and understanding of the role of the regions in the European Union must be done without considering these capital regions, which from an economic and statistical viewpoint are far from the other regions, i.e. eccentric, outside the national environments. But, they translate the economic power of those countries.

From the above situation, the regions of the European Union that recorded disproportionately high values compared to the rest of the analyzed countries also stand out:

Luxemburg	**87.100 euros**
Cork (Southern Ireland)	**84.500 euros**
Dublin (Eastern & Midland Ireland)	**77.400 euros**

But there are other economic and social explanations for these three situations. In the case of Luxembourg, the economic result relates to the activity of people from the neighboring countries – France, Germany, Belgium – but it is related only to the resident population, and the GDP of the two Irish regions is artificially increased by reporting the performance of some companies based in this country for fiscal and opportunity advantages, after the exit of the United Kingdom (UK) (Pălăngean, 2023).

2. Methodology

We used information, opinions and experiences, both our own from the academic activity, but also other people's, either CEOs, managers, or employees in various firms/companies.

The opinions are diverse and subjective but the endogenous, affective and motivational aspect is decisive in individual actions, but also in supporting the business activity which, in turn (the business environment), through feedback can ensure the elements of the work climate and favorable development.

The discussions held also focused on the generational typology, fashionable today, in order to understand how the generations that make up the workforce see the happiness and its impact on life and profession.

3. The Human Resource Push System towards Progress

A particularly important aspect, which must also take into account the current generational characteristics, especially of the Millennials and Gen Z, as well as the internal resource which is the permanent feeling of happiness, depending on what objectives each of us and them – proposed, is that of the management phenomenon, from "The Great Resignation" to "The Great Mismatch".

"The Great Resignation" substantiated and disseminated in 2021 by Professor Anthony Klotz – a professor of business administration at Texas A & M University – was specific to the pandemic period, but also to the post-pandemic period. It is the very process that no employer or entrepreneur wants to occur, through which employees leave their jobs very quickly, not integrating the work environment caused by wages considered to lack motivation, and by the climate that does not comply to what that person considers to be conducive to a career plan and achievement.

Currently, there is also a worrying phenomenon that unfolds is that of "The Great Mismatch". This means that *the labor supply and demand are disengaged* (emphasis added). This is clearly seen in Romania, where more and more higher education graduates fail to find jobs suitable to their training (Popa, 2024).

Thus, the employers can't find workers for the available jobs they have, and the unemployed and graduates don't want to fill those jobs, either:

- they have to commute (something that would not be too much of an impediment);
- they are higher education people, or who had a well-paid job and do not want to have a a secondary education underpaid job;
- they are experienced people in their field of expertise, some of which had management positions and who are replaced by young people with digital knowledge and skills, with the ability to synthesize and find the optimal option in the issues they face at work. These outcasts won't find work soon to fall back on;
- a specific situation for the labor market in Romania (which we do not believe to be singular) is represented by the accession, in the not too distant future, we hope, to the Schengen land area. This will mean that the migrants who came from the East, from Asia, will be able to leave (they have already expressed this intention) to work and live in the developed states of the Western Europe. Again, the job crisis will deepen, because no employees filled certain jobs, but also because the labor force over 50 years old will prevail.

So, the situations that lead us to directly support the proportionality between the analyzed variables are those related to firms/companies which through propagation and aggregation reach the macroeconomic level.

Speaking of entities and a recent factor of production, the CEO, there is the case of the CEO of Nvidia, but also one of the founders, Jensen Huang, considered a "self-made" billionaire in the USA and an unconventional CEO (Jucan, 2024).

We praise Taiwan-born Jensen Huang for his managerial skills not only for the fact that he is at the head of the tech giant Nvidia, the world leader in Artificial Intelligence Computing, but also for the way he thinks through the purpose of this company, but also the human resources in general (Jucan, 2024).

More precisely, what caught our attention was the piece of advice he gave to young people; it was a rather unorthodox and impactful advice, in the sense that they should experience "pain and suffering" to shape their character, but also that parents they don't have to push their kids into programming.

Regarding his first piece of advice, one can note that it is taken from the Taoist philosophy, which states, in summary, that in order to be well/do well, you need first to go through pain and decline in life.

Trying to be as real as possible, as unconventional, is a credo for Jensen Huang, who managed to propel Nvidia from a market capitalization of 1 trillion dollars to more than 2 trillion dollars nowadays. Certainly, this extraordinary propulsion was due to the focus of the activity on AI (Artificial Intelligence) and the use of top specialists in this field.

In fact, the chips released by Nvidia have come to the attention of American universities, where the research laboratories have successfully used them. Then moving on to the use of AI technology, the success was appropriate.

Passing to the macro level of the national economies, we cannot help to salute the Scandinavian States which, along with Finland (already the happiness champion for the seventh consecutive time) are in this top of happiness published in March 2024.

In these cases, especially in the case of Finland, we are actually talking about the harmonious cooperation of the entire society, both the citizens and the state institutions, which come to meet and support the citizens. We relate to public goods, such as the education, the healthcare, that are the very pillars of *the Human Capital*, as well as the security, which supports people's trust that their money is used wisely and for the stated purposes.

In the same way, and at the micro level, without the phenomenon of *bossing* and pressure from other employees, or even from competing entities, the happiness comes from the satisfaction of the accomplished work, in achieving targets, an aspect that leads to profitability for the company as well as to possible increases in employees' incomes.

The defining aspect that reinforces the definition at the beginning of the paper is that *the happiness is a permanent state in these northern European countries*. We believe that, both at the economic entity level and at the macroeconomic level, they are important (www.g4media.ro 2024):

a. *The people's trust* (emphasis added), primarily in the state institutions, but also the social trust, within the business or extended community;
b. The reduction of income inequalities between social categories, especially between the people who earn high incomes/salaries and the others. Here, one can note that the middle social class is well articulated in the society.

Let us see another aspect relevant to the present issue: we relate to *the countries experiencing the highest standard of living in the world*, determined on the basis of the HDI (Human Development Index). It has as calculation variables the GDP, the social progress including the life expectancy, the education level and the gross national income per person. According to the Report of March 13, 2024, the HDI for the year 2022 recorded an increase compared to the previous analysis, but the progress was slow and uneven because of the great challenges of this stage.

The top 10 countries in this ranking are as follows (www.digi24.ro 2024):

Switzerland; *Norway; Iceland*; Hong Kong; *Denmark; Sweden; Germany*; Ireland; Singapore; Australia.

Finland ranks 13th, which is a good ranking given its achievements in the economic and social fields. A shortcoming of this index is that it does not take into account the economic inequalities, or the disparities between ethnicities or the genders.

There are also rich countries, with a high level of GDP, but they are not to be found in the top of the world's happiness. According to the top in this field, the first place is awarded to the USA, followed by China, Japan, Germany and India (https://www.worldometers.info/gdp/gdp-by-country/#google_vignette). The study relates to the nominal GDP, i.e. the totality of the final goods and services obtained, in current prices, and it only relates to *the quantitative aspect* of increasing the size of an economy. Finland ranks 47th, even if in terms of GDP/capita it registers a value that can propel it higher in the ranking.

What we are interested in is the fact that the happiness and the endogenous motivations support the structural, qualitative aspects of any increase in size, whether they are macroeconomic or microeconomic.

We emphasize that the incentives, the salary increases, the increased responsibilities in the microeconomic environment, the establishment of the recession and the austerity measures in the macroeconomic environment can lead to negative mental states, to the decrease of happiness related to the reduction of one's time allocated to the family and for oneself (Kahneman et al., 2006).

But one has to find the inner strength plus the options that are offered for various services of revitalization and recovery, so that the balance that we were talking about and that is essential between the family/personal life and the professional life continues is set straight.

4. Conclusions

This co-operation and homogeneous operation of the Nordic States should be an example for other economies and societies. The wealth and prosperity doubled by the effective and efficient feedback of state institutions results in *the state of happiness* that becomes the "engine" for the movement of the entire economic and social system towards progress, prosperity and competitiveness.

In fact, what we presented in the first part of our paper is the need for happiness to be the result of achieving a balance between personal life and personal activity, without constraints or pressures, so that everyone can follow their dreams.

The well-being, the prosperity, together with the trust in the projects undertaken, in the state institutions that meet the citizens' needs through the education, health and security systems strengthen the state of happiness that the Nordic States experience.

The fiscal policy of progressive taxation, the boosting of the economic activity and the motivating of companies and their employees should occur so that the tax base is as high as possible and the added value is as high as possible. That translates into prosperity and the motivation to take pleasure in a well-done, efficient work.

Acknowledgments

We would like to thank Mr. Dan Gîrtan, the manager of a service provision company for his ideas related to the issue analyzed, as well as to Professor Veysel Kaya and his collaborators for the opportunity given to us and the publishing of these analysis in the coordinated books for them to be known by specialists and by all those interested in this topic.

References

Jucan, Sebastian (March 20, 2024). *Miliardar "self-made" in SUA, vedetă în țara natală* (in Romanian in original, meaning *A self-made billionaire in the USA, A Star In His Native Country*), https://hotnews.ro/miliardar-self-made-n-sua-vedeta-n-tara-sa-natala-cine-este-jensen-huang-ceo-ul-neconventional-al-nvidia-10963 retrieved March 26, 2024.

Kahneman, Daniel et al. (2006). *Would You Be Happier If You Were Richer? Science, 312*, www.researchgate.net/publication/6974433_/ retrieved March 31st, 2024.

Luca, Iulian (2023). *Regiunile de sud-est și nord-est ale României, pe ultimile locuri din UE, în privința competitivității* (in Romanian in orig., meaning *The south-east and north-east regions of Romania, on the last places in EU in terms of competitiveness*), http://www.capital.ro//regiunile-de-sud-est-si-nord-est-aleromaniei-pe-ultimile-locuri-din-ue-in-privinta-competitivitatii/ accesat 20 februarie 2024.

Morgan, Kendra (2023). *What is the definition of happiness? Can money buy happiness?* Quora, www.quora.com/What-is-the-definition-of-happiness-Can-money-buy-happiness/ retrieved March 15, 2024.

Nortje, Alicia (2023). *Happiness economics: Can money buy happiness*? www.positivepsychology.com/happiness-economics/ retrieved April 2nd, 2024.

Pălăngean, Dan (December 2023). *Regiunea București-Ilfov în topul european al PIB/locuitor*(in Romanian in orig., meaning *Bucharest-Ilfov region in the European top of GDP/capita*), Financial Intelligence, www.financialintelligence.ro/regiunea-bucuresti-ilfov-in-topul-european-ca-pib-pe-locuitor/ retrieved March 10, 2024.

Popa, Dan (March 29, 2024). *Analiza de la Marea Demisioneală la Marea Nepotrivire (…)* (in Romanian în original, which means *From The Great Resignation to The Great Mismatch*), https://hotnews.ro/analiza-de-la-marea-demisioneala-la-marea-nepotrivire-statistica-tocmai-a-publicat-numarul-locurilor-de-munca-pentru-care-angajatorii-nu-reusesc-sa-gaseasca-oameni-9321 retrieved March 31st, 2024.

Rampono, Justin (2023). *Cost of contentedness*, https://www.smoney.com.au/blog/the-price-of-happiness-in-every-country/ retrieved March 29, 2024.

Tversky, A., & Kahneman, Daniel (2019, based on initial paper of 1974). *Judgement Under Uncertainty: Heuristics and Biases*, Books and Boots, https://astrofella.wordpress.com/2019/04/05/judgement-under-uncertainty-heuristics-and-biases-amos-tversky-daniel-kahneman/ retrieved March 24, 2024.

*** (March 2024) *Țările cu cel mai bun nivel de trai* (in Romanian in orig., meaning *The countries with the best Standard of Living*), https://www.digi24.ro/stiri/externe/tarile-cu-cel-mai-bun-nivel-de-trai-pe-ce-loc-este-romania-2729155 retrieved April 1st, 2024.

*** (March 2024) *De ce oamenii din țările nordice sunt cei mai fericiți și ce putem învăța de la ei?* (in Romanian in orig., meaning *Why are people from Nordic countries the happiest and what can we learn from them?*) https://www.g4media.ro/de-ce-oamenii-din-tarile-nordice-sunt-cei-mai-fericiti-si-ce-putem-invata-de-la-ei-taxarea-progresiva-si-calitatea-institutiilor-printre-factorii-principali.html retrieved March 31st, 2024.

Aliya Akhmedieva, Abdurashid Kadirov, Bahtiyor Mamurov,
Ulugbek Musabekov

Improving Investment Strategy for the Economic Development of Uzbekistan

1. Introduction

The investment strategy is a crucial tool for establishing the necessary institutional conditions that drive investment plans, norms, programs, and other related activities. It should not only prioritize socio-economic development or investment projects, but also provide a holistic view of the investment process in conjunction with the growth of the country's competitiveness.

In line with the Decree of the President of the Republic of Uzbekistan No. PP-4937, "On measures to implement the investment program of the Republic of Uzbekistan for 2021–2023" issued on December 28, 2020, the forecast parameters for the development of capital investments, attraction of investments and loans, and centralized and non-centralized investments are planned to be developed, amounting to 928.7 trillion soums, including $37.5 billion of foreign investments.

As a result of the radical reforms implemented to transform and restructure various industries, economic growth is expected to be achieved by creating competitive production chains and increasing investments.

2. Literature Review

Attracting investment is a critical issue for the world economy, particularly for increasing the economic growth of countries. Researchers like V.A. Tolmachev (2017), L.V. Polunin (2012), V.P. Savchuk, S.I. Primenko, E.G. Velichko (2016), V. Trenev and Likhachev (2007), and A.P. Ivanov (Ivanov et al., 2017) have studied the challenges related to investment climate attractiveness. Meanwhile, N. Yusupova (2020) has examined the issues concerning foreign investment attraction in Uzbekistan. Sh. Mustafakulov (2017) has focused on creating necessary conditions for foreign investment attraction in the country. K.Y. Lee (2000) has looked at inflation as an important indicator affecting investment climate.

The works of M. Moore and H. Schmitz emphasize the significance of investment strategy formation and implementation in achieving strategic goals of investment activities. They consider investment strategy as one of the functional strategies of strategic management (Moore & Schmitz, 2016). Additionally, scholars like W. Sharp, G. Birman, and Z. Bodi classify investment strategy as a key functional strategy, along with innovation and financial strategies (Birman, 2003; Body, 2002; Sharp, 2001).

3. Data and Methodology

This research employs various methods such as the systematic approach, statistical analysis, structural analysis, comparative analysis, expert and predictive assessment, as well as economic and mathematical modeling.

4. Results and Discussion

Based on the analysis conducted, it is projected that Uzbekistan's GDP growth will range between 4.8 % to 5 % in 2021, provided that there is no reintroduction of quarantine measures throughout the country (refer to Fig. 1).

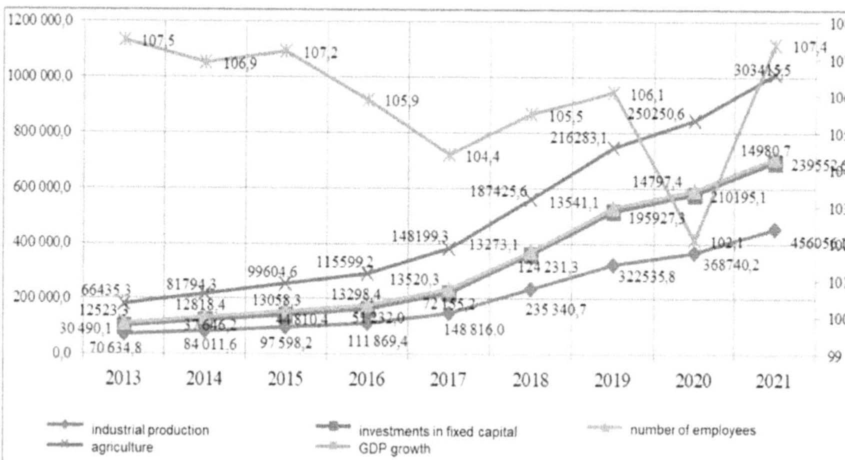

Figure 1. The macroeconomic indicators of the development of Uzbekistan's economy in billion soums

The rate of decline in Uzbekistan's economy slowed down from 11.2 % in Q1 2020 to 3.5 % in the current quarter. Investments from the budget and government-guaranteed loans decreased, with their share dropping from 18 % in Q1 2020 to 6.2 % this year. However, investments from non-centralized sources increased by 13.6 % compared to the corresponding period last year. Foreign direct investments and loans increased by 30.6 %, investments at the expense of the population increased by 20 %, and investments by enterprises increased by 6.3 %. Additionally, commercial banks issued loans 11 % more than in the same period last year.

The decrease in centralized investments was due to a higher social burden on the budget and restrictions on attracting foreign loans under state guarantees, which resulted in an improvement in the structure of investments. The growth in the volume of non-centralized investments indicates an increase in the investment activity of businesses and the population, as well as the attractiveness of the country for foreign investors, who have already positively assessed the resilience of the economy to the crisis (Abaturov, 2021).

Based on the above statistics, the investment sector is the most affected part of Uzbekistan's economy in 2021, emphasizing the need to develop this sector. The World Bank projects that GDP growth in Uzbekistan will recover to 4.8 % in 2021, after falling sharply from 5.8 % in 2019 to 1.6 % in 2020 due to quarantine restrictions and disruptions in trade operations caused by the pandemic. However, growth may be affected by uncertainties related to the pace of global economic recovery and the success of the national COVID-19 vaccination campaign. GDP growth is projected higher in 2022 (up to 5.5 %) as vaccination rates accelerate and global economic disruptions ease.

The concept of an investment strategy applies to various participants in the investment process, including investors, financial intermediaries, as well as state and legislative bodies that regulate these processes (Izaak & Chernyshov, 2013).

To develop an investment strategy for the development of the Republic of Uzbekistan, the following algorithm can be proposed (refer to Fig. 2):

Set the goals of the investment strategy based on the overall goals of economic development, taking into account the country's economic potential, comparative advantages, and priorities.

Analyze the current state of the investment climate, including macroeconomic indicators, legal and regulatory framework, business environment, infrastructure, and social factors. Identify strengths, weaknesses, opportunities, and threats (SWOT analysis) that affect the investment activity.

Define the target sectors and areas of investment based on the strategic goals, comparative advantages, market demand, and potential impact on economic growth, employment, and social welfare. Prioritize the sectors and areas based on their importance and potential.

Develop the investment portfolio that specifies the types, amounts, sources, and timing of investments in the target sectors and areas. Consider the balance

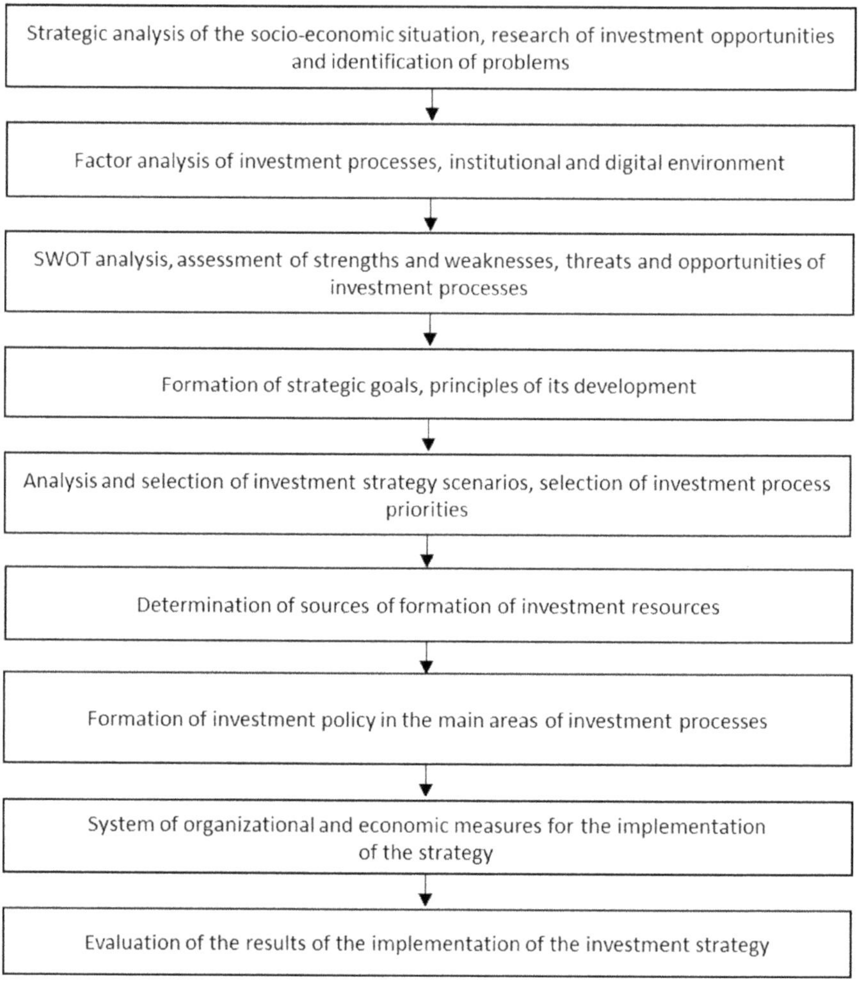

Figure 2. An Algorithm for Formulating an Investment Strategy for the Development of the Republic of Uzbekistan

between real and financial investments, short-term and long-term investments, domestic and foreign investments, public and private investments, and other factors.

Identify the financing mechanisms and instruments that are appropriate for the investment portfolio, such as budgetary funds, development funds, public-private partnerships, foreign loans and investments, venture capital, crowdfunding, and others. Evaluate the risks and benefits of each mechanism and instrument and select the optimal ones.

Design the implementation plan that outlines the steps, responsibilities, timelines, and performance indicators of the investment strategy. Monitor and evaluate the implementation progress and outcomes regularly and adjust the strategy if necessary.

Ensure the coordination and cooperation among the relevant stakeholders and institutions, such as government agencies, private sector entities, civil society organizations, and international partners. Foster the trust, transparency, and accountability in the investment process.

By following this algorithm, the investment strategy for the development of the Republic of Uzbekistan can be formulated systematically, based on the analysis, goals, priorities, and actions that are aligned with the overall strategy of economic development.

An investment strategy serves as a long-term roadmap for the development of investment processes in a particular territory. It outlines the parameters that the subject of management deems necessary for the future and how they will be achieved in unstable conditions. The primary goal of developing an investment strategy is to achieve the target parameters of the investment process and maintain them in the face of potential adverse changes in the external environment.

The fundamental principles of developing an investment strategy involve considering a system of measures aimed at implementing medium and long-term socio-economic development tasks while accounting for the rational contribution of industries and regions to solving these tasks. It takes into account the real prerequisites and limitations of their development.

An investment strategy is a document that defines general goals, objectives, directions of investment processes, and mechanisms for their implementation. This arises from the analysis of resource opportunities, the existing socio-economic situation, and possible scenarios for the development of external conditions. The strategy changes depending on the socio-economic situation at a particular stage of development, the emerging relationship between government, business and the community, and the external economic situation. Thus, adjusting the strategy as external and internal conditions change is mandatory.

An investment strategy is not a document of "direct action" but serves as a basis for the development of a whole system of documents. These include strategic plans for the development of regions, individual industries, comprehensive targeted programs, long-term and current plans for socio-economic development, plans for the activities of various levels of government, and legislative initiatives.

To respond adequately to the challenges of the modern world, the proposed approach to the development of investment strategies incorporates an innovative, motivational, economic, organizational, administrative, and other qualitative components. Developing investment strategies and assessing their quality should take into account new principles, approaches to targets, and results of work when developing a national strategy for socio-economic development.

The strategy is a product of partnership between representatives of legislative and executive authorities, management of large enterprises, banks, business associations, universities, research institutes, the local community, and non-governmental organizations. Legally, a strategy is a document in which various branches of government, business circles, public organizations undertake obligations to jointly promote direct or most important (strategic) projects and other events.

Tools for implementing the strategy at various levels include investment programs for the development of regions and industries, targeted programs for socio-economic development, business plans, and projects of commercial and public organizations. The strategy, as an interim document, is continuously monitored.

An analysis of development trends can influence the future development of the country in the forecast period. The results of the analysis should lead to specific conclusions such as whether the forecast growth rates of individual sectors of the economy ensure the growth of investments by the forecast period and which sectors and individual enterprises can become the "locomotives" of GDP growth.

The significance of the analysis for the development of investment processes depends on factors of the external and internal environment. External factors such as the macroeconomic situation, actions of republican executive and legislative authorities that influence investment processes, economic and geographical position of the republic, and the degree of inclusion in the system of global commodity, financial, and information markets should be included.

The profitable instrument of investment policy is of great importance for the development of production. Three groups of factors that can be considered from the standpoint of macro, meso, and micro-levels underlie the formation and rapid spread throughout the world of business.

When developing a strategy for investment, it is important to consider macro-level, meso-level, and micro-level factors. Macro-level factors include macroeconomic policies, legal and regulatory frameworks, and patterns that affect the overall economy. Meso-level factors focus on regional features, while micro-level factors aim to address enterprise-level needs.

Conducting an analysis of these factors can help identify the most significant ones that require special attention when developing a strategy. It can also help correct the assessment of the potential of industries and regions to use their competitive advantages for further development. Assessing the current state and development potential of the country, including its strengths and weaknesses, is crucial in setting strategic goals for national economic development.

A SWOT analysis is an effective and affordable way to evaluate the socio-economic situation, growth potential, and starting conditions for developing a strategy. It helps identify idle resources and threats, fills information gaps, and complements traditional analysis.

Considering the current stage of modernization of the national economy, two types of strategies can be distinguished: the traditional socio-economic strategy that maintains the existing structure of the economy and modernizes leading industries, and the innovative strategy that integrates institutional, motivational, economic, organizational, administrative, and other components into a new vector of development that goes beyond existing trends.

In the future, specific scientific and methodological tools for investment strategy can be developed based on these methodological provisions. These tools should be used by all parties involved in the investment process and integrated into the system of state regulation (as illustrated in Fig. 3).

Investment opportunities in Uzbekistan are currently being actively utilized, which is contributing to the growth and development of small businesses and private entrepreneurship. Notably, this trend is particularly evident in the agricultural processing, building materials, food, and textile industries, which have quickly expanded their production capacity and have been able to offer high-quality, affordable products to domestic consumers.

This study aims to examine, analyze, and evaluate the factors that impact the size of the gross domestic product. To achieve this objective, we have identified the following key factors: the volume of gross domestic product (in billion soums) – Y; the average annual number of employees (in thousands) – X1; the volume of industrial production (%) – X2; the volume of agricultural production (in billion soums) – X3; investments in fixed capital (in billion soums) – X4; the volume of services (in billion soums) – X5; the total income of the population (in thousand soums) – X6.

Through our research, we have developed a regression equation using the EViews program to analyze the impact of these factors on the outcome index. This equation will help to identify the most significant factors that affect the gross domestic product and provide a basis for developing effective investment strategies to promote sustainable economic growth and development in Uzbekistan.

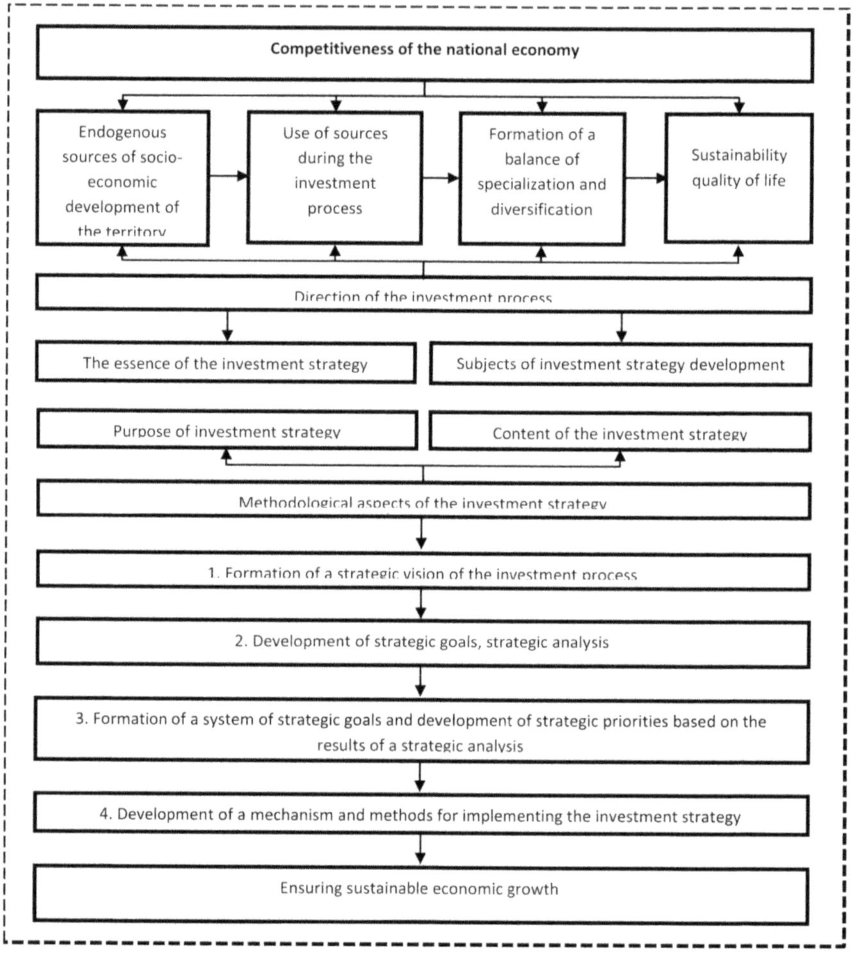

Figure 3. Structural Matrix of the Methodology for Developing an Investment Strategy

After evaluating the constructed regression equation based on the evaluation criteria, it was found that several parameters, including X1, X2, and X5, were insignificant according to the Student's criterion. Moreover, the Fisher criterion was positive, but the autocorrelation according to the Durbin-Watson criterion was 2.52, indicating negative autocorrelation. As a result, the overall stability of the regression equation was deemed questionable. Therefore, we re-examined the selected influencing factors and created a new regression equation.

Using a linear and stepwise multifactor econometric model for forecasting the gross domestic product volume can take into account the impact of macroeconomic factors in the medium and long term. The evaluation of the newly created regression equation revealed that parameters X3, X4, and X6 were insignificant according to the Student's criterion. Furthermore, the Fisher criterion was positive, but the autocorrelation according to the Durbin-Watson criterion was 2.52, indicating negative autocorrelation. As with the previous equation, the general stability of the regression equation was found to be unstable.

After evaluating the obtained regression equation based on all the relevant criteria, we found that both the regression equation and its coefficients were stable. Hence, we can express the multifactor regression equation as follows:

$$\begin{matrix} Y \\ t \end{matrix} = \begin{matrix} -5878,304 + 0,67995X_3 + 0,53991X_4 + 0,78665X_6 \\ (-2,573) \quad (5,839) \quad (13,702) \quad (9,942) \end{matrix}$$

Based on the trend models we have constructed for the factors influencing the gross regional product of the country, we have formulated a forecast that is presented in the following Table 1.

Table 1. Forecast results based on a multifactorial econometric model between factors affecting the country's gross domestic product

Forecast years	**Gross domestic product Y**		**The volume of agricultural production (in billion soums) X3**	**Investments in fixed capital (in billion soums) X4**	**The total income of the population (in thousand soums) X6**
	A forecast based on a trend model	**A forecast based on an empirical model**	**A forecast based on a trend model**	**A forecast based on a trend model**	**A forecast based on a trend model**
2023	1005115,6	1004534,1	400523,7	372163,1	682821,2
2024	1158785,4	1157955,3	456936,4	439503,4	782873,6
2025	1324700,1	1323587,2	517503,5	512743,5	890807,4
2026	1502859,4	1501428,6	582225,3	591883,4	1006621,5

The multi-factor econometric model that we developed evaluated the impact of scientific research factors on the country's gross domestic product. Based on trend models and 2020 prices, we predict that the country's gross domestic product will increase to 1.36 times in 2023 and 2.04 times in 2026 compared to 2021.

The volume of agricultural production is expected to increase by 1.32 times in 2023 and 1.92 times in 2026 compared to 2021. Likewise, investments in Fixed Capital are expected to increase by 1.55 times in 2023 and 2.47 times in 2026 compared to 2021. We predict that the total income of the country's population will increase by 1.32 times in 2023 and 1.94 times in 2026 compared to 2021 (Fig. 4).

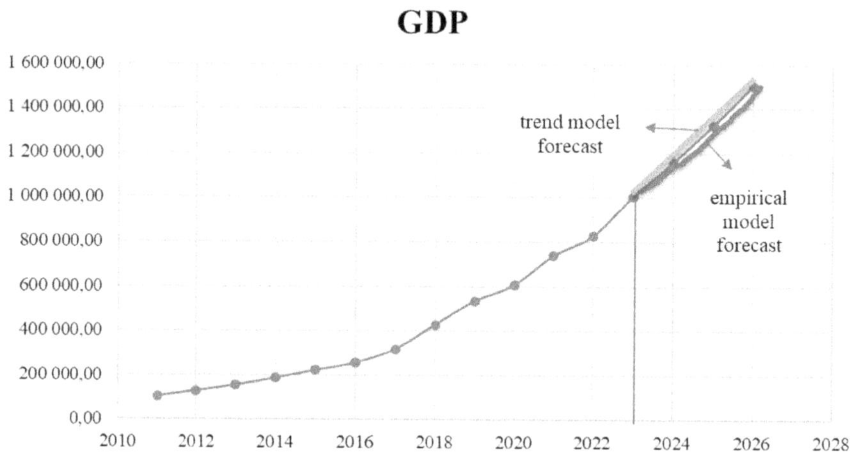

Figure 4. Structural Matrix of the Methodology for Developing an Investment Strategy

The results of the constructed multi-factor empirical model indicate that a 1 % increase in agricultural production will lead to a 0.29 % increase in the Gross Domestic Product (GDP), while a 1 % increase in fixed capital investments will lead to a 0.155 % increase in the GDP. Moreover, the model shows that a 1 % increase in the general income of the population will result in a 0.572 % increase in the GDP. To obtain forecast results, we created trend models of the influencing factors based on the constructed econometric model.

5. Conclusion

In conclusion, enhancing the efficiency of investment activities in the republic requires the right choice of strategy to concentrate efforts and resources on realizing the potential for economic development, thereby ensuring the growth of the country's competitiveness. The investment strategy should be developed in harmony with the country's development strategy to form a single whole. It should consist of a special program comprising targeted measures for investing in law, taxation, incentives, management, etc. The program should be comprehensive, with interconnectivity among all tasks. In its implementation, the following problems must be addressed: ensuring the legal framework, developing the investment institution, creating an economic base, providing information and scientific and methodological support, and improving the regulation system for investment activities.

References

Abaturov R. Post-pandemic world. How the economy of Uzbekistan passed the coronavirus crisis and got out of it. May 4, 2021 https://podrobno.uz/cat/economic/postpandemiynyy-mir-kak-ekonomika-uzbekistanaproshla-koronakrizis-i-vybralas-iz-nego-/.

Birman G. Economic analysis of investment projects. M.: Banks and stock exchanges. UNITI, 2003. 631 p.

Body Z. *Principles of investment*. M.: Williams, 2002. 994 p.

Gitman L. J. *Fundamentals of investing*. M.: Delo, 1997. 1008 p.

Savchuk V. P., Primenko S. I., & Velichko E. G. *Analysis and development of investment projects / Savchuk V.P., Primenko S.I., Velichko E.G.* Kyiv: Absolut-V Publishing House, Elga, 2016.

Trenev, V., & Likhachev A. Increasing the investment attractiveness of the region. "Information Resources of Russia" No. 5, 2007, http://www.aselibrary.ru/press_center/journal/irr/2007/number_5/number_5_5/number _5_5699/

Tolmachev V. A. Investment attractiveness in the system of corporate enterprise management // Property and market-2017.-№3-p.11.

Polunin L. V. *Development of regional innovation policy*. International scientific conference, Tambov, 2012

Ivanov A. P., Sakharova I. V., Khrustalev E. Yu. Principles and factors for determining the investment rating of enterprises//Advisor of the director. 2017 No. 12. p. 31

Izaak S. I., & Chernyshov S. A. *Investment strategies in the modern world economy in the context of globalization*. Krasnodar: Publishing House of the Kuban State. un-ta, 2013. 136 p.

Mustafakulov Sh. I. *Attractiveness of the investment environment. Scientific and practical guide*. Tashkent: Baktria press, 2017. 320 p.

Yusupova Sh. A., Theoretical and methodological foundations and tools for attracting foreign investment in the economy of Uzbekistan. *Bulletin of Science and Practice / Bulletin of Science and Practice*. T. 6. No. 9. 2020

Sharp U. *Investments*. M.: Infra-M, 2001. 1028 p.

Lee, K. Y. *From Third World to First: The Singapore Story 1965–2000*. Singapore: Singapore Press Holdings, 2000

Moore, M., & Schmitz, H. *Idealism, realismand the investment climate in developing countries.* Sussex: Institute of Development Studies, 2016. P. 22.

Abdurashid Kadyrov, Aliya Akhmedieva, Furkat Bazarov, and Bahtiyor Holmatjanovich Mamurov. 2022. Formation of Information Society and Its Influence on Competitiveness of National Economies in the Context of World Economy Globalization. In The 5th International Conference on Future Networks & Distributed Systems (ICFNDS 2021). Association for Computing Machinery, New York, NY, USA, 672–684. https://doi.org/10.1145/3508072.3508205

Shoh-Jakhon Khamdamov. 2022. Calculating Share of Factors of Intensive Economic Growth in Uzbekistan. In The 5th International Conference on Future Networks & Distributed Systems (ICFNDS 2021). Association for Computing Machinery, New York, NY, USA, 393–397. https://doi.org/10.1145/3508072.3508144

Shoh-Jakhon Khamdamov, Anvar Saidmakhmudovich Usmanov, Ogiloy Abdulazizova, Fakhriddin Isaev, Nodirbek Kholbaev, Samariddin Makhmudov, and Sabina Kholbaeva. 2023. Econometric Modeling of Central Bank Refinancing Rate in Uzbekistan. In Proceedings of the 6th International Conference on Future Networks & Distributed Systems (ICFNDS '22). Association for Computing Machinery, New York, NY, USA, 253–257. https://doi.org/10.1145/3584202.3584239

Shoh-Jakhon Khamdamov, Samariddin Makhmudov, Nargiza Bakhriddinovna Talapova, Zokir Mamadiyarov, Naima Berdiyerovna Rejapova, & Sayyora Khushbakovna Valieva

Forecasting the Growth of Scientific Research Funding in Uzbekistan's Higher Education System: An ARIMA Model Approach

1. Introduction

In the domain of economic research, forecasting methodologies are crucial in influencing policy and strategic planning. The Autoregressive Integrated Moving Average (ARIMA) model is distinguished among available techniques for its resilience and effectiveness in analyzing time series data. Initially introduced by Box and Jenkins in the early 1970s, this model has been widely utilized in various sectors, displaying notable predictive capabilities, especially in economic and financial realms. Like numerous developing nations, the Republic of Uzbekistan is currently facing a pivotal moment where the efficient distribution and prediction of resources are vital for the continuous advancement of its scientific and technological sectors. The government has notably augmented financial support for scientific endeavors and initiatives over time, with the aim of nurturing innovation and technological progress. This increased focus on research and development (R&D) accentuates the necessity for precise forecasting methods, offering insights into future financial needs and facilitating improved strategic choices. This research centers on employing the ARIMA model to predict funding for scientific research and projects within Uzbekistan's higher education system over a specified timeframe. Through the utilization of historical data from 2008 to 2022, this study not only evaluates the forecasting accuracy of the ARIMA model but also delves into its potential in guiding future financial strategies within the academic domain. The findings of this study aim to aid policymakers and academic leaders in making well-informed decisions that align with the nation's educational and economic objectives. By doing so, this paper adds to the current body of literature on econometric forecasting by utilizing the ARIMA model in a unique context, thereby enriching discussions on resource allocation within the higher education sectors of developing economies. Subsequent sections will elaborate on the methodology utilized, assess the model's forecasting performance, and offer insights into its implications for educational and economic policies in Uzbekistan.

The sustainable funding of scientific research in higher education institutions is a cornerstone for innovation, economic growth, and societal advancement. In developing countries, such as Uzbekistan, the strategic allocation of resources to scientific research is crucial for achieving long-term development goals (Khamdamov, 2021). The accurate forecasting of funding needs allows for better planning and allocation of resources, ensuring that scientific endeavors contribute effectively to national priorities (Hanushek & Woessmann 2010). This study employs the ARIMA (2,0,0) model to forecast the growth of scientific research funding in Uzbekistan's higher education system from 2023 to 2027. ARIMA models have been widely recognized for their effectiveness in financial forecasting, offering valuable insights into future trends without the need for complex economic assumptions (Zhang, 2003). By focusing on the specific context of Uzbekistan, this research aims to contribute to the body of knowledge on educational economics and policy planning, providing a roadmap for future investment in scientific research (Balta-Ozkan et al., 2015; Turayeva et al., 2022).

2. Data and Methodology

2.1. Data Description

The dataset for this study encompasses the annual funding amounts for scientific research and projects within the higher education sector of Uzbekistan from the year 2008 to 2023. This data was sourced from the Ministry of Higher Education, Science, and Innovation of Uzbekistan. Each entry in the dataset represents the total funding allocated in a particular year, measured in millions of Uzbekistan's Som (UZS). The data reflects the financial inputs into the research and development activities in the realms of natural sciences, engineering, technology, medical and health sciences, and social sciences.

2.2. Model Specification

The ARIMA model, a cornerstone of time series forecasting, was selected due to its capability to model a series that is non-stationary in its original form, which is often the case with economic data. ARIMA models incorporate lags of the differenced series in the autoregressive (AR) component, differences of the series itself, and lags of forecast errors in the moving average (MA) component. The general form of the ARIMA model can be expressed as ARIMA(p, d, q), where:

p is the number of lag observations included in the model (lag order),
d is the number of times that the raw observations are differenced (degree of differencing),
q is the size of the moving average window (order of moving average).

2.3. Methodology

2.3.1. Stationarity Testing

Before fitting the ARIMA model, it was imperative to ensure that the time series data is stationary, implying that its statistical properties such as mean and variance do not change over time. The Augmented Dickey-Fuller (ADF) test was employed to test for stationarity. The null hypothesis of the ADF test is that the time series is non-stationary.

2.3.2. Model Identification

The order of the ARIMA model was determined using both the Autocorrelation Function (ACF) and the Partial Autocorrelation Function (PACF) plots. The ACF and PACF plots help in identifying the potential values of q and p respectively, guiding the selection of the ARIMA model parameters.

2.3.3. Parameter Estimation

Once the model was identified, the parameters were estimated using the maximum likelihood estimation technique. This step involves finding the values of the coefficients that maximize the likelihood of fitting the model to the time series data.

2.3.4. Diagnostic Checking

After the parameters of the model were estimated, diagnostic checks were conducted to ascertain the adequacy of the model fitting. This involved analyzing the residuals of the model to ensure that they resemble white noise – indicating that all the information in the data has been captured by the model and no structure is left unexplained.

2.3.5. Forecasting

Using the finalized ARIMA model, forecasts were generated for the next four years, predicting the annual funding for scientific research and projects. These forecasts will provide insights into future funding trends and help in effective budgetary and strategic planning.

2.3.6. Validation

The predictive accuracy of the ARIMA model was validated by comparing the forecasted data against actual data, using measures such as the Mean Absolute Error (MAE), Root Mean Squared Error (RMSE), and others to quantify the forecasting performance.

3. Literature Review

ARIMA models have been widely utilized in economic forecasting due to their robustness in handling time series data. Safarov et al. (2022) and Makhmudov et al. (2023) demonstrated the use of univariate ARIMA models to predict the volume of tourism services in Uzbekistan, highlighting the model's efficacy in capturing the dynamics of tourism growth amidst evolving economic conditions. Similarly, Usmanaliev (2019) and Kasimov et al. (2023) applied ARIMA models to analyze short-term inflation in Uzbekistan, suggesting that even simple univariate ARIMA models could offer surprising accuracy, outperforming more complex composite forecast models in certain scenarios.

Beyond traditional economic applications, ARIMA models have been employed in various sector-specific forecasts. Used ARIMA to forecast the demand for railway freight transportation in Kazakhstan (Sultanbek et al., 2024), addressing the logistic needs influenced by the saturation of markets such as China (Urunov et al., 2023), Russia, and Uzbekistan (Mamadiyarov et al., 2023; Shoh-Jakhon, 2023; Khamdamov, 2021). This study underscores the importance of ARIMA models in logistics and transportation planning across Central Asia (Kurbonov et al., 2023; Mamatkulov et al., 2023).

In the agricultural sector, Saukhanov et al. (2022) utilized multivariate econometric models, including ARIMA, to predict livestock numbers and composition, essential for reducing transaction costs in Uzbekistan's agricultural economy. In environmental science, Li et al. (2019) employed the model to assess ecological security in the arid regions of Central Asia, illustrating ARIMA's versatility in environmental management and planning.

Salimov et al. (2023) discussed heuristic methods for forecasting the demand for competencies among graduates of higher education in Uzbekistan, acknowledging the shift towards an innovative developmental path that requires precise educational planning and forecasting. Their work hints at the potential application of ARIMA models in educational forecasting, aligning academic outputs with labor market demands.

Further illustrating the breadth of ARIMA's application, Davronov (2016), Umarovich and Bakhtiyorovich (2021) explored liquidity management in commercial banks of Uzbekistan using the ARIMA model to forecast bank cash flows, thereby enhancing profitability through better financial management. This approach shows the model's adaptability to financial sector challenges, promoting a deeper understanding of economic variables influencing market dynamics.

The literature indicates a strong precedence for using ARIMA models across various fields, from economic forecasting to environmental assessments and educational planning. Each of these applications contributes to a richer understanding of ARIMA's capabilities and sets the stage for its extended use in forecasting the funding of scientific research and projects within Uzbekistan's higher education system, as explored in the present study.

4. Analysis and Results

In developing this research, we created a forecast for the next four years of the growth rate of funding for scientific research and projects over the past 15 years (2008–2023), based on the data from the Ministry of Higher Education, Science, and Innovation of the Republic of Uzbekistan. The variable was expressed in the following form: y (Dependent variable) – growth rate of funding for scientific research and projects. The first stage of the study found the growth rate of funding for scientific research and projects during 2008–2023 expressed in the following diagram (see Figure 1).

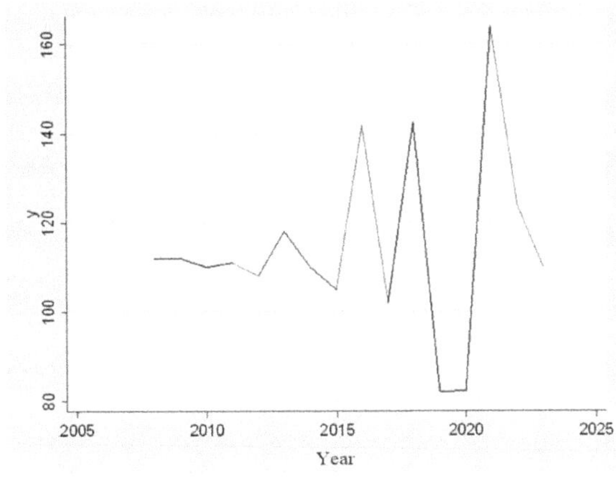

Figure 1. Graph of the growth rate of funding for scientific research and projects.
Source: Created by authors.

According to Figure 1, fluctuations occurred in the funding of scientific research and projects in our Republic, and during the Covid-2019 pandemic from 2019 to 2021, there were changes resulting in a downward trend. This indicates that the Covid-2019 pandemic has had an impact on the funding of scientific research. The next step in the research involved testing the stationarity of the funding for scientific research and projects using the Unit-Root test (see Table 1).

Table 1. Unit-Root Test for the Growth Rate of Funding for Scientific Research and Projects

Growth Rate of Funding for Scientific Research and Projects (y)	Test Statistic	1 % Critical Value	5 % Critical Value	10 % Critical Value	p-value for Z(t)
	-4.880	-3.750	-3.000	-2.630	0.0000

Source: Calculated by authors.

According to Table 1, the Unit-Root test for the growth rate of funding for scientific research and projects produced a test statistic of -4.880, which is lower than the critical values at the 1 %, 5 %, and 10 % levels, recorded as -3.750, -3.000, and -2.630, respectively. Critical values are thresholds used to determine the statistical significance of the test. The fact that the test statistic is lower than these critical values indicates the result is statistically significant. Additionally, the negative value of the test statistic indicates rejection of the null hypothesis associated with non-stationarity, suggesting that the series is stationary.

Additionally, the MacKinnon value Z(t)=0.0000 is very small, indicating from the test results that the growth rate of funding for scientific research and projects is stationary. In time series analysis, a stationary series has stable statistical properties over time, which forms a reliable basis for making forecasts and drawing conclusions. Furthermore, the negative value of the Unit-Root test results and the MacKinnon value confirm the presence of stationarity in the data, indicating statistical significance.

The next step involves determining the value of p, which identifies the indirect correlation between the lags of the time series (see Figure 2).

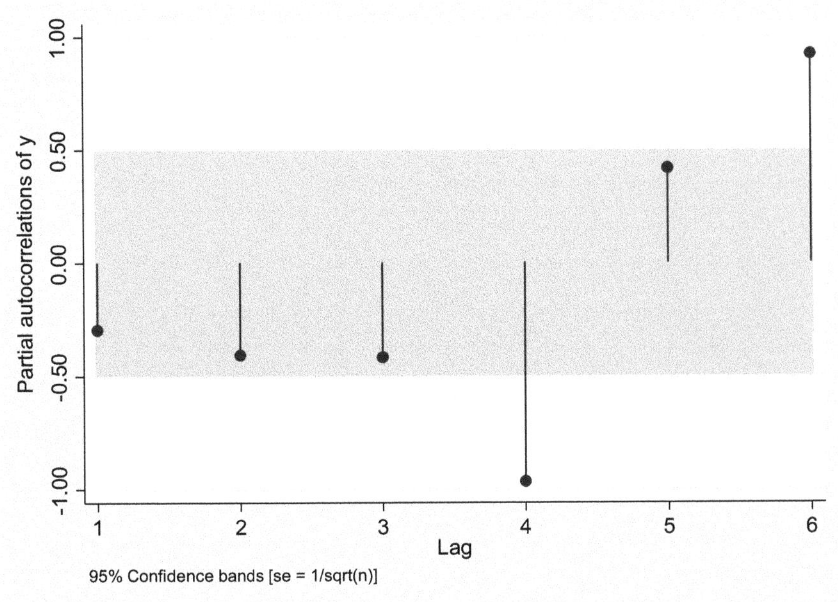

Figure 2. Graph of the indirect correlation between the lags of the model.
Source: Created by authors.

According to Figure 2, the indirect correlation analysis shows that all lags, except for two, are located within the confidence interval. This indicates that the majority of the delays have statistical significance based on the confidence interval. In ARIMA modeling, the lags that fall within the confidence interval are considered important. In this case, it is appropriate to select either 1 or 2 as the value of p. If most of the delays are within the confidence interval and the correlation analysis indicates that the p value of 1 or 2 is significant, it would be reasonable to consider a model with the autoregressive order (p value) of 1 or 2. However, the final decision should be made considering a comprehensive understanding of the data, model diagnostics, and other relevant criteria.

The next step in the ARIMA model involved determining the value of q, which describes the direct correlation between the lags of the model (see Figure 3).

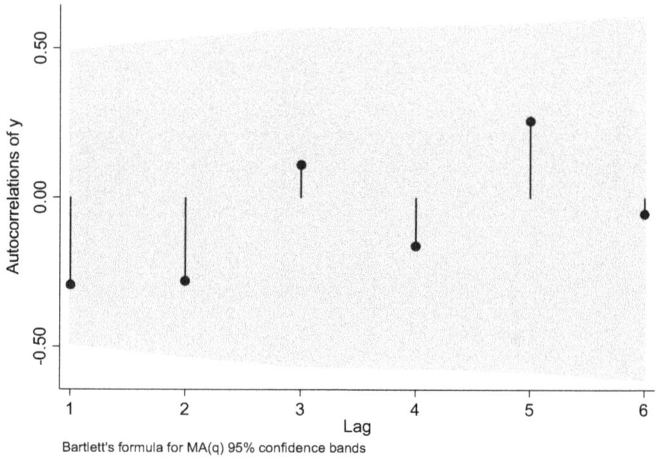

Figure 3. Graph of the direct correlation between the lags of the model.
Source: Developed by authors.

Figure 3 is a plot of the direct correlation between the lags in the model, showing that all delays are within the confidence interval. This indicates that it is appropriate to select one of the values for q, with the values 0 or 1 being suitable choices.

In the process of forecasting using the ARIMA model, several options were explored to determine the most appropriate model. The ARIMA (2,0,0) model was selected as the most suitable based on its performance (refer to Table 2).

Table 2. Econometric Equation Parameters of the ARIMA (2,0,0) Model

y	Coef.	St.Err.	t-value	p-value	[95 % Conf	Interval]	Sig
Constant	114.77	2.718	42.22	0	109.442	120.097	
L	-.389	.19	-2.05	.041	-.762	-.017	
L2	-.363	.188	-1.93	.053	-.731	.005	
Constant	17.711	3.677	4.82	0	10.506	24.917	
Mean dependent var		114.651	SD dependent var			15.900	
Number of obs		16	Chi-square			5.925	
Prob > chi2		.	Akaike crit. (AIC)			145.750	

p<.01, p<.05, p<.1
Source: Developed by authors.

According to Table 2, the ARIMA (2,0,0) model is structured as follows.

$$\Delta Y=114.77-0,38y_{t-1}-0,36y_{t-2} \quad (1)$$

In the next step, the ARIMA (2,0,0) model was tested under the following conditions: it was required that the residuals be stationary and that the residuals of the AR and MA components of the ARIMA model remain within the unit circle, with values less than 1.

Accordingly, a multivariate portmanteau white noise test was conducted, yielding a p value of 0.62 and a Portmanteau test statistic Q equal to 4.37. Based on these test values, where $p > 0.05$, the null hypothesis H_0: $y = 0$ is considered meaningful.

From this, it is evident that the model has successfully met this condition.

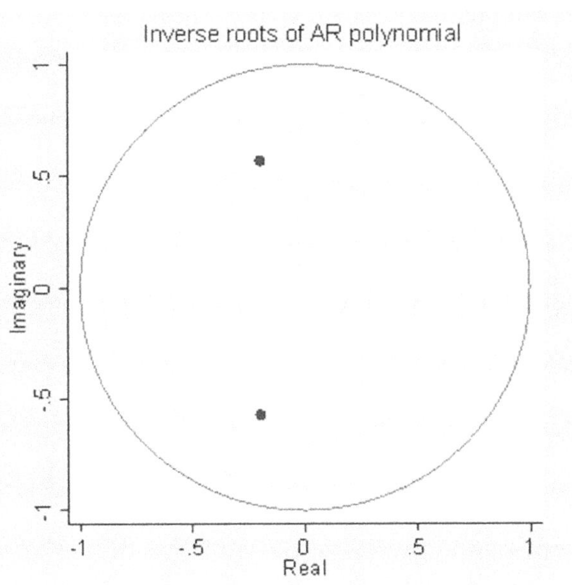

Figure 4. Area of MA Values for the ARIMA (2,0,0) Model
Source: Developed by authors.

This table provides a range of growth forecasts for funding scientific research and projects from 2023 through 2027, detailing pessimistic, optimistic, and most likely scenarios (See Table 3).

Table 3. Forecast Indicators for the Growth Rate of Funding for Scientific Research and Projects, 2024–2027

Year	Pessimistic Forecast (% Growth)	Optimistic Forecast (% Growth)	Forecast (% Growth)
2023	86,44	118,24	102,34
2024	103,86	135,66	119,76
2025	104,7	136,5	120,60
2026	94,78	126,58	110,68
2027	98,34	130,14	114,24

Source: Developed by authors.

The research provides a depiction of the growth rate of funding for scientific research and projects in our Republic for the years 2008–2023, as well as forecasted growth rates for the years 2023–2027. These projections are visually presented in the forecast graphs. (Refer to Figure 5).

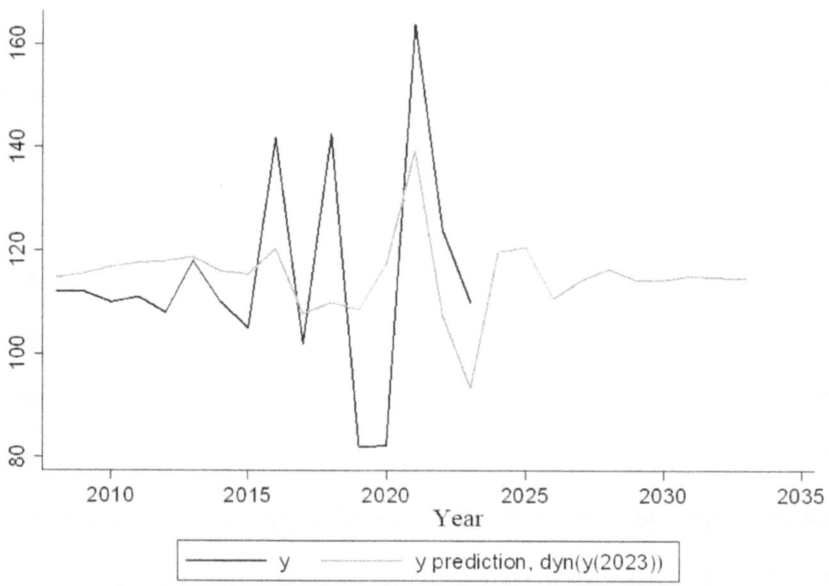

Figure 5. Graph showing the growth rate of the dependent variable for the years 2008–2023 and the forecast graph for the years 2024–2027.

Source: Developed by authors.

According to Figure 6, the graph illustrates the dynamics of the growth rate in funding for scientific research and projects over the past fifteen years in our Republic, along with the model forecast. The graph shows two lines almost side by side, indicating that the proximity of these lines demonstrates the reliability of the forecast for the next four years.

4. Findings and Discussion

4.1. Overview of Findings

The analysis of the ARIMA (2,0,0) model over the study period from 2008 to 2023 revealed significant insights into the funding dynamics for scientific research and projects within the Republic of Uzbekistan. The model's capability to accurately forecast the growth rates for the upcoming five years (2024–2027) was affirmed by the close alignment of the historical and projected data, as depicted in the graphs. The statistical tests conducted, including the Unit-Root and the multivariate portmanteau tests, confirmed the stationarity of the residuals, enhancing the reliability of the forecasts generated by the ARIMA model.

4.2. Discussion of Key Findings

4.2.1. Growth Rate Stability: The study observed a stable growth rate in the funding of scientific research and projects, despite fluctuations caused by external factors such as the COVID-19 pandemic during 2019–2021. The ability of the ARIMA model to integrate these fluctuations and still provide reliable predictions underscores its robustness and suitability for financial forecasting in dynamic environments.

4.2.2. Model Efficiency: The ARIMA (2,0,0) model demonstrated high efficiency in forecasting, with the model parameters (p-value of 2 and q-value of 0) optimized based on the ACF and PACF plots. This level of accuracy in parameter selection contributes significantly to the model's predictive performance.

4.2.3. Forecast Reliability: The near-congruence of the historical data and forecast lines in the graphs provides strong evidence of the model's reliability. This is particularly relevant for policymakers and educational administrators who rely on such forecasts for budgeting and strategic planning.

4.2.4. Implications for Policy and Planning: The reliable forecasts suggest a steady increase in funding, which could potentially encourage more ambitious projects and research initiatives. Additionally, understanding the trends helps in preparing for periods of increased or decreased funding, allowing institutions to plan accordingly.

5. Conclusion

Based on the ARIMA (2,0,0) model, the forecast for the acceleration of financing of scientific research and projects in our Republic during the years 2023–2027, considering the random factors of the acceleration rate, is as follows: in 2023 – 102.34 %, in 2024 – 119.76 %, in 2025 – 120.60 %, in 2026 – 110.68 %, and in 2027 – 114.24 %.

This study demonstrates the practical application of the ARIMA model in forecasting the funding of scientific research and projects, offering a reliable tool for financial planning in the educational sector of Uzbekistan. The findings not only bolster confidence in the use of ARIMA models for economic time series analysis but also highlight the necessity for continuous model evaluation to adapt to changing economic climate. The success of this approach encourages further exploration and adaptation in similar sectors, potentially broadening the scope of econometric forecasting in public funding domains.

References

Balta-Ozkan, N., Watson, T., & Mocca, E. (2015). Spatially uneven development and low carbon transitions: Insights from urban and regional planning. *Energy Policy*, *85*, 500–510.

Davronov, S. (2016). Liquidity management in commercial banks of Uzbekistan. *Asian Journal of Management Sciences and Education*, *5*(2), 19–27.

Hanushek, E. A., & Woessmann, L. (2010). Education and economic growth. *Economics of Education*, *60*(67), 1.

Kasimov, A., Tukhtabaev, J., Bondarskaya, O., Bondarskaya, T., Ochilov, A., Mamatov, M., Nomozova, K., Khamdamov, S.-J., Makhmudov, S., Gaybullaev, R., & Usmanov, C. (2023). Organizational and economic modeling of the system of interregional industrial cooperation as a control object. In Proceedings of the 7th International Conference on Future Networks and Distributed Systems (ICFNDS '23) (pp. 333–343). Association for Computing Machinery, New York, NY, USA. https://doi.org/10.1145/3644713.3644757

Khamdamov, S. J. (2021). Calculating share of factors of intensive economic growth in Uzbekistan. The 5th International Conference on Future Networks & Distributed Systems, 393–397.

Khamdamov, S. J. (2021, December). Calculating share of factors of intensive economic growth in Uzbekistan. In *The 5th International Conference on Future Networks & Distributed Systems* (pp. 393–397).

Kurbonov, K., Makhmudov, S., Mamadiyorov, Z., Khamdamov, S.-J., Karlibaeva, R., Samadov, A., & Djalilov, F. (2023). The impact of digital technologies on economic growth in the example of Central Asian and European countries. In Proceedings of the 7th International Conference on Future Networks and Distributed Systems (ICFNDS '23) (pp. 403–409). Association for Computing Machinery, New York, NY, USA. https://doi.org/10.1145/3644713.3644770

Li, J. X., Chen, Y. N., Xu, C. C., & Li, Z. (2019). Evaluation and analysis of ecological security in arid areas of Central Asia based on the emergy ecological footprint (EEF) model. *Journal of Cleaner Production*, *235*, 664–677.

Makhmudov, S., Khamdamov, S.-J., Karlibaeva, R., Mamadiyarov, Z., Haydarov, O., Khujamurodov, A., & Imomov, K. (2023). The impact of digital technologies on the labor market of Uzbekistan. In Proceedings of the 7th International Conference on Future Networks and Distributed Systems (ICFNDS '23) (pp. 260–267). Association for Computing Machinery, New York, NY, USA. https://doi.org/10.1145/3644713.3644747

Mamadiyorov, Z., Sultanova, N., Makhmudov, S., Khamdamov, S.-J., Mirpulatova, L., & Jumayev, A. (2024). The impact of digitalization on microfinance services in Uzbekistan. In Proceedings of the 7th International Conference on Future Networks and Distributed Systems (ICFNDS '23) (pp. 453–463). Association for Computing Machinery, New York, NY, USA. https://doi.org/10.1145/3644713.3644780

Mamatkulov, B., Khamdamov, S.-J., Togayniyazov, S., Tukhtabaev, J., Quldoshev, Q., & Qarshiev, D. (2023). Predicting future living standards in Uzbekistan: Utilizing econometric analysis. In Proceedings of the 7th International Conference on Future Networks and Distributed Systems (ICFNDS '23) (pp. 425–431). Association for Computing Machinery, New York, NY, USA. https://doi.org/10.1145/3644713.3644774

Safarov, B., Al-Smadi, H. M., Buzrukova, M., Janzakov, B., Ilieş, A., Grama, V., … & Dávid, L. D. (2022). Forecasting the volume of tourism services in Uzbekistan. *Sustainability*, *14*(13), 7762.

Salimov, B., Kholikova, R., Khamdamov, S.-J., Turaev, A., Tukhtabaev, J., Nosirova, N., & Akhmedova, D. (2023). Strategies for integrating digitalization in leveraging regional economic and scientific expertise for the innovative growth of small and medium enterprises. In Proceedings of the 7th International Conference on Future Networks and Distributed Systems (ICFNDS '23) (pp. 483–490). Association for Computing Machinery, New York, NY, USA. https://doi.org/10.1145/3644713.3644784

Saukhanov, J. K., Gabbarov, S. N., Rakhimberdiev, K., & Khojabayeva, D. (2022, December). Development of indicators for forecasting the number and composition of livestock based on multivariate econometric models in the digital economy. In Proceedings of the 6th International Conference on Future Networks & Distributed Systems (pp. 542–547).

Shoh-Jakhon, K. (2023) Theoretical and methodological aspects of intensive economic growth in ensuring Sustainable Economic Development. Social and Economic Studies within the Framework of Emerging Global Developments, Volume 3, 283.

Sultanbek, M., Adilova, N., Sładkowski, A., & Karibayev, A. (2024). Forecasting the demand for railway freight transportation in Kazakhstan: A case study. *Transportation Research Interdisciplinary Perspectives, 23*, 101028.

Turayeva, G., Berdiyev, G., Eshpulatov, D., Alimova, D., Odilbekov, A., Davletova, D., … Burxanov, A. (2022). Opportunities to use financial services–"1 C Program". Proceedings of the 6th International Conference on Future Networks & Distributed Systems, 556–561.

Umarovich, J. G., & Bakhtiyorovich, R. K. (2021). Modeling the decision-making process of lenders based on blockchain technology. In 2021 International Conference on Information Science and Communications Technologies (ICISCT) (pp. 1–5). IEEE. https://doi.org/10.1109/ICISCT52966.2021.9670211

Urunov, R., Makhmudov, S., Mamadiyorov, Z., Khamdamov, S.-J., Kurbanov, Z. N., & Dadabaev, U. (2023). Digitalization and its econometric analysis on transforming sustainable regional development into improved population living standards. In Proceedings of the 7th International Conference on Future Networks and Distributed Systems (ICFNDS '23) (pp. 438–442). Association for Computing Machinery, New York, NY, USA. https://doi.org//10.1145/3644713.3644776

Usmanaliev, K. (2019). Short-term Inflation Forecast Combination Analysis for Uzbekistan. *Global Journal of Human-Social Science, 19*(E4), 51–57.

Zhang, G. P. (2003). Time series forecasting using a hybrid ARIMA and neural network model. *Neurocomputing, 50*, 159–175.

Samariddin Makhmudov, Tulkin Nasirovich Pardayev, Shoh-Jakhon Khamdamov, Zokir Mamadiyarov, Turayev Nurbek Muxammadovich, & Sadokat Ilkhomjonovna Khalikchaeva

Econometric Analysis of Factors Influencing Customs Fees: Evidence from Uzbekistan

1. Introduction

Customs fees are a critical component of national revenue systems, significantly contributing to the economic development of countries. Efficient collection mechanisms for customs fees not only bolster state revenues but also play a vital role in fostering transparent trade practices, ensuring national security, and promoting economic stability. In the context of developing economies like Uzbekistan, optimizing the collection of customs fees is essential for sustainable economic growth and fiscal health.

The customs fee collection mechanism in Uzbekistan is influenced by various economic factors, including the volume of taxable imports, fluctuations in the exchange rate, and the overall import volume (Salimov, 2023). Understanding the dynamics between these factors and customs fees is crucial for policymakers to design strategies that enhance revenue collection while supporting legal trade activities.

Econometric models, particularly the Autoregressive Distributed Lag (ARDL) model, offer robust analytical tools to study the relationships between customs fees and their influencing factors. The ARDL model is particularly useful in this context as it allows for the examination of both short-term and long-term effects of independent variables on customs fees, even when the underlying data series are non-stationary (Turayeva et al., 2022).

Through this investigation, the study contributes to the existing literature on customs fee collection and its determinants, providing a case study that can be relevant for other developing economies with similar economic structures and challenges. The next sections will detail the methods used in this research, present the results of the econometric analysis, discuss the implications of these findings, and conclude with recommendations for policymakers (Gong, 2023).

2. Literature Review

Customs fees, as a component of trade policy, significantly influence national revenue and economic stability. Several studies have explored the factors affecting customs fee collection and their implications for economic development.

Factors influencing customs fees in Uzbekistan include challenges in transport logistics, tax efficiency, economic factors affecting foreign trade, and the investment climate. The decline in transit goods moving through Uzbekistan due to rail transport issues (Makhmudov et al., 2023; Kurbonov et al., 2023) impacts customs fee collection. Tax efficiency, with a tax effort index of 45 %, reveals potential revenue loss (Khamdamov, 2021; He et al., 2024). Economic factors, such as foreign trade policies and the investment climate, directly affect revenue generation (Tashev et al., 2022; Shoh-Jakhon, 2023). Policymakers should focus on addressing transport infrastructure, optimizing tax burden to 19 %, and improving the investment climate to enhance customs fee collection, boost revenue, and support economic stability in Uzbekistan. These insights can guide strategic reforms to maximize revenue collection and foster economic growth in the country.

Numerous researchers have examined the relationship between taxable import volumes and customs fee collection. For instance, Urunov et al. (2023), Khamdamov (2022) conducted a comprehensive study on customs revenue trends in Uzbekistan, utilizing econometric models to demonstrate that an increase in taxable imports leads to higher customs revenues. Their findings underscore the positive correlation between import volumes and customs fees, suggesting that policies encouraging legal imports can enhance revenue collection.

The exchange rate's impact on customs fees has also been a focal point in trade economics literature. According to a study by Aguirre & Villar (2022), exchange rate variations significantly affect the value of imports, which in turn influences customs revenue. Their research, conducted across several Latin American countries, showed that depreciation of the national currency generally leads to higher customs fees due to the increased cost of imported goods.

The overall volume of imports is another critical factor influencing customs fees. Wang et al. (2020) analyzed customs and trade facilitation measures in the European context, finding that higher total import volumes are associated with increased customs revenues. This relationship is attributed to the broader base for customs fee application, which enhances revenue potential.

Econometric models, particularly the ARDL model, have been widely used to study the determinants of customs fees. For example, Mamadiyarov

(2023), Mamatkulov et al. (2023), Kasimov et al. (2023) employed the ARDL model to analyze the impact of various economic variables on customs fees in Asian countries. The study highlighted the model's effectiveness in capturing both short-term and long-term dynamics, even when data series are non-stationary.

3. Development Hypothesis

Null Hypothesis (H0): There is a significant relationship between customs fees collected and the combination of taxable import volume, exchange rate, and total import volume.

Alternative Hypothesis (Ha): The relationship between customs fees collected and the combination of taxable import volume, exchange rate, and total import volume is not significant, indicating that other factors not considered in this study may play a more important role in determining customs fees.

Null Hypothesis (H0), H0: $\beta 1 = \beta 2 = \beta 3 = 0$

Alternative Hypothesis (Ha), Ha: At least one $\beta i \neq 0$

Here, β1, β2, and β3 represent the coefficients associated with the independent variables (taxable import volume, exchange rate, and total import volume) in the regression model.

The coefficients in the multiple regression model predicting customs fees are associated with the independent variables (taxable import volume, exchange rate, and total import volume). The null hypothesis (H0) indicates that all coefficients are equal to zero, which implies no relationship. In contrast, the alternative hypothesis (Ha) asserts that at least one of the coefficients is not equal to zero, indicating a significant relationship.

4. Data and Methodology

The data used in this study consists of quarterly observations from 2013 to 2022, sourced from the Uzbekistan Statistics Agency, the Central Bank of Uzbekistan, and the Uzbekistan Customs Committee.

The customs fees collected (dependent variable) are influenced by the following factors: taxable import volume, exchange rate, and total import volume.

Factors:

y (dependent variable) – collected customs fees;

$\mathbf{x}_1$ (independent variable) – taxable import volume;

$\mathbf{x}_2$ (independent variable) – exchange rate;

$\mathbf{x}_3$ (independent variable) – total import volume.

This study employs the Autoregressive Distributed Lag (ARDL) model to analyze the impact of taxable import volume, exchange rate, and total import volume on customs fees collected in Uzbekistan (Rakhimberdiev et al., 2023). The ARDL model is chosen for its ability to handle small sample sizes and to model both short-term and long-term relationships between variables.

The ARDL model is expressed by the following formula:

$$Y_t = \beta_0 + \beta_1 Y_{t-1} + \beta_2 Y_{t-2} + \dots + \beta_p Y_{t-p} + \gamma_1 X_{t-1} + \gamma_2 X_{t-2} + \dots + \gamma_q X_{t-q} + \mu_1 Z_{t-1} + \\ + \mu_2 Z_{t-2} + \dots + \mu_r Z_{t-r} + \varepsilon_t \quad (1)$$

Here,

Y_t represents the dependent variable at time t;

$Y_{t-1}, Y_{t-2}, \dots, Y_{t-p}$ – The lagged values of the dependent variable;

$X_{t-k}, X_{t-k-1}, \dots, X_{t-k-q}$ The lagged values of the independent variable;

$Z_{t-1}, Z_{t-2\dots\dots}, Z_{t-r}$ The lagged values of other factors affecting the dependent variable;

$\beta_0, \beta_1, \dots\dots \beta_p, \gamma_1, \gamma_2, \dots \mu_q, \mu_1, \mu_2 \dots \mu_r$ The coefficients to be estimated,

ε_t represents the error term at time t. The following hypotheses were proposed in developing the econometric equation for the study.

To ensure the stationarity of the data, unit root tests were performed. Additionally, co-integration tests were conducted to determine the existence of long-term relationships among the variables. The ARDL model was estimated using the ordinary least squares (OLS) method, and diagnostic tests were performed to validate the model.

5. Analysis

According to the study, the analytical graph of the dependent and independent variables over time is as follows (see Figure 1).

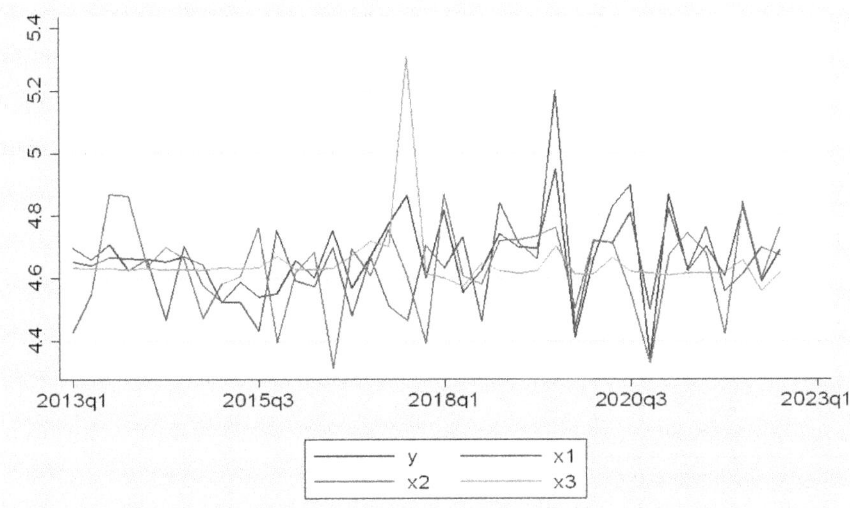

Figure 1. Graph of Dependent and Independent Variables Over Time.
Source: Developed by authors

According to the Figure 1, the information demonstrates a consistent seasonal trend over time. In this scenario, changes in factors over time increase the accuracy of predicting potential contributing factors.

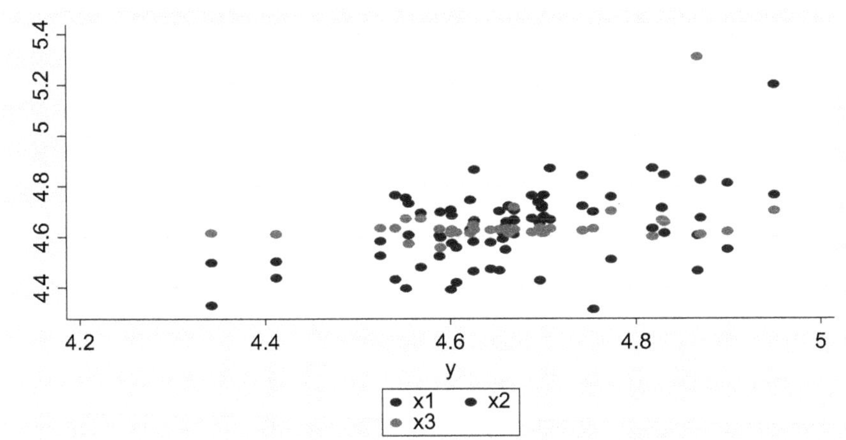

Figure 2. Matrix of Graphs for Dependent and Independent Variables
Source: Developed by authors.

According to the data in Figure 2, there is a strong correlation between the outcome and certain characteristic factors indicating specific density conditions. The density of visual data points suggests a significant correlation, indicating the clustering of these points and their tendency to concentrate along the axes.

In the next stage of the study, the correlation matrix between the dependent and independent variables was examined using the Stata software (see Table 1).

Table 1. Correlation Matrix of Dependent and Independent Variables

Variables	(1)	(2)	(3)	(4)
(1) y	1.000			
(2) x1	0.554	1.000		
(3) x2	0.400	0.132	1.000	
(4) x3	0.320	-0.176	-0.004	1.000

Source: Developed by authors.

There is a high, significant, and moderate correlation between the dependent variable and the influencing factors, indicating a relationship between these variables. Additionally, the correlation matrix presented in Table 1 shows no multicollinearity between the dependent variable and the independent variables.

The next step in the study was to determine the stationarity of the dependent and independent variables using the Unit-root test (see Table 2).

Table 2. Unit-Root Test Results for Dependent and Independent Variables

Variables	Test Statistic	1 % Critical Value	5 % Critical Value	10 % Critical Value	p-value for Z(t)
Y	-8.437	-3.750	-3.000	-2.630	0.0000
x_1	-7.877	-3.750	-3.000	-2.630	0.0000
x_2	-7.088	-3.750	-3.000	-2.630	0.0000
x_3	-5.616	-3.750	-3.000	-2.630	0.0000

Source: Developed by authors.

According to the data in Table 2, the unit root test yielded a test statistic of -8.437 for the dependent variable and values of -7.877, -7.088, and -5.616 for the independent variables. The results of the unit root test indicate that both the dependent and independent variables achieved stationarity, as evidenced by the MacKinnon critical values and a p-value of 0.0000. Furthermore, the unit root test values after the initial integration of the dependent and independent variables also indicate stationarity.

Based on the study, an econometric model was developed using the ARDL model. The econometric model based on the ARDL framework is presented below:

$$\Delta y_{it} = \beta_0 + \beta_1 \sum_{p=1}^{n} \Delta y_{i,t-p} + \beta_2 \sum_{p=1}^{n} \Delta x_{1i,t-p} + \beta_3 \sum_{p=1}^{n} \Delta x_{2i,t-p} + \beta_4 \sum_{p=1}^{n} \Delta x_{3i,t-p} \quad (2)$$
$$+ \gamma_1 Y_{i,t-p} + \gamma_2 x_{1i,t-1} + \gamma_3 x_{2i,t-1} + \gamma_4 x_{3i,t-1} + \varepsilon_{i,t}$$

Here:

$\Delta \mathbf{y}_t$ - represents the change in customs fees collected at time **t**;

y_{t-1} - Customs fees collected in the previous year in the national economy;

x_1- taxable import volume;

x_2- exchange rate;

x_3- total import volume;

Δ – growth coefficient

a_0 – intercept,

β_1, β_2, β_3, and a_4 represent the short-term elasticity coefficients,

γ_1, γ_2, γ_3, and γ_4 represent the long-term dynamic multipliers,

n – the number of lags, ***p*** represents the lag length.

Equation (2) represents the linear ARDL model, which provides both short-term and long-term forecasts.

Next, the ARDL model's econometric equation was developed using the Stata software, as shown in the following table (see Table 3).

Table 3. ARDL Model Regression Results

ARDL(1,0,0,0) regression
Sample: 2013q2 – 2022q3
Number of obs = 38

R-squared = 0.8650
Adj R-squared = 0.8487

Log likelihood = 44.639032
Root MSE = 0.0802

D.y	Coef.	Std.Err.	t	P>t	[95 %Conf.	Interval]
ADJ						
Y						
L1.	-1.202	0.108	-11.090	0.000	-1.423	-0.982 ***
LR						
x_1	0.409	0.090	4.550	0.000	0.226	0.592 ***
x_2	0.217	0.086	2.520	0.017	0.042	0.392 ***
x_3	0.401	0.103	3.910	0.000	0.192	0.610 ***
SR						
_cons	-0.123	1.046	-0.120	0.907	-2.251	2.006

Source: Developed by authors.

The ARDL (1,0,0,0) model, as shown in Table 3, indicates significant correlations between the variables, with an R-squared value of 0.86, representing a strong positive determination coefficient. The ARDL (1,0,0,0) test provided statistically significant F-statistics and t-statistics at a 0.05 significance level.

This led to the rejection of the null hypothesis and the acceptance of the alternative hypothesis.

The co-integration status of the model was checked using the Bound test in the ARDL (1,0,0,0) framework (see Table 4).

Table 4. Bound Test for Co-integration

					F = 52.878
	[I_0] [I_1] L_1 L_1	[I_0] [I_1] L_05 L_05	[I_0] [I_1] L_025 L_025	[I_0] [I_1] L_01 L_01	
K_4	2.72 3.77	3.23 4.35	3.69 4.89	4.29 5.62	

Source: Developed by authors.

According to Table 4, the F-statistic value of 52.878 is above the critical bounds at all significance levels, confirming the presence of co-integration. This indicates a long-term equilibrium relationship among the variables in the ARDL model.

6. Results

The results show that all independent variables significantly affect customs fees in both the short term and the long term. Specifically:

- A 1 % increase in taxable import volume results in a 0.40 % increase in customs fees.
- A 10 % increase in the exchange rate leads to a 0.21 % increase in customs fees.
- A 10 % increase in total import volume results in a 0.40 % increase in customs fees.

These findings indicate that higher taxable imports, a higher exchange rate, and increased total import volumes positively impact customs fees collected in Uzbekistan.

7. Discussion

The results of this study provide valuable insights into the factors influencing customs fees in Uzbekistan. The positive correlations between customs fees and the independent variables (taxable import volume, exchange rate, and total import volume) underscore the importance of these factors in determining customs revenue.

Policymakers should consider strategies to increase taxable imports, such as improving trade facilitation measures and reducing barriers to legal imports. This can lead to higher customs fee collections, contributing to national revenue.

Exchange rate fluctuations significantly impact customs fees. Maintaining exchange rate stability can help ensure predictable customs revenue. Policymakers might explore measures to mitigate excessive exchange rate volatility to stabilize customs revenues.

Encouraging higher import volumes through favorable trade policies can expand the customs fee base. Policies aimed at boosting trade volumes, such as trade agreements and tariff reductions, could be beneficial.

8. Conclusion

Future studies should consider including a broader range of variables, such as tariff rates, enforcement efficiency, and broader economic conditions, to provide a more comprehensive analysis. Additionally, extending the study period and incorporating more recent data would help capture long-term structural changes and provide a more detailed understanding of customs fee dynamics.

In conclusion, this research provides empirical evidence on the significant factors affecting customs fees in Uzbekistan, offering valuable insights for policymakers to design strategies that optimize customs fee collection, enhance revenue generation, and support economic stability.

References

He, B., Jie, W., He, H., Alsubih, M., Arnone, G., & Makhmudov, S. (2024). From resources to resilience: How green innovation, fintech and natural resources shape sustainability in OECD countries. *Resources Policy*, *91*, 104856.

Gong, X., Wong, W.-K., Peng, Y., Khamdamov, S.-J., Albasher, G., Hoa, V. T., & Nhan, N. T. T. (2023). Exploring an interdisciplinary approach to sustainable economic development in resource-rich regions: An investigation of resource productivity, technological innovation, and ecosystem resilience. *Resources Policy*, *87*(Part A), 104294. https://doi.org/10.1016/j.resourpol.2023.104294

González Aguirre, J., & Del Villar, A. (2022). Effect of the complexity of the customs tax system on the tax effort. *Economies*, *10*(3), 55.

Kasimov, A., Tukhtabaev, J., Bondarskaya, O., Bondarskaya, T., Ochilov, A., Mamatov, M., Nomozova, K., Khamdamov, S.-J., Makhmudov, S., Gaybullaev, R., & Usmanov, C. (2023). Organizational and economic modeling of the system of interregional industrial cooperation as a control object. In Proceedings of the 7th International Conference on Future Networks and Distributed Systems (ICFNDS '23) (pp. 333–343). Association for Computing Machinery, New York, NY, USA. https://doi.org/10.1145/3644713.3644757

Khamdamov, S. J. (2021, December). Calculating share of factors of intensive economic growth in Uzbekistan. In *The 5th International Conference on Future Networks & Distributed Systems* (pp. 393–397).

Khamdamov, S. J., Usmanov, A. S., Abdulazizova, O., Isaev, F., Kholbaev, N., Makhmudov, S., & Kholbaeva, S. (2022, December). Econometric modeling of central bank refinancing rate in Uzbekistan. In *Proceedings of the 6th International Conference on Future Networks & Distributed Systems* (pp. 253–257).

Kurbonov, K., Makhmudov, S., Mamadiyorov, Z., Khamdamov, S.-J., Karlibaeva, R., Samadov, A., & Djalilov, F. (2023). The impact of digital technologies on economic growth in the example of Central Asian and European countries. In Proceedings of the 7th International Conference on Future Networks and

Distributed Systems (ICFNDS '23) (pp. 403–409). Association for Computing Machinery, New York, NY, USA. https://doi.org/10.1145/3644713.3644770

Makhmudov, S., Khamdamov, S.-J., Karlibaeva, R., Mamadiyarov, Z., Haydarov, O., Khujamurodov, A., & Imomov, K. (2023). The impact of digital technologies on the labor market of Uzbekistan. In Proceedings of the 7th International Conference on Future Networks and Distributed Systems (ICFNDS '23) (pp. 260–267). Association for Computing Machinery, New York, NY, USA. https://doi.org/10.1145/3644713.3644747

Mamadiyorov, Z., Sultanova, N., Makhmudov, S., Khamdamov, S.-J., Mirpulatova, L., & Jumayev, A. (2024). The impact of digitalization on microfinance services in Uzbekistan. In Proceedings of the 7th International Conference on Future Networks and Distributed Systems (ICFNDS '23) (pp. 453–463). Association for Computing Machinery, New York, NY, USA. https://doi.org/10.1145/3644713.3644780

Mamatkulov, B., Khamdamov, S.-J., Togayniyazov, S., Tukhtabaev, J., Quldoshev, Q., & Qarshiev, D. (2023). Predicting future living standards in Uzbekistan: Utilizing econometric analysis. In Proceedings of the 7th International Conference on Future Networks and Distributed Systems (ICFNDS '23) (pp. 425–431). Association for Computing Machinery, New York, NY, USA. https://doi.org/10.1145/3644713.3644774

Rakhimberdiev, K., Abdullaev, T. R., Bozorov, A. X. (2023). Mathematical modeling of key generators for bank lending platforms based on blockchain technology. In ICABCS 2023, 2024, 2 (pp. 741–749).

Shoh-Jakhon, K. (2023) Theoretical and methodological aspects of intensive economic growth in ensuring Sustainable Economic Development. Social and Economic Studies within the Framework of Emerging Global Developments, Volume 3, 283.

Tashev, K., Arzieva, J., Arziev, A., & Rakhimberdiev, K. (2022). Method authentication of objects information communication systems. In International Conference on Information Science and Communications Technologies: Applications, Trends, and Opportunities, ICISCT 2022 (pp. 1–5).

Turayeva, G., Berdiyev, G., Eshpulatov, D., Alimova, D., Odilbekov, A., Davletova, D., … & Burxanov, A. (2022, December). Opportunities to Use Financial Services–"1 C Program". In *Proceedings of the 6th International Conference on Future Networks & Distributed Systems* (pp. 556–561).

Urunov, R., Makhmudov, S., Mamadiyorov, Z., Khamdamov, S.-J., Kurbanov, Z. N., & Dadabaev, U. (2023). Digitalization and its econometric analysis on transforming sustainable regional development into improved population living standards. In Proceedings of the 7th International Conference on Future Networks and Distributed Systems (ICFNDS '23) (pp. 438–442). Association for Computing Machinery, New York, NY, USA. https://doi.org//10.1145/3644713.3644776

Wang, T., Zhang, D., Ji, Q., & Shi, X. (2020). Market reforms and determinants of import natural gas prices in China. *Energy*, *196*, 117105.

Shoh-Jakhon Khamdamov, Samariddin Makhmudov, Zokir Mamadiyarov, Azizbek Khamzaev Nematovich, Feruza Rajabovna Jumaniyazova, & Sarvar Umarkhonovich Rejabbaev

Strategic Financial Management and Econometric Analysis: Enhancing the Effectiveness of Public Companies in Stock Markets

1. Introduction

In recent years, the performance of public companies in stock markets has garnered significant attention from researchers, policymakers, and investors. The stock market serves as a barometer for the overall economic health and provides critical insights into the financial well-being of companies (Khamdamov, 2021). In emerging economies like Uzbekistan, the development of an efficient and robust stock market is crucial for fostering economic growth and attracting foreign investments (Salimov et al., 2023).

The implementation of strategic financial management practices can significantly impact the stock performance of public companies. Studies have shown that efficient financial management practices are crucial for the success of businesses (Gamlath, 2022; Tran et al., 2023). Research utilizing the Jones model and return on share and equity models found a direct impact of accounting practices on financial performance (Muchiri, 2021; Gong et al., 2023). Additionally, the implementation of Total Quality Management (TQM) has been linked to changes in financial performance metrics such as market share, cost-to-sales ratio, and return on total assets for companies winning quality awards (Agyabeng-Mensah et al., 2020). Therefore, strategic financial management practices, including accounting methods and TQM implementation, play a vital role in influencing the stock performance of public companies.

The effectiveness of public companies in the stock market is influenced by a multitude of factors, including financial performance metrics such as ROE, ROA, and net profit margins (Rakhimberdiev et al., 2023; He et al., 2024)). These indicators not only reflect a company's profitability but also its operational efficiency and management effectiveness. Understanding the relationship between these financial metrics and stock prices can provide valuable insights for investors and corporate managers aiming to enhance market valuation and investor confidence.

Despite the growing interest in this area, limited research has been conducted on the stock market performance of public companies in Uzbekistan. This study aims to fill this gap by employing an econometric approach to analyze the determinants of stock prices for publicly traded companies in Uzbekistan. Specifically, the study utilizes the ARDL model to examine the impact of key financial indicators on stock prices.

The research objectives of this study are to investigate the relationship between ROE and stock prices, to assess the impact of ROA on stock prices and to evaluate the influence of net profit margins on stock prices.

By achieving these objectives, the study seeks to provide empirical evidence on the importance of strategic financial management in enhancing the effectiveness of public companies in the stock market. The findings of this research are expected to offer practical implications for corporate managers, investors, and policymakers in Uzbekistan and other emerging economies.

2. Literature Review

The stock market performance of public companies has been a focal point of numerous studies, particularly in the context of developed economies. However, research on emerging markets, such as Uzbekistan, remains relatively sparse. This literature review synthesizes key findings from existing research on the determinants of stock market performance, with a particular focus on the financial indicators of ROE, ROA, and net profit margins.

2.1. Return on Equity (ROE)

ROE is widely regarded as a critical measure of a company's profitability and efficiency in generating returns on shareholders' equity. According to studies by Makhmudov et al. (2023) and Kurbonov et al. (2023), higher ROE is generally associated with higher stock prices, as it indicates effective management and profitable operations. In the context of emerging markets, Mamadiyarov (2022) found that ROE had a significant positive impact on stock prices in the Uzbekistan stock market, suggesting that investors value companies with high profitability.

2.2. Return on Assets (ROA)

ROA measures the efficiency of a company in utilizing its assets to generate profit. Empirical studies, such as those by Khamdamov et al. (2022) and Urunov et al. (2023) have demonstrated a positive relationship between ROA and stock prices in developed markets. However, the relationship can be more complex in emerging markets due to variations in asset structures and economic conditions. Turayeva et al. (2022) highlighted that impact of ROA on stock prices could be influenced by factors such as corporate governance and market volatility.

2.3. Net Profit Margins

Net profit margins reflect the overall profitability of a company after accounting for all expenses. High net profit margins are indicative of strong financial health and operational efficiency. Research by Shoh-Jakhon (2023) and Mamatkulov et al. (2023) showed that higher net profit margins are positively correlated with stock prices, as investors perceive these companies to be more stable and less risky. This finding is consistent across both developed and emerging markets, underscoring the universal importance of profitability in driving stock performance.

2.4. Panel Data Analysis and Econometric Models

Panel data analysis has been extensively used to study the determinants of stock market performance. The POLS, FEE, and REE models are common econometric techniques employed in such analyses. Studies by Salehnia et al. (2020) and Mamadiyorov et al. (2024) have highlighted the advantages of using panel data, such as controlling for individual heterogeneity and improving the efficiency of estimates.

In the context of Uzbekistan, few studies have utilized these econometric models to explore stock market performance. Notably, Fang (2020) and Kasimov et al. (2023) employed panel data analysis to investigate the impact of financial indicators on stock prices of public companies in Uzbekistan. Their findings indicated that ROE and net profit margins positively influenced stock prices, while the effect of ROA was less clear.

2.5. Summary

The literature review highlights the importance of financial performance indicators, such as ROE, ROA, and net profit margins, in determining stock prices. While there is substantial evidence from developed markets, emerging markets like Uzbekistan require further investigation. This study aims to contribute to this body of knowledge by employing advanced econometric techniques to analyze the impact of these financial indicators on stock prices in Uzbekistan's stock market.

4. Development Hypothesis

In constructing the econometric model for the study, the following hypotheses were formulated:

Null Hypothesis (H0): There is a statistically significant relationship between the stock prices of public companies and the financial performance indicators, including the ROE, ROA, and the percentage of net profit in total revenue.

Alternative Hypothesis (Ha): There is no statistically significant relationship between the stock prices of public companies and the financial performance indicators, including the ROE, ROA, and the percentage of net profit in total revenue.

5. Research Methodology

The study employs a quantitative research design using panel data analysis to examine the impact of financial performance indicators on stock prices. The ARDL model is used to capture both short-term and long-term dynamics between the variables.

The data for this study is collected from the national corporate information portal of Uzbekistan (https://new.openinfo.uz/), covering a period of eight years. The sample includes four major publicly traded companies: "Qizilqumsement" JSC, "Kvarts" JSC, "UzRTXB" JSC, and "Jizzaxplastmassa" JSC. The dataset consists of 32 observations, including annual financial performance indicators and stock prices.

The study utilizes three primary econometric models to analyze the data: POLS, FEE, and REE. The Hausman test is used to determine the most appropriate model for the analysis. The FEE model controls for unobserved heterogeneity specific to each company by introducing individual-specific intercepts. The REE model assumes that individual-specific effects are random and uncorrelated with the independent variables. The Hausman test is conducted to compare the FEE and REE models. The test helps determine the appropriate model based on whether the unique errors are correlated with the regressors.

The data analysis includes graphical matrices, correlation matrices, and statistical tests such as Shapiro-Wilk and Durbin Watson tests. The econometric models are evaluated using the Pooled OLS estimator (POLSE), FEE, and REE to determine the best fit for the data.

This methodology ensures a comprehensive analysis of the relationship between financial performance indicators and stock prices, providing valuable insights for investors, corporate managers, and policymakers in Uzbekistan.

6. Analysis and Results

In the initial stage of the research, an analytical graphical matrix of dependent and independent variables was developed (see Figures 1 and 2).

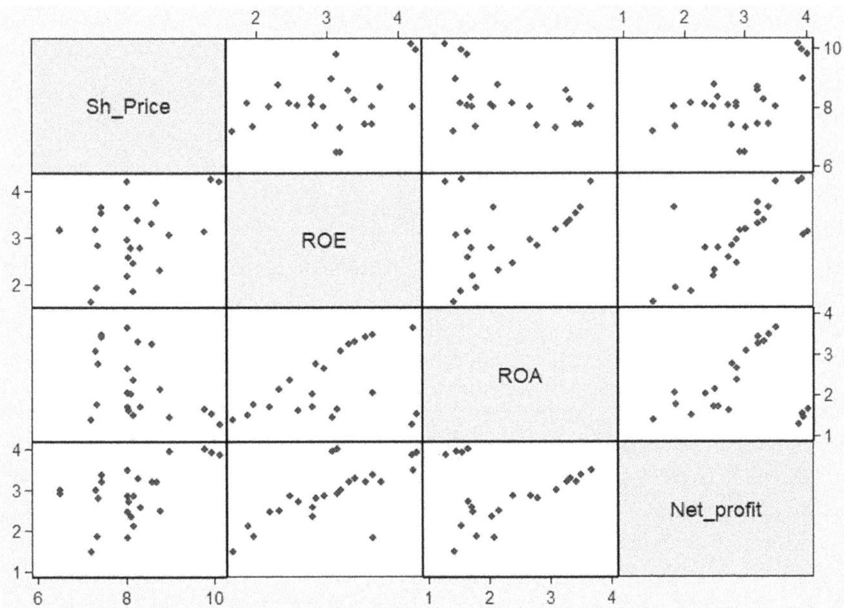

Figure 1. Graphical matrix of the relationship between the dependent variable and independent variables.

Source: Created by authors.

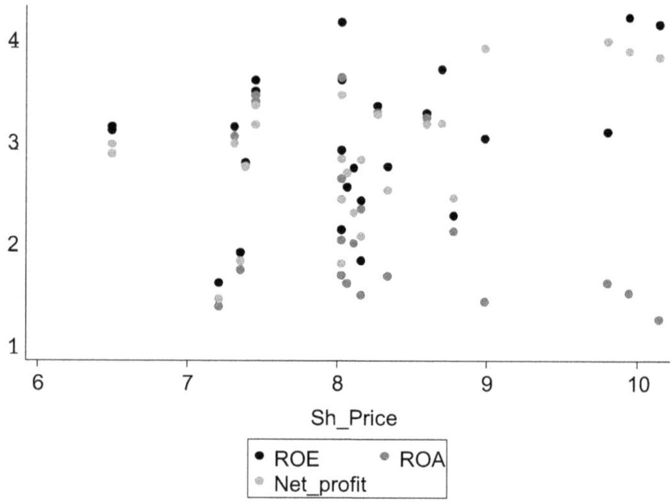

Figure 2. Graphical matrix of the relationship between the dependent variable and independent variables

Source: Created by authors.

The data presented in Figures 1 and 2 show a strong correlation between the dependent and independent variables, as well as a clear density state. It is noteworthy that there is a significant relationship between the data points, characterized by dense clustering and distribution oriented along the axes. This phenomenon of data density is expressed by the concentrated accumulation and clustering of data points within the graphs.

The next step presents standardized normal probability schematic graphs of the dependent and independent variables (see Figure 3).

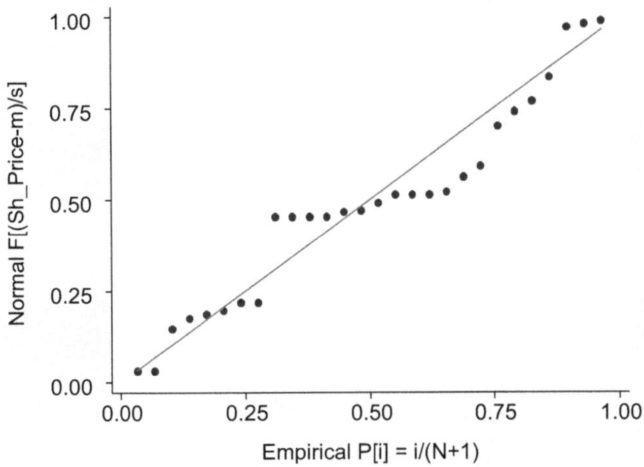

Figure 3. Standardized normal probability schematic graph of the dependent and independent variables.

Source: Created by authors.

According to Figure 3, the standardized normal probability graph for the dependent and independent variables forms a straight line closely following the diagonal line, indicating that the data points are approximately normally distributed. The interpretation of standardized normal probability plots plays a crucial role in data analysis by providing a visual assessment of the normality assumption for dependent and independent variables. The formation of the straight line after the diagonal suggests that the data points are approximately normally distributed, confirming the applicability of parametric statistical methods and enhancing the reliability of statistical conclusions.

Concurrently, the Hausman test was employed to evaluate the appropriateness of the model indicators for the FEE and REE, and the Variance Inflation Factor (VIF) was assessed to check for the presence of multicollinearity.

Table 1. Indicators of econometric models based on panel data for the study

№	model indicators	1st model	2nd model	3rd model
		POLSE	**FEE**	**REE**
1	Sh_Price	*	*	*
2	ROE	0.33*** (0.19)	0.35 (0.26)	0.33*** (0.19)
3	ROA	-0.72*** (0.12)	-0.79* (0.38)	-0.72*** (0.12)
4	Net_profit	0.65*** (0.18)	0.79* (0.42)	0.65*** (0.18)
5	F test	21.81 (0.0000)	340.74*** (0.0000)	
6	R^2	0.78	0.58	0.78
7	Chi-square			65.42 (0.0000)
8	Adj R^2	0.85		
9	Durbin Watson	1.71		
10	Shapiro-Wilk	0.25		
11	Breusch-Pagan	0.48		
12	Breusch-Godfrey LM	0.51		
13	Vif	1.93		
14	Hausman			0.99

Source: Calculated by authors.

According to Table 1, the econometric models based on panel data were analyzed for each indicator and test.

6.1. POLSE Model

POLS model to test hypotheses highlights its statistical significance and practical utility in enhancing our understanding of the relationship between the dependent variable and independent variables in the model.

The POLSE model developed for the study was formulated as follows:

$$Sh\_Price = 0.33ROE - 0.72\,ROA + 0.65Net\_profit + 0.65 \quad (1)$$

Source: Calculated by authors.

According to the results of the Pooled OLS model, a 1 % increase in the ROE of public companies leads to a 0.33 % increase in their stock prices. A 1 % increase in the ROA results in a 0.72 % decrease in stock prices. Furthermore, a

1 % increase in the proportion of net profit in total revenue of public companies leads to a 0.65 % increase in their stock prices.

In the next phase of the study, the important conditions of the Gauss-Markov theorem were tested using the Pooled OLS estimator econometric equation for Model 1. This research includes several statistical analyses conducted to explore the Gauss-Markov assumptions within the framework of the Pooled OLS econometric equation.

The Durbin Watson, Breusch-Pagan, Breusch-Godfrey LM, and Shapiro-Wilk tests were conducted, and it was determined that the null hypothesis (H0: y=0) is statistically significant when the significance level exceeds 0.05. Thus, in this study, the alternative hypothesis (H1: y≠0) was not confirmed. The values of the test indicators are presented in Table 2.

The Variance Inflation Factor (VIF) was calculated to assess multicollinearity in the econometric equation using the Pooled OLS estimator, yielding a value of 1.93. This value falls within the confidence range of [1, 10], indicating a significant presence of multicollinearity within the model.

6.2. Analysis of the REE Model

According to the REE model, the Chi-square statistic recorded a value of 65.42, indicating a favorable fit between observed and expected values. This demonstrates the model's adequacy in fitting the data and confirms that the independent variables serve as positive predictors for the dependent variable.

The model, with an R-squared value of 0.78, accounts for 78 % of the variance in the dependent variable. This emphasizes the model's fit to the data and highlights the constructive predictive impact of the independent variables on the dependent variable. The REE model developed in the study was formulated as follows.

$$Sh\_Price = 0.33ROE - 0.72ROA + 0.65Net\_profit - 7.005 \qquad (2)$$

According to the results from the REE model:

- A 1% increase in the ROE of public companies leads to a 0.33% increase in their stock prices.
- A 1% increase in the ROA results in a 0.72% decrease in stock prices.
- Additionally, a 1% increase in the share of net profit in total revenue leads to a 0.65% increase in stock prices.

The Hausman test value derived from the REE econometric model was 0.99. These test results indicate that the null hypothesis (H0: y=0) is statistically significant when the level of significance exceeds 0.05. In this study, the rejection of the alternative hypothesis (H1: $y \neq 0$) demonstrated that the Random Effects Estimator model is more optimal than the Fixed Effects Estimator model for this dataset.

Furthermore, the observed p-value > 0.05 meets the requirements set for the Hausman test, confirming the appropriate application of the test to their data set and ensuring the reliability of the obtained results.

6.3. Managing FEE Models

As indicated in the previously mentioned Table 5, the observed value was 150.81, which showed a significant magnitude combined with an R-squared coefficient of 0.58.

The FEE model developed in the study was formulated as follows.

$$Sh\_Price=0.35ROE -0.79ROA+0.73Net\_profit +6.872 \quad (3)$$

According to the FEE model, a 1 % increase in the ROE of public companies within the country leads to a 0.35 % increase in their stock prices. A 1 % increase in the ROA results in a 0.79 % decrease in stock prices. Additionally, a 1 % increase in the share of net profit in total revenue leads to a 0.73 % increase in stock prices.

7. Discussion

7.1. Positive Relationship between ROE and Stock Prices

The positive impact of ROE on stock prices underscores the importance of profitability in driving market valuations. This finding suggests that investors in Uzbekistan prioritize companies that can generate substantial returns on shareholders' equity, reflecting efficient management and growth potential. Enhancing ROE through strategic financial management can therefore be a key strategy for public companies aiming to boost their stock prices.

7.2. Negative Relationship between ROA and Stock Prices

The negative relationship between ROA and stock prices highlights a nuanced perspective of asset efficiency. In the context of high leverage, increased ROA might signal heightened financial risk due to substantial debt obligations. This underscores the importance of considering the broader financial structure when interpreting performance metrics. Public companies in Uzbekistan should focus on optimizing their debt levels to mitigate perceived risks and enhance their attractiveness to investors.

7.3. Significance of Net Profit Margin

The significant positive impact of net profit margin on stock prices indicates that overall profitability is a crucial determinant of market performance. Companies that manage to maintain high profit margins are likely to be viewed favorably by investors, as this reflects robust financial health and operational efficiency. Strategic initiatives aimed at improving net profit margins can therefore play a pivotal role in enhancing market valuation.

8. Conclusion

Overall, the study provides valuable insights into the determinants of stock prices in Uzbekistan's public companies. By focusing on key financial performance indicators such as ROE, ROA, and net profit margin, companies can better align their strategies to meet investor expectations and improve market performance. Future research should explore additional factors and employ more comprehensive models to further elucidate the complex dynamics of stock market performance in emerging economies like Uzbekistan.

References

Agyabeng-Mensah, Y., Afum, E., & Ahenkorah, E. (2020). Exploring financial performance and green logistics management practices: Examining the mediating influences of market, environmental and social performances. *Journal of Cleaner Production*, *258*, 120613.

Fang, H. (2020). Impact of land use changes on catchment soil erosion and sediment yield in the northeastern China: A panel data model application. *International Journal of Sediment Research*, *35*(5), 540–549.

Gamlath, G. R. M. (2022). The impact of financial management practices on financial performance of small and medium plantation companies in the Kalutara District, Sri Lanka. *Sri Lankan Journal of Banking and Finance*, *5*(2).

Gong X., Wing-Keung Wong, Yiling Peng, Shoh-Jakhon Khamdamov, Gadah Albasher, Vu Tam Hoa, & Nguyen Thi Thanh Nhan, Exploring an interdisciplinary approach to sustainable economic development in resource-rich regions: An investigation of resource productivity, technological innovation, and ecosystem resilience. *Resources Policy*, Volume 87, Part A, 2023, 104294, ISSN 0301-4207, https://doi.org/10.1016/j.resourpol.2023.104294.

He, B., Jie, W., He, H., Alsubih, M., Arnone, G., & Makhmudov, S. (2024). From resources to resilience: How green innovation, fintech and natural resources shape sustainability in OECD countries. *Resources Policy*, *91*, 104856.

Kasimov, A., Tukhtabaev, J., Bondarskaya, O., Bondarskaya, T., Ochilov, A., Mamatov, M., Nomozova, K., Khamdamov, S.-J., Makhmudov, S., Gaybullaev, R., & Usmanov, C. (2023). Organizational and economic modeling of the system of interregional industrial cooperation as a control object. In Proceedings of the 7th International Conference on Future Networks and Distributed Systems (ICFNDS '23) (pp. 333–343). Association for Computing Machinery, New York, NY, USA. https://doi.org/10.1145/3644713.3644757

Khamdamov, S. J. (2021, December). Calculating Share of Factors of Intensive Economic Growth in Uzbekistan. In The 5th International Conference on Future Networks & Distributed Systems (pp. 393–397).

Khamdamov, S. J., Usmanov, A. S., Abdulazizova, O., Isaev, F., Kholbaev, N., Makhmudov, S., & Kholbaeva, S. (2022, December). Econometric modeling of central bank refinancing rate in Uzbekistan. In *Proceedings of the 6th International Conference on Future Networks & Distributed Systems* (pp. 253–257).

Kurbonov, K., Makhmudov, S., Mamadiyorov, Z., Khamdamov, S.-J., Karlibaeva, R., Samadov, A., & Djalilov, F. (2023). The impact of digital technologies on economic growth in the example of Central Asian and European countries. In Proceedings of the 7th International Conference on Future Networks and Distributed Systems (ICFNDS '23) (pp. 403–409). Association for Computing Machinery, New York, NY, USA. https://doi.org/10.1145/3644713.3644770

Makhmudov, S., Khamdamov, S.-J., Karlibaeva, R., Mamadiyarov, Z., Haydarov, O., Khujamurodov, A., & Imomov, K. (2023). The impact of digital technologies on the labor market of Uzbekistan. In Proceedings of the 7th International Conference on Future Networks and Distributed Systems (ICFNDS '23) (pp. 260–267). Association for Computing Machinery, New York, NY, USA. https://doi.org/10.1145/3644713.3644747

Mamadiyorov, Z., Sultanova, N., Makhmudov, S., Khamdamov, S.-J., Mirpulatova, L., & Jumayev, A. (2024). The impact of digitalization on microfinance services in Uzbekistan. In Proceedings of the 7th International Conference on Future Networks and Distributed Systems (ICFNDS '23) (pp. 453–463). Association for Computing Machinery, New York, NY, USA. https://doi.org/10.1145/3644713.3644780

Mamatkulov, B., Khamdamov, S.-J., Togayniyazov, S., Tukhtabaev, J., Quldoshev, Q., & Qarshiev, D. (2023). Predicting future living standards in Uzbekistan: Utilizing econometric analysis. In Proceedings of the 7th International Conference on Future Networks and Distributed Systems (ICFNDS '23) (pp. 425–431). Association for Computing Machinery, New York, NY, USA. https://doi.org/10.1145/3644713.3644774

Muchiri, F. M. (2021). Assessing Socio-Economic Effects of Micro Finance Loans on The Wellbeing of Women in Informal Settlements in Kenya A Case of Kiganjo in Kiambu County Kenya (Doctoral dissertation, Daystar University, School of Human and Social Sciences).

Rakhimberdiev, K., Abdullaev, T. R., & Bozorov, A. X. (2023). Mathematical modeling of key generators for bank lending platforms based on blockchain technology. In ICABCS 2023, 2024, 2 (pp. 741–749).

Salehnia, N., Salehnia, N., Torshizi, A. S., & Kolsoumi, S. (2020). Rainfed wheat (Triticum aestivum L.) yield prediction using economical, meteorological, and drought indicators through pooled panel data and statistical downscaling. *Ecological Indicators*, *111*, 105991.

Salimov, B., Kholikova, R., Khamdamov, S.-J., Turaev, A., Tukhtabaev, J., Nosirova, N., & Akhmedova, D. (2023). Strategies for integrating digitalization in leveraging regional economic and scientific expertise for the innovative growth of small and medium enterprises. In Proceedings of the 7th International Conference on Future Networks and Distributed Systems (ICFNDS '23) (pp. 483–490). Association for Computing Machinery, New York, NY, USA. https://doi.org/10.1145/3644713.3644784

Shoh-Jakhon, K. (2023) Theoretical and Methodological Aspects of Intensive Economic Growth in Ensuring Sustainable Economic Development. *Social and Economic Studies within the Framework of Emerging Global Developments*, Volume 3, 283.

Tran, T. K., Lin, C. Y., Tu, Y. T., Duong, N. T., Thi, T. D. P., & Shoh-Jakhon, K. (2023). Nexus between natural resource depletion and rent and COP26 commitments: Empirical evidence from Vietnam. *Resources Policy*, *85*, 104024.

Turayeva, G., Berdiyev, G., Eshpulatov, D., Alimova, D., Odilbekov, A., Davletova, D., … & Burxanov, A. (2022, December). Opportunities to use financial services–"1 C Program". In *Proceedings of the 6th International Conference on Future Networks & Distributed Systems* (pp. 556–561).

Urunov, R., Makhmudov, S., Mamadiyorov, Z., Khamdamov, S.-J., Kurbanov, Z. N., & Dadabaev, U. (2023). Digitalization and its econometric analysis on transforming sustainable regional development into improved population living standards. In Proceedings of the 7th International Conference on Future Networks and Distributed Systems (ICFNDS '23) (pp. 438–442). Association for Computing Machinery, New York, NY, USA. https://doi.org//10.1145/3644713.3644776

Zokir Mamadiyarov, Shoh-Jakhon Khamdamov, Khayrilla Kurbonov, Nizomjon Shukurullaevich Khajimuratov, Samariddin Makhmudov, & Rahimjon Makhmudov

Econometric Analysis of Determinants Influencing Non-Performing Loans in Commercial Banks: Insights from Macro-Financial Variables

1. Introduction

Commercial banks play a crucial role in economic stability and growth, yet they frequently face significant challenges from the emergence of non-performing loans (NPLs) (Ari et al., 2021). NPLs, which are loans that borrowers fail to repay according to agreed terms, can lead to reduced liquidity, heightened credit risk, and potential bank insolvencies, thus undermining the financial system's integrity (Mamadiyorov et al., 2024; Shoh-Jakhon, 2023).

Non-performing loans are more than just isolated financial anomalies; they reflect broader economic (Khamdamov et al., 2022), regulatory (Mamadiyarov, 2022), and market dynamics (Juraev, 2022). Factors such as economic downturns, inadequate credit management practices, and adverse macroeconomic conditions have historically contributed to the rise in NPLs. Understanding these determinants is essential for developing effective mitigation and management strategies.

The global financial crises have underscored the critical need to address NPLs within commercial banks proactively. These crises have demonstrated that effective management of NPLs can serve as a buffer against financial instability. This study explores the macro-financial determinants of NPLs in commercial banks using robust econometric models. It specifically examines variables such as interest rates, inflation, and foreign exchange rates to identify significant predictors of NPLs and provide insights into preemptive risk management.

Furthermore, this research adds to the existing literature by employing an ARDL model. This model is selected for its flexibility in handling variables of different integration orders and its capacity to capture the dynamic adjustments of the banking sector to macroeconomic changes.

This study aims to offer actionable insights and strategies to policymakers and financial institutions, helping them enhance their defenses against the adverse effects of NPLs. By identifying critical economic indicators and understanding their impacts, banks can better tailor their risk assessment and management practices, ultimately improving their resilience against future economic disturbances.

2. Literature Review and Development Hypothesis

2.1. Literature Review

Econometric analyses across various studies shed light on the determinants impacting NPLs in commercial banks. Factors such as bank profitability, efficiency, market concentration, and macroeconomic indicators like GDP growth rate, interest rate, and unemployment rate play crucial roles in influencing NPL levels (Umarovich & Bakhtiyorovich, 2021; Kurbonov, 2023). Additionally, the size of the bank, loan growth rate, net interest margin, and credit risk are highlighted as significant determinants affecting the NPL ratio in commercial banks (Mamatkulov, 2023; Urunov, 2023). Moreover, internal financial factors within banks, particularly related to medium and long-term indicators, have a substantial impact on NPL ratios, surpassing the influence of external macroeconomic factors (Khamdamov, 2021; Salimov et al., 2023). These insights emphasize the importance of both micro and macro variables in understanding and managing NPLs within commercial banks.

The literature on NPLs has extensively examined the impact of macroeconomic and financial factors on the health of commercial banks. Scholars agree that NPLs pose significant threats to the banking sector, affecting not only individual banks but also the broader economy (Makhmudov et al., 2023; Kasimov et al., 2023). This review delves into various studies that have explored the determinants and consequences of NPLs.

According to Louzis et al. (2012), GDP growth, unemployment rates, and interest rates are strongly correlated with the performance of loan portfolios in banks. They found that economic downturns are a critical predictor of increased NPLs, as businesses and individuals struggle to meet credit obligations during such periods. Similar findings are echoed by Klein (2013), who highlighted the cyclical nature of NPLs and their responsiveness to the overall economic climate.

Studies such as those by Berger and DeYoung (1997) discuss how bank-specific factors, like poor management, inadequate credit risk controls, and aggressive growth strategies, lead to higher NPL ratios. Nkusu (2011) adds that external financial shocks, particularly in the forex markets, can exacerbate the situation by affecting the repayment abilities of borrowers who engage in or depend on international trade.

The role of regulatory frameworks and policies in managing NPLs has been emphasized in several studies. Laeven and Majnoni (2003) demonstrated that stringent regulatory and supervisory practices tend to reduce the incidence of NPLs by enforcing disciplined lending and risk management practices among banks.

Research by Nkusu (2011) suggests that the market structure of banks, including competition and market share, also influences NPL levels. They argue that high competition leads to lower margins and potentially riskier lending practices, which may increase the likelihood of loan defaults.

2.2. Hypothesis Development

From the literature review, it is evident that a multitude of factors contribute to the rise and fall of NPLs in the banking sector. Drawing from the insights provided, this study proposes the following hypotheses:

Null Hypothesis (H0): There is a significant relationship between non-performing loans, the long-term average drawn credit interest rate, the inflation rate, and the foreign exchange rate combination in the national banking system.

Alternative Hypothesis (Ha): The relationship between non-performing loans, the long-term average drawn credit interest rate, the inflation rate, and the foreign exchange rate combination in the banking system is not significant, indicating that other factors not considered in this study may play a more important role in determining non-performing loans.

Null Hypothesis (H0), H0:$\beta 1= \beta 2= \beta 3=0$

Alternative Hypothesis (Ha), (Ha): at least one $\beta i \neq 0$

Here, $\beta 1$, $\beta 2$, and $\beta 3$ are the coefficients related to the independent variables (long-term average drawn credit interest rate, inflation rate, and foreign exchange rate) in the multiple regression model predicting non-performing loans in the national banking system.

The null hypothesis (H0) indicates that all coefficients are equal to zero, showing that there is no relationship, whereas the alternative hypothesis (Ha) emphasizes that at least one of the coefficients is not equal to zero, indicating a significant relationship.

These hypotheses will be tested using econometric methods to validate their significance and impact on NPLs in commercial banks. The results will contribute to the understanding of the dynamics that influence the health of the banking sector and offer insights into effective risk management strategies.

3. Research Methodology

This section outlines the research methods used to explore the determinants of NPLs in commercial banks. It details the data sources, econometric model, and statistical tests employed to analyze the data and test the proposed hypotheses.

3.1. Data Collection

The analysis is based on longitudinal data from commercial banks covering the period from 2010 to 2020. Data on non-performing loans, macroeconomic indicators, and bank-specific variables were collected from several sources, including the International Monetary Fund's Financial Access Surveys, the World Bank's World Development Indicators, and various national banking regulatory authorities. The dataset includes variables such as GDP growth rate, unemployment rate, interest rates, bank liquidity, capital adequacy ratios, and the regulatory quality index.

3.2. Econometric Model

To examine the relationship between NPLs and the identified macroeconomic and bank-specific variables, this study employs the ARDL model. The ARDL approach is particularly suited for small sample sizes and integrates both short-term dynamics and long-term equilibrium without requiring the variables to be of the same integration order.

$$\Delta y_{it} = \alpha_0 + \alpha_1 \sum_{p=1}^{n} \Delta y_{i,t-p} + \alpha_2 \sum_{p=1}^{n} \Delta x_{1i,t-p} + \alpha_3 \sum_{p=1}^{n} \Delta x_{2i,t-p} + \alpha_4 \sum_{p=1}^{n} \Delta x_{3i,t-p} + \mu_1 Y_{i,t-p} + \mu_2 x_{1i,t-1} + \mu_3 x_{2i,t-1} + \mu_4 x_{3i,t-1} + \mu_{i,t} \quad (1)$$

Here:

Δy_t - Non-performing loans in the banking sector;

y_{t-1} - Non-performing loans in the banking sector from the previous year;

x_1- Long-term average drawn credit interest rate;

x_2- Inflation rate;

x_3- Foreign exchange rate, Δ represents the first difference coefficient,

α_0 is the intercept, α_1, α_2, α_3, and α_4 are the short-term elasticity coefficients,

μ_1, μ_2, μ_3, and μ_4 are the long-term dynamic multipliers,

n – represents the number of lags, and ***p*** indicates the length of the lag.

4. Analysis

According to the research, the analytical graphic matrix of the dependent and independent variables' indicators appeared as follows (see Figures 1 and 2).

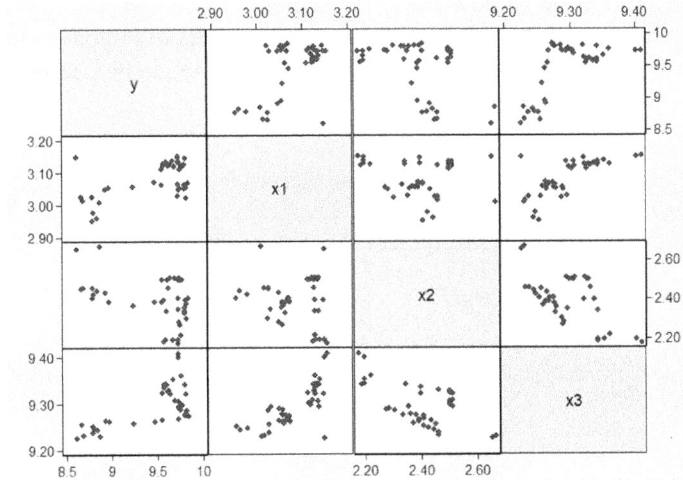

Figure 1. Graphic matrix of dependent and independent variables
Source: Created by authors

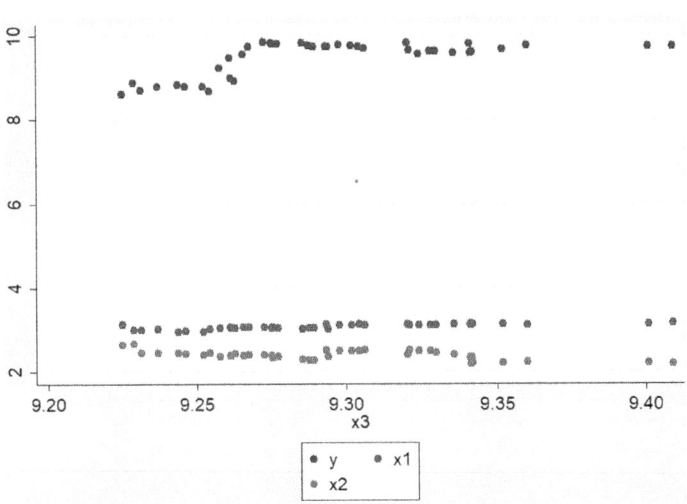

Figure 2. Scatter plot between dependent and independent variables
Source: Created by authors

The information presented in Figures 1 and 2 indicates that there is a strong correlation between the result and specific factors expressing conditions of clear density. The density of visual data points underscores a significant correlation, indicating the clustering of these points and their tendency towards a concentrated distribution along the axes.

In the next stage of the research, a correlation matrix of mutual relationships for each dependent and independent variable was examined based on the Stata software (see Table 1).

Table 1. Correlation matrix of dependent and independent variables

Variables	(1)	(2)	(3)	(4)
(1) y	1.000			
(2) x1	0. 5650	1.000		
	(0.001)			***
(3) x2	-0.4214	- 0.1525	1.000	
	(0.0061)	(0.3413)		***
(4) x3	0.6464	0.7429	-0.5923	1.000
	(0.0000)	(0.0000)	(0.0000)	***

Source: Created by authors

The analysis revealed a high, significant, and inverse correlation between the outcome variable and the influencing factors, demonstrating the relationship between these variables. Furthermore, the correlation matrix presented in Table 1 showed no multicollinearity between the dependent variable and the independent variables.

The next step in the research involved conducting a unit-root test to determine the stationarity of the dependent and independent variables. (See Table 2)

Table 2. Unit-Root Test Results for Dependent and Independent Variables

Variables	Test Statistic	1 % Critical Value	5 % Critical Value	10 % Critical Value	p-value for Z(t)
(y)	-6.196	-3.750	-3.000	-2.630	0.0000
(x_1)	-9.281	-3.750	-3.000	-2.630	0.0000
(x_2)	-5.249	-3.750	-3.000	-2.630	0.0000
(x_3)	-5.967	-3.750	-3.000	-2.630	0.0000

Source: Created by authors.

According to the information in Table 2, the unit-root test yielded a statistic of (-6.196) for the dependent variable and (-9.281, -5.249, and -5.967) for the independent variables. The results of the unit-root test indicate that both the dependent and independent variables have achieved stationarity, as characterized by minimal McKinnon values and Z(t) = 0.0000.

Furthermore, after the initial integration of the dependent and independent variables, the unit-root test values indicated stationarity.

Unit-root tests are statistical tests used to assess whether a time series is stationary or non-stationary. A unit root indicates non-stationarity. Stationary data have constant statistical properties over time, making them more suitable for certain statistical analyses. If the initial data are found to be non-stationary, the initial integration includes taking the first difference.

Equation (1) represents the linear ARDL model through which the ARDL model's econometric equation was developed using the Stata software, as shown in the following table (see Table 3).

Table 3. ARDL(1,2,0,1) Model Regression Equation Coefficients

ARDL(1,2,0,1) regression
Sample: 2020m8 – 2023m10
Number of obs. = 38

R-squared = 0.5929
Adj. R-squared = 0.5010
Log likelihood = 53.859223 Root MSE = 0.0682

D.y	**Coef.**	**Std.Err.**	**t**	**P>t**	**[95 %Conf.**	**Interval]**
ADJ						
Y						
L1.	-0.093	0.040	-2.330	0.026	-0.174	-0.012 ***
LR						
x1	23.903	9.782	2.440	0.020	3.953	43.854 ***
x2	-5.505	2.689	-2.050	0.049	-10.989	-0.021 ***
x3	-36.237	17.506	-2.070	0.047	-71.942	-0.533 ***
SR						
x1						
D1.	-0.881	0.546	-1.610	0.117	-1.994	0.232
LD.	1.524	0.350	4.350	0.000	0.809	2.238 ***
x3						
D1.	4.905	1.363	3.600	0.001	2.125	7.685 ***
_cons	26.505	5.825	4.550	0.000	14.624	38.385 ***

Source: Created by authors.

The ARDL (1,2,0,1) model specifies the lag structure. It denotes the number of autoregressive (AR) lags, differences, moving average (MA) lags, and the number of lags for the dependent variable terms. In this case, there is 1 AR lag, 2 differences, 0 MA lags, and 1 lag of the dependent variable term.

R-squared Value 0.59: The R-squared value measures how well the independent variables explain the variations in the dependent variable. With an R-squared value of 0.59, approximately 59 % of the variability in the dependent variable is explained by the independent variables in the model. This significant R-squared value indicates a positive and significant correlation between the variables.

ARDL (1,2,0,1) Test Results: The ARDL test conducted has statistical significance at the 0.05 level, providing F-statistics and t-statistics. The F-statistic is related to the overall significance of the model, while the t-statistic assesses the individual significance of the coefficients.

Rejecting the Null Hypothesis (H0) and Accepting the Alternative Hypothesis (H1):

The rejection of the null hypothesis (H0) and the acceptance of the alternative hypothesis (H1) suggest that the estimated coefficients in the model are significantly different from zero. In the context of the ARDL model, this often indicates that a statistically significant relationship exists between the variables, and the effect supports the alternative hypothesis, rejecting the null hypothesis of no effect.

Furthermore, the ARDL (1,2,0,1) model, as indicated by the R-squared value and the statistically significant F-statistics and t-statistics, demonstrates a positive and significant correlation between the variables. Rejecting the null hypothesis supports the presence of meaningful relationships in the specified lag structure, which confirm the impact of the independent variables on the dependent variable.

The F-statistic is a measure used in cointegration tests, such as the Bound test, to assess the existence of long-term relationships (cointegration) between variables. In this case, the calculated F-statistic value was 6.989. Exceeding the critical bounds with this F-statistic confirms the presence of cointegration. Cointegration suggests that despite short-term fluctuations, there is a long-term relationship between the variables, indicating that they move together over time.

Outcome: In the national banking sector, a 1 % increase in the long-term average drawn credit interest rates leads to a 23.90 % increase in non-performing loans. Similarly, a 1 % increase in inflation leads to a 5.50 % decrease in non-performing loans in the national banking sector. Additionally, a 1 % increase in the foreign exchange rate results in a 36.23 % decrease in non-performing loans in the national banking sector.

The next step in the research involved checking the CUSUM diagnostic test for the ARDL(1,2,0,1) model. (See Figures 4 and 5).

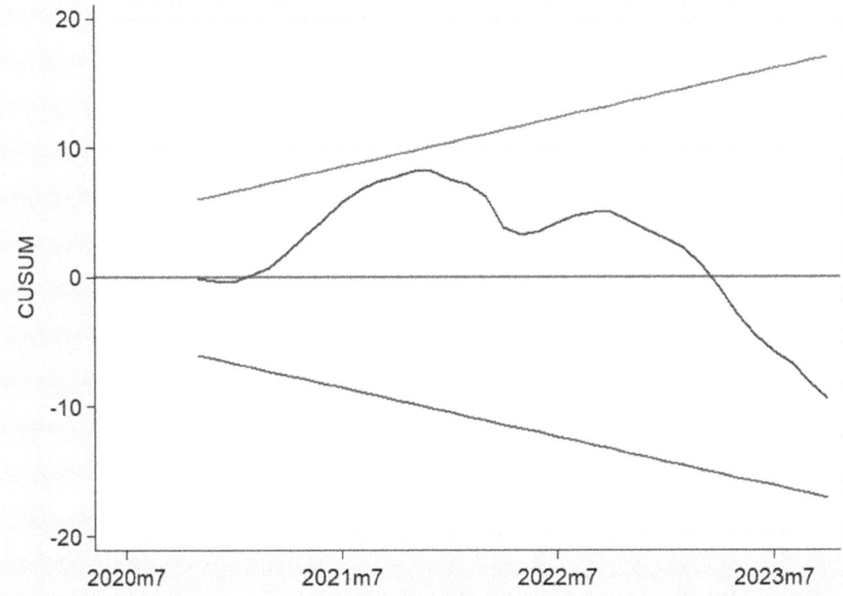

Figure 3. CUSUM Diagnostic Test Graph
Source: Created by authors.

In Figure 4, the CUSUM line remains within the critical boundaries throughout the sample period. This consistency indicates that there are no significant structural breaks in the model, and the null hypothesis (H0) cannot be rejected. Therefore, it can be concluded that the ARDL model's parameters are stable over time.

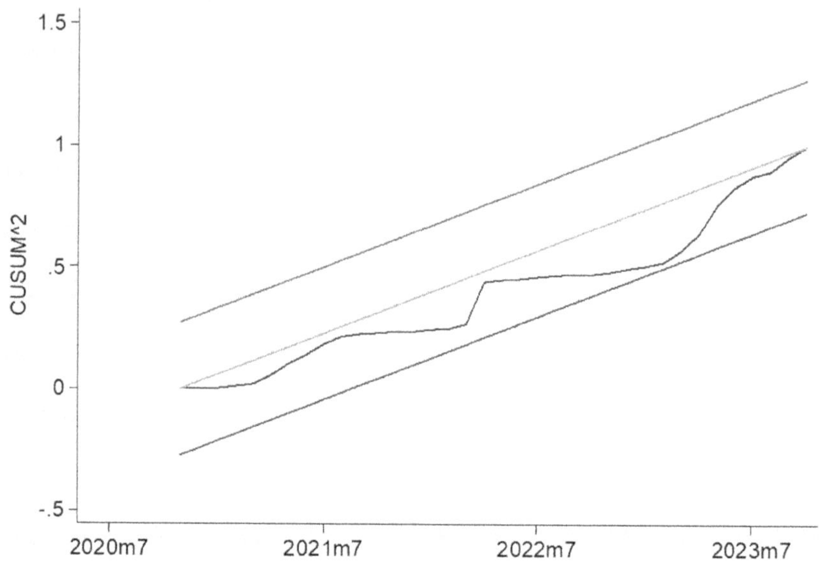

Figure 4. Graph of the CUSUM Diagnostic Test
Source: Created by authors.

Figure 5 illustrates the Cumulative Sum of Squares (CUSUMSQ) diagnostic test graph. Similar to the CUSUM test, the CUSUMSQ test is used to detect parameter instability in the ARDL model over the sample period. While the CUSUM test focuses on cumulative sums of recursive residuals, the CUSUMSQ test considers the squared residuals, making it sensitive to sudden changes or gradual shifts in variance.

5. Findings and Discussions

In the ARDL(1,2,0,1) model, the applied CUSUM (Cumulative Sum) diagnostic test included the following hypotheses:

Null Hypothesis (H0): There are no structural breaks or instability.

(H0): This confirms that there are no structural changes or shifts in the ARDL model coefficients over time. In other words, the model's parameters remain constant throughout the period.

Alternative Hypothesis (H1): Structural breaks or instability exist.

The Alternative Hypothesis (H1) in the ARDL (1,2,0,1) model indicates the presence of one or several systematic breaks or shifts in the coefficients. This suggests that there are fundamental changes in the relationships between variables at certain points during the sample period.

The interpretation of the information presented in Figures 4 and 5 shows that the statistics of the CUSUM diagnostic test have consistently remained within the critical boundaries, and no notable changes have been detected. Furthermore, the null hypothesis H0, which confirms the stability of the systematic conditions, remains unchanged.

In the study, we examined the Gauss-Markov's essential conditions for the ARDL model and achieved the following results:

The result of the Durbin Watson test for the ARDL (1,2,0,1) model showed a value of 0.22. Additionally, the study recorded a value of 0.10 for the Shapiro-Wilk W test and conducted the Breusch-Pagan test, which yielded a value of 0.30.

During the study, the primary hypothesis H0: $y = 0$ and its alternative H1: $y \neq 0$ were tested at a significance level where $r > 0.05$. After conducting the Durbin Watson, Shapiro-Wilk W, and Breusch-Pagan tests, the rejection of the alternative hypothesis was based on a criterion of $p > 0.05$. Thus, it can be concluded that our research confirms the Gauss-Markov estimate that there is no correlation between the error terms and the independent variables, indicating that the econometric model successfully passed Gauss-Markov's essential conditions.

6. Conclusion

The analyses and conclusions drawn from the study of the interaction between non-performing loans, long-term average drawn credit interest rates, inflation rates, and foreign exchange rates in the national banking sector have led to the following recommendations and suggestions based on the ARDL (1,2,0,1) model:

A 1 % increase in the interest rate for long-term drawn credits is associated with a 23.90 % increase in non-performing loans. This outcome suggests that higher interest rates on long-term credits lead to an increase in non-performing loans within the banking sector. Borrowers may face difficulties in servicing their debts, which creates a foundation for an increase in non-performing loans.

a 1 % increase in inflation is associated with a 5.50 % decrease in non-performing loans. This result indicates that inflation may have a mitigating effect on non-performing loans. Inflation could potentially decrease the real value of outstanding debts, making them more manageable for borrowers and reducing the likelihood of loan defaults.

A 1 % increase in the exchange rate correlates with a significant 36.23 % decrease in non-performing loans. This result suggests that the strengthening of the national currency due to an increase in the exchange rate positively affects the reduction of non-performing loans. A strong currency can contribute to improved economic conditions, making it easier for borrowers to fulfill their payment obligations.

The results indicate that interest rates, inflation, and exchange rates play a significant role in affecting the level of non-performing loans in the national banking sector. High-interest rates increase the risk of non-performing loans, whereas inflation and a strong exchange rate show mitigating effects.

Practitioners and financial institutions need to carefully consider the impact of changes in interest rates on non-performing loans, monitor inflation rates, and maintain a stable currency environment to reduce the occurrence of non-performing loans in the banking sector.

References

Ari, A., Chen, S., & Ratnovski, L. (2021). The dynamics of non-performing loans during banking crises: A new database with post-COVID-19 implications. Journal of Banking & Finance, *133*, 106140.

Berger, A. N., & DeYoung, R. (1997). Problem loans and cost efficiency in commercial banks. Journal of Banking & Finance, *21*(6), 849–870.

Juraev, G., & Rakhimberdiev, K. (2022). Prospects of application of blockchain technology in the banking. In International Conference on Information Science and Communications Technologies: Applications, Trends, and Opportunities, ICISCT 2022 (pp. 1–5).

Kasimov, A., Tukhtabaev, J., Bondarskaya, O., Bondarskaya, T., Ochilov, A., Mamatov, M., Nomozova, K., Khamdamov, S.-J., Makhmudov, S., Gaybullaev, R., & Usmanov, C. (2023). Organizational and economic modeling of the system of interregional industrial cooperation as a control object. In Proceedings of the 7th International Conference on Future Networks and Distributed Systems (ICFNDS '23) (pp. 333–343). Association for Computing Machinery. https://doi.org/10.1145/3644713.3644757

Khamdamov, S. J. (2021, December). Calculating Share of Factors of Intensive Economic Growth in Uzbekistan. In The 5th International Conference on Future Networks & Distributed Systems (pp. 393–397).

Khamdamov, S. J., Usmanov, A. S., Abdulazizova, O., Isaev, F., Kholbaev, N., Makhmudov, S., & Kholbaeva, S. (2022, December). Econometric Modeling of Central Bank Refinancing Rate in Uzbekistan. In Proceedings of the 6th

International Conference on Future Networks & Distributed Systems (pp. 253–257).

Klein, N. (2013). Non-performing loans in CESEE: Determinants and impact on macroeconomic performance. International Monetary Fund.

Kurbonov, K., Makhmudov, S., Mamadiyorov, Z., Khamdamov, S.-J., Karlibaeva, R., Samadov, A., & Djalilov, F. (2023). The impact of digital technologies on economic growth in the example of Central Asian and European countries. In Proceedings of the 7th International Conference on Future Networks and Distributed Systems (ICFNDS '23) (pp. 403–409). Association for Computing Machinery. https://doi.org/10.1145/3644713.3644770

Laeven, L., & Majnoni, G. (2003). Loan loss provisioning and economic slowdowns: too much, too late?. *Journal of Financial Intermediation*, *12*(2), 178–197.

Louzis, D. P., Vouldis, A. T., & Metaxas, V. L. (2012). Macroeconomic and bank-specific determinants of non-performing loans in Greece: A comparative study of mortgage, business and consumer loan portfolios. *Journal of Banking & Finance*, *36*(4), 1012–1027.

Makhmudov, S., Khamdamov, S.-J., Karlibaeva, R., Mamadiyarov, Z., Haydarov, O., Khujamurodov, A., & Imomov, K. (2023). The impact of digital technologies on the labor market of Uzbekistan. In Proceedings of the 7th International Conference on Future Networks and Distributed Systems (ICFNDS '23) (pp. 260–267). Association for Computing Machinery. https://doi.org/10.1145/3644713.3644747

Mamadiyarov, Z. T. (2022). Risk management in the remote provision of banking services in the conditions of digital transformation of banks. In The 5th International Conference on Future Networks & Distributed Systems (ICFNDS 2021) (pp. 311–317). Association for Computing Machinery. https://doi.org/10.1145/3508072.3508119

Mamadiyorov, Z., Sultanova, N., Makhmudov, S., Khamdamov, S.-J., Mirpulatova, L., & Jumayev, A. (2024). The impact of digitalization on microfinance services in Uzbekistan. In Proceedings of the 7th International Conference on Future Networks and Distributed Systems (ICFNDS '23) (pp. 453–463). Association for Computing Machinery. https://doi.org/10.1145/3644713.3644780

Mamatkulov, B., Khamdamov, S.-J., Togayniyazov, S., Tukhtabaev, J., Quldoshev, Q., & Qarshiev, D. (2023). Predicting future living standards in Uzbekistan: Utilizing econometric analysis. In Proceedings of the 7th International Conference on Future Networks and Distributed Systems (ICFNDS '23) (pp. 425–431). Association for Computing Machinery. https://doi.org/10.1145/3644713.3644774

Nkusu, M. M. (2011). *Nonperforming loans and macrofinancial vulnerabilities in advanced economies*. International Monetary Fund.

Salimov, B., Kholikova, R., Khamdamov, S.-J., Turaev, A., Tukhtabaev, J., Nosirova, N., & Akhmedova, D. (2023). Strategies for integrating digitalization in leveraging regional economic and scientific expertise for the innovative growth of small and medium enterprises. In Proceedings of the 7th International Conference on Future Networks and Distributed Systems (ICFNDS '23) (pp. 483–490).

Shoh-Jakhon, K. (2023). Theoretical and Methodological Aspects of Intensive Economic Growth in Ensuring Sustainable Economic Development. *Social and Economic Studies within the Framework of Emerging Global Developments* Volume 3, 283.

Umarovich, J. G., & Bakhtiyorovich, R. K. (2021). Modeling the decision-making process of lenders based on blockchain technology. In *2021 International Conference on Information Science and Communications Technologies (ICISCT)* (pp. 1–5). IEEE. https://doi.org/10.1109/ICISCT52966.2021.9670211

Urunov, R., Makhmudov, S., Mamadiyorov, Z., Khamdamov, S.-J., Kurbanov, Z. N., & Dadabaev, U. (2023). Digitalization and its econometric analysis on transforming sustainable regional development into improved population living standards. In Proceedings of the 7th International Conference on Future Networks and Distributed Systems (ICFNDS '23) (pp. 438–442). Association for Computing Machinery. https://doi.org/10.1145/3644713.3644776

Samariddin Makhmudov, Shoh-Jakhon Khamdamov, Ravshanbek Sadullaevich Urunov, Zokir Mamadiyarov, Hakimjon Hakimov, & Dilorom Mahammadzhanovna Mutalova

Econometric Analysis of Sustainable Development in Digital Economies: A Multi-Factorial Approach to Improving Regional Standards of Living

1. Introduction

In recent years, the concept of sustainable development has gained paramount importance across the globe as economies strive to balance growth with environmental sustainability and social inclusivity. This balance is particularly pivotal in the context of the digital economy, which has radically transformed the socio-economic landscapes of both developed and developing nations. The digital economy offers unique opportunities for regions to enhance their economic activities, improve governance, and ensure broader access to services, thereby potentially improving the overall standard of living and sustainability.

Despite its potential, the integration of digital technologies in regional development strategies has been uneven, with significant variations in outcomes. This disparity is pronounced in Uzbekistan, a country actively pursuing the "Digital Uzbekistan – 2030" strategy, aimed at digitalizing various sectors including industry, agriculture, and services to foster economic growth and enhance quality of life.

However, the impact of such digital transformation initiatives on sustainable development and standards of living has not been comprehensively studied. While previous research has explored various aspects of the digital economy, there remains a gap in statistically robust, econometric assessments of how digitalization affects regional sustainable development. Moreover, existing studies often lack a predictive approach that can offer insights into future trends and outcomes based on current digitalization efforts.

This study aims to fill these gaps by:

- assessing the current state of regional development in the digital context of Uzbekistan;

- developing econometric models that quantify the impact of digital initiatives on key indicators of sustainable development such as GDP growth per capita, employment rates, and income levels;
- forecasting future trends to provide a basis for policy-making and strategic planning in the context of sustainable digital economies.

By leveraging extensive regional data and employing sophisticated econometric techniques, this research contributes to a nuanced understanding of the dynamic interplay between digitalization and sustainable development. The findings are intended to inform policymakers, stakeholders, and academics, facilitating more effective strategies for harnessing digital technologies to achieve sustainable economic progress.

2. Literature Review

A multi-factorial approach to enhancing regional standards of living in digital economies should consider various key factors. Firstly, the role of digitalization in public management can significantly impact quality of life (Alhassan & Adam, 2021; Gong et al., 2023). Secondly, the development of a digital economy can lead to reduced environmental pollution and improved environmental quality, thus positively affecting living standards (Luo et al., 2022). Additionally, the influence of modern technologies on rights protection and the need for regional rulemaking to address challenges posed by the borderless cyber environment should be taken into account (Juraev & Rakhimberdiev, 2022) Moreover, the assessment of regional development based on industry specifics, cluster analysis, and the impact of investments and digitalization in sectors like agriculture are crucial for enhancing living standards in different regions (Mamatkulov et al., 2023; Shoh-Jakhon, 2023; Kurbonov et al., 2023). By integrating these factors, regions can effectively navigate the complexities of digital transformation to uplift their standards of living.

The application of econometric analysis plays a crucial role in enhancing the sustainable development of digital economies(Makhmudov et al., 2023; Urunov et al., 2023; Mamadiyorov et al., 2024). Econometric models are utilized to assess the impact of globalization, digital technologies, and trade openness on sustainable growth, highlighting the significant contribution of the digital economy to sustainable development (Khamdamov et al., 2022; Kasimov et al., 2023, Mamadiyarov et al., 2023). Moreover, the use of classical statistical and econometric methods in analyzing socio-economic processes is time-consuming, prompting the need for faster and more effective tools like artificial intelligence to optimize forecasting estimates and evaluation procedures. Specifically, in the context of urban development, econometric analysis has shown that the digital economy promotes sustainable urban development by enhancing green technology innovation and upgrading industrial structures, especially in non-resource-based cities and larger cities in the eastern region.

2.1. Global Perspective

According to Upadhyay et al. (2021), digital technologies enhance economic performance by improving efficiency and access to information. Mamadiyarov et al. (2022) and Tran et al. (2023) discuss how digital infrastructure investments have accelerated economic growth in Asian and European regions, but caution about uneven benefits across different socio-economic groups.

2.2. Regional Studies

Focusing on the CIS countries, Samara et al. (2023), Saukhanov et al. (2023) and Turayeva et al. (2022) examined the digital economy's role in regional development, highlighting significant disparities in digital adoption and its impacts. They noted that regions with robust digital infrastructure and policies experienced better economic outcomes.

2.3. Uzbekistan Context

Local studies, such as those by Khamdamov (2021) and Salimov et al. (2023), specifically address the statistical evaluation of regional development in Uzbekistan under digital economy conditions. They emphasize the need for improved methodologies to accurately capture the socio-economic impacts of digital initiatives.

3. Development Hypothesis

This study is guided by the hypothesis that digitalization significantly influences regional sustainable development and the standard of living in Uzbekistan. The hypothesis is developed based on the theoretical framework discussed in the literature and the observed patterns in preliminary data:

H1: Digital economy initiatives positively correlate with an increase in GDP per capita across regions in Uzbekistan.
H2: Enhanced digital infrastructure leads to lower unemployment rates due to new job creation in the digital sector and related industries.

H3: The standard of living, measured through income levels and poverty rates, improves significantly in regions with advanced digital initiatives.

These hypotheses will be tested using econometric models that incorporate multiple variables and controls to ensure robustness. The outcome will provide empirical evidence to support or refute the theoretical assertions made in existing literature, thereby contributing to a deeper understanding of the digital economy's role in sustainable regional development.

4. Data and Research Methodology

Data for this study is sourced from the National Statistics Committee of Uzbekistan and various regional databases that track economic indicators influenced by digitalization efforts. Key variables include GDP per capita, employment rates, income levels, digital infrastructure penetration, and demographic statistics. Historical data from 2010 to 2021 is used, with projections made for 2022–2026 based on current trends.

The core of our methodology involves developing multifactorial econometric models that integrate time series analysis to predict the outcomes of digital economy policies on regional development indicators. The models are specified as follows:

- Dependent Variables: GDP per capita, unemployment rate, and standard of living indicators.
- Independent Variables: Measures of digital infrastructure (e.g., internet penetration rate, digital services adoption), policy implementation indices, demographic factors, and regional economic policies.
- Control Variables: Global economic conditions, national economic policies unrelated to digitalization, and other socio-political factors that could influence the outcomes.

Used the Ordinary Least Squares (OLS) method for linear regressions, ensuring the best linear unbiased estimators under the Gauss-Markov theorem conditions. For logistic models, the maximum likelihood estimation (MLE) technique is used.

5. Analysis and Results

The forecast study selected factors such as the population growth rate, employment rate, unemployment rate, and the share of small business and private entrepreneurship in GDP. Therefore, we will develop the forecast scenarios for these factors through the algorithm mentioned, using the STATA software (Table 1).

Table 1. Forecasting methods for factor indicators of the Republic of Uzbekistan

№	Types of Forecast Models	MAPE	MAD	MSD
	Growth rate of GDP per capita, %			
1	$Y_t = 105{,}142 - 0{,}0579221{*}t$	1,44	1,50	3,32
2	$Y_t = 101{,}282 + 0{,}949139{*}t - 0{,}0457755{*}t^2$	0,78	0,82	1,08
3	$Y_t = 105{,}133 * (0{,}999441^t)$	1,44	1,51	3,32
4	Smoothing Constants Alpha (level) 0,3 Gamma (trend) 0,5 Delta (seasonal) 0,6	1,17	1,22	2,69
	Growth rate of total income per capita, %			
1	$Y_t = 142{,}010 - 1{,}40312{*}t$	4,9	6,2	61,17
2	$Y_t = 148{,}983 - 3{,}22208{*}t + 0{,}0826800{*}t^2$	4,5	5,7	53,8
3	$Y_t = 141{,}885 * (0{,}989318^t)$	4,8	6,2	60,06
4	Smoothing Constants Alpha (level) 0,37 Gamma (trend) 0,27 Delta (seasonal) 0,50	4,2	4,9	51,03
	Unemployment rate, %			
1	$Y_t = -0{,}981429 + 0{,}468442{*}t$	125,6	1,12	1,6
2	$Yt = -0{,}525414 + 0{,}349481{*}t + 0{,}00540729{*}t^2$	117,8	1,08	1,59
3	$Yt = 0{,}267624 * (1{,}21373^t)$	66,08	1,73	5,29
4	Smoothing Constants Alpha (level) 0,5 Gamma (trend) 0,8 Delta (seasonal) 0,4	22,53	0,8	2,1
	Share of small business and private entrepreneurship in GDP, %			
1	$Y_t = 31{,}4748 + 1{,}58455{*}t$	6,76	3,37	18,14
2	$Y_t = 23{,}9877 + 3{,}53770{*}t - 0{,}0887798{*}t^2$	5,14	2,4	9,7
3	$Y_t = 32{,}6365 * (1{,}03510^t)$	7,8	3,9	25,02
4	Smoothing Constants Alpha (level) 0,5 Gamma (trend) 0,3 Delta (seasonal) 0,4	4,6	2,4	11,2

Source: Developed by authors.

If we carefully analyze Table 1, the Holt-Winters seasonal smoothing method appears to be the most optimal for all factor indicators, as it shows the least error in terms of MAPE, MAD, and MSD quality indicators compared to other forecast scenarios.

Based on the econometric models presented in Table 1, we will present the forecast scenarios for factors such as the growth rate of GDP per capita, the growth rate of total income per capita, the unemployment rate, and the share of small business and private entrepreneurship in GDP in Table 2.

Table 2. Medium-term forecast scenarios for sustainable development indicators of the Republic of Uzbekistan

Years	Forecast	Optimistic	Pessimistic
Growth rate of GDP per capita, %			
2022	97,738	102,294	93,183
2023	98,430	102,644	93,237
2024	99,221	103,623	95,954
2025	99,913	103,871	95,798
2026	101,396	104,377	98,414
Growth rate of total income per capita, %			
2022	111,274	134,736	81,7759
2023	111,346	134,743	84,6201
2024	113,190	137,216	89,3070
2025	113,262	137,929	91,6370
2026	115,177	140,916	95,6183
Unemployment rate, %			
2022	12,2075	17,2704	11,1446
2023	11,8430	16,6038	11,0821
2024	11,4654	14,9466	9,9841
2025	10,1008	14,3333	9,8684
2026	9,7232	12,7491	8,6973
Share of small business and private entrepreneurship in GDP, %			
2022	49,2855	58,2572	40,3138
2023	50,5169	58,6039	42,4299
2024	51,5190	58,7869	44,2511
2025	52,7504	59,2896	46,2112
2026	53,7526	59,6868	47,8183

Table 2. Continued

Years	Forecast	Optimistic	Pessimistic
		Poverty rate, %	
2022	11,4	12,5	12,2
2023	11,2	12,1	11,7
2024	10,8	11,7	11,4
2025	10,5	11,2	10,9
2026	9,7	10,7	10,6

Source: Developed by authors.

As evident from the data in Table 2, it is projected that in our Republic, the growth rate of GDP per capita will increase from 97.8 % in 2022 to 101.4 % by 2026, and the growth rate of total income per capita will correspondingly rise from 111.3 % to 115.2 %. The share of small business and private entrepreneurship in GDP is expected to increase from 58.3 % to 59.7 % (optimistic scenario). The unemployment rate is forecasted to decrease from 11.1 % in 2022 to 8.7 % by 2026 (pessimistic scenario), and the poverty rate is projected to decrease correspondingly from 11.4 % to 9.7 %.

6. Discussion of Results

The forecasting study conducted within the framework of the "Digital Uzbekistan – 2030" strategy, focusing on industrial, agricultural, and service sectors, has brought forward insightful econometric models that quantify the potential future trends based on the current data and the specified model predictors like population growth rate, employment, unemployment levels, and the contribution of small businesses and private entrepreneurship to GDP.

The statistical forecasts, thoroughly detailed in Tables 1 and 2 of our study, have revealed a systematic increase in GDP per capita and total income per capita. Notably, the growth rate of GDP per capita is predicted to increase from 97.8 % in 2022 to 101.4 % by 2026, while the growth of total income per capita is expected to rise from 111.3 % to 115.2 % within the same period. These indicators not only reflect a strengthening economic environment but also highlight the effective role of digital transformation initiatives in boosting economic growth.

Additionally, our projections include an optimistic outlook for the unemployment rate, forecasted to decrease from 11.1 % in 2022 to 8.7 % by 2026, and a reduction in the poverty rate from 11.4 % to 9.7 %, suggesting an improvement in overall economic welfare and stability. These results underline the significant impact of digitalization on employment and income distribution, with the enhancements in digital infrastructure and technology adoption contributing to more efficient market processes and greater business opportunities.

The role of small business and private entrepreneurship is also expected to increase slightly from 58.3 % of GDP to 59.7 %, emphasizing the critical role of these sectors in sustainable economic development. These sectors are often seen as vital for innovation, job creation, and economic dynamism, and their growth reflects the successful integration of business-friendly policies and digital technologies.

The econometric models used in this research, particularly the Holt-Winters seasonal smoothing method, provided the best fit for the data according to the error metrics of MAPE, MAD, and MSD discussed. This method's effectiveness in capturing seasonal patterns and trends has allowed for more accurate and reliable forecasts, essential for planning and policy development.

7. Conclusion

In conclusion, the research underscores the importance of digital economic strategies in fostering sustainable development across various sectors. By effectively integrating digital projects within private and public sectors, Uzbekistan is setting a robust foundation for continued economic growth and improved quality of life, thereby achieving the goals outlined in its national development strategies. The data-driven approach in this study not only supports current policy measures but also provides a valuable baseline for future research and decision-making processes in the rapidly evolving economic conditions.

The research conducted has led to the following conclusions regarding the statistical assessment of sustainable development in the regions:

- The Holt-Winters seasonal smoothing method was identified as the most optimal for forecasting factor indicators. This method provided the best balance between accuracy and computational efficiency, making it particularly suitable for handling the seasonal variations observed in the economic data.
- The studies demonstrated a decrease in the poverty rate in the Republic of Uzbekistan, from 12.2 % in 2022 to 10.6 % by 2026. This reduction highlights the effectiveness of the economic policies and social programs implemented, which have significantly contributed to improving living standards and reducing poverty.

- The unemployment rate is projected to decrease from 11.1 % in 2022 to 8.9 % by 2026 as a result of the measures taken. This forecast, based on econometric models, underscores the positive impact of initiatives aimed at creating jobs and enhancing workforce skills in response to the evolving demands of the digital economy.
- The growth in the share of small business and private entrepreneurship in the regional economy, increasing from 58.3 % in 2022 to 59.7 % by 2026, was confirmed. This growth indicates the success of strategies aimed at fostering an entrepreneurial environment and supporting small business development as critical components of economic diversification and resilience.

These outcomes not only reflect the progress made in achieving the strategic goals outlined in the "Digital Uzbekistan – 2030" framework but also reinforce the importance of continued investment in digital infrastructure and policy innovation to sustain economic growth and improve the quality of life for all citizens.

References

Alhassan, M. D., & Adam, I. O. (2021). The effects of digital inclusion and ICT access on the quality of life: A global perspective. *Technology in Society*, *64*, 101511.

Gong, X., Wong, W. K., Peng, Y., Khamdamov, S. J., Albasher, G., Hoa, V. T., & Nhan, N. T. T. (2023). Exploring an interdisciplinary approach to sustainable economic development in resource-rich regions: An investigation of resource productivity, technological innovation, and ecosystem resilience. *Resources Policy*, *87*, 104294.

Juraev, G., & Rakhimberdiev, K. (2022). Mathematical modeling of credit scoring system based on the Monge-Kantorovich problem. In 2022 IEEE International IOT, Electronics and Mechatronics Conference (IEMTRONICS) (pp. 1–7). IEEE. https://doi.org/10.1109/IEMTRONICS55184.2022.9795800

Kasimov, A., Tukhtabaev, J., Bondarskaya, O., Bondarskaya, T., Ochilov, A., Mamatov, M., Nomozova, K., Khamdamov, S.-J., Makhmudov, S., Gaybullaev, R., & Usmanov, C. (2023). Organizational and economic modeling of the system of interregional industrial cooperation as a control object. In Proceedings of the 7th International Conference on Future Networks and Distributed Systems (ICFNDS '23) (pp. 333–343). Association for Computing Machinery, New York, NY, USA. https://doi.org/10.1145/3644713.3644757

Khamdamov, S. J. (2021, December). Calculating Share of Factors of Intensive Economic Growth in Uzbekistan. In The 5th International Conference on Future Networks & Distributed Systems (pp. 393–397).

Khamdamov, S. J., Usmanov, A. S., Abdulazizova, O., Isaev, F., Kholbaev, N., Makhmudov, S., & Kholbaeva, S. (2022, December). Econometric Modeling of Central Bank Refinancing Rate in Uzbekistan. In Proceedings of the 6th International Conference on Future Networks & Distributed Systems (pp. 253–257).

Kurbonov, K., Makhmudov, S., Mamadiyorov, Z., Khamdamov, S.-J., Karlibaeva, R., Samadov, A., & Djalilov, F. (2023). The impact of digital technologies on economic growth in the example of Central Asian and European countries. In Proceedings of the 7th International Conference on Future Networks and Distributed Systems (ICFNDS '23) (pp. 403–409). Association for Computing Machinery, New York, NY, USA. https://doi.org/10.1145/3644713.3644770

Luo, K., Liu, Y., Chen, P. F., & Zeng, M. (2022). Assessing the impact of digital economy on green development efficiency in the Yangtze River Economic Belt. *Energy Economics*, *112*, 106127.

Makhmudov, S., Khamdamov, S.-J., Karlibaeva, R., Mamadiyarov, Z., Haydarov, O., Khujamurodov, A., & Imomov, K. (2023). The impact of digital technologies on the labor market of Uzbekistan. In Proceedings of the 7th International Conference on Future Networks and Distributed Systems (ICFNDS '23) (pp. 260–267). Association for Computing Machinery, New York, NY, USA. https://doi.org/10.1145/3644713.3644747

Mamadiyarov, Z. T., Sulaymanov, S. A. U., Askarov, S. A. U., & Uktamova, D. B. K. (2022). Impact of COVID-19 pandemic on accelerating the digitization and transformation of banks. In The 5th International Conference on Future Networks & Distributed Systems (ICFNDS 2021) (pp. 706–712). Association for Computing Machinery, New York, NY, USA. https://doi.org/10.1145/3508072.3508211

Mamadiyarov, Z., Hakimov, H. and Askarov, S. (2023) "Development of Retail Banking Services in the Context of Digital Transformation". *Financial and Credit Activity Problems of Theory and Practice*, *1*(54), pp. 51–67. doi: 10.55643/fcaptp.1.54.2024.4288.

Mamadiyorov, Z., Sultanova, N., Makhmudov, S., Khamdamov, S.-J., Mirpulatova, L., & Jumayev, A. (2024). The impact of digitalization on microfinance services in Uzbekistan. In Proceedings of the 7th International Conference on Future Networks and Distributed Systems (ICFNDS '23) (pp. 453–463). Association for Computing Machinery, New York, NY, USA. https://doi.org/10.1145/3644713.3644780

Mamatkulov, B., Khamdamov, S.-J., Togayniyazov, S., Tukhtabaev, J., Quldoshev, Q., & Qarshiev, D. (2023). Predicting future living standards in Uzbekistan: Utilizing econometric analysis. In Proceedings of the 7th International Conference on Future Networks and Distributed Systems (ICFNDS '23) (pp. 425–431). Association for Computing Machinery, New York, NY, USA. https://doi.org/10.1145/3644713.3644774

Salimov, B., Kholikova, R., Khamdamov, S.-J., Turaev, A., Tukhtabaev, J., Nosirova, N., & Akhmedova, D. (2023). Strategies for integrating digitalization in leveraging regional economic and scientific expertise for the innovative growth of small and medium enterprises. In Proceedings of the 7th International Conference on Future Networks and Distributed Systems (ICFNDS '23) (pp. 483–490). Association for Computing Machinery, New York, NY, USA. https://doi.org/10.1145/3644713.3644784

Samara, E., Andronikidis, A., Komninos, N., Bakouros, Y., & Katsoras, E. (2023). The role of digital technologies for regional development: A system dynamics analysis. *Journal of the Knowledge Economy*, 14(3), 2215–2237.

Saukhanov, J., Gabbarov, S., Rakhimberdiev, K., & Khojabayeva, D. (2022). Development of indicators for forecasting the number and composition of livestock based on multivariate econometric models in the digital economy. In ICFNDS '22: Proceedings of the 6th International Conference on Future Networks & Distributed Systems (pp. 542–547). ACM. https://doi.org/10.1145/3584202.3584283

Shoh-Jakhon, K. (2023) Theoretical and Methodological Aspects of Intensive Economic Growth in Ensuring Sustainable Economic Development. Social and Economic Studies within the Framework of Emerging Global Developments Volume 3, 283.

Tran, T. K., Lin, C. Y., Tu, Y. T., Duong, N. T., Thi, T. D. P., & Shoh-Jakhon, K. (2023). Nexus between natural resource depletion and rent and COP26 commitments: Empirical evidence from Vietnam. *Resources Policy*, *85*, 104024.

Turayeva, G., Berdiyev, G., Eshpulatov, D., Alimova, D., Odilbekov, A., Davletova, D., … & Burxanov, A. (2022, December). Opportunities to use Financial Services–"1 C Program". In *Proceedings of the 6th International Conference on Future Networks & Distributed Systems* (pp. 556–561).

Upadhyay, A., Mukhuty, S., Kumar, V., & Kazancoglu, Y. (2021). Blockchain technology and the circular economy: Implications for sustainability and social responsibility. *Journal of Cleaner Production*, *293*, 126130.

Urunov, R., Makhmudov, S., Mamadiyorov, Z., Khamdamov, S.-J., Kurbanov, Z. N., & Dadabaev, U. (2023). Digitalization and its econometric analysis on transforming sustainable regional development into improved population living standards. In Proceedings of the 7th International Conference on Future Networks and Distributed Systems (ICFNDS '23) (pp. 438–442). Association for Computing Machinery, New York, NY, USA. https://doi.org//10.1145/3644713.3644776

Samariddin Makhmudov, Shoh-Jakhon Khamdamov, Menglikulov Bakhtiyor Yusupovich, Norov Akmal Ruzimamatovich, Zokir Mamadiyarov, & Nadir Muratovich Shamsiev

Enhancing Credit Mechanisms in Commercial Banks: An Econometric Analysis of Banking Operations and Economic Impact

1. Introduction

The efficiency and robustness of credit mechanisms within commercial banks play a crucial role in the economic development of countries, especially in emerging markets. These mechanisms not only facilitate individual and corporate financing but also significantly influence macroeconomic stability and growth (Luo et al., 2021). Financial globalization and regulatory changes, the impact of these banking operations on economic outcomes has attracted considerable attention from policymakers and researchers alike.

Recent shifts in global banking regulations and financial technology advancements have redefined how banks operate and deliver credit, making the need for empirical research more pressing. Studies have shown varied impacts of credit provision on economic indicators, suggesting that the effectiveness of credit mechanisms can differ widely based on regulatory environments (Chen et al., 2021), bank characteristics (Mamadiyorov et al., 2024) and economic conditions (Mamatkulov et al., 2023).

This study aims to fill the gap in literature by employing a comprehensive econometric analysis to explore how commercial banks' credit mechanisms affect economic outcomes. Specifically, it seeks to understand the relationship between banking operations, such as credit volume and risk management, and broader economic performance indicators like GDP growth and inflation within the context of a developing economy.

By identifying and analyzing these dynamics, the research intends to provide insights that could inform better regulatory frameworks and enhance the operational strategies of banks, thus supporting sustained economic growth and financial stability.

2. Literature Review

Enhancing credit mechanisms in commercial banks involves evaluating the effectiveness of credit and deposit practices, analyzing the impact of banking sector credit on the real sector, and assessing the management of credit operations. Studies highlight the importance of credit in economic development, the need for improved banking sector credit to boost the economy, and the significance of effective lending for economic growth (Ho & Saadaoui, 2022; Khamdamov et al., 2022; Mamadiyarov et al., 2023). Econometric analysis aids in understanding the relationship between variables like commercial bank credit and real gross domestic product, emphasizing the positive impact of credit on economic growth (Wang et al., 2022; Kurbonov et al., 2023; Salimov et al., 2023; Shoh-Jakhon, 2023). Furthermore, dynamic analysis of financial indicators in non-stationary conditions is crucial for adjusting development strategies and minimizing risks in banking operations . By continuously monitoring and improving credit mechanisms, commercial banks can contribute significantly to economic development and stability.

The relationship between commercial banking operations and economic stability has been extensively studied, yet results remain mixed and context-specific. Belkhir et al. (2022) and Turayeva et al. (2022) explored how financial dependence affects growth and found that countries with more developed credit markets experience faster economic expansions. Similarly, Adabor (2022) demonstrated that banking regulation and supervision play a pivotal role in determining the efficiency of credit distribution and its impact on economic cycles.

More recent studies have focused on the operational mechanisms within banks themselves. Researchers like Urunov et al. (2023) and Khamdamov (2021) have analyzed how innovations in financial products influence banking stability and economic growth. They argue that while innovations can enhance efficiency, they also introduce new risks that need to be managed carefully.

Despite extensive research, few studies have employed econometric models to dissect the impacts of specific credit mechanisms on economic outcomes in developing economies, where financial systems exhibit unique characteristics compared to their developed counterparts.

3. Development Hypothesis

Based on the literature, this study posits that:

3.1. H1: There is a positive relationship between the efficiency of credit mechanisms in commercial banks and economic growth. Efficient credit mechanisms are hypothesized to correlate with higher GDP growth rates, as they enable more effective distribution of financial resources across the economy.

3.2. H2: Strong regulatory frameworks enhance the positive impact of credit mechanisms on economic outcomes. This hypothesis stems from the assumption that better-regulated environments prevent excessive risk-taking and ensure that credit growth aligns with real economic activities.

3.3. H3: The introduction of digital banking services influences the relationship between credit mechanisms and economic stability. It is hypothesized that digital services reduce transaction costs and expand access to credit, which in turn supports economic growth but may also introduce volatility if not adequately regulated.

3. Data and Research Methodology

3.1. Data Collection

This study utilizes a panel dataset of twelve commercial banks over a period of six years, from 2017 to 2022. The data include quarterly financial statements, bank operation metrics, and macroeconomic indicators relevant to the banking sector and economic outcomes. Sources include central bank reports, financial supervision authorities' disclosures, and banks' publicly available reports.

3.2. Econometric Model

To analyze the impact of credit mechanisms on economic growth, this study employs several econometric models. The primary analysis uses Pooled Ordinary Least Squares (Pooled OLS) (Kasimov et al., 2023), Fixed Effects (FE), and Random Effects (RE) models to capture both cross-sectional and time-series variations within the data. These models help to assess the influence of banks' credit operations on GDP growth, inflation rates, and other economic variables, adjusting for potential heterogeneity and omitted variable bias.

3.3. Variable Specification

Dependent Variable: The primary dependent variable is economic growth, measured by changes in GDP.

Independent Variables: Key independent variables include credit volume, risk management metrics, regulatory compliance scores, and digital banking adoption rates.

Control Variables: To account for external economic influences, control variables such as inflation rates, interest rates, and unemployment rates are included.

3.4. Hypothesis Testing

To test the hypotheses posited in the literature review:

H_0 involves interaction terms between credit mechanisms and regulatory scores to determine the regulatory impact on the credit-economic growth relationship.
H_1 tests the effect of digital banking services by including these as independent variables and observing their interaction with traditional credit variables and economic outcomes.

3.5. Statistical Analysis

Statistical significance will be assessed at the 0.05 level using t-tests for individual coefficients. Model adequacy will be checked using R-squared values, F-statistics for overall model fit, and the Hausman test (Makhmudov et al., 2023) to decide between FE and RE models based on the presence of systematic differences between groups.

4. Analysis

The independent and dependent variables in the model are as follows:

- y – Credit operations of commercial banks (dependent variable);
- x1 – Deposit operations of commercial banks;
- x2 – Remote banking services of commercial banks;
- x3 – Number of plastic cards in commercial banks;
- x4 – Number of information kiosks and ATMs in commercial banks;

From 2017 to 2022, over a period of 20 quarters, an analytical graphical chart was developed to analyze the indicators of dependent and independent variables for 12 commercial banks in the national economy. This chart provides a visual representation of the trends and patterns in the banking sector's data over time. (Refer to Figure 1 for details).

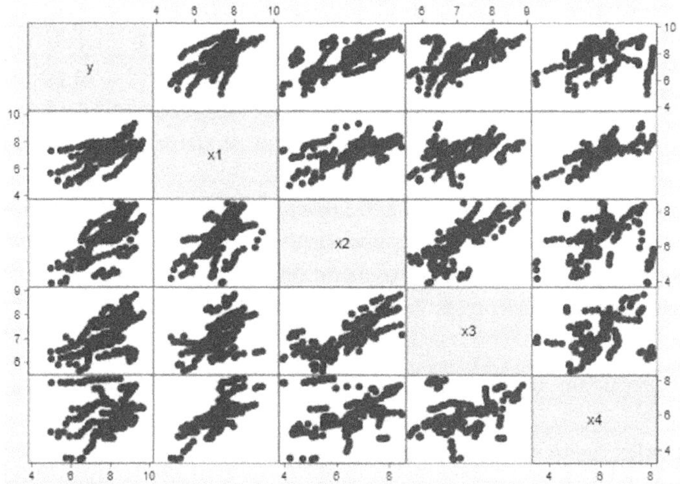

Figure 1. Graphical matrix of the relationship between the dependent variable and independent variables.

Source: Developed by author

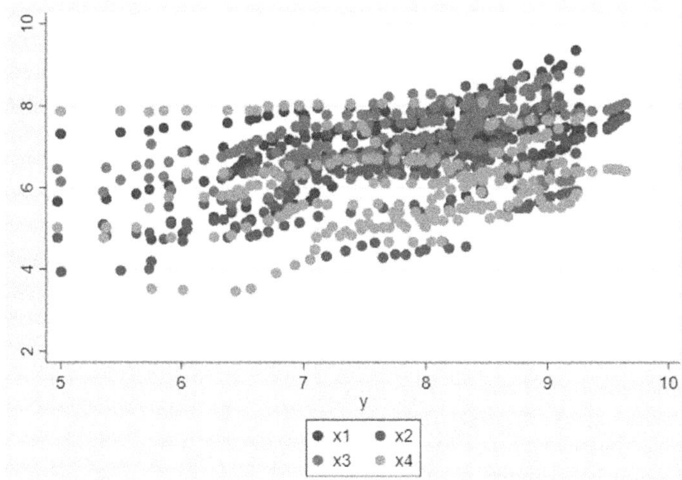

Figure 2. Graphical matrix of the relationship between the dependent variable and independent variables.

Source: Developed by the authors.

The data presented in Figures 1 and 2 illustrate a noticeable correlation between the dependent and independent variables, showing a clear density effect. The density effect is related to the concentration or clustering of data points in specific areas of the graph. In simpler terms, there exists a significant correlation where data points show a strong accumulation or dense dispersion along the axes.

Additionally, in the next stage of the research, a correlation matrix was analyzed for both dependent and independent variables (see Table 1). This analysis further explores the interdependencies and interactions between these variables, providing a deeper insight into the dynamics at play within the data.

Table 1. Correlation matrix of the relationships between dependent and independent variables

Variables	(1)	(2)	(3)	(4)	(5)
(1) y	1.000				
(2) x1	0.558	1.000			
	(0.000)				
(3) x2	0.603	0.562	1.000		
	(0.000)	(0.000)			
(4) x3	0.529	0.476	0.775	1.000	
	(0.000)	(0.000)	(0.000)		
(5) x4	0.193	0.712	0.266	0.212	1.000
	(0.003)	(0.000)	(0.000)	(0.001)	

Source: Developed by the authors.

The research findings indicate a strong, significant, and straightforward correlation between the dependent and independent variables. Furthermore, the correlation matrix shows no presence of multicollinearity among the influencing factors. Additionally, the model exhibits a confidence coefficient of 81 %, demonstrating a positive correlation with the quality indicators of the constructed econometric equations.

Subsequent steps in the study included analyzing panel data and applying various estimation methods such as the Pooled OLS Estimator (POLSE), Fixed Effects Estimator (FEE), and Random Effects Estimator (REE), alongside assessing the primary variables. Notably, important conditions and tests, including the Gauss-Markov tests such as Breusch Pagan and Durbin Watson, were evaluated. Moreover, the model's suitability was checked using the Hausman test. Additionally, the presence of multicollinearity was examined using the Variance Inflation Factor (VIF) test (refer to Table 2).

Table 2. Indicators of econometric models based on panel data for the study

Model Indicators	**1st model**	**2nd model**	**3rd model**
	POLSE	**FEE**	**REE**
y (Dependent Variable)	*	*	*
x1 (Independent Variable)	0.66 (0.09)	0.86 (0.05)	0.85 (0.06)
x2 (Independent Variable)	0.27 (0.07)	0.24 (0.02)	0.24 (0.04)
x3 (Independent Variable)	0.14 (0.10)	-0.15 (0.02)	-0.14 (0.07)
x4 (Independent Variable)	-0.31 (0.07)	-0.01 (0.09)	-0.02 (0.04)
F test	55.14 (0.0000)	243.28 (0.0000)	
R^2	0.68	0.81	
Chi-square			967.68 (0.0000)
Adj R^2	0.67		
Breusch Pagan	0.11		
Durbin Watson	0.25		
Vif	2.63		
Hausman			0.39

Source: Developed by the authors.

From the data in Table 2, each indicator and test for the econometric models based on panel data were analyzed. This analysis involved a detailed evaluation of how each independent variable (x1, x2, x3, x4) influences the dependent variable (y) within the models. The tests included in this analysis helped determine the statistical significance, potential multicollinearity, and overall model fit, ensuring the reliability and validity of the econometric models used in the study.

In the next phase of the research, using the Stata software, the Durbin Watson and Breusch-Pagan tests were conducted for the Pooled OLS model while adhering to the Gauss-Markov conditions. The analysis results showed a Durbin Watson value of 0.25 and a Breusch-Pagan value of 0.11. According to the test results, the null hypothesis H0: $y=0$, H1: $y\neq0$ was found significant with a p-value >0.05. Consequently, the alternative hypothesis for the Durbin Watson and Breusch-Pagan tests was rejected, confirming compliance with the Gauss-Markov conditions.

Within the scope of the research, the Variance Inflation Factor (VIF) test was used to check for multicollinearity under the Gauss-Markov assumption in the model. The test identified a VIF value of 2.63, indicating the absence of multicollinearity in the developed model. Additionally, based on the analysis of the POLSE model, the primary hypothesis H0: $y=0$, H1: $y\neq0$ was determined to be significant with a p-value <0.10. As a result, the alternative hypothesis was rejected. Considering that the VIF test result fell below the threshold of 0.10, this condition of Gauss-Markov is satisfied.

5. Findings and Discussion

The analysis and conclusions obtained for the mutual influence of the existing commercial banks in our Republic in terms of trade operations, credit operations, deposit operations, remote services, the number of plastic cards, and the number of information kiosks and ATMs are as follows:

Based on panel data, the econometric model using the Pooled OLS estimator (POLSE) is as follows:

$$y=0.66x1+0.27x2+0.14x3-0.31x4+2.20$$

- An increase of 1% in deposit operations of existing commercial banks in our Republic leads to an increase of 0.66% in credit operations of these banks.
- An increase of 1% in remote services provided by existing commercial banks in our Republic results in a 0.27% increase in credit operations of these banks.
- An increase of 1% in the number of plastic cards issued by existing commercial banks in our Republic leads to a 0.14% increase in credit operations of these banks.
- An increase of 1% in the number of information kiosks and ATMs of existing commercial banks in our Republic results in a decrease of 0.31% in credit operations of these banks.

Based on panel data, the econometric model using the Random Effects Estimator (REE) is as follows:

$$y=0.85x1+0.24x2-0.14x3-0.02x4+1.27$$

- An increase of 1% in deposit operations of existing commercial banks in our Republic leads to an increase of 0.85% in credit operations of these banks.

- An increase of 1% in remote services provided by existing commercial banks in our Republic results in a 0.24% increase in credit operations of these banks.
- An increase of 1% in the number of plastic cards issued by existing commercial banks in our Republic leads to a 0.14% increase in credit operations of these banks.
- An increase of 1% in the number of information kiosks and ATMs of existing commercial banks in our Republic results in a decrease of 0.02% in credit operations of these banks.

Based on panel data, the econometric model using the Fixed Effects Estimator (FEE) is as follows:

$$y=0.86x1+0.24x2-0.15x3-0.19x4+1.28$$

- An increase of 1% in deposit operations of existing commercial banks in our Republic leads to an increase of 0.86% in credit operations of these banks.
- An increase of 1% in remote services provided by existing commercial banks in our Republic results in a 0.24% increase in credit operations of these banks.
- An increase of 1% in the number of plastic cards issued by existing commercial banks in our Republic leads to a 0.15% increase in credit operations of these banks.
- An increase of 1% in the number of information kiosks and ATMs of existing commercial banks in our Republic results in a decrease of 0.19% in credit operations of these banks.

When we analyze the above three models based on panel data, the Random Effects Estimator (REE) econometric model is considered the most optimal model for assessing the influence of credit operations of existing commercial banks in our Republic today:

$$y=0.55x1+0.25x2+0.026x3-0.26x4+0.26x5-3.843$$

According to the results, we came to the conclusion that the Random Effects Estimator (REE) models are suitable for analyzing them.

Furthermore, the p-value obtained from the Hausman test is \(p = 0.39\), indicating no significant difference between the estimated coefficients of the two models. Therefore, in the process of analyzing the research model's data, while adhering to correct procedures and assumptions, the optimal conclusion about the random effects estimator (REE) regarding their random effects is drawn.

This conclusion identifies the specific data set used in the research and model specifications. Moreover, it is crucial to consider additional factors such as the accuracy, reliability, and theoretical consistency of the model in evaluating its suitability for a particular analysis.

The analysis revealed a positive and statistically significant relationship between credit volume provided by commercial banks and GDP growth. This result supports Hypothesis 1, suggesting that efficient credit mechanisms are indeed associated with higher economic growth. The coefficients in the Fixed Effects model were particularly telling, showing a strong positive impact of credit expansion on economic outcomes.

The interaction terms between credit volume and regulatory compliance scores were significant, indicating that stronger regulatory frameworks amplify the positive effects of credit mechanisms on economic growth. This finding validates Hypothesis 2 and underscores the importance of sound regulatory practices in enhancing the effectiveness of credit distribution.

The coefficients for digital banking services were positive and significant, suggesting that the adoption of digital banking positively influences economic growth. This supports Hypothesis 3 and highlights the transformative role of digital banking in the financial sector. However, the analysis also indicated some potential for increased volatility in economic outcomes associated with rapid digital adoption, calling for cautious regulatory approaches.

The positive relationship between credit volume and economic growth is consistent with previous studies that highlighted the role of banking sector efficiency in supporting macroeconomic stability. However, the significant role of regulatory frameworks and digital banking services provides new insights into the dynamics of modern banking and its impact on economic systems. These findings suggest that while digital transformation in banking can spur economic growth, it must be paired with robust regulatory frameworks to mitigate associated risks and ensure sustainable development.

The results imply that policymakers should focus on enhancing the efficiency of credit distribution mechanisms in commercial banks and strengthen regulatory frameworks to support sustainable economic growth. Additionally, embracing digital innovation in banking should be accompanied by updated regulations that address the unique challenges and opportunities presented by digital finance.

6. Conclusion

This study has comprehensively analyzed the dynamics of credit operations within commercial banks in the context of developing economies, utilizing econometric models to elucidate the interactions between various banking operations. Our research demonstrates significant correlations between bank deposits, remote services, and the issuance of credit, underscoring the pivotal role these factors play in enhancing the economic stability and growth of financial institutions.

The findings suggest that an increase in bank deposits directly correlates with an enhanced ability of banks to provide credit, highlighting the importance of robust deposit bases in supporting lending capacities. Similarly, advancements in remote banking services have been shown to positively influence credit operations, suggesting that technological integration into banking services can significantly augment financial outreach and efficiency.

Additionally, our analysis points to the critical influence of regulatory frameworks and market conditions on the effectiveness of credit operations. As such, policymakers should consider these factors when designing regulations to ensure they foster an environment conducive to financial stability and growth.

In light of these conclusions, it is recommended that banks continue to innovate their deposit and service offerings to enhance their credit capabilities. Moreover, regulatory bodies should aim to create policies that support the stability and growth of the banking sector while encouraging the adoption of new technologies that facilitate more efficient and widespread credit distribution.

This research contributes to the broader understanding of the economic impact of banking operations in emerging markets and lays the groundwork for future studies to explore the nuanced interactions between banking practices and economic outcomes.

References

Adabor, O. (2022). Exploring the asymmetric effect of lending rate on economic growth in Ghana: Evidence from nonlinear autoregressive distributed lag model. *Cogent Business & Management*, *9*(1), 2087464.

Belkhir, M., Naceur, S. B., Candelon, B., & Wijnandts, J. C. (2022). Macroprudential policies, economic growth and banking crises. *Emerging Markets Review, 53*, 100936.

Chen, Y., Cheng, L., Lee, C. C., & Wang, C. S. (2021). The impact of regional banks on environmental pollution: Evidence from China's City commercial banks. *Energy Economics, 102*, 105492.

Ho, S. H., & Saadaoui, J. (2022). Bank credit and economic growth: A dynamic threshold panel model for ASEAN countries. *International Economics, 170*, 115–128.

Kasimov, A., Tukhtabaev, J., Bondarskaya, O., Bondarskaya, T., Ochilov, A., Mamatov, M., Nomozova, K., Khamdamov, S.-J., Makhmudov, S., Gaybullaev, R., & Usmanov, C. (2023). Organizational and economic modeling of the system of interregional industrial cooperation as a control object. In Proceedings of the 7th International Conference on Future Networks and Distributed Systems (ICFNDS '23) (pp. 333–343). Association for Computing Machinery, New York, NY, USA. https://doi.org/10.1145/3644713.3644757

Khamdamov, S. J. (2021, December). Calculating Share of Factors of Intensive Economic Growth in Uzbekistan. In *The 5th International Conference on Future Networks & Distributed Systems* (pp. 393–397).

Khamdamov, S. J., Usmanov, A. S., Abdulazizova, O., Isaev, F., Kholbaev, N., Makhmudov, S., & Kholbaeva, S. (2022, December). Econometric Modeling of Central Bank Refinancing Rate in Uzbekistan. In *Proceedings of the 6th International Conference on Future Networks & Distributed Systems* (pp. 253–257).

Kurbonov, K., Makhmudov, S., Mamadiyorov, Z., Khamdamov, S.-J., Karlibaeva, R., Samadov, A., & Djalilov, F. (2023). The impact of digital technologies on economic growth in the example of Central Asian and European countries. In Proceedings of the 7th International Conference on Future Networks and Distributed Systems (ICFNDS '23) (pp. 403–409). Association for Computing Machinery, New York, NY, USA. https://doi.org/10.1145/3644713.3644770

Luo, S., Yu, S., & Zhou, G. (2021). Does green credit improve the core competence of commercial banks? Based on quasi-natural experiments in China. *Energy Economics*, *100*, 105335.

Makhmudov, S., Khamdamov, S.-J., Karlibaeva, R., Mamadiyarov, Z., Haydarov, O., Khujamurodov, A., & Imomov, K. (2023a). The impact of digital technologies on the labor market of Uzbekistan. In Proceedings of the 7th International Conference on Future Networks and Distributed Systems (ICFNDS '23) (pp. 260–267). Association for Computing Machinery, New York, NY, USA. https://doi.org/10.1145/3644713.3644747

Mamadiyarov, Z., Hakimov, H., & Askarov, S. (2023). Development of retail banking services in the context of digital transformation. *Financial and Credit Activity Problems of Theory and Practice*, *1*(54), pp. 51–67. doi: 10.55643/fcaptp.1.54.2024.4288.

Mamadiyorov, Z., Sultanova, N., Makhmudov, S., Khamdamov, S.-J., Mirpulatova, L., & Jumayev, A. (2024). The impact of digitalization on microfinance services in Uzbekistan. In Proceedings of the 7th International Conference on Future Networks and Distributed Systems (ICFNDS '23) (pp. 453–463). Association for Computing Machinery, New York, NY, USA. https://doi.org/10.1145/3644713.3644780

Mamatkulov, B., Khamdamov, S.-J., Togayniyazov, S., Tukhtabaev, J., Quldoshev, Q., & Qarshiev, D. (2023). Predicting future living standards in Uzbekistan: Utilizing econometric analysis. In Proceedings of the 7th International

Conference on Future Networks and Distributed Systems (ICFNDS ‘23) (pp. 425–431). Association for Computing Machinery, New York, NY, USA. https://doi.org/10.1145/3644713.3644774

Salimov, B., Kholikova, R., Khamdamov, S.-J., Turaev, A., Tukhtabaev, J., Nosirova, N., & Akhmedova, D. (2023). Strategies for integrating digitalization in leveraging regional economic and scientific expertise for the innovative growth of small and medium enterprises. In Proceedings of the 7th International Conference on Future Networks and Distributed Systems (ICFNDS ‘23) (pp. 483–490). Association for Computing Machinery, New York, NY, USA. https://doi.org/10.1145/3644713.3644784

Shoh-Jakhon, K. (2023). Theoretical and methodological aspects of intensive economic growth in ensuring Sustainable Economic Development. Social and Economic Studies within the Framework of Emerging Global Developments, Volume 3, 283.

Turayeva, G., Berdiyev, G., Eshpulatov, D., Alimova, D., Odilbekov, A., Davletova, D., … & Burxanov, A. (2022, December). Opportunities to use Financial Services–“1 C Program”. In *Proceedings of the 6th International Conference on Future Networks & Distributed Systems* (pp. 556–561).

Urunov, R., Makhmudov, S., Mamadiyorov, Z., Khamdamov, S.-J., Kurbanov, Z. N., & Dadabaev, U. (2023). Digitalization and its econometric analysis on transforming sustainable regional development into improved population living standards. In Proceedings of the 7th International Conference on Future Networks and Distributed Systems (ICFNDS ‘23) (pp. 438–442). Association for Computing Machinery, New York, NY, USA. https://doi.org//10.1145/3644713.3644776

Wang, H., Qi, S., Zhou, C., Zhou, J., & Huang, X. (2022). Green credit policy, government behavior and green innovation quality of enterprises. *Journal of Cleaner Production*, *331*, 129834.

Zokir Mamadiyarov, Shoh-Jakhon Khamdamov, Samariddin Makhmudov, Rahimjon Makhmudov, Muyassarhon Ganievna Umarkhodjaeva, & Makhbuba Mirkhalilovna Ismailova

Forecasting Non-Performing Loans in Uzbekistan's Commercial Banks: An ARIMA Model Approach

1. Introduction

Foreign operations demonstrate that the successful economic performance of financial institutions and commercial banks is crucial for the overall efficiency of the financial system (Chen & Yuan, 2021). Problematic loans are closely monitored as they can disrupt this balance. Commercial banks are working to mitigate serious financial risks for the stability and efficiency of financial institutions .

The stability and efficiency of financial institutions are crucial indicators of the overall health of a country's economy. In Uzbekistan, the prevalence of NPLs within commercial banks has been a significant challenge, impacting financial stability and economic growth. NPLs, which refer to loans that are in default or close to being in default, present substantial risks to the banking sector. They hinder banks' ability to lend, reduce profitability, and increase the likelihood of financial crises.

Given the critical importance of managing NPLs, accurate forecasting models are essential tools for policymakers and banking institutions. Forecasting NPLs can help in planning and implementing effective risk management strategies, ensuring that banks remain resilient in the face of economic fluctuations. This study aims to apply the ARIMA model to forecast the dynamics of NPLs in Uzbekistan's commercial banks, providing a robust methodological approach to support financial stability.

The ARIMA model, known for its effectiveness in time series forecasting, offers a reliable means of predicting future trends based on historical data. By employing this model, we aim to deliver precise forecasts that can guide financial institutions and policymakers in making informed decisions. This study utilizes historical financial data from the Central Bank of Uzbekistan to develop the ARIMA model and project NPL trends from January 2024 to December 2027.

This research contributes to the existing body of knowledge on financial risk management by introducing a data-driven approach to forecasting NPLs in the context of Uzbekistan's banking sector. The findings are expected to provide actionable insights for enhancing credit risk management practices and ensuring the long-term stability of the financial system.

2. Literature Review and Development Hypothesis

The accurate forecasting of NPLs is a critical area of study in financial risk management. Numerous studies have employed various econometric models to predict NPL trends and assess their impact on financial stability. In the context of Uzbekistan, there has been limited research focusing on the application of advanced forecasting models to predict NPL dynamics.

Forecasting non-performing loans in Uzbekistan's commercial banks can benefit from advanced machine learning techniques, as shown in studies on emerging countries' financial institutions (Mamadiyarov, 2021; Mamadiyorov et al., 2024). Additionally, factors like government ownership and operating costs significantly impact banking profitability in Uzbekistan (Shoh-Jakhon, 2023). Understanding the chaotic nature of financial time series can aid in predicting non-performing loans, as evidenced by research on economic institutions in Iran (Ahmadi et al., 2022). Moreover, the negative relationship between financial performance and non-performing loans in Tanzanian commercial banks highlights the importance of managing credit risk effectively (Chindengwike, 2022). While non-performing loans have a positive effect on the return on equity in Yemeni commercial banks, they do not significantly impact return on assets or lending behavior (Zaid & Khan, 2022).

Effective management of NPLs in the banking industry is influenced by various factors. Research indicates that key factors include macroeconomic indicators like real GDP, unemployment, and consumer prices (He et al., 2024; Syed, 2021; Kurbonov et al., 2023). Additionally, bank-specific factors such as audit committee efficiency, CEO duality, and independent commissioners play a crucial role in stabilizing and minimizing NPLs (Khamdamov, 2022). Moreover, the quality of a bank's financial condition, risk management, and industry development are significant in setting non-performing loan policies, impacting financial stability (Makhmudov et al., 2023). Factors like corruption, political stability, lending interest rates, and GDP also affect NPL levels, emphasizing the importance of internal and external considerations in managing NPLs effectively (Tran et al., 2023; Mamatkulov et al., 2023). Overall, a comprehensive approach that considers both macroeconomic and bank-specific factors is essential for successful NPL management in the banking sector (Salimov et al., 2023).

Previous studies have demonstrated the effectiveness of the ARIMA model in forecasting financial time series data. For instance, Romdhane et al. (2020) utilized regression techniques to forecast recovery rates on NPLs, highlighting the importance of considering historical payment behaviors. Similarly, Gamba-Santamaria et al. (2024) emphasized the need for banks with higher risk profiles to pay higher deposit insurance premiums, using credit rating methods to identify stable banks.

Alan, (2022) examined the role of NPLs in Turkey's banking sector, identifying key macroeconomic variables that influence NPL levels. Their findings indicated that economic growth, interest rates, and unemployment rates are significant predictors of NPL volumes. Armağan (2023) further explored the macro-financial linkages and the cyclical nature of NPLs, suggesting that macroeconomic shocks can significantly impact NPL ratios.

In light of these studies, this research hypothesizes that the ARIMA model can effectively forecast NPL trends in Uzbekistan's commercial banks (Wanke et al., 2023). By leveraging historical data, the ARIMA model is expected to provide accurate and reliable predictions, thereby aiding in the development of proactive risk management strategies (Bu et al., 2023).

3. Research Methodology

3.1. Sample Selection and Data Collection

The data for this study were obtained from the Central Bank of Uzbekistan, covering the period from June 2020 to December 2023. The dataset includes monthly figures on NPLs across commercial banks in Uzbekistan. This period was chosen to capture the recent trends and dynamics in NPL levels, providing a robust basis for forecasting.

3.2. Variables

The primary variable of interest in this study is the volume of NPLs, which serves as the dependent variable. The ARIMA model parameters include the autoregressive (AR) component, the differencing (I) component, and the moving average (MA) component. These parameters are denoted as p, d, and q, respectively.

3.3. Method

The ARIMA model was applied to the time series data to forecast NPL levels from January 2024 to December 2027. The model parameters (p, d, q) were determined through a systematic process of identification, estimation, and diagnostic checking. The optimal model was selected based on criteria such as the Akaike Information Criterion (AIC) and the Bayesian Information Criterion (BIC) (Rakhimberdiev et al., 2023). The chosen ARIMA(2,0,1) model was validated through diagnostic tests to ensure its suitability for forecasting.

4. Analysis and Results

In the initial phase of the study, the graph of NPLs over a 42-month period in the national banking system is presented below (see Figure 1).

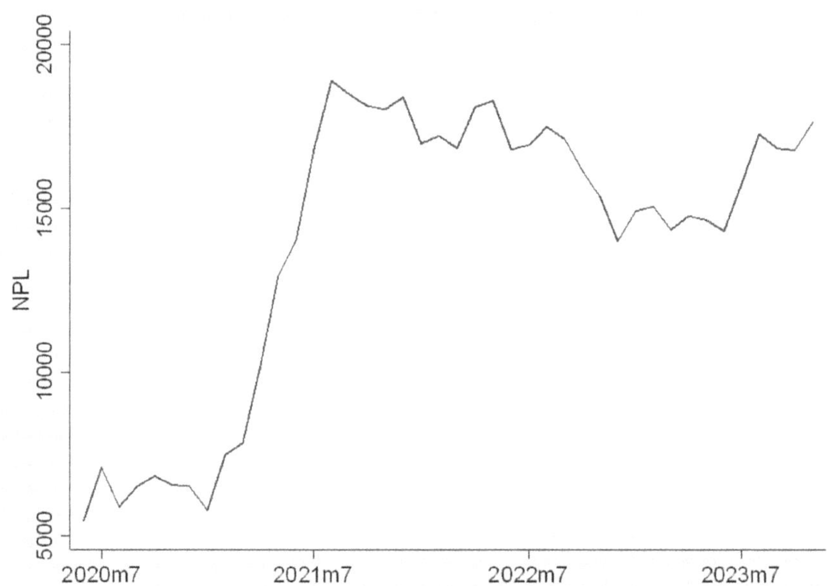

Figure 1. Quantitative Indicator of Non-Performing Loans in the National Banking System

Source: Developed by authors.

The analysis of Figure 1 indicates that non-performing loans in the national banking system showed a trend-like change over this period. Notably, the growth dynamics of non-performing loans peaked in the first half of 2021, but by 2023, there was a significant decline in this indicator.

According to the analytical data, the changes in non-performing loans are trend-like, and the diagram monitors the status of loans that have encountered issues such as payment delays or deferred payments.

According to the highest indicator in the first half of 2021, the growth dynamics of non-performing loans reached their peak in the first six months of 2021. This indicates that the number or share of loans significantly increased during this period, reflecting a rise in the proportion of non-performing loans within the national banking system. By 2023, there was a significant decline in the indicator of non-performing loans. This suggests an overall improvement in credit operations relative to the loan portfolio, and the number of non-performing loans significantly decreased compared to the peak observed in the first half of 2021. This positive development suggests that the reforms in the central banking system are on the right track and may include effective intervention measures, economic recovery, and changes in lending practices.

In the next step of the study, the stationarity of non-performing loans in the national banking system was checked, and the Unit-Root test was used to determine it (see Table 1).

Table 1. Unit-Root Test for Quantitative Indicator of Non-Performing Loans in the National Banking System

NPL	Test Statistic	1 % Critical Value	5 % Critical Value	10 % Critical Value	p-value for Z(t)
	-4.846	-3.648	-2.958	-2.630	-2.612

Source: Developed by authors.

According to Table 1, the unit-root test indicates that the non-performing loans indicator in the national banking system is statistically significant, confirmed by the obtained value of -4.846. The results show that this value is smaller than the critical thresholds of 1 %, 5 %, and 10 %, indicating statistical significance.

Additionally, the MacKinnon value, with Z(t)=0.0000, is very small, indicating that the quantitative indicator of non-performing loans in the national banking system demonstrates stationarity. In time series analysis, a stationary series has stable statistical properties over time, which is essential for reliable forecasting and drawing conclusions. The results of the Unit-Root test and the MacKinnon value show that the data are statistically significant, indicating the presence of stationarity in the non-performing loans indicator.

In the next stage, ARIMA (p,d,q) parameters were established and evaluated to forecast the econometric model using the ARIMA model. The values of ARIMA (p,d,q) were set based on the characteristics of the analyzed time series data. According to Table 1, d=1 was selected because the stationary properties of the ARIMA model were achieved by first-degree differencing of the time series data.

The subsequent step involved determining the value of p, which identifies the indirect correlation between the model's time lags (see Figure 2).

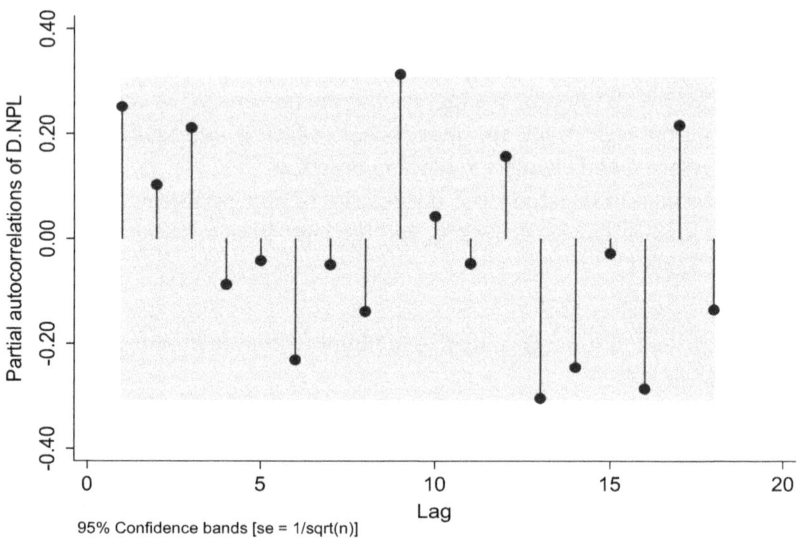

Figure 2. Graph of Indirect Correlation Between the Model's Lags
Source: Developed by authors.

Based on Figure 2, except for one lag, all other lags fall within the confidence intervals. Confidence intervals are statistical ranges that likely contain the true value with a certain level of confidence. From this perspective, lags refer to the time intervals between observations, and most lags are statistically significant because they fall within the confidence intervals. Recognizing and incorporating these important lags is crucial in creating and interpreting ARIMA models. Acknowledging the significance of lags that fall within confidence intervals is very important in the ARIMA model. In this case, it is appropriate to accept a p-value of 0 or 1. Given that most lags fall within the confidence interval and correlation analysis indicates the importance of a p-value of 0 or 1, this choice is reasonable.

In the next step of the ARIMA model, the value of q, which describes the direct correlation between the model's lags, was determined (see Figure 3).

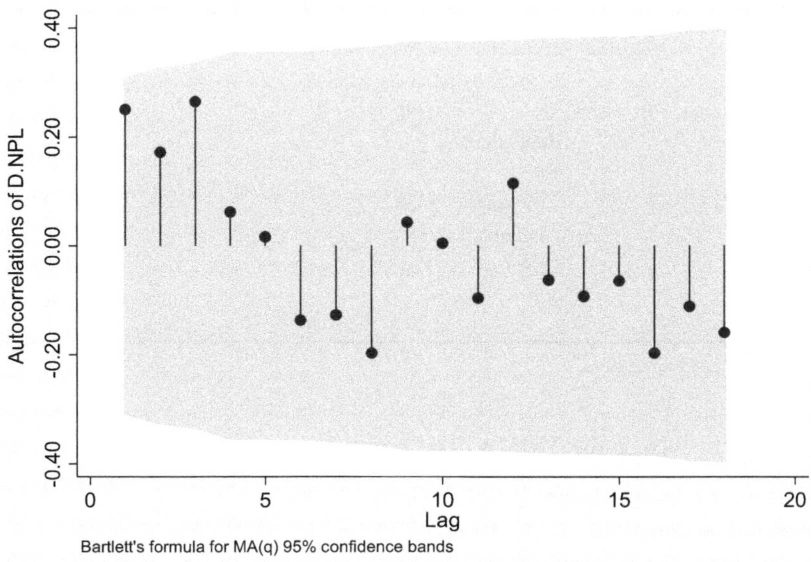

Figure 3. Graph of Direct Correlation Between the Model's Lags
Source: Developed by authors.

Figure 3 shows the positive correlation between the model's lags, with all lags falling within the confidence intervals. Additionally, it is emphasized that selecting one of the values for "q" is appropriate, and according to the figure, choosing a value of 0 or 1 is considered suitable.

In forecasting the model, ARIMA(0,1,1), ARIMA(1,1,1), ARIMA(2,1,1), ARIMA(1,0,1), and ARIMA(2,0,1) models were used to precisely select the ARIMA model. Among these, the ARIMA(2,0,1) model, which produced the best results, was selected (see Table 2).

Table 2. Econometric Equation Indicators of the ARIMA (2,0,1) Model

NPL	Coef.	St.Err.	t-value	p-value	[95 % Conf	Interval]	Sig
Constant	13634.344	2182.901	6.25	0	9355.937	17912.751	***
L	1.847	.161	11.48	0	1.532	2.163	***
L2	-.869	.153	-5.66	0	-1.169	-.568	***
L	-.672	.272	-2.47	.014	-1.206	-.138	**
Constant	1028.458	155.331	6.62	0	724.014	1332.901	***
Mean dependent var	13934.643	SD dependent var	4486.285				
Number of obs	42	Chi-square	5351.527				
Prob > chi2	.	Akaike crit. (AIC)	715.214				
*** *p<.01*, ** *p<.05*, * *p<.1*							

Source: Developed by authors.

According to Table 2, the ARIMA (2,0,1) model has the following form.

$$\Delta Y=13634.34+1,84y_{t-1}-0,86y_{t-2}-0,67e_{t-1} \quad (1)$$

In the next stage, the ARIMA (2,0,1) model was tested based on the following criteria. It is assumed that the residuals exhibit stationarity, and the autoregressive (AR) and moving average (MA) residuals of the ARIMA model fall within the unit circle with values less than 1. After this criterion, a multivariate Portmanteau white noise test was conducted. According to this test, performed with a significance level of p=0.95, the Portmanteau test yielded a statistical value of Q=10.03. According to this criterion, the primary hypothesis H0: y=0 and H1: y≠0 was considered significant, with test values showing p˃0.05. Evidently, this model effectively met this condition.

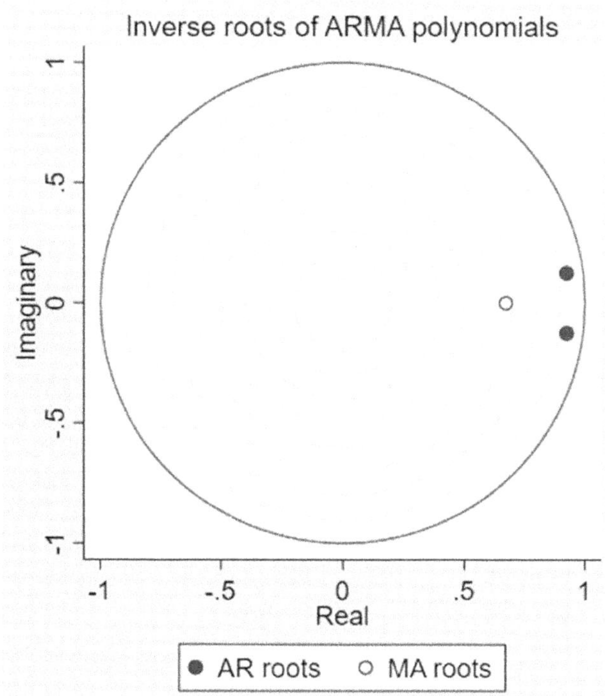

Figure 4. Range of MA Values for the ARIMA (2,0,1) Model
Source: Developed by authors.

Using the Stata software, the ARIMA (2,0,1) model was applied to forecast the quantitative indicator of non-performing loans in the national banking system for the period from January 2024 to December 2027, excluding random factors (see Table 3).

Table 3. Quarterly Forecast Indicators of Non-Performing Loans in the Banking System for 2024–2027

Period	Pessimistic Forecast (in billion soums)	Optimistic Forecast (in billion soums)	Forecast (in billion soums)
01.01.2024	22 092,92	13 200,36	17 646,64
01.04.2024	21 546,06	12 653,50	17 099,78
01.07.2024	20 615,25	11 722,69	16 168,97
01.10.2024	19 586,42	10 693,86	15 140,14
01.01.2025	18 663,19	9 770,63	14 216,91
01.04.2025	17 961,67	9 069,11	13 515,39
01.07.2025	17 521,36	8 628,80	13 075,08
01.10.2025	17 325,01	8 432,45	12 878,73
01.01.2026	17 321,05	8 428,49	12 874,77
01.04.2026	17 443,88	8 551,32	12 997,60
01.07.2026	17 629,56	8 737,00	13 183,28
01.10.2026	17 825,79	8 933,23	13 379,51
01.01.2027	17 996,53	9 103,97	13 550,25
01.04.2027	18 122,36	9 229,80	13 676,08
01.07.2027	18 197,97	9 305,41	13 751,69
01.10.2027	18 228,17	9 335,61	13 781,89

Source: Developed by authors.

Based on the data presented in Table 3, the quarterly forecast indicators for non-performing loans in the national banking system show a decreasing trend from 2024 to 2027. According to the forecast created using the ARIMA model, there is an indication of a consistent decline in the expected level of non-performing loans in the national banking sector during this period.

The forecasted declining trend and the systematic reforms in credit operations are interconnected. The observed tendency of a decreasing volume of non-performing loans suggests that the systematic changes being implemented in credit practices within the national banking system are having a significant and positive impact. In other words, the anticipated improvement in credit operations indicates that the reforms are successfully addressing issues related to non-performing loans, which can lead to greater stability in the banking sector.

This correlation indicates that the ARIMA model used for forecasting non-performing loans serves as a valuable tool in evaluating the effectiveness of systematic reforms. The downward trend in the forecasted indicators reflects an optimistic outlook, suggesting that the anticipated reforms may help create a stable credit environment within the national banking system.

The study presents the graphs of non-performing loans in the national banking system and the forecasted indicators for 2024–2027. (See Figure 5).

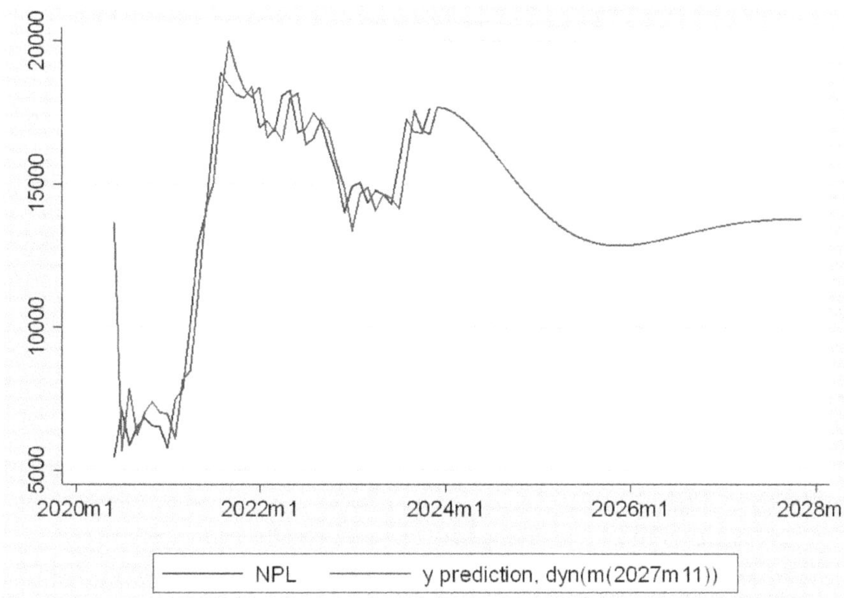

Figure 5. Problematic credit indicators for the period from June 2020 to December 2023, as well as the forecast chart for the period from January 2024 to December 2027
Source: Developed by authors.

According to Figure 5, the graph depicts the dynamics of problematic credits in the banking system, as well as the forecast model for the next four years, without taking into account random factors due to the almost linear nature of the trend graph. This indicates the reliability of the forecast indicators implemented for the next four years.

According to the research results, using the ARIMA (2,0,1) model, the following forecast for the problematic credit indicators of the National Bank for the years 2023–2027 was made without taking into account random factors:

- In 2024, it is forecasted at 15,140.14 billion soums.
- In 2025, it is forecasted at 12,878.73 billion soums.
- In 2026, it is forecasted to be approximately 13,379.51 billion soums.
- In 2027, it is forecasted at 13,781.89 billion soums.

The results show a variable trend in the problematic credit index forecasted for the years 2024–2027, indicating potential challenges in the National Bank system. This information provides financial institutions and commercial banks with an opportunity to anticipate and make informed decisions about potential issues that may arise.

5. Discussion

The ARIMA(2,0,1) model provided accurate forecasts for NPL levels, indicating a declining trend over the forecast period from January 2024 to December 2027. The results suggest that the quality of the loan portfolio in Uzbekistan's commercial banks is expected to improve, reflecting effective credit risk management practices and economic stabilization measures.

The model's predictive accuracy was validated through various diagnostic tests, confirming that the ARIMA(2,0,1) model is well-suited for forecasting NPL trends in the given context. The findings align with previous studies that have highlighted the effectiveness of ARIMA models in financial forecasting.

The decline in NPL levels can be attributed to several factors, including improved economic conditions, regulatory reforms, and enhanced risk management practices within the banking sector. These results underscore the importance of continuous monitoring and proactive management of credit risks to maintain financial stability.

6. Conclusion

This study demonstrates the effectiveness of the ARIMA model in forecasting NPLs in Uzbekistan's commercial banks. The findings provide valuable insights for policymakers and financial institutions, highlighting the need for ongoing efforts to manage credit risks and enhance the stability of the banking sector. Future research could explore the integration of additional econometric models and macroeconomic variables to further refine the forecasts and support strategic decision-making.

References

Ahmadi, F., Pourmahmood Aghababa, M., & Kalbkhani, H. (2022). Identification of chaos in financial time series to forecast nonperforming loan. Mathematical Problems in Engineering, 2022.

Alan, A. (2022). A macro stress test application on the financial system of Turkey: A credit risk perspective (Master's thesis).

Armağan, İ. Ü. (2023). Price prediction of the Borsa Istanbul banks index with traditional methods and artificial neural networks. Borsa Istanbul Review.

Bu, Y., Du, X., Li, H., Yu, X., & Wang, Y. (2023). Research on the FinTech risk early warning based on the MS-VAR model: An empirical analysis in China. *Global Finance Journal*, *58*, 100898.

Chen, W., & Yuan, X. (2021). Financial inclusion in China: An overview. *Frontiers of Business Research in China*, *15*, 1–21.

Chindengwike, J. D. (2022). Nexus between non-performance loans and financial performance of commercial banks listed at Dse, Tanzania: Ardl approach. *Journal of Corporate Finance Management and Banking System (JCFMBS)*, ISSN, 2799–1059.

Gamba-Santamaria, S., Melo-Velandia, L. F., & Orozco-Vanegas, C. (2024). Decomposition of non-performing loans dynamics into a debt-servicing capacity and a risk taking indicators. *The Quarterly Review of Economics and Finance*.

He, B., Jie, W., He, H., Alsubih, M., Arnone, G., & Makhmudov, S. (2024). From resources to resilience: How green innovation, fintech and natural resources shape sustainability in OECD countries. *Resources Policy*, *91*, 104856.

Khamdamov, S. J., Usmanov, A. S., Abdulazizova, O., Isaev, F., Kholbaev, N., Makhmudov, S., & Kholbaeva, S. (2022, December). Econometric modeling of central bank refinancing rate in Uzbekistan. In *Proceedings of the 6th International Conference on Future Networks & Distributed Systems* (pp. 253–257).

Kurbonov, K., Makhmudov, S., Mamadiyorov, Z., Khamdamov, S.-J., Karlibaeva, R., Samadov, A., & Djalilov, F. (2023). The impact of digital technologies on economic growth in the example of Central Asian and European countries. In Proceedings of the 7th International Conference on Future Networks and Distributed Systems (ICFNDS '23) (pp. 403–409). Association for Computing Machinery, New York, NY, USA. https://doi.org/10.1145/3644713.3644770

Makhmudov, S., Khamdamov, S.-J., Karlibaeva, R., Mamadiyarov, Z., Haydarov, O., Khujamurodov, A., & Imomov, K. (2023). The impact of digital technologies on the labor market of Uzbekistan. In Proceedings of the 7th International Conference on Future Networks and Distributed Systems (ICFNDS '23) (pp. 260–267). Association for Computing Machinery, New York, NY, USA. https://doi.org/10.1145/3644713.3644747

Mamadiyarov, Z. (2021). Analysis of factors affecting remote banking services in the process of bank transformation in Uzbekistan. *Financial and Credit Activity Problems of Theory and Practice*, *1*(36), pp. 14–26. doi: 10.18371/fcaptp.v1i36.227607.

Mamadiyorov, Z., Sultanova, N., Makhmudov, S., Khamdamov, S.-J., Mirpulatova, L., & Jumayev, A. (2024). The impact of digitalization on microfinance services in Uzbekistan. In Proceedings of the 7th International Conference on Future Networks and Distributed Systems (ICFNDS '23) (pp. 453–463). Association for Computing Machinery, New York, NY, USA. https://doi.org/10.1145/3644713.3644780

Mamatkulov, B., Khamdamov, S.-J., Togayniyazov, S., Tukhtabaev, J., Quldoshev, Q., & Qarshiev, D. (2023). Predicting future living standards in Uzbekistan: Utilizing econometric analysis. In Proceedings of the 7th International Conference on Future Networks and Distributed Systems (ICFNDS '23) (pp. 425–431). Association for Computing Machinery, New York, NY, USA. https://doi.org/10.1145/3644713.3644774

Rakhimberdiev, K., Abdullaev, T. R., & Bozorov, A. X. (2023). Mathematical modeling of key generators for bank lending platforms based on blockchain technology. In ICABCS 2023, 2024, 2 (pp. 741–749).

Romdhane, S., & Kenzari, K. (2020). The determinants of the volatility of non-performing loans of tunisian banks: Revolution versus covid-19. *Review of Economics and Finance*, *18*, 92–111.

Salimov, B., Kholikova, R., Khamdamov, S.-J., Turaev, A., Tukhtabaev, J., Nosirova, N., & Akhmedova, D. (2023). Strategies for integrating digitalization in leveraging regional economic and scientific expertise for the innovative growth of small and medium enterprises. In Proceedings of the 7th International Conference on Future Networks and Distributed Systems (ICFNDS '23) (pp. 483–490). Association for Computing Machinery, New York, NY, USA. https://doi.org/10.1145/3644713.3644784

Shoh-Jakhon, K. (2023). Theoretical and methodological aspects of intensive economic growth in ensuring Sustainable Economic Development. Social and Economic Studies within the Framework of Emerging Global Developments Volume 3, 283.

Syed, A. A. (2021). Determinants of nonperforming loans: A review of empirical evidence. New Challenges for Future Sustainability and Wellbeing, 277–306.

Tran, T. K., Lin, C. Y., Tu, Y. T., Duong, N. T., Thi, T. D. P., & Shoh-Jakhon, K. (2023). Nexus between natural resource depletion and rent and COP26 commitments: Empirical evidence from Vietnam. *Resources Policy*, *85*, 104024.

Wanke, P., Rojas, F., Tan, Y., & Moreira, J. (2023). Temporal dependence and bank efficiency drivers in OECD: A stochastic DEA-ratio approach based on generalized auto-regressive moving averages. *Expert Systems with Applications*, *214*, 119120.

Zaid, M., & Khan, M. F. (2022). Non-performing loans effects on profitability and lending behavior of commercial banks: Empirical evidence. *Studies in Economics and Business Relations*, *3*(2), 28–35.

Andrea Betti, Pablo Biderbost, & Esther Vaquero

Is Visual Thinking Useful for Teaching International Relations? Evidence from an Implementation through Movies and Documentaries in an Undergraduate Class

1. Introduction

Active learning, understood as "student activity and engagement in the learning process" (Prince, 2004, p. 223), has become one of the main features of contemporary teaching. This term is often used in opposition to traditional teaching formats in which professors expose contents through frontal lectures, during which students passively listen and take notes (King, 1993, p. 30). The idea is to design teaching strategies capable of helping students advance from "dependent learners", requiring "a large amount of direction from the teacher", to "independent learners" (Lage et al., 2000). This implies helping students actively participate in what they learn through activities that can foster some "higher-order skills", such as analysis or evaluation.

Among these teaching strategies, Visual Thinking (VT) is increasingly acquiring popularity. Conceived as "the ability to see visual shapes as images of the patterns of forces that underlie our existence" (Arnheim, 1969, p. 315), VT was initially applied to teaching as "an inquiry-based method" to "develop students' thinking skills by looking at and discussing art" (Tisham et al., 1999, p. 1). The term soon came to include other visual materials, such as pictures, comics, or movies, as instruments that can complement traditional teaching tools, such as manuals and frontal lectures, and provide students with a supposedly more engaging and entertaining learning experience.

The large production of movies about international topics has made their use increasingly common in International Relations (IR) classrooms, with the goal of helping students make sense of complex issues related to global politics. Nevertheless, the exact influence of film on student learning has more rarely been studied. Surprisingly few empirical analyses are devoted to this growing trend.

This chapter presents the results of an exploratory study aimed at assessing whether a teaching format designed around movies and documentaries in an

IR undergraduate class can contribute to improving students' academic performance. The results are measured in terms of grades and students' perceptions about other relevant skills, such as critical thinking, self-efficacy, and learning perception.

Through a mixed-method approach, based on a quantitative and qualitative analysis, this study comes to the tentative conclusion that using movies and documentaries in an IR undergraduate class offers benefits in terms of improvement of students' personal knowledge, with positive repercussions on their perceptions about critical thinking, self-efficacy, and learning perception. Nevertheless, the effects of these visual materials on students' academic performance, in terms of grades, are less evident.

2. Literature Review

First conceptualised in the fields of Psychology (Arnheim, 1969) and Education (Yenawine, 2013), visual literacy, understood as "the ability … to think and learn in terms of images", was considered important to teach students how to "interpret and develop ideas, solve problems, and process information" (Hortin, 1980). After being employed in a wide range of disciplines, VT reached the field of IR, thanks to scholars that underscored the necessity of a "visual turn" in the discipline (James, 2019; Bleiker, 2018). Long dominated by the assumption on the rationality of actors and by a positivist mindset centred around the methodological requirements to discover causal and generalisable relations based on measurable aspects of reality (Kirkpatrick, 2015), most IR theory tended to consider emotions and experiences as irrelevant factors (Callahan, 2015).

Especially after the end of the Cold War, several Security, Peace, and IR Theory scholars argued in favour of considering factors, such as ideas and emotions in the study of international political phenomena. Although their impact might be more difficult to measure, as compared to material wealth or military capabilities, these factors can have considerable influence on shaping political views and decision-making (Hansen, 2021; Bleiker & Hutchinson, 2008). This turn was accompanied by a pluralist methodological approach that suggested the use of "visual language" (Weber, 2008) for the study of international politics, with special attention devoted to popular culture items, such as comics (Schmid, 2020), video games (Valeriano & Habel, 2016), or movies (Weldes & Rowley, 2015).

In U.S. universities, several IR scholars studied the relevance of movies as instruments to promote foreign policy goals and values, especially during and after wars (Campbell, 2022; Carter & Dodds, 2014; Shapiro, 2009). Critical scholars too have more recently researched the use of movies as tools that can influence social perceptions, either to stigmatise specific groups for political purposes (Carter & Dodds, 2014) or to give voice to marginalised actors (Harman, 2018). The relevance of movies for research purposes made it important also for teaching across a wide array of disciplines, including IR.

Among the benefits of using movies in the IR classrooms, several scholars have signalled their capacity to improve students' understanding of complex concepts (Boaz, 2020) or regions (Simpson & Kaussler, 2009) and their ability to think critically (Boaz, 2020; Weber, 2001; Valeriano, 2013). In addition, movies have been considered useful to improve students' engagement, participation (Waalkes, 2003), and their capacity of analysis and debate (Lieberfeld, 2007; Sunderland et al., 2009). Among the drawbacks of using movies in the IR classrooms, scholars have indicated the possibility that movies provide simplified versions of issues and characters, being more focused on entertaining than educating (Boyer, 2002; Sunderland et al., 2008). Movies have not always been deemed helpful, as students might find them boring. Moreover, they do not easily allow students to distinguish facts from representations (Lieberfeld, 2007).

Nevertheless, most initial publications on this subject were descriptions of teaching implementations, rather than empirical analyses of the impact of movies on students' learning. Empirical studies based on qualitative methods detected that movies can be beneficial for students' engagement as they provide a link between concepts and reality, with positive effects in terms of their critical thinking (Gokcek & Howard, 2013; Kuzma & Haney, 2001). Others warned that movies can also provide students with inaccurate information that could hinder their capacity of understanding complex issues (Iretzberger, 2021). Other studies based on combinations of qualitative and quantitative analyses detected that movies could improve students' understanding of concepts related to the class contents (Swimelar, 2012; Kiasatpour, 1999), together with their grades, engagement, and critical and interpretive thinking skills (Inoue & Krain 2014; Swimelar, 2012). Nonetheless, movies could at times give confusing information because they tend to simplify facts and characters, making it difficult to connect academic concepts with film scripts (Swimelar, 2012).

3. Research Methodology

To detect the effects of using movies and documentaries on students' achievement in terms of grades and on their perceptions in terms of critical thinking, self-efficacy, and learning, we conducted an experiment with 62 students enrolled in a second-year core class of Comparative Political System that belongs to a Dual Degree in International Relations (IR) and Global Communication

(GC). The University where the experiment took place approved and authorised the ethical and pedagogical aspects of the experiment. Students who voluntarily agreed to participate gave their written consent and received full information on the experiment during all process. We could collect all the data for 59 of them.

The class was organised in two sections, each of them lasting 7 weeks. In the first, contents were taught through a semi-traditional format, based on two hours per week of frontal lectures taught by the professor about the contents of the section, that is the classification of different political and electoral systems. Lectures were complemented with 2 hours per week of active learning techniques, such as presentations and class debates assigned and directed by the professor. Then, students were required to work in groups and write a 2500-word take-home essay on the contents explained in class. Finally, groups were required to prepare a 20-minute class presentation to share with the rest of the class the results of their analyses of the class contents.

In the second section, about the political and institutional differences between democracy and dictatorship, all four weekly hours were based on movies and documentaries. Class time was dedicated to watching two Netflix documentaries, one about democracy and one about dictatorship. After each session, the professor directed some class debates on the contents of the documentaries. We, then, selected 12 movies about democracy and 12 about dictatorship[1]. Each group had to watch one movie at home for each subject and write a 2500-word take-home essay analysing their contents on the basis of a scheme of analysis provided by the professor. After submitting the essay, groups had to share their analyses of the two selected movies with their classmates through a 20-minute class presentation, highlighting the differences between democracy and dictatorship.

4. Findings: Data Collection and Analysis[2]

To assess the impact of the two different teaching formats in terms of grades, we collected data about students' academic achievement before, during, and after the experiment. To assess students' achievement before the experiment, we considered the average of all the final grades that they had obtained throughout their Degrees in IR and GC, before taking the class Comparative Political Systems that we used for this study. To assess their achievement during the experiment, we

1 The complete list of movies and documentaries used for this experiment cannot be included for space reasons, but authors can make it available upon request.

2 Supplemental materials on the quantitative and qualitative studies are available upon request.

considered the grades that they achieved in two different moments, first, after concluding the first section (NVT), designed around face-to-face lecturing and other active learning techniques, and second, after concluding the second section (VT), designed around visual materials. This allowed us to assess their learning of the class contents in each of the two sections. Lastly, we considered the grades that students obtained in the final exam (FINAL) that took place at the end of the class Comparative Political Systems. This way, we could assess their aggregated learning of the class contents in both teaching formats.

Table 1. Description of students' performance prior, during and after the experiment[3]

	Minimum	Maximum	Mean	Standard Deviation
Degree in IR	6.48	9.24	8.1392	0.65229
Degree in GC	7.19	9.36	8.2729	0.57690
NVT	5.00	10.00	7.5805	1.80841
VT	5.00	9.50	7.0847	1.31929
Final	5.60	10.00	8.1563	1.14918

As Table 1 indicates, students' grades in the section based on movies and documentaries worsened, being the difference between the grades in the section not based on visual materials (NVT) and the grades that they had obtained before the experiment higher than 1.0 points. Nevertheless, when considering students' grades in the final exam at the end of the class, their performance was similar to the grades that they had obtained before the experiment.

These results lead us to the tentative conclusion that, when the class is taught through a combination of different teaching formats and techniques, students tend to improve as compared to when the class is based on a sole and specific teaching format.

To analyse students' perceptions about the effects of movies and documentaries on their critical thinking, self-efficacy, and learning perception we performed a focus group. While our initial goal was to include 8 students based on a "purposive sampling criterion", capable of considering a "good deal of variety in the resulting sample" (Bryman, 2012, p. 418), by selecting students with different grades and performance, only 4 took our invitation. We, thus,

3 Data range from 0.00, being the lowest grade, to 10.00, being the highest grade. The minimum grade to pass an exam is 5.00.

followed a "convenience sampling" based on students' will to participate (Miles & Huberman, 2017, Chapter 2).

The focus group detected a consensus on the benefits of movies and documentaries in terms of helping students to connect the class contents with the facts and people represented in them (4 times). First, it helped them understand concepts, such as the differences between democracy and dictatorship (11 times). Second, it fostered their engagement and motivation with the class (10 times) and their capacity to maintain attention in class (10 times). Movies also stimulated their will to autonomously deepen their knowledge of the issues and characters represented in them (8 times), for example, by looking for additional information and material (7 times). This favoured their capacity of personal reflection (12 times).

Students related these benefits to an improvement in their critical thinking, understood as their capacity to analyse, evaluate, and form a judgement on complex issues (3 times). In terms of self-efficacy, students provided that they felt less shy and more motivated to contribute to class debates with their own arguments (6 times). Overall, these aspects contributed to increasing their "sensation of learning" (10 times).

Nevertheless, in line with the results of our quantitative study, students did not detect a clear impact of movies and documentaries on their grades (4 times). Learning about facts and characters augmented their knowledge but more on a personal, rather than academic basis (3 times). Students saw movies and documentaries as tools that could improve their knowledge of issues and people but not necessarily as products from which to extract generalisations or conclusions about the class contents (6 times). Along these lines, they all convened that VT formats based on movies and documentaries should complement but not replace other teaching formats (4 times). For them, detecting several benefits in a VT format did not mean to consider it necessarily more effective than other teaching formats. They, rather, argued in favour of a class design that can combine different teaching strategies, such as the professor's face-to-face exposition of contents, more common active learning techniques, such as presentations, debates, or simulations, and the use of movies and other visual products (6 times).

5. Discussion and Conclusions

In line with previous studies, students in our experiment appreciated the use of movies and documentaries, in terms of helping them understand complex issues (Sunderland et al., 2009; Boaz, 2020; Swimelar, 2012; Kiasatpour, 1999) or other regions of the world (Simpson & Kaussler, 2009). Providing them with useful information on facts and characters, these products have the potential to develop skills that they consider deeply relevant for their life, such as the capacity to autonomously deepen their knowledge (Lieberfeld, 2007) and their critical thinking and interpretative skills (Inoue & Krain, 2014; Gokcek & Howard, 2013; Kuzma & Haney, 2001). This positively influenced their perception of learning and the possibility of expanding personal knowledge, which directly benefited their engagement, motivation, and attention (Iretzberger, 2021; Waalkes, 2003). These factors importantly contributed to improving their sense of self-efficacy.

Nevertheless, this sensation of improving their personal knowledge and self-efficacy did not necessarily mean an improvement in their academic performance in terms of grades, as both our quantitative and qualitative analyses seem to confirm. This corroborates previous studies that did not see a lineal relation between the capacity of movies to improve students' understanding of complex and real-world issues and the possibility of extracting conclusions on how academic contents should be explained and applied (Inoue & Krain, 2014). Some scholars have explained this potential contradiction by observing that movies and documentaries are not always accurate representations of facts and people (Iretzberger, 2021). In addition to being potential vehicles of knowledge, they are also artistic depictions of reality. As such, the possibility of establishing clear connections between academic concepts and artistic scripts cannot be taken for granted (Swimelar, 2013, p. 24).

Unlike other studies that identified the positive effects of using movies on grades (Lobasz & Valeriano, 2015), students in our experiment frequently mentioned the difficulty to connect fictional representations with academic concepts. In this sense, they did not see a clear relation between a teaching format based on movies and documentaries and their academic performance (Lieberfeld, 2007, p. 573). This is possibly why our quantitative study detected a worsening of students' grades in the class section based on VT.

Far from being a refutation of teaching strategies based on movies and documentaries, our study goes in the direction of using these materials with prudence. This not only implies planning in advance the design of VT formats, but also finding a balance between visual and more traditional teaching materials, such as the contents that professors share in class or the readings that they assign. Several scholars have reached similar conclusions, when warning that visual materials are certainly useful but can also lead to a simplification of complex academic contents (Roberts, 2017; Kuzma & Haney, 2002, p. 93). The fact that the issues and characters represented in a movie can help students develop their personal knowledge does not necessarily lead to a better academic performance.

In line with previous analyses on the use of active learning strategies, the qualitative results of our study detected a students' preference for integrating different teaching strategies, both traditional and innovative (Jenkins, 2015). This preference was reflected in the results of the quantitative study. Despite a worsening in the VT format, after being exposed to all the different teaching formats and strategies used in our experiment, students eventually improved their academic performance in terms of grades. These results should sound as an invitation to strike an adequate equilibrium between textual and visual teaching materials, capable of avoiding a simplification of academic contents and achieving a productive combination among different course formats (Swimelar, 2013, p. 24).

The possibility to generalise the results of this study is limited by the relatively reduced sample and duration of the experiment. This will require to repeat the experiment with more participants and observations. Nevertheless, as an exploratory study, it can provide useful data and information for the relevant debate on how to improve students' learning in IR.

References

Arnheim, R. (1969). *Visual thinking*. LA: University of California Press.

Bleiker, R. (ed.). (2018). *Visual global politics*. London: Taylor & Francis.

Bleiker, R., & Hutchinson, E. (2008). Fear no more: Emotions and world politics. *Review of International Studies, 34*, 115–135.

Boaz, C. (2020). How speculative fiction can teach about gender and power in international politics: A pedagogical overview. *International Studies Perspectives, 21*(3), 240–57.

Boyer, M.A. (2002). At the movies: A continuing dialogue on the challenges of teaching with film. *International Studies Perspectives, 3*, 89–94.

Bryman, A. (2012). *Social research methods*. Oxford: Oxford University Press.

Callahan, W. A. (2015). The visual turn in IR: Documentary filmmaking as a critical method. *Millennium: Journal of International Studies, 43*(3), 891–910.

Campbell, J. R. (2022). *Politics go to the movies: International relations and politics in genre films and television*. Lanham: Lexington Books.

Carter, S., & Dodds, K. (2014). *International politics and film: Space, vision, power*. NY: Columbia University Press.

Gokcek, G., & Howard, A. (2013). Movies to the rescue: Keeping the cold war relevant for twenty-first century students. *Journal of Political Science Education, 9*(4), 436–52.

Hansen, L., & Spanner, J. (2021). National and post-national performances at the Venice Biennale: Site-specific seeing through the photo essay. *Millennium: Journal of International Studies, 49*(2), 305–336.

Harman, S. (2018). Making the invisible visible in international relations: Film, Co-Produced Research and Transnational Feminism. *European Journal of International Relations*, *24*(4), 791–813.

Hortin, J.A. (1980). *Visual literacy and visual thinking*. Eric.

Inoue, C., & Krain, M. (2014). One world, two classrooms, *Thirteen Days*: Film as an active teaching and learning tool in cross-national perspective. *Journal of Political Science Education*, *10*(4), 424–44.

Iretzberger, M. (2021). Film and its unused potential for teaching international relations: Exploring new possibilities in a classroom experiment. *Journal of Political Science Education*, *17*(1), 567–82.

James, P. (2019). Systemist international relations. *International Studies Quarterly*, *63*(4), 781–804.

Jenkins, S. (2015). Flipping the introductory American politics class: Student perceptions of the flipped classroom. *PS: Political Science and Politics*, *48*(4), 607–611.

Kiasatpour, S. (1999). The internet and films: Teaching Middle East politics interactively. *PS: Political Science and Politics*, *32*(1), 83–9.

King, A. (1993). From sage on the stage to guide on the side. *College Teaching*, *41*(1), 30–35.

Kirkpatrick, E. (2015). Visuality, photography, and media in international relations theory: A Review. *Media, War & Conflict*, *8*(2), 199–212.

Kuzma, L. M., & Haney, P. J. (2002). Comments by Kuzma and Haney: Using Film in the Classroom. International Studies Perspectives, 2(1), 92–94.

Lage, M. J., Glenn J., Platt, & Treglia, M. (2000). Inverting the classroom: A gateway to creating an inclusive learning environment. *The Journal of Economic Education*, *31*(1), 30–43.

Lieberfeld, D. (2007). Teaching about war through film and literature. *PS: Political Science and Politics*, *40*(3), 571–574.

Lobasz, J., & Valeriano, B. (2015). Teaching International relations with film and literature: using non-traditional texts in the classroom. In Ishiyama, J., Miller, W. J., & Simon, E. (eds.), *Handbook on teaching and learning in political science and international relations* (pp. 399–409). Northampton: Edward Elgar.

Miles, A., & Huberman, M. A. (2017). *Qualitative data analysis*. London: Sage.

Prince, M. (2004). Does active learning work? A review of the research. *Journal of Engineering Education*, *93*(3), 223–231.

Roberts, D. (2017). 'The Message is in the Medium': Evaluating the use of visual images to provoke engagement and active learning in politics and international relations lectures. *Politics*, *38*(2), 232–249.

Schmid, J. (2020). (Captain) America in crisis: Popular digital culture and the negotiation of *Americanness*. *Cambridge Review of International Affairs*, *33*(5), 690–712.

Shapiro, M. J. (2009). *Cinematic Geopolitics*. London: Routledge.

Simpson, A. W., & Kaussler, B. (2009). IR teaching reloaded: Using films and simulations in the teaching of international relations. *International Studies Perspectives*, *10*(4), 413–27.

Sunderland, S., Rothermel, J. C., & Lusk, A. (2009). Making movies active: Lessons from simulations. *PS: Political Science and Politics*, *42*(3), 543–547.

Swimelar, S. (2013). Visualizing international relations: Assessing student learning through film. *International Studies Perspectives*, *14*(1), 14–38.

Tisham, S., MacGillivray, D., & Palmer, P. (1999). Investigating the Educational Impact and Potential of the Museum of Modern Art's Visual Thinking Curriculum, Final Report, Harvard Project Zero.

Valeriano, B. (2013). Teaching introduction to international politics with film. *Journal of Political Science Education*, *9*(1), 52–72.

Valeriano, B., & Habel, P. (2016). Who are the enemies? The visual framing of enemies in digital games. *International Studies Review*, *18*(3), 462–486.

Waalkes, S. (2003). Using film clips as cases to teach the rise and "Decline" of the State. *International Studies Perspectives*, *4*(2), 156–174.

Weber, C. (2001). The highs and lows of teaching IR Theory: Using popular films for theoretical critique. *International Studies Perspectives*, *2*(3), 281–287.

Weber, C. (2008). Popular visual language as global communication: The remediation of United Airlines Flight 93. *Review of International Studies*, *34*, 137–153.

Weldes, J., & Rowley, C. (2015). How does popular culture relate to world politics? *E-International Relations*, April 29.

Yenawine, P. (2013). *Visual thinking strategies: Using art to deepen learning across school disciplines*. Boston: Harvard Education Press.

Juliya S. Tsertseil & Aleksei Ilyich Bolvachev

Influence of the System of State Support Measures for Small and Medium-sized Businesses on the Formation of Financial Conditions for Functioning

1. Introduction

The issues of development of small and medium-sized businesses are reflected in the works of many authors, in particular: Antonova M.P., Barinova V.A., Gromov V.V., Zemtsov S.P., Krasnoselskikh A.N., Milogolov N.S., Potapova A.A., Tsareva Yu.V. (Antonova et al., 2022), Razmanova S.V., Volkova A.A., Nesterova O.V. (Razmanova et al., 2022), etc.

In the scientific work of Antonova M.P., Barinova V.A., Gromov V.V. and other authors (Antonova et al., 2022) consider the constraining factors in the opportunities for the development of small and medium-sized businesses in the Russian Federation in the areas of implementation of the national project "SMEs and support for individual entrepreneurial initiative" and the achievement of its target indicators: the number of employees in the field of small and medium-sized businesses, the share small and medium enterprises in GDP, the share of exports of small and medium enterprises in the total volume of non-commodity exports.

Many authors study the prospects for the development of small and medium-sized businesses on the example of specific territories. For example, Razmanova S.V., Volkov A.A., Nesterova O.V. (Razmanova et al., 2022) explore the constraining factors in the development of SMEs in the Komi Republic, among which are the tax burden and a high degree of concentration (monopolization) of the market.

It should be noted that all authors agree that initially the development of small and medium-sized businesses as an institution is influenced by the lack of formation of the institutional environment. This aspect is reflected in the works of Akimova E.N., Zhura S.E., Nikolaev O.V., Timchenko V.O., Shataeva O.V. (Akimova et al., 2022). As evaluation indicators, the authors introduce criteria such as: the established taxation system, property relations, the system of contractual relations, the system of state support measures, sources of financing activities, as well as the labor market as an integral element of the development of SMEs as an institution.

Thus, the main goal of this study is to develop and scientifically substantiate theoretical approaches and practical recommendations that ensure the financial and economic sustainability of small and medium-sized enterprises in the manufacturing sector with the participation of anchor corporations in the framework of the framework-cluster approach.

The objectives of this study are:

- to study theoretical and methodological approaches in ensuring the financial and economic sustainability of small and medium-sized businesses in the framework of the implementation of the framework-cluster approach;
- to study existing trends in the formation of state support measures in the development of small and medium-sized businesses;
- to develop an algorithm for financial and economic clustering of small and medium enterprises in the manufacturing sector with the participation of corporations;
- to classify potential and actual cooperative ties of small and medium business with anchor corporations;
- to develop directions for improving the financial and economic clustering of small and medium-sized businesses in the manufacturing sector in cooperation with anchor corporations;
- to assess the potential for the development of territorial clusters of the Russian Federation on the basis of the constructed model of financial and economic clustering of small and medium-sized businesses in the manufacturing sector.

2. Findings and Discussion

Features of the legal regulation of the development of small and medium-sized businesses in the Russian Federation are reflected in Article 7 of the Federal Law of July 24, 2007 No. 209-FZ (as amended on December 29, 2022) "On the Development of SMEs in the Russian Federation", which highlights areas for supporting small and medium entrepreneurship, as shown in Table 1.

Table 1. List of measures of state support for small and medium-sized businesses of the Russian Federation

Measure name	**State regulation**
Special tax regimes	This type of support is regulated by the Tax Code of the Russian Federation of July 31, 1998 No. 146-FZ (as amended on December 28, 2022) and is applied in cases and in the manner provided for by the Tax Code of the Russian Federation, as well as other acts of legislation on taxes and fees
Simplified accounting and cash transactions for small businesses	Reflected in Article 6 of the Federal Law of the Russian Federation of December 6, 2011 No. 402-FZ (as amended on December 5, 2022)
Simplified procedure for compiling statistical reporting	Reflected in Article 5 of the Federal Law of July 24, 2007 No. 209-FZ (as amended on December 29, 2022)
Preferential payment procedure for privatized state and municipal property	This activity is regulated in accordance with: – Federal Law of the Russian Federation of July 22, 2008 No. 159-FZ (as amended on December 29, 2022); – Decree of the Government of the Russian Federation of August 21, 2010 No. 645 (as amended on September 22, 2022)
Features of the participation of small businesses in procurement	Regulation is carried out in accordance with Article 30 "Participation of SE subjects, socially oriented non-profit organizations in procurement" of the Federal Law of the Russian Federation dated 04/05/2013 No. 44-FZ (as amended on 12/28/2022)
Measures to ensure the rights and legitimate interests of small and medium-sized businesses in the implementation of state supervision	Regulation is carried out in accordance with the Federal Law of the Russian Federation dated December 26, 2008 No. 294 – FZ (as amended on November 4, 2022) "On the Protection of the Rights of Legal Entities and Individual Entrepreneurs in the Implementation of State Control (Supervision) and Municipal Control".
Measures to provide financial support for small and medium-sized businesses	In accordance with Article 7 of the Federal Law of July 24, 2007 No. 209-FZ (as amended on December 29, 2022), measures to provide financial support also apply to organizations that form the infrastructure for supporting SMEs
Measures to develop the infrastructure to support small and medium-sized businesses	Regulation is carried out in accordance with Article 15 of the Federal Law of July 24, 2007 No. 209-FZ (as amended on December 29, 2022)

Source: Compiled by the author based on the data of (Federal Law, 2007)

According to Table 1, a fairly wide range of areas for supporting SMEs in the Russian Federation has been formed to date. In legal regulation, there are no differences in measures to support small businesses and medium-sized businesses, although their shares in the total turnover of companies in the Russian Federation differ, which is reflected in Graphs 1–4.

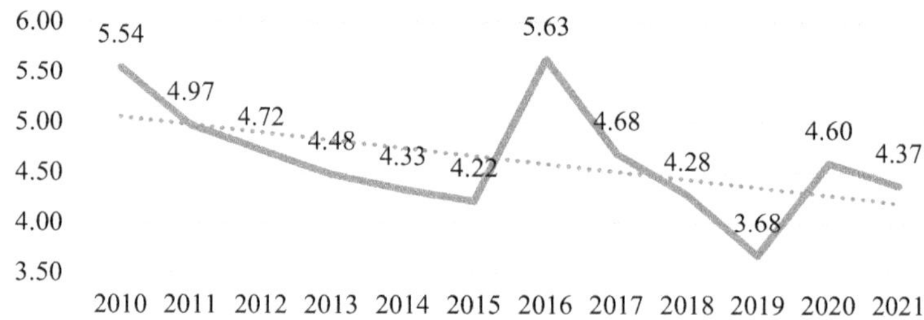

Graph 1. Dynamics of the share of medium-sized enterprises in the turnover of companies, excluding small and medium-sized businesses in the Russian Federation for the period 2010–2021, %

Source: Compiled by the author based on the data of (Rosstat, 2021)

According to the data presented in Graph 1, the share of medium-sized enterprises in the total turnover of companies, excluding small and medium-sized enterprises, varies in the range from 3.68 % to 5.63 %. As we can see, the structural ratio of medium-sized enterprises and large companies practically does not change throughout the analyzed period. In 2021, the share of medium-sized enterprises was 4.37 % and had a downward trend. At the same time, it should be noted that there was a positive trend in the formation of the turnover of companies, excluding small and medium-sized businesses, which is reflected in Graph 2.

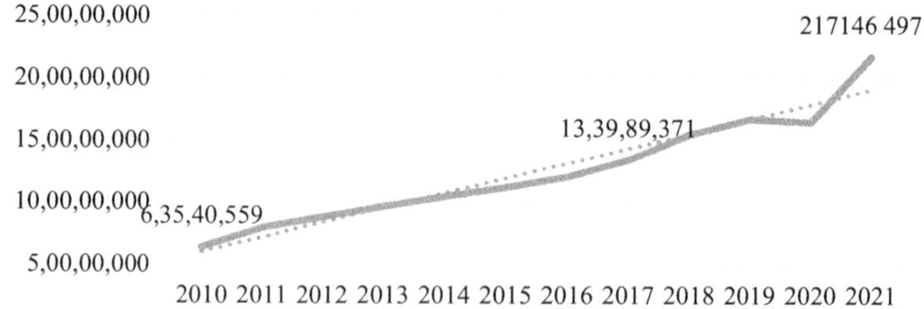

Graph 2. Dynamics of turnover of companies excluding small and medium-sized businesses in Russia for the period from 2010 to 2021, million rubles

Source: Compiled by the author based on the data of (Rosstat, 2021)

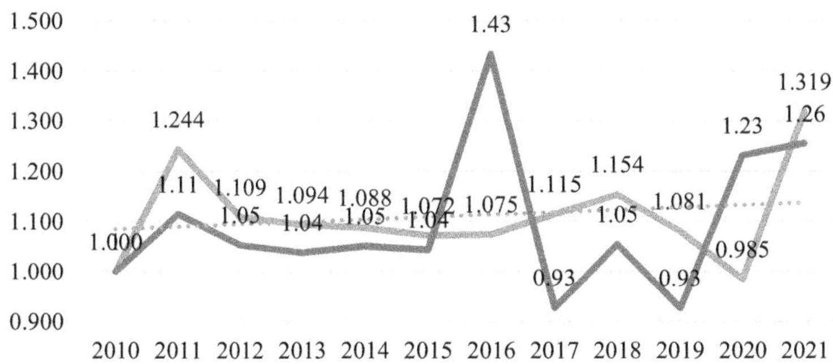

Graph 3. Dynamics of growth rates of medium-sized enterprises and companies, excluding small and medium-sized businesses in Russia for the period from 2010 to 2021, %

Source: Compiled by the author based on the data of (Rosstat, 2021)

In Graph 3, the red line reflects the growth rate of medium-sized enterprises. The blue line reflects the growth rate of companies excluding small and medium enterprises in Russia.

According to Graph 3, the growth rates of medium-sized enterprises and large companies in 2021 are above 25 % and amount to 26 % and 32 %, respectively.

Graph 4. Dynamics of the share of small enterprises in the turnover of companies, excluding small and medium-sized businesses in Russia for the period 2010–2021, %

Source: Compiled by the author based on the data of (Rosstat, 2021)

According to Graph 4, the share of turnover of small enterprises is decreasing from 20.59 % in 2017 to 13.77 % in 2021. At the same time, the share of turnover of small enterprises is higher than the share of medium-sized enterprises in the turnover of companies in the Russian Federation, excluding small and medium-sized businesses. However, small enterprises react to changes in environmental factors more strongly than medium-sized enterprises, regardless of whether such changes are positive or negative.

Graph 5 shows the dynamics of the growth rate of turnover of small enterprises and companies excluding SMEs for the period from 2011 to 2021. In Graph 5, the red line reflects the growth rate of companies excluding small and medium-sized enterprises in Russia of medium-sized enterprises. The blue line reflects the growth rate of small businesses.

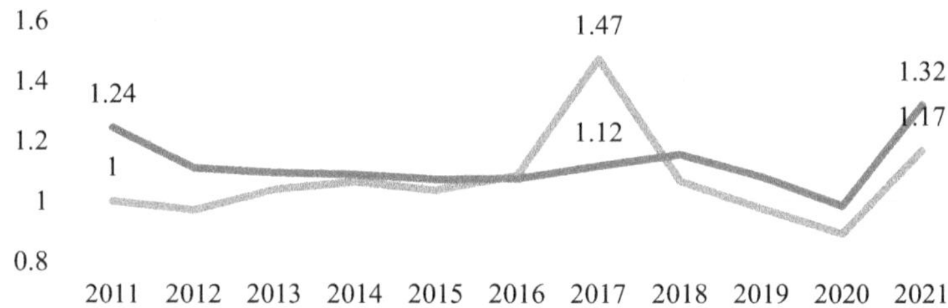

Graph 5. Dynamics of growth rates of small enterprises and companies, excluding small and medium-sized businesses in the Russian Federation for the period 2010–2021, %

Source: Compiled by the author based on the data of (Rosstat, 2021)

One of the directions for the implementation of state policy in the development of small and medium-sized businesses is the increase in the objects of infrastructural support for small and medium-sized businesses, among which clusters stand out in the first place.

The process of forming a cluster with the participation of small and medium-sized businesses can be represented as a sequence of actions reflected in Table 2.

Table 2. Algorithm for the formation of a cluster with the participation of small and medium-sized businesses

Stage name	Stage content
Preparatory stage: identification of potential and actual participants of the cluster	– financial and organizational support for small and medium businesses; – identification of a cluster based on quantitative and qualitative measurements

Table 2. Continued

Stage name	Stage content
Main stage: development of cooperation ties	– increasing the capacity, scale of activities and skills of suppliers, mainly representatives of small businesses; – increase in additional areas of interaction; – development and support of labor potential in strategic industries
Transformation stage: formation of sustainable forms of interaction between cluster members	– formation and assessment of the production potential of the cluster development; – formation and evaluation of the financial and economic potential of the cluster development; – ensuring the financial and economic sustainability of small and medium enterprises in the manufacturing sector

Source: Compiled by the author

The territory clustering involving small and medium businesses model is presented in Table. 3.

Table 3. Territory clustering involving small and medium businesses model

State programs for the development of the territory, the implementation of cluster policy, strategies for innovative development, etc.			
Special economic zone of industrial-production type or technology-innovative type, administrative resource			
Groups of cluster members			
Production (public) companies of the real sector of the economy	Educational sector in the field of vocational training and retraining of personnel	Innovation infrastructure: business incubators, manufacturers' associations, technology parks, technopolises: "innovation block"	Small and medium business

Source: Compiled by the author

As we can see, production (public) companies of the real sector of the economy are also participating in the process of clustering small and medium-sized businesses. An analysis of the dynamics of profitability indicators of this group of participants is presented in Graph 6–8 below.

The following indicators of profitability were chosen as indicators that determine the potential for the development of corporations:

- return on assets;
- operating income return.

Below is an analysis of corporate profitability indicators for 2021 based on data from the Refinitive information and analytical terminal. For a sample of 501 corporations, data are presented on the indicator "return on assets", which is reflected in Graph 6.

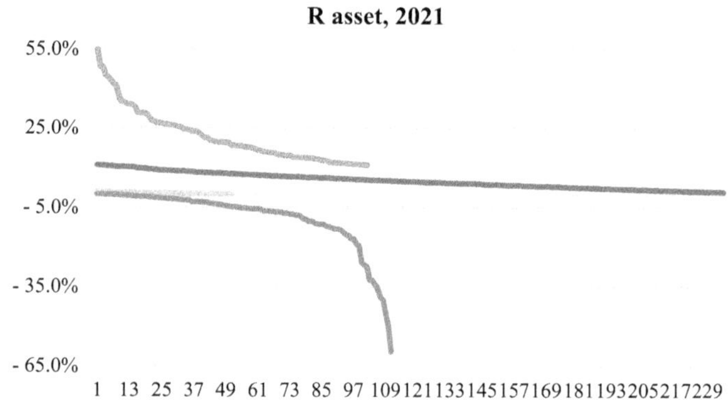

Graph 6. Distribution of Russian corporations by return on assets in 2021, %
Source: Compiled by the author

The author analyzed the indicator "Operating profit return" for a sample of 553 Russian corporations in 2021, which is shown in Graph 7.

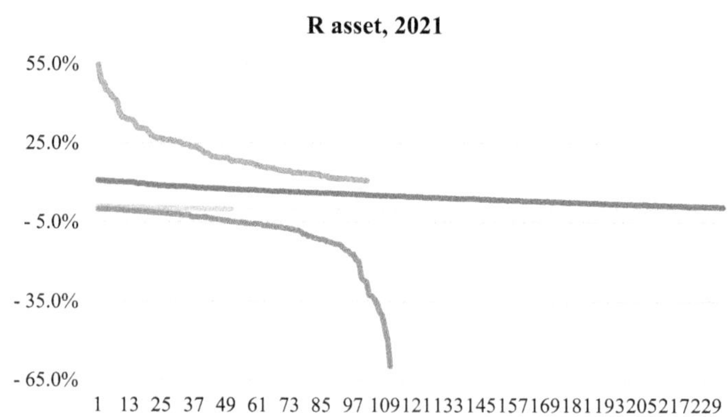

Graph 7. Distribution of corporations in the Russian Federation by operating profit return in 2021, %
Source: Compiled by the author

As a clarifying indicator, the author considered the indicator "average operating profit return" for the last 5 years, the period 2016–2021. The data are presented for 565 corporations of the Russian Federation in Graph 8.

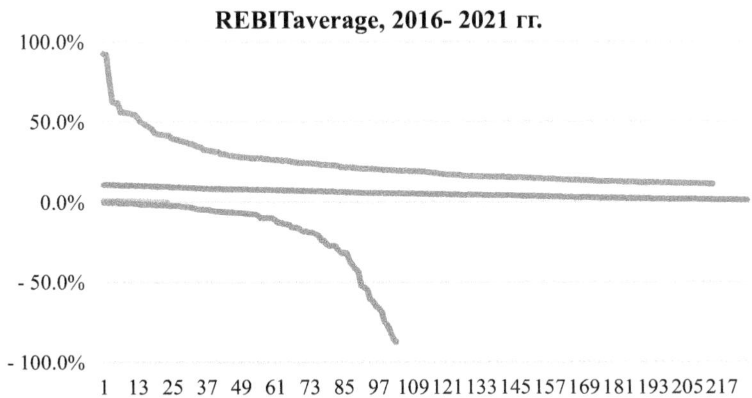

Graph 8. Distribution of corporations in the Russian Federation by the level of average return on operating profit for the period 2016–2021

Source: Compiled by the author

According to the above data, today the activities of large companies generate average profitability indicators, which necessitates further analysis and transformation of cooperative relationships. We propose an extension of cooperative relationships based on the inclusion of small and medium-sized businesses engaged in the manufacturing sector.

In Figure 1, as an example, a model of the territorial cluster of the Sverdlovsk region is formed.

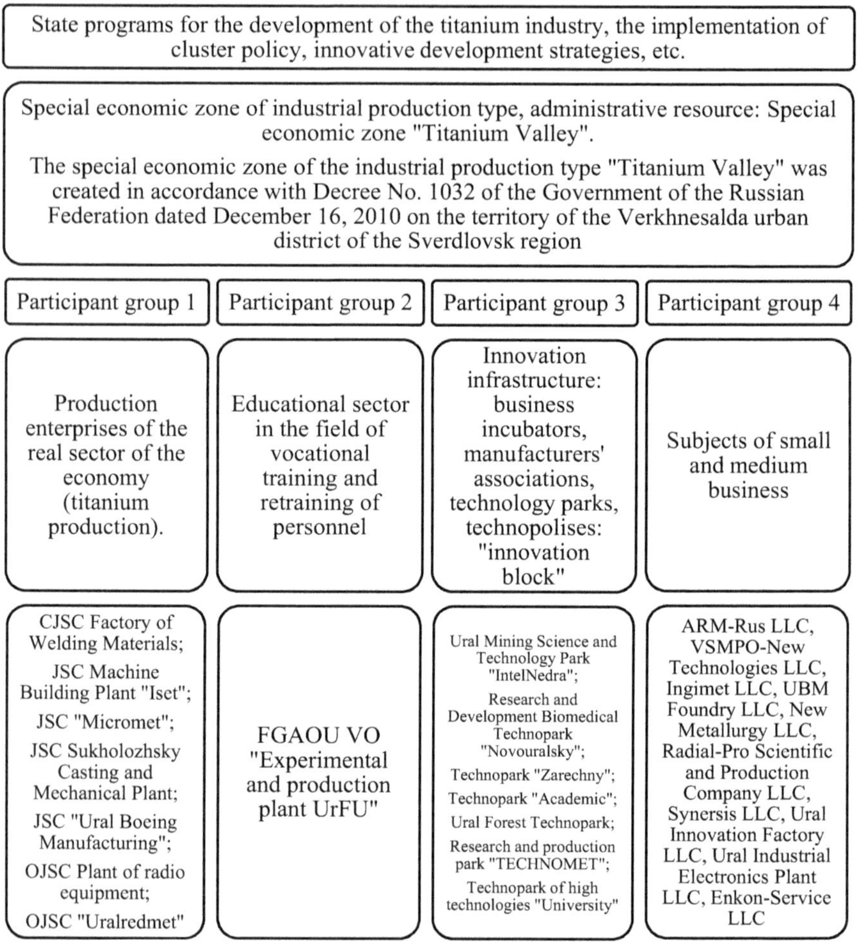

Figure 1. Model of the territorial cluster of the Sverdlovsk region

Source: Compiled by the author on the basis of official data of enterprises – cluster members (Administration of the Lipetsk region, 2023)

As part of the "Development Strategy of JSC Federal Corporation for the Development of SMEs until 2025" dated June 17, 2021, the main restrictions in the development of SMEs include:

- low availability of funding;
- limited access to sales markets;

- low level of digitalization;
- unavailability of qualified labor resources.

When determining sources of financing for SMEs, one should understand the ratio of turnover of medium, small and micro enterprises, which is reflected in Graph 9. According to Graph 9, the ratio of turnover of small businesses and micro enterprises is comparable and amounted to 45.3 % and 45.0 %, respectively, in 2021, there is a tendency to equalize this ratio over the period 2011–2021. The share of medium-sized enterprises in the total turnover of SMEs is significantly lower and amounts to 9.7 % in 2021, while a progressive declining trend has been observed since 2011. Thus, in 2011 the share of medium-sized enterprises in the total turnover of SMEs was 14.8 %.

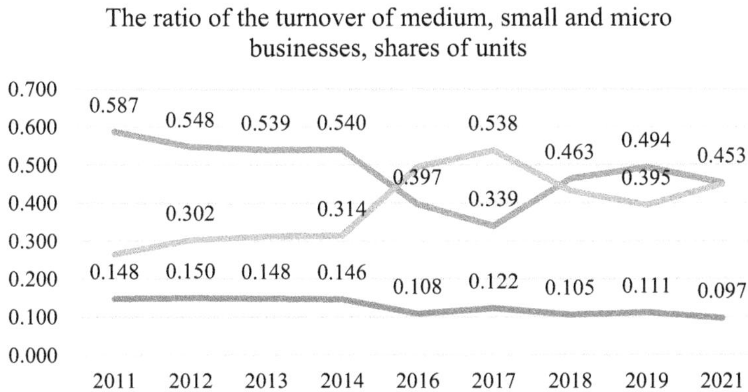

Graph 9. Specific ratio of subjects of SMEs of the Russian Federation, shares of units.
Source: Compiled by the author on the basis of data from the Federal Tax Service of the Russian Federation

In Graph 9, the blue line represents medium-sized businesses, the orange line represents small businesses, and the gray line represents micro-enterprises.

According to Graph 9, over 90 % of the turnover of SMEs is accounted for by small businesses and micro-enterprises, and no more than 10 % – by medium-sized enterprises. According to the Federal Law of the Russian Federation dated July 26, 2017 No. 207, micro-enterprises are distinguished among small enterprises, the number of which is up to 15 people.

3. Conclusion

The "Forecast of the long-term socio-economic development of the Russian Federation for the period up to 2030", developed by the Ministry of Economic Development of Russia, notes that small business is characterized, first of all, by belonging to the region, which makes it possible to single it out as a strategic resource for the development of territories. As part of this Forecast, the main areas of state support for small and medium-sized businesses for the period from 2013 to 2030 were identified. Today, it is necessary to consider small and medium-sized businesses in conjunction with large companies, which will ensure the financial sustainability of small and medium-sized businesses in the long term and ensure the implementation of government programs aimed at achieving target indicators to increase the total number of jobs, the number of small and medium enterprises.

When considering the mechanism for the formation and implementation of state support measures, the following areas can be distinguished:

- property support,
- information and consulting support,
- concessional lending.

References

Akimova, E. N., Shataeva, O. V., Nikolaev, M. V., & Timchenko, V. O. (2022). Problems of development of small and medium-sized businesses in Russia, the necessity and essence of institutional transformations. *Vestnik MGOU. Series: Economy. [Vestnik MGOU. Seriya: Ekonomika]*, 3, 6–20. (in Russian)

Antonova, M. P., Barinova, V. A., & Gromov, V. V. (2022) *Development of small and medium business in Russia in the context of the implementation of the national project [Razvitie malogo i srednego predprinimatel'stva v Rossii v kontekste realizacii nacional'nogo proekta]*. Publishing house "Delo" RANEPA (pp. 88) Moscow (in Russian)

Federal Law (2007) No. 209-FZ of July 24 (as amended on December 29, 2022) *"On the Development of Small and Medium Enterprises in the Russian Federation" (O razvitii malogo i srednego predprinimatel'stva v Rossijskoj Federacii)*. Available at: http://www.consultant.ru/document/cons_doc_LAW_52144/5c9e578cad93f63bf294b59c0b15714fe54fb4a7/ (accessed 1 March 2023). (in Russian)

Rosstat. (2021). *Institutional transformations in the economy*. Available at: https://rosstat.gov.ru/statistics/instituteconomics (accessed 29 May 2023) (in Russian)

Trisha Ramsuraj

Examining Strategies to Enhance the Contribution of Small and Medium Enterprises (SMEs) in a Globalized Economy

1. Introduction

Small and medium-sized businesses (SMEs) are an essential source of economic activity and play a significant role in employment creation in nations of all development levels. In most countries, SMEs employ between 60 % and 70 % of workers. Additionally, there is proof that SMEs encourage greater economic inclusivity, for instance by encouraging the involvement of women in the workforce and as entrepreneurs (Enaifoghe, 2023a). Even though SMEs have a significant impact on modern economies and societies, they are often underrepresented in international trade.

Specifically, they make up a negligible amount of exports in comparison to their percentage of total activity and employment. This is partially due to the fact that SMEs typically lack the resources necessary to cover the high costs of doing business internationally. In addition, smaller businesses have a harder time navigating international marketplaces than larger businesses since they are less equipped to handle intricate regulatory requirements. Globally, small and medium-sized businesses (SMEs) are important to the field of economic development.

As a result of economic globalization, researchers have been interested in SMEs' role on the development platform since the 1990s (Alfred & Wilson, 1996). During this time, SMEs have faced opportunities as well as challenges due to changes in the global economy (Dominguez & Mayrhofer, 2017). It is common knowledge to examine globalization in terms of the political, cultural, and production systems of the modern world (Aspers & Kohl, 2015).

Furthermore, trade liberalization brought forth by the WTO trade system since 1995 has been included in the concept of globalization (Martin, 2001). The idea of globalization highlights the spread of political and economic cultures throughout with relation to dependence modes. Todaro and Smith (2015) assert that fresh opportunities presented by globalization exist for the eradication of world poverty through trade and financing, as well as via sharing of scientific, technological, cultural, and social aspects, it may also directly and indirectly benefit developing nations.

1.2. Research and Methodology

In this study, which is qualitative in nature, the secondary resource content data analysis method was employed. This approach enables researchers to examine and interpret textual materials that may be in the public or private domain (Garg, 2016). This implies that the researcher evaluates the materials they review for relevance in light of their importance to the investigation (Mogalakwe, 2006). The majority of secondary sources used to gather the qualitative data were books, papers, magazines, policy briefs, journals, articles, news bulletins, and government documents on the strategies to enhance the role of Small and Medium Enterprises (SMEs) as they are vital to national economies all over the world, because they create jobs, generate value, and foster innovation.

The paper reviewed several research papers published in different databases such as Google scholar, Scorpus and other reputable publishing companies. Over 100 pieces of literature were sourced in different domains using advanced searches from Google scholars and Scorpius on the subject. The collected data were analysed based on content and relevance, but only 70 pieces of literature were used that were found relevant to inform the study.

2. Literature Consideration

In recent decades, income growth, more specialized market demand, and evolving technologies have allowed SMEs to strengthen their comparative advantages and lessen the structural disadvantages resulting from resource constraints and limited ability to reap economies of scale. These improvements have broadened and deepened the skill-set, accelerated innovation, created opportunities to scale up, and enhanced the contribution of SMEs to innovation dynamics (Ndebele & Enaifoghe, 2023). The majority of SMEs are using this tactic to increase their company competitiveness in the market since globalization has accelerated due to the development of information and communication technology (Sung et al., 2016).

In addition, the process of globalization has accelerated due to the fall of socialist economies, the interplay between the market economy, financial liberty, and the deregulation of capital movements (Sung et al., 2016). As a result, businesses cannot ignore globalization and avoid facing difficulties (Maarof & Mahmud, 2016). According to Sceulovs and Gaile-Sarkane (2014), globalization is acknowledged as a motivating factor for businesses' competitiveness. Globalization and trade liberalization during the past few decades have increased consumer expectations and business competition (Karaev Schmidt & Sofka, 2009).

As opposed to rivals even within the same industry, Sener et al. (2014) noted that the international economic environment promotes enterprises to enhance their competition. Following the industrialization of the world, advancements in production infrastructure and capacity led to an increase in the percentage of industrial activities in the economy. The economy now places more emphasis on urban than on rural areas as a result. Additionally, it has fundamentally altered the nature and structure of urban economic activity.

2.1. Relationship between New Economic Structure and Social Interactions

In cities, this new economic structure gave rise to new social interactions and relationships. Cities have grown to be more populous places than ever before. Poor living conditions, social unrest, and inequality have resulted from this. These unfavorable ideas have begun to define the word "city". In order to enhance living conditions in cities, governments and politicians have created new policies and urban projects. A new area of study in both politics and science is urbanization. The Turkish economy, like the economies of other developed and emerging nations, is driven by SMEs. Compared to large firms, they have more flexible production opportunities, which allows them to swiftly reach full competition conditions and adjust to changes in demand.

The primary driver of increased employment is SMEs. SMEs are therefore seen to be essential to meeting the "growth" and "employment" targets. Approximately 26 million SMEs are active in the EU, employing 109 million people and contributing two thirds of the country's GDP. Furthermore, SMEs have a significant impact on the advancement and application of innovative technology because of their creative and adaptable architecture.

Globalization of the economy presents a great deal of potential as well as challenges for business operations (Mundim et al., 2000). Aside from the real effects of globalization, the acceptance of financial agreements presents SMEs with a new challenge: how to stay competitive in wide marketplaces (Maarof & Mahmud, 2016).

2.3. The Capacity of SMEs to Survive in the Marketplace

In particular, the capacity of SMEs to survive in the marketplace and expand their operations internationally have been the main subjects of concern. Since SMEs lack the resources, innovative capabilities, initial difficulties in going global, and international strategies capabilities of large-scale firms, the threat of large-scale firms – MNCs (Multi-National Corporations) and TNCs (Trans-National Corporations) – has been noted in the literature (Ren et al., 2015).

SMEs do, however, have opportunities to engage with larger companies, which enhances their competitiveness in the market by allowing SMEs to pick up on the competitive tactics used by the larger company (Singh et al., 2008). Since SMEs make a substantial contribution to the economies of both developed and developing countries, the impact of economic competition on them in the globalization era has thus drawn far more attention than it has to other kinds of ventures (Sener et al., 2014; Asare et al., 2015; Bilal & Al Mqbali, 2015; Auzzir et al., 2018; Gamage et al., 2019).

The primary problem with SMEs, especially in developing nations, is that a significant portion of them close down relatively quickly after they start operating, according to sources in the literature (Prasanna et al., 2019). This is mostly because of the new competitive obstacles that have arisen in the globalized economy's free market environment. In that regard, three competitive issues – namely, sustainability challenges, global challenges, and technical challenges – that business entities face in the global economy have been identified by recent literature (Noe et al., 2017).

The ability of businesses to defend their home markets while breaking into newly emerging global markets like China, India, Brazil, and Russia is referred to as the "global challenge" (Noe et al., 2017). Thus, by conducting a systematic assessment of the literature in the disciplines of SMEs, the primary goal of this study is to investigate the major worldwide issues that SMEs face, particularly in the era of economic globalization. In this regard, the study examines each global challenge to show how it affects SME performance, identifies the approaches taken by SMEs in various contexts, and proposes important issues that SMEs should take into account while addressing the global difficulties.

3. Discussion of Research Findings

3.1. The Status of SMEs in Economic Development

In the current global economy, SMEs are essential to both developed and emerging nations' industrial practices. As the most active businesses in the world economy, they are important for the advancement of any nation's human well-being. Recent data indicates that SMEs make about 90 % of businesses and employ over 60 % of the labor force worldwide (Munro, 2013). Therefore, SMEs have a critical role in reducing poverty and promoting sustainable economic growth (Enaifoghe, 2023b; St-Pierre et al., 2015).

Fiseha and Oyelana (2015) noted that SMEs work with local community development in rural economies across the globe. Since SMEs assist people in meeting their basic needs and provide support to marginalized groups such as the disabled, female household heads, the uneducated, and rural families, their role in promoting local development is even more crucial to the elimination of poverty, inequality, and unemployment in rural areas (Fiseha & Oyelana, 2015). By supporting the Sustainable Development Goals of the UN, SMEs promote equitable and sustainable economic growth and lessen inequality (Fonseca & Carvalho, 2019).

3.2. Capacity of SMEs and Sustainable Development

It must be noted that SMEs can effectively solve the main development concerns with the right support that encourage the sustainability of SMEs and innovation. As a result, all countries recognize that SMEs can effectively solve the main development concerns, especially in rural areas, when formulating national policies (Fiseha & Oyelana, 2015). In line with what scholar like Enaifoghe and Ramsuraj (2023); Stuart (2011) noted, encouraging SMEs contributes to the creation of jobs, the elimination of poverty, and the improvement of living standards, especially for women and other vulnerable groups, by raising wage income as well as self-employment.

Starting a business has grown more appealing than working for several fruitful years in ordinary jobs that tend to terminate at any time, as stated by Miller et al. (2003). The most important finding is that SMEs help the economy by allowing it to make use of local resources like raw materials, create savings locally, offer opportunities for self-employment, and provide apprenticeship programs for the training of semi-skilled laborers (Asare et al., 2015). According to several studies (Enaifoghe & Vezi-Magigaba, 2023; Eniola & Entebang, 2015; Fiseha & Oyelana, 2015; Asare et al., 2015; Auzzir et al., 2018), this industry is the most prolific in terms of job creation in any economy.

Moreover, SMEs create a local technological foundation, promote involvement from marginalized groups, offer opportunities for entrepreneurship and management training, and alter how own capital resources are used (Fiseha & Oyelana, 2015). Small and medium-sized enterprises (SMEs) are essential providers of parts, assemblies, and components to large-scale companies in the production sector. This is because SMEs can create these essentials at a lower cost than larger companies can make the same product (Singh et al., 2008).

According to Wang et al. (2018), subcontracting manufacturing is a wonderful venture strategy for SMEs. Through the reverse transmission of technological wisdom, SMEs also provide TNCs with opportunities to approach localized knowledge in terms of local technologies and know-how (Chew & Yeung, 2001).

3.3. Approaches to Impact Global SME Sustainability

Governments are using regulations, standards, and climate-related disclosure requirements more frequently as nations strive to cut carbon emissions and lessen the effects of climate change. This has significant implications for businesses. Even though only a tiny portion of SMEs are now directly affected by these regulations, larger companies in their value chains and financial institutions will probably put more pressure on SMEs to measure, report on, and enhance their environmental performance (Enaifoghe, 2023). This means that in order to finance their green initiatives, SMEs will need to get appropriate financing and incorporate sustainability concerns into their operations on a growing basis.

With very little progress made in lowering their carbon footprint, the majority of SMEs are still in the early stages of their journey towards net zero. This is mostly due to the fact that they still have a great deal of unfilled information and awareness regarding the green transition and the business case for going green. Due to the diversity and ever-changing character of global difficulties, economic literature lacks a singular theory to describe how these challenges affect commercial enterprises and the strategic options such firms take.

4. Application of Keynesian Business Cycle Theory

The adoption and application of Keynesian business cycle theory was to explain the theoretical approach to the sustainability of SMEs survival. Keynes (1933) introduced the Keynesian business cycle theory as a new hypothesis to explain the economic crisis, based on the Great Depression of the 1930s. The global economy is subject to periodic economic and financial crises, which provide a significant challenge to all businesses worldwide, especially small and medium-sized enterprises in the increasingly interconnected global economy.

Marginal efficiency of capital and effective demand are the two ideas that the Keynesian theory uses to analyze the situation. In particular, the theory blames the economic downturn on low effective demand, which leads to high unemployment and poor productivity as a result of the economy's stock piling up. It is also associated with a liquidity trap, or a lack of financial liquidity among the economy's investors. The global economic crisis puts SMEs' ability to sustain their production at risk or temporarily halts it since SMEs are more susceptible to external shocks.

4.1. The Utilization of Monetary and Fiscal Policy Tools

As a result, the theory recommends utilizing monetary and fiscal policy tools to particularly increase aggregate demand through government intervention in the economy. Therefore, one of the global business concerns of the 21st century is the economic crisis, for which the Keynesian theory of business cycle offers an explanation at the aggregate level. One of the global problems facing corporate entities is this, which can be addressed by policy. During the most recent economic slowdown brought on by COVID-19, most nations employed the Keynesian perspective for managing economic crises.

Since it facilitates the distribution of resources to productive areas of the economy, the theory of comparative advantage may be utilized as a tool to modify the production system to competition. When a nation produces goods or services at a lower opportunity cost than other nations, it is said to have a comparative advantage. This helps a business boost sales margins by enabling it to offer goods and services at a cheaper cost than its rivals. Moving low-cost product goods while taking into account other particular product qualities like pricing and quality are crucial for gaining a competitive edge through firm internationalization under the WTO trade regime.

4.2. Applied Strengths, Weaknesses, Opportunities, Threats (SWOT) Analysis

A methodology called SWOT analysis (strengths, weaknesses, opportunities, and threats) is used to assess a company's competitive position and create strategic planning. The SWOT analysis evaluates possibilities for the future as well as internal and external influences. The acronym SWOT, which stands for strengths, weaknesses, opportunities, and threats, is an analysis tool used by organizations to determine their internal and external environmental elements.

Internal aspects include strengths and weaknesses, while external factors include opportunities and threats. Before putting their corporate strategies into action, a lot of businesses in today's business environment perform a SWOT analysis as part of their strategic planning process (Bernroider, 2002; Houben et al., 1999; Roth & Washburn, 1999). Culture, structure, resources, and functional areas all influence how well consumers' requirements are met, and these aspects are the focus of the internal study (Hai, 2011).

Organizations can detect business opportunities and hazards in the environment with the aid of external analysis. Nonetheless, because the ultimate objective of strategic planning and SWOT analysis is to obtain a lasting competitive advantage, both large and small businesses can conduct a SWOT analysis for their company prior to executing corporate strategy.

Porter's generic strategies aid in identifying an organization's strategic position so that it can obtain a competitive edge (Porter, 1985). Michael Porter identifies four general strategies – cost leadership, differentiation, cost focus, and differentiation focus – that are based on the type of market in which they compete (wide or narrow) and the source of advantage they have (the price and distinction). This is the competitive scope that the company chooses, and it sets it apart from competitors that target a certain limited or wide industrial segment.

Small and medium-sized businesses (SMEs), in addition to larger companies, also need to assess their strategic positioning. As such, it is imperative to ascertain the strategies that these companies are implementing. Mumbua (2013) asserts that cost leadership and differentiation, as opposed to cost emphasis and differentiation focus, are the most effective generic strategy for SMEs. Cost leadership yields a higher return on assets than differentiation strategy, according to Dess and Davis (1984).

5. Concluding Remarks

The goal of this study was to understand the succession processes and the strategies to enhance the contribution of SMEs in the current competitive business environment – globalized economy by critically analyzing the body of literature on global issues for SMEs. Additionally, to identify policies connected to sustainability, the study took into account the survival strategies of small and medium-sized enterprises (SMEs) in the industrial platform. Specifically,

The world is moving toward a more international economy these days, and no business could avoid the difficulties that come with globalization by ignoring it. Since SMEs are essential to production, job creation, poverty reduction, innovation, and economic progress in all nations, the impact of globalization on SMEs is a widely discussed issue in economic evaluations. The ability of SMEs to both access new rising markets worldwide and safeguard their home markets from shocks both internal and external was referred to as the global challenge.

References

Alfred, M. P., & David, T. W. (1996). A longitudinal study of the impact of market structure, firm structure, strategy, and market orientation culture on the dimension of small-firm performance. *Journal of the Academy of Marketing Science, 24*, 27–43.

Asare, R., Akuffobea, M., Quaye, W., & Atta-Antwi, K. (2015). Characteristics of micro, small and medium enterprises in Ghana: Gender and implications for economic growth. *African Journal of Science, Technology, Innovation and Development, 7*, 26–35.

Aspers, P., & Kohl, S. (2015). Economic theories of globalization. In *The Routledge international handbook of globalization studies*, 1st ed. Edited by Bryan S. Turner and Robert J. Holton. London: Routledge, vol. 1, pp. 41–59.

Auzzir, Z., Haigh, R., & Amaratunga, D. (2018). Impacts of disaster to SMEs in Malaysia. *Proedia Engineering, 212*, 1131–1138.

Bernroider, E. W. N. (2002). Factors in SWOT analysis applied to micro, small-to-medium, and large software enterprises. *European Management Journal, 20*, 562–573.

Bilal, Z. O., & Al Mqbali, N. S. (2015). Challenges and constraints faced by Small and Medium Enterprises (SMEs) in AL Batinah Governorate of Oman. *World Journal of Entrepreneurship, Management, and Sustainable Development, 11*, 120–130.

Chew, Y. T., & Yeung, Henry, W. C. (2001). The SME advantage: Adding local touch to foreign transnational corporations in Singapore. *Regional Studies, 35*, 431–448.

Dess, G. G., & Davis, P. S. (1984). Porter's generic strategies as determinants of strategic group membership and organizational performance. *Academy of Management Journal, 27*, 467–488.

Dominguez, N., & Mayrhofer, U. (2017). Internationalization stages of traditional SMEs: Increasing, decreasing and re-increasing commitment to foreign markets. *International Business Review, 26*, 1051–1063.

Enaifoghe, A. (2023a). The challenges hampering the South African economic growth integration process in the sub-region. *International Journal of Research in Business and Social Science* (2147–4478), *12*(7), 235–243.

Enaifoghe, A., & Ramsuraj, T. (2023). Examining the function and contribution of entrepreneurship through Small and Medium Enterprises as drivers of local economic growth in South Africa. *African Journal of Inter/Multidisciplinary Studies, 5*(1), 1–11.

Enaifoghe, A., & Vezi-Magigaba, M. F. (2023). Conceptualizing the role of entrepreneurship and SME in fostering South Africa's local economic development. *Research in Business & Social Science.* (IJRBS), Vol. 12, No. 4 (2023), 96–105.

Enaifoghe, A. O. (2023b). Exploring entrepreneurship and Small and Medium Enterprises in advancing local economic development. In Hasim Özüdoğru, Muhammed Veysel Kaya, & Ufuk Kaya (eds.), *Social & economic studies within the framework of emerging global developments* – Volume 4. Peter Lang Publihers. Pp. 177–190. ISBN 978-3-631-90842-6.

Eniola, A. A., & Entebang, H. (2015). Small firm performance-financial innovation and challenges. *Procedia-Social and Behavioral Sciences, 195*, 334–342.

Fiseha, G. G., & Oyelana, A. A. (2015). An assessment of the roles of Small and Medium Enterprises (SMEs) in the Local Economic Development (LED) in South Africa. *Journal of Economics, 6*, 280–290.

Fonseca, L., & Carvalho, F. (2019). The reporting of SDGs by quality, environmental, and occupational health and safety-certified organizations. *Sustainability, 11*, 5797.

Gamage, S. K. N., Ekanayake, E. M. S., Abeyrathne, G. A. K. N. J., Prasanna, R. P. I. R. Jayasundara, J. M. S. B., & Rajapakshe, P. S. K. (2019). *Global challenges and survival strategies of the SMEs in the era of economic globalization: A systematic review.* Mihintale: Rajarata University of Sri Lanka.

Garg, R. (2016). Methodology for research I. *Indian Journal of Anaesthesia*, *60*(9), 640–645. https://doi.org/10.4103/0019-5049.190619

Hai, H. L. (2011). Assessing the SMEs competitive strategies on the impact of environmental factors: A quantitative SWOT analysis application. In *Environmental Management in Practice.* Rijeka: IntechOpen.

Houben, G., Lenie, K., & Vanhoof, K. (1999). A knowledge based SWOT-analysis system as an instrument for strategic planning in small- and medium-sized enterprises. *European Management Journal, 20*, 562–573.

Karaev, S. T., & Sofka, W. (2009). Liability of foreignness as a barrier to knowledge spillovers: Lost in translation? *Journal of International Management,* 15, 460–474.

Keynes, J. M. (1933). *The means of prosperity*. London: Macmillan.

Maarof, M. G., & Mahmud, F. (2016). A review of contributing factors and challenges in implementing Kaizen in Small and Medium Enterprises. *Procedia Economics and Finance, 35*, 522–531.

Martin, W. (2001). *Trade policies, developing countries, and globalization*. Washington: Development Research Group, World Bank.

Miller, D., Steier, L., & Le Breton-Miller, I. (2003). Lost in time: Intergenerational succession, change, and failure in family businesses. *Journal of Business Venturing, 16*, 33–39.

Mogalakwe, M. (2006). Research report. The use of documentary research methods in social research. *African Sociological Review, 10*(1), 221–230.

Mumbua, M. S. (2013). Competitive strategies applied by small and medium-sized firms in Mombasa County, Kenya. Master's thesis, School of Business, Univerity of Nairobi, Nirobi, Kenya.

Mundim, A. A. R., & Stochetti, A. (2000). SMEs in global market: Challenges, opportunities and threats. *Brazilian Electronic Journal of Economics, 3*, 418–425.

Munro, D. (2013). *A guide to financing SMEs.* New York: Palgrave Macmillan.

Ndebele, C. N., & Enaifoghe, A. (2023). The adoption of innovative strategies for enhanced service delivery in the South Africa public sector: Challenges and prospects. *Social Sciences and Education Research Review* (SSERR). Volume 10, Issue 2. Pp 114–121.

Noe, R. A., Hollenbeck, John R., Gerhart, Barry, & Wright, Patrick M. (2017). *Human resource management: Gaining a competitive advantage,* 9th ed. New York: McGraw-Hill.

Porter, M. E. (1985). *Competitive advantage*. New York: The Free Press, pp. 1–32.

Prasanna, R. P. I. R., Jayasundara, J. M. S. B., Gamage, Sisira, K. N., Ekanayake, E. M. S., Rajapakshe, P. S. K., & Abeyrathne, G. A. K. N. J. (2019). Sustainability of SMEs in the competition: A systemic review on technological challenges and SME performance. *Journal of Open Innovation: Technology, Market and Complexity, 5*, 100.

Ren, S., Eisingerich, A. B., & Isai, H. T. (2015). How do marketing research and development capabilities, and degree of internationalization synergistically affect the innovation performance of Small and Medium-Sized Enterprises (SMEs)? A panel data study of Chinese SMEs. *International Business Review, 24*, 642–651.

Roth, B. N., & Washburn, S. A. (1999). Developing strategy. *Journal of Management Consulting, 10*, 50–54.

Sceulovs, D., & Gaile-Sarkane, E. (2014). Impact of e-Environment on SMEs business development. 2014. *Proceedia Social and Behavioral Science, 156*, 409–413.

Sener, S., Savrul, M., & Aydın, O. (2014). Structure of Small and Medium-Sized Enterprises in Turkey and global competitiveness strategies. *Procedia-Social and Behavioral Sciences, 150*, 212–221.

Singh, R. K., Garg, S. K., & Deshmukh, S. G. (2008). Strategy development by SMEs for competitiveness: A review. *Benchmarking: An International Journal, 15*, 525–547.

St-Pierre, J., Foleu, L, Abdulnour, G., Nomo, S., & Fouda, M. (2015). SME development challenges in Cameroon: An entrepreneurial ecosystem perspective. *Transnational Corporations Review, 7*, 441–462.

Stuart, E. (2011). *Making growth inclusive: Some lessons from countries and the literature*. Oxfam Research Report. Nairobi: Oxfam, pp. 1–43.

Sung, C. Y., Kim, K. C., & In, S. (2016). Small and Medium-Sized Enterprises policy in Korea from the 1960s to the 2000s and beyond. *Small Enterprise Research, 23*, 262–275.

Todaro, M. P., & Smith, S. C. (2015). *Economic development*. Washington: Pearson.

Wang, Y., Van Assche, A., & Turkina, E. (2018). Antecedents of SME embeddedness in inter-organizational networks: Evidence from China's Aerospace Industry. *Journal of Small Business and Entrepreneurship, 30*, 53–75.

www.ingramcontent.com/pod-product-compliance
Ingram Content Group UK Ltd.
Pitfield, Milton Keynes, MK11 3LW, UK
UKHW020154290926
15471UKWH00005B/860

9 783631 924785